FEMINIST PERSPECTIVES ON EVIDENCE

Cavendish
Publishing
Limited

London • Sydney

Titles in the *Feminist Perspectives in Law* series

Child Law

Criminal Law

Employment Law

Equity and Trusts

Evidence

Foundational Subjects of Law

Health Care Law

Law and Theory

Literary Jurisprudence

Public Law

FEMINIST PERSPECTIVES ON EVIDENCE

Edited by

Mary Childs
Lecturer in Law
University of Manchester

and

Louise Ellison
Lecturer in Law
University of Reading

Cavendish
Publishing
Limited

London • Sydney

First published in Great Britain 2000 by Cavendish Publishing Limited,
The Glass House, Wharton Street, London WC1X 9PX, United Kingdom
Telephone: + 44 (0)20 7278 8000   Facsimile: + 44 (0)20 7278 8080
Email: info@cavendishpublishing.com
Website: www.cavendishpublishing.com

British Library Cataloguing in Publication Data

Feminist perspectives on evidence – (Feminist perspectives series)
1 Evidence (Law) – England   2 Evidence (Law) – Wales
I Childs, Mary   II Ellison, Louise
347.4'2'06

ISBN 1 85941 527 X

Printed and bound in Great Britain

SERIES EDITORS' PREFACE

One of the unfortunate aspects of most law degrees is the split between substantive and procedural law. Most students, if not all, study criminal law, but only those intending to take the professional examinations tend to study evidence. For most students, it is viewed as a subject concerned with rules about what one can do and what one is not allowed to do. Of course, in practice, many evidence courses go beyond this diet and talk about fundamental issues of notions of truth and the power in play through the rules and practices of presenting 'evidence of truth' in court. This collection displays, very clearly, the fundamental issues which lie behind the operation of the rules.

The editors of the collection, in Chapter 1, quote Orenstein: 'Feminism, like evidence, is concerned with how stories are heard and how society determines credibility.' The collection of papers which they have brought together display both how rich the area of evidence law is in terms of feminist perspectives and how far the material and debates have developed and are developing. As they themselves say: '... one of the most fundamental challenges of feminist thinking for the law of evidence is the insistence that epistemological matters are inextricably intertwined with identity and standpoint ... there cannot be an unproblematic approach to the reception and evaluation of evidence.' In these terms, not only is this collection a very valuable contribution to those working within the field of the law of evidence, it is also of great value to those of us who are interested in developing feminist perspectives on law *per se*.

We were very pleased when Mary Childs and Louise Ellison suggested this collection to us. The papers which they have brought together, and their own very succinct introduction, makes clear that the time is ripe for such a collection. We have no doubt that it will provide a valuable resource to all those working in this area of law. We hope it will be a spur to those who still teach the limited diet of rules in their courses and an inspiration to students to rethink their own perspectives on why evidence should be studied. But we do not want the readership to be limited to those working specifically in the area. Any feminist working on law, or indeed anyone interested in the telling/hearing of stories in an institutional setting, will find invaluable material in this collection.

Our thanks to the contributors, the editors and, as always, to those at Cavendish who have done so much to support the series, especially Cara Annett and Jo Reddy.

Anne Bottomley and Sally Sheldon

CONTRIBUTORS

Mary Childs is Lecturer in Law at the University of Manchester. Her research and teaching interests include criminal law, evidence and feminist theory.

Susan Easton is a barrister and Senior Lecturer in Law at Brunel University. She is the author of *The Case for the Right to Silence* (1998) and *The Problem of Pornography: Regulation and the Right to Free Speech* (1994) and is the editor of the International Journal of Discrimination and the Law.

Louise Ellison is Lecturer in Law at the University of Reading. Her primary research and teaching interests are criminal law and evidence. She is currently working on a book entitled *Vulnerable Witnesses and the Adversarial Process*.

Pamela R Ferguson holds the Chair in Scots Law at the University of Dundee. Her research interests include criminal law and procedure, and medical law. Professor Ferguson is a member of the Criminal Court Rules Council and the Convenor of the Scottish Criminal Law Forum.

Rosemary Hunter is Professor of Law and Director of the Socio-Legal Research Centre at Griffith University, Brisbane, Australia. Her research interests are in the areas of feminist legal theory, anti-discrimination law, women's employment, and procedures and dispute resolution.

Kit Kinports is a Professor at the University of Illinois College of Law. Her primary research and teaching interests are criminal law, feminist jurisprudence and civil rights litigation. The second edition of her co-authored casebook, *Criminal Law: Cases and Materials*, was published in 2000.

Kathy Mack is Associate Professor of Law at Flinders University, South Australia, and was previously Senior Lecturer in Law at the University of Adelaide. Her special interests are women and the law, criminal procedure and evidence, civil procedure and dispute resolution, and legal education. Recent publications include 'Choice, consent and autonomy in a guilty plea system' (2000) 17 Law in Context 75, which she co-authored with Dr Sharyn Roach Anleu.

Donald Nicolson is Lecturer in Law at the University of Bristol. He has published articles on the South African judiciary, civil liberties in criminal law, battered women who kill their abusers, and professional legal ethics, as well as on the philosophy and teaching of fact-finding in law. He recently co-wrote *Professional Legal Ethics: Critical Interrogations* (1999) and is co-editor of *Feminist Perspectives on Criminal Law* (2000). Donald is also the founder and Director of the University of Bristol Law Clinic.

Fiona E Raitt is Senior Lecturer at the University of Dundee. She previously practised as a solicitor for 13 years. She researches and publishes in the areas of evidence, feminist theory and family law. Fiona co-authored (with S Zeedyk) *The Implicit Relation of Psychology and Law: Woman and Syndrome Evidence* (2000) and is currently working on a third edition of *The Law of Evidence in Scotland.*

Sharyn Roach Anleu is Associate Professor of Sociology at Flinders University, South Australia, and past President of the Australian Sociological Association. The author of *Law and Social Change* (2000) and *Deviance, Conformity and Control* (3rd edn, 1999), she recently collaborated with Kathy Mack on a national study of guilty plea negotiations in Australia.

Anne Scully is Lecturer in Law at Brunel University, where she teaches jurisprudence, public law and legal method. Her research interests include feminist legal theory and the development of constitutional law and judicial review principles from a feminist standpoint.

ACKNOWLEDGMENTS

We are grateful to all our contributors for their unwavering enthusiasm and commitment to the production of this volume. A number of the essays in this collection were presented at a one day workshop held at the University of Reading in March 1999. We would like to thank everyone involved for their generous and stimulating participation. We would also like to thank Cavendish Publishing for sponsoring the event, and the Law Department at Reading for providing the venue.

Thanks must also go to the team at Cavendish Publishing for their support and guidance. Jo Reddy has supported the *Feminist Perspectives* series with incredible energy and enthusiasm; Ruth Massey has been patient, encouraging and always good humoured.

Anne Bottomley and Sally Sheldon have been helpful and inspirational series editors, and we wish to express our gratitude to them.

We would also like to thank our colleagues in the Law Departments of Reading and Manchester for their encouragement.

Mary Childs and Louise Ellison
September 2000

CONTENTS

Series Editors' Preface   *v*

List of Contributors   *vii*

Acknowledgments   *ix*

Table of Cases   *xiii*

Table of Legislation   *xxi*

Table of Abbreviations   *xxiii*

1   **EVIDENCE LAW AND FEMINISM**   1

by Mary Childs and Louise Ellison

2   **GENDER, EPISTEMOLOGY AND ETHICS: FEMINIST PERSPECTIVES ON EVIDENCE THEORY**   13

by Donald Nicolson

3   **RAPE AND THE ADVERSARIAL CULTURE OF THE COURTROOM**   39

by Louise Ellison

4   **GENDER BIAS IN THE HEARSAY RULE**   59

by Fiona E Raitt

5   **THE 'PRIVILEGE' IN THE PRIVILEGE DOCTRINE: A FEMINIST ANALYSIS OF THE EVIDENTIARY PRIVILEGES FOR CONFIDENTIAL COMMUNICATIONS**   79

by Kit Kinports

6   **EVIDENTIARY HARASSMENT: THE USE OF THE RULES OF EVIDENCE IN AN INFORMAL TRIBUNAL**   105

by Rosemary Hunter

7 **RESOLUTION WITHOUT TRIAL, EVIDENCE LAW AND THE CONSTRUCTION OF THE SEXUAL ASSAULT VICTIM**   127

   by Kathy Mack and Sharyn Roach Anleu

8 **CORROBORATION AND SEXUAL ASSAULTS IN SCOTS LAW**   149

   by Pamela R Ferguson

9 **THE USE OF SEXUAL HISTORY EVIDENCE IN RAPE TRIALS**   167

   by Susan Easton

10 **EXPERT DISTRACTIONS: WOMEN WHO KILL, THEIR SYNDROMES AND DISORDERS**   191

   by Anne Scully

11 **THE CHARACTER OF THE ACCUSED**   211

   by Mary Childs

Bibliography   237
Index   263

TABLE OF CASES

A v Caboolture Shire Council (1992) EOC 92-403 122

Adams v HM Advocate [1999] SCCR 188 154

Agosto, In re 553 F Supp 1298 (D Nev 1983) 102

Ahluwalia [1992] 4 All ER 889 ....16, 17, 20, 21, 67, 192, 193, 197–201, 205

Aldridge v Booth (1986) EOC 92-177 122

Allred v State 554 P 2d 411 (Alaska 1976) 82, 91

Annesley v Earl of Anglesea 17 Howells State
    Trials 1139 (Ex 1743) 85

Application of A and M, In re 4034 NYS 2d 375
    (App Div 1978) 102

Begg v Tudhope 1983 SCCR 32 ....160, 161

Beggs [1989] Crim LR 898 222

Bellis [1996] 1 All ER 552 213

Bennett v HM Advocate 1989 SCCR 608 159

Bevacqua v Klinkert (1993) EOC 92-515 122

Billam [1986] 1 WLR 349 168

Bishop [1975] QB 274 233

Blair v HM Advocate 1993 SCCR 483 165

Blau v US 340 US 332 (1951) 98

Blough v Food Lion Inc 142 FRD 622 (ED Va 1992) 88

Boardman [1894] AC 57 ....224, 227

Boyle v HM Advocate 1976 SLT 126 154

Boyle v Ishan Ozden (1986) EOC 92-165 122

Brandy v HREOC (1995) 183 CLR 245 106

Briginshaw v Briginshaw (1938) 60 CLR 336 115

Britzman and Hall [1983] 1 All ER 369 ....232, 234

Brotherston v HM Advocate 1995 SCCR 613 165

Brown (1989) 89 Cr App R 97 171

Brown v Lemeki and the Government of Papua New
    Guinea, Rees v Lemeki and the Government of Papua
    New Guinea, Johnston v Lemeki and the
    Government of Papua New Guinea (1997) unreported 122

Buchanan v Mayfield 925 SW 2d 135 (Tex Ct App 1996) 92

Camplin [1845] 1 Den 89 150

Cannon 1992 JC 138; 1992 SLT 709; 1992 SCCR 505 ....159–60, 162

Charles Sweenie (1858) 3 Irv 109 150

Clark [1955] 2 QB 459 232
Clarke [1817] 2 Stark 244 169
Commonwealth v Oatterson 572 A 2d 1258 (Pa Super Ct 1990) 89
Commonwealth v Stewart 690 A 2d 195 (Pa 1997) 89
Cook [1959] 2 QB 340 232
Couch v US 409 US 322 (1973) 86
Courtney-Smith (No 2) (1990) 48 A Crim R 49 139
Croissant v Germany, 25 September 1992, Series A, Vol 237 187
Crofts (1996) 88 A Crim R 232 133

Darnell v State 674 NE 2d 19 (Ind Ct App 1996) 92
Diggle [1995] 16 Cr App R (S) 163 174
DPP v Boardman [1975] AC 421; [1974] 2 WLR 673 219
DPP v Morgan [1975] 2 All ER 347 169
DPP v P [1991] 2 AC 477 . . . . .176, 186, 219
Doe, John (see Grand Jury Proceedings of John Doe v US)
Doorson v The Netherlands (1996) 22 EHRR 330 51
Duffy [1949] 1 All ER 932 . . . . .191, 192, 196, 198

Eckmann v Board of Education 106 FRD 70 (ED Mo 1985) 88
Edington v Mutual Life Insurance Co 67 NY 185 (1876) 91
Elkins v US 364 US 206 (1960) 83
Erato, In re 2 F 3d 11 (2d Cir 1993) 101

Fletcher [1859] Bell CC 63 150
Fox v HM Advocate 1998 SLT 335; 1998 SCCR 115 . . . . .75, 150, 154, 163
Funderburk [1990] 2 All ER 482; (1990) 90 Cr App R 467 .170, 231

Giakas [1988] VR 973 139
Gilbreath v Guadalupe Hospital Foundation
    Inc 5 F 3d 785 (5th Cir 1993) 91
Gracey 1987 JC 45; 1987 SLT 749; 1987 SCCR 260 159
Grand Jury Investigation, In re 918 F 2d 374 (3d Cir 1990) 89
Grand Jury Proceedings of John Doe v US,
    In re 842 F 2d 244 (10th Cir 1988) 101
Grand Jury Proceedings, Unemancipated Minor Child,
    In re 949 F Supp 1487 (ED Wash 1996) 102
Grand Jury, In re 103 F 3d 1140 (3d Cir 1997) 82, 101
Gray v Ritossa (1994) EOC 92-635 . . . . .115, 116

Gray v State of Victoria and Pettman [1999] VCAT 33 . . . . .114–16, 118–21, 123, 124
Gruenke [1991] 3 SCR 263 87
Gunning [1980] Crim LR 592 49

Hamilton [1969] Crim LR 486 49
Harradine (1992) 164 LSJS 382 139
Harrison v Watson (1979) unreported, 19 June,
    NSW Anti-Discrimination Board 109
Henry (1968) 53 Cr App R 150 151
Higgins v Fricker (1992) 63 A Crim R 473 139
Hill v Guilfoyle (1988) EOC 92-233 122
Hill v Water Resources Commission (1985) EOC 92-127 122
Hirock and Others [1970] 1 QB 67 49
HM Advocate v Logan 1935 JC 100 150
Hobbs v Tinling [1929] 2 KB 151 48
Holder [1983] 3 NSWLR 245 139
Horne v HM Advocate [1989] SCCR 608 159
Horne v Press Clough Joint Venture (1994) EOC 92-591 .122
Hudson [1912] 2 KB 464 232
Humphreys [1995] 4 All ER 1008 . . . . .194, 195, 197–201, 204
Hunt v Maricopa County Employees Merit System
    Commission 619 P 2d 1036 (Ariz 1980) 87

Inquest Proceedings, In re 676 A 2d 790 (Vt 1996) 101
Isaacs v Sosnowski t/a QA Industrial Chemicals (1998) unreported,
    17 November, Victorian Civil and Administrative Tribunal 112, 116

Jaffee v Redmond 518 US 1 (1996) 93– 96, 103
Johnson v Avery 393 US 483 (1969) 86

Kalia [1975] Crim LR 181 48
Kessler v Troum 392 A 2d 662 (NJ Super Ct Law Div 1978) 92
Kostovski v Netherlands (1992) 14 EHRR 396 50
Krausz (1973) 57 Cr App R 466 176
Krepp v Valcic t/a Capel Bakery (1993) EOC 92-520 (WA) 122

Larter and Castleton [1995] Crim LR 75 150
Lasseur [1991] Crim LR 53 180
Lavallee [1990] 1 SCR 852; (1990) 55 CCC 3d 97 . . . . .67, 194
Lindsey, In re 158 F 3d (DC Cir 1998) 79, 84

Lococo v XL Disposal Corp 717 NE 2d 823 (Ill Ct App 1999) 92
Lockwood v Walker 1910 SC (J) 3; 1910 6 Adam 124; 1909 2 SLT 400 153
Longman v R (1989) 168 CLR 79 180
Luc Thiet Thuan [1996] 3 WLR 45 201

McAvoy v HM Advocate 1991 SCCR 123 165
McKenna v State of Victoria (Victoria Police), Mansfield,
    Fyfe and Arnold (1998) EOC 92-927 114–16
Mackie v HM Advocate 1994 SCCR 227 164
McLaren v Zucco (1994) EOC 92-650 122
McLellan v HM Advocate 1992 SLT 991; 1992 SCCR 171 ....160, 161
Makanjuolo [1995] 2 Cr App R 469 152
Makin v AG for New South Wales [1894] AC 57 ....218–20, 227
Mechanical and General Inventions Co Ltd and Lehwess
    v Austin and Austin Motor Co Ltd [1935] AC 346; 48
Medical-Express Inc v Tarpley 629 So 2d 331 (La 1993) 92
Milton Brown [1998] 2 Cr App R 364 168
Moore 1990 JC 371; 1991 SLT 278; 1990 SCCR 586 159
Moorhead v Lane 125 FRD 680 (CD Ill 1989) 85, 87
Moorov v HM Advocate 1930 JC 68; 1930 SLT 596 160
Morhall [1996] 1 AC 90 193
Morton [1986] VR 863 139
Morton v HM Advocate 1938 JC 50 ....74, 153, 154
Murphy v Colorific Lithographics Pty Ltd and Hevey
    (1997) unreported, 11 April, Supreme Court of Victoria 112, 114–17, 119, 122
Murtha, In re 279 A 2d 889 (NJ Sup Ct App Div 1971) 88

Nelson v HM Advocate 1988 SCCR 536 154
Nicholls (1991) 53 A Crim R 455 139

Olugboja (1981) 73 Cr App R 344 150
Orr v Liva Tool and Diemakers Pty Ltd
    (1985) EOC 92-126 122
Osolin [1993] 4 SCR 595 182

Parker [1997] Crim LR 760 201
Patterson v Caterpillar Inc 70 F 3d 503 (7th Circ 1995) 91
Patterson v Hookey (1996) unreported 115

People v Fitzgerald 422 NYS 2d 309
(Westchester County Court 1979) 101, 102
People v Hanf 611 NYS 2d 85 (County Ct 1994) 92
People v Hilligas 670 NYS 2d 744 (Sup Ct 1998) 101
People v McAlpin 812 P 2d 563 (Cal 1991) 228
People v Sanders 457 NE 2d 1241 (Ill 1983) 101, 103
People v Suarez 560 NYS 2d 68 (Sup Ct 1990) 99
Perks [1973] Crim LR 388 49
Phillips v Alabama Department of Pensions and
Security 394 So 2d 51 (Ala Civ App 1981) 83
Phillips v State 701 SW 2d 875 (Tex Crim App 1985) 99
Polen, In re 670 NE 572 (Ohio Ct App 1996) 92
Pommell [1999] Crim LR 576 228
Preston [1909] 1 KB 568 232

R [1991] 4 All ER 481 178
Rabbitt (1931) 23 Cr App R 112 49
Ralston v HM Advocate 1987 SCCR 467 154
Recorder of Bristol, The, Re Z (1999) unreported, CA 228
Riley (1887) 16 Cox CC 191 169
Ritossa v Gray (1992) EOC 92-452 122
Rivers v Rivers 354 SE 2d 784 (SC 1987) 90
Robertson v HM Advocate 1998 SCCR 390 157
Robinson v Meca 632 NYS 2d 728 (App Div 1995) 92
Rouse [1904] 1 KB 184 232
Rubin v United States 524 US 1301 79
Russo v Petracca (1997) unreported 114, 115, 117, 124
Rutledge v State 525 NE 2d 326 (Ind 1988) 89

SMS [1992] Crim LR 310 172
Sambasivam v Public Prosecutor, Federation of Malaya
[1950] AC 458 229–31
Scott v Hammock 870 P 2d 947 (Utah 1994) 89
Seaboyer [1970] AC 304 . . . . .11, 180–82
Seaboyer (1991) 83 Dom LR (46th) 193 . . . . .174, 175, 188
Sealed Case, In re 148 F 3d 1073 (DC Cir 1998) 79
Selvey v DPP [1970] AC 304 . . . . .180, 188, 232, 233
Shannon (1979) 21 SASR 442 . . . . .139, 140

Sharp (1994) 98 Cr App R 144 49

Sheean (1908) 21 Cox CC 561 ....180, 233

Simms v Datagap and Giamirra (1997) 2 May,
    Anti-Discrimination Tribunal 116

Simpson (1993) 68 A Crim R 439 139

Simrin v Simrin 43 Cal Rptr 376 (Dist Ct App 1965) 89

Sinnappan v State of Victoria: Decision on Remedy
    (1994) EOC 92-658 107

Slater (1984) 36 SASR 524 139

Slavutych v Baker [1976] 1 SCR 254 82

Smith (1916) 11 CAR 229 230

Smith [1998] 4 All ER 387 ....193, 201

Smith v Lees 1997 SCCR 139 ....75, 153, 156, 158, 161–63

Stannard (1837) 7 C & P 673 213

State ex rel Barker v McAuley 51 Tenn (4 Heisk) 424 (1871) 98

State v Buss 887 P 2d 920 (Wash Ct App 1995) 88, 89

State v Clark 570 NW 2d 195 (ND 1997) 94

State v Edwards 819 SW 2d 841 (Mo Ct App 1996) 95

State v Gotfrey 598 P 2d 1325 (Utah 1979) 95

State v Hankins 642 SW 2d 606 (Mo 1982) 99

State v Hereford 518 So 2d 515 (La Ct App 1987) 89

State v Howland 658 P 2d 194 (Ariz Ct App 1982) 95

State v Jackson 687 A 2d 485 (Conn) (1997) 82

State v Jaggers 506 NE 2d 832 (Ind Ct App 1987) 92

State v Lassai 366 So 2d 1389 (La 1978) 83, 94

State v Maxon 756 P 2d 1297 (Wash 1988) 101

State v McKinnon 525 NE 2d 821 (Ohio Ct App 1987) 92

State v Melendez 834 P 2d 154 (Ariz 1992) 87

State v Ross 947 P 2d 1290 (Wash Ct App 1997) 92

State v Sandberg 392 NW 2d 298 (Minn Ct App 1986) 94

State v Spell 399 So 2d 551 (La 1981) 87

State v Wanrow 88 Wash 2d 221; 559 P 2d 548 (1977) 67

State v Watkins 614 P 2d 835 (Ariz 1980) 99, 103

State v Williams 688 So 2d 1277 (La Ct App 1997) 99

State v Willoughby 532 A 2d 1020 (Me 1987) 101

Stein v Bowman 38 US (13 Pet) 209 (1839) 100

Strate v Cahoon 799 P 2d 1911 (Wash Ct App 1990) 92

State of Victoria v McKenna [1999] VSC 310 ....113, 115

Stephen v HM Advocate 1987 SCCR 570 159
Stobo v HM Advocate 1994 JC 28; 1994 SLT 28;
    1993 SCCR 1105 . . . . .160, 161
Straffen [1952] 2 QB 911 222
Sweeney v X 1982 SCCR 509 150
Swidler and Berlin v US 524 US 399 79

Teper v R [1952] AC 480 61
Thompson v R [1918] AC 221 . . . . .223, 224
Thomson v HM Advocate 1998 SCCR 56 162
Thornton [1992] 1 All ER 306 . . . . .16, 67, 195–97, 201
Thornton (No 2) [1996] 2 All ER 1023 . . . . .16, 17, 18, 37, 67, 196, 197,
                                                                         200, 201, 204, 205, 207
Three Juveniles v Commonwealth 455 NE 2d 1203
    (Mass 1983) 101, 102
Trammel v United States 445 US 40 (1980) 82, 84, 88, 97, 98
Turner [1944] KB 463 233
Turner [1970] 2 QB 321 141
Turner [1975] QB 834; [1975] 1 All ER 70 . . . . .196, 216

Upjohn Co v United States 449 US 383 (1981) 84
US v Acker 52 F 3d 509 (4th Cir 1995) 99
US v Arthur Young and Co 465 US 805 (1984) 86
US v Hamilton 19 F 3d 350 (7th Cir 1994) 99

Van Mechelen v The Netherlands (1997) 25 EHRR 547 51
Verplank, In re 329 F Supp 433 (CD Calif 1971) 90
Viola [1982] 3 All ER 73 . . . . .171, 177

Wade v Ridley 32 A 975 (Me 1895) 85
Wainwright [1998] Crim LR 665 232
Welfare Rights Organization v Crisan 661 P 2d 1073
    (Cal 1983) 87
Whalen v Roe 429 US 589 (1977) 91
White v R [1999] 1 Cr App R 153 74
Wiles v Wiles 448 SE 2d 681 (Ga 1994) 94
Wilson v Phoenix Contracting Services Pty Ltd
    and Haig [1998] VSC 81 . . . . .113, 114, 116, 117, 119, 124
Winchester (1992) 58 A Crim R 345 139

Winfield (1939) 27 Cr App R 139 214
Wolfle v US 291 US 7 (1934) 98

Yates v HM Advocate 1997 SLT (Notes) 42 . . . . .158, 162

Z (2000) The Times, 23 June, HL 228

TABLE OF LEGISLATION

Charter of Rights and
Freedoms (Canada)
ss 7, 11 180
Civil Evidence Act 1968 2
Civil Evidence Act 1972 2
Civil Evidence Act 1995 2
Contempt of Court Act 1981—
s 8 231
Crimes Act 1958 (Vic)—
s 61(1)(b) 133
Crimes Act 1990 (NSW)—
s 405B 133
s 439 139
Crimes (Rape) Act 1991
(Vic) 54, 131, 132
Crimes (Sexual Offences)
Act 1991(Vic) 54
s 37C 54
Criminal Code (Canada)—
s 276......................175, 176,
180, 182
s 277 180
Criminal Code (Tas)—
s 371A 133
Criminal Code Act
Compilation
Act 1913 (WA)—
s 19b(1)(b) 139
Criminal Evidence Act 1898 228
s 1(3)(ii) 180, 232, 233
Criminal Justice and
Public Order Act
1994 (UK)—
s 32 213
s 32(1)(b) 151
s 48 139
s 142 ....150, 170
Criminal Procedure
Act 1865—
s 6 231

Criminal Procedure (Scotland)
Act 1995 62
s 259 62
ss 274, 275 183
Criminal Sexual Conduct
Act 1974 (Michigan) 180

Disability Discrimination
Act 1992 (Aus) 106

Equal Opportunities Act
1984 (Vic) 122
s 20(1) 108
Equal Opportunities Act
1995 (Vic)—
s 85 108
s 103 121
ss 109, 119–24 110
s 138 106
ss 141, 142 107
s 142(1) 108
s 144 106
s 182 107
s 218 108
Evidence Act 1906 (WA)—
s 36BD 133
Evidence Act 1929 (SA)—
s 34i(6) 133
Evidence Act 1958 (Vic)—
s 37A..........................123
Evidence Act 1971 (ACT)—
s 76C..........................133
Evidence (Confidential
Communications)
Act 1998 (Vic) 124

Firearms Act 1968—
s 21 213

Homicide Act 1957—
s 2 192
s 3 191

Human Rights Act 1998 4

Official Secrets Act 1911—
  s 1(2) 213

Penalties and Sentences
  Act 1992 (Qld)—
  s 13 139

Racial Discrimination Act
  1975 (Aus) 106

Sentencing Act 1991 (Vic)—
  s 5(2)(e) 139
Sentencing Act 1995 (NT)—
  s 5(2)(j) 139
Sex Discrimination Act
  1984 (Aus) 106, 122
Sex Offenders Act 1997 222
Sexual Offences Act 1956 149
  s 1 . . . . .150, 175
Sexual Offences (Amendment)
  Act 1976 . . . . .167, 169, 186
  s 2 . . . . .170–72, 181, 188
Sexual Offences (Evidence and
  Procedure) Act 1994 (NT)—
  s 4 133

Sexual Offences (Scotland)
  Act 1976—
  s 5 161
Street Offences Act 1959 213

Theft Act 1968—
  s 27(3) 213

Youth Justice and Criminal
  Evidence Act 1999 . . . . .51, 53, 57,
                              167, 168, 180,
                              183–86, 235
  ss 16, 17 52
  s 17(1) 183
  s 17(3) 52
  s 17(4) 52, 183
  s 19(1), (3) 52
  s 20(2), (5) 183
  ss 23–25 52
  ss 26–28 53
  s 32 54
  ss 34, 38(3), 39 184
  s 41 . . . . .184, 185
  s 41(4) 186
  s 41(5) 185
  s 62 . . . . .52, 185

TABLE OF ABBREVIATIONS

A & NZ J Crim	Australia and New Zealand Journal of Criminology
AC	Appeal Cases
AIJA	Australian Institute for Judicial Administration
AJFL	Australian Journal of Family Law
All ER	All England Reports
Alt LJ	Alternative Law Journal
Am J Psychiatry	American Journal of Psychiatry
Am UJ Gender & Law	American University Journal of Gender and the Law
Anglo-Am L Rev	Anglo-American Law Review
Aus Fem LJ	Australian Feminist Law Journal
Br J Crim	British Journal of Criminology
Br J Soc Psy	British Journal of Social Psychology
CFLQ	Child and Family Law Quarterly
CJLS	Canadian Journal of Law and Society
CJWL	Canadian Journal of Women and the Law
CLR	Commonwealth Law Reports
CMLR	Common Market Law Reports
Cr App R	Criminal Appeal Reports
Crim LJ	Criminal Law Journal
Crim LR	Criminal Law Review
CSP	Critical Social Policy
E & P	International Journal of Evidence and Proof
EHRR	European Human Rights Reports
EJST	European Journal of Social Theory
EL Rev	European Law Review
FLS	Feminist Legal Studies
FR	Feminist Review

Harv L Rev	Harvard Law Review
HLR	Housing Law Reports
HREOC	Human Rights and Equal Opportunities Commission
HRQ	Human Rights Quarterly
ICLQ	International and Comparative Law Quarterly
ICR	Industrial Compensation Reports
Int J Soc Law	International Journal of the Sociology of Law
J Inst Stud Leg Ethics	Journal of the Institute for the Study of Legal Ethics
J Transnational L & P	Journal of Transnational Law and Policy
JC	Justiciary Cases
JLS	Journal of Law and Society
JSWFL	Journal of Social Welfare and Family Law
KB	King's Bench
Law & Phil	Law and Philosophy
Law & Soc Inq	Law and Social Inquiry
Law & Soc Rev	Law and Society Review
LGR	Local Government Reports
Loyola U Chi LJ	Loyola University Chicago Law Journal
LRB	London Review of Books
LS	Legal Studies
LQR	Law Quarterly Review
MLR	Modern Law Review
NLJ	New Law Journal
NLR	New Left Review
NSWLR	New South Wales Law Reports
NYLS L Rev	New York Law School Law Review
OJLS	Oxford Journal of Legal Studies

PL	Public Law
QB	Queen's Bench
RP	Radical Philosophy
SCCR	Scottish Criminal Case Reports
SLS	Social and Legal Studies
SLT	Scots Law Times
W & ML Rev	William and Mary Law Review
Web JCLI	Web Journal of Current Legal Issues
WLR	Weekly Law Reports
YBEL	Yearbook of European Law
YJCEA 1999	Youth Justice and Criminal Evidence Act 1999

CHAPTER 1

EVIDENCE LAW AND FEMINISM

Mary Childs and Louise Ellison

INTRODUCTION

This book is part of a growing series which began with the publication in 1996 of *Feminist Perspectives on the Foundational Subjects of Law.*[1] As with the other collections in the series, we have sought to draw together a range of voices and perspectives linked by both their focus on a particular area of law and by their feminist approach to that subject. We have attempted not to provide a comprehensive account of the subject area, but to draw together a body of work which will examine the subject at varying levels of abstraction and from a variety of perspectives.

WHAT IS EVIDENCE?

As a leading textbook on the law of evidence observes, the word 'evidence' is not specifically or even primarily legal in meaning.[2] It refers simply to information which may persuade a person that something is more or less likely to be true. In this broad sense, evidence is something we all rely upon daily, whether it is the evidence of our own sense in relation to the world around us or information we derive from the statements or actions of others. We make decisions about evidence whenever we use available information, or seek our further information, in order to make judgments about the 'truth' of past events or presents states of affairs.

Correspondingly, questions of evidence and proof have been the focus of much scientific and philosophical debate in circles far removed from those of law. The subject has been considered by social and physical scientists, by historians and theologians, and by mathematicians and epistemologists. The question of what we can know and how we can know it, or make judgments about its probability, is relevant to virtually every intellectual discipline. In

---

1   Bottomley, A (ed), *Feminist Perspectives on the Foundational Subjects of Law*, 1996, London: Cavendish Publishing.
2   Dennis, I, *The Law of Evidence*, 1999, London: Sweet & Maxwell.

this sense, evidential debates within law are logically connected to much broader debates about the limitations and refinements of human attempts to understand all aspects of the world around us. As Bentham said, 'the field of evidence is no other than the field of knowledge'.[3]

Although our subject is part of this broader field of inquiry about the assessment of probability and the limits of human knowledge, the subject of this book is what may be called 'judicial evidence'; specifically, the question of what may be used as evidence to persuade the trier of fact in legal proceedings. The laws which relate to this question are concerned principally with the question of what evidence may be introduced at trial and by whom, but they also concern questions such as the weight to be given to certain items of evidence, restrictions on the gathering and creation of some types of evidence and attempts to control the uses of evidence by judicial fact-finders.

The law of evidence may be regarded as the area of legal study which is most 'lawerly', in the sense that it embodies and reflects attitudes which are at the heart of any legal system. If one takes the view that enforcement by courts and tribunals is fundamental to the operation of any law (even if only rarely, as a matter of last resort), then the evidential rules and practices adopted by those tribunals are inexorably implicated in the workings of such substantive rules. Some rules of evidence may be regarded as, effectively, rules of substantive law due to their effects (such as the now repealed irrebuttable presumption of English law that a boy under 14 years of age could not commit rape); others may have such significant effects on the enforcement of laws that they might as well be regarded as substantive rules themselves. It may be virtually impossible in some areas to classify a rule as either substantive or evidential, where the two are intimately interwoven.

Students often remark that their understanding of substantive law subjects has shifted significantly after they study evidence; only then do they become aware of some of the factors which shaped the presentation of facts in the case reports they studied. For instance, they begin to understand why some perspectives on the events might have been missing – perhaps the absent witness was a spouse who could not be compelled to testify, a defendant who feared cross-examination as to previous convictions, an accomplice who was incompetent as a prosecution witness, a child who could not be sworn. They appreciate how the admissibility of certain types of evidence dramatically affected the use of certain lines of argument – an obvious example is the reception of evidence of Battered Woman's Syndrome in support of claims of self-defence or diminished responsibility.

---

3   Bentham, J, 'An introductory view of the rationale of evidence for the use of non-lawyers as well as lawyers', in Mill, J (ed), *The Works of Jeremy Bentham*, 1810, London: Simkin, Marshall, Pt 6.

The relaxation of evidential rules and restrictions has proceeded steadily in civil cases, especially in England and Wales.[4] Evidential technicalities now have decreasing impact upon the operation of substantive rules of tort or contract. But it is still the case that a basic grasp of evidence is essential for students to understand the way in which the law has developed, and awareness of evidential rules can afford students insight into legal attitudes surrounding the substantive rules. Presumptions of legitimacy and marriage reflect certain values and concerns about families; and the courts' desire for certainty and 'objectivity' in contract disputes can be seen in the parol evidence rule (rendering inadmissible extrinsic evidence which conflicts with the express terms of a written agreement).

Exclusionary rules of evidence remain central to the application of criminal law in most common law jurisdictions, and it is arguable that, in most criminal trials, the outcome turns not upon any contested issue of substantive law, but rather upon points of procedure and evidence. Evidential issues are influential at all stages of criminal proceedings, as police officers and other investigators must comply with rules concerning the collection and disclosure of evidence or run the risk that information obtained in contravention of those rules will be inadmissible. Decisions about whether to proceed with prosecutions will be determined principally by the likelihood of conviction, and in such assessments the sufficiency and quality of the available evidence will be of central importance. Equally, the evidence presented at trial will be crucial to the sentencing process if the accused is convicted.

Evidential rules and practices touch every area of law, as lawyers negotiate and practise in 'the shadow' of litigation. For this reason, the rules of evidence are of crucial importance even to those lawyers who never appear in court: the contracts they draft must be considered in light of their potential admission as evidence; the formalities they observe in executing wills are formalities which have evidential significance.

---

4   See, eg, the Civil Evidence Acts of 1968, 1972 and 1995, which all reduced the impact of common law exclusionary rules.

THE DEVELOPMENT OF EVIDENCE
LAW AND SCHOLARSHIP

The rules of evidence in the various legal systems discussed in this collection are for the most part based upon a body of judge made law from the 18th and 19th centuries, overlaid in some cases with statutory reforms of the 20th and 21st centuries. These rules of evidence have developed in a piecemeal and sometimes inconsistent fashion,[5] and have been shaped by the adversarial nature of the common law trial,[6] as well as by the use of the jury system. One outside observer has described the resulting body of law as exhibiting three distinctive properties: complexity; fear of the misuse of evidence; and attempts to structure the fact-finders' analysis.[7] Attempts have been made in recent years to simplify these rules (especially in civil trials) and to acknowledge the reality that jury trials are the exception rather than the norm in most jurisdictions, even in criminal cases. But the general principles hold true.

The study of the Anglo-American law of evidence and the production of specialised scholarly writings on judicial evidence originated in the latter half of the 18th century and have been dominated since by what Twining has called 'the rationalist tradition'.[8] This tradition (feminist critiques of which are explored in Chapter 2 of this collection) is characterised by cognitivist epistemology, a correspondence theory of truth, inductive reasoning, the aspiration to rational decision making and the pursuit of truth as a means to the end of justice.[9] Within this tradition there have, however, been long standing and closely argued debates over a variety of issues.

At the end of the 20th century, and continuing into the 21st, evidence scholarship and policy have been affected by a number of notable influences. One is the interaction of the law of evidence with the growing body of law concerned with human rights and civil liberties. In Canada, the Charter of Rights and Freedoms had a significant impact on certain areas of evidence law; and the coming into force of the Human Rights Act 1998 in the UK seems likely to have an equally dramatic impact on the way that lawyers argue about certain aspects of evidence and procedure, especially in criminal cases. Other crucial developments are the advance of forensic science and the growth, principally but not exclusively in the US, of research into the way in which judicial processes operate – the way in which juries receive and

---

5   As William Twining has observed, 'the history of the law of evidence is the history of a series of largely isolated responses to particular problems at different time' (*Theories of Evidence: Bentham and Wigmore*, 1985, London: Weidenfeld & Nicolson, p 1).

6   McEwan, J, *Evidence and the Adversarial Process*, 2nd edn, 1998, Oxford: Hart.

7   Damaska, M *Evidence Law Adrift*, 1997, New Haven: Yale UP, p 24.

8   *Ibid*, Twining.

9   *Ibid*, Twining, p 16.

interpret evidence, for example.[10] Equally significant is the growth of what has been termed 'the new evidence scholarship';[11] work which seeks to bring to the study of evidence the insights of the social sciences and the mathematical study of probability theory. A rich and growing body of evidence scholarship considers the application of Bayes Theorem to the evaluation of evidence and proof.[12] Questions about narrative and interpretation have been addressed in the humanities as well, and those developments have begun to find their way into discussions about the telling of stories in court.[13] Economists, psychologists and specialists from many other disciplines have been engaged in interdisciplinary debates with lawyers.[14]

Feminism and evidence

What does it mean to have a feminist perspective on the law of evidence? No doubt most, if not all, readers of this introduction will have their own ideas of what might be meant by such a phrase. But, as with other terms more familiar to most lawyers – 'reasonable', 'foreseeable', 'unjust', to offer but a few – individuals are likely to find that their ideas of what is meant by the phrase do not always exactly match those of other reasonable individuals. For this reason, it seems sensible to start with some thoughts about what the title of this book means to us.

We prefer a broad and flexible description of the word 'feminist', one which is capable of encompassing a number of different approaches. Broadly conceived, the word can be used to refer to work which is concerned with past and present social constructions of 'women' and, more specifically, which exhibits a commitment to the principle that these social constructions should not lead to inequality or oppression. Within this category can be found theories and approaches which might variously be described as liberal, socialist, radical or postmodern, or as belonging to some other strand of feminism.

---

10 Hastie, R (ed), *Inside the Juror*, 1993, Cambridge: CUP; Wagenaar, WA, van Koppen PJ and Crombag HFM, *Anchored Narratives*, 1993, Hemel Hempstead: Harvester Wheatsheaf.

11 Lempert, R, 'The new evidence scholarship: analyzing the process of proof' (1986) 66 Boston L Rev 439.

12 See Friedman, RD, 'Answering the Bayesioskeptical challenge' (1997) 1 E & P 276; Stein, A, 'Judicial fact finding and the Bayesian method: the case for deeper scepticism about their combination' (1996) 1 E & P 25.

13 Pennington, N and Hastie, R, 'The story model for juror decision making', in Hastie, R (ed), *Inside the Juror*, 1993, Cambridge: CUP.

14 See Twining, W, 'Recent trends in evidence scholarship', in *Proceedings of the First World Conference on New Trends in Criminal Investigation and Evidence*, 1997, Lelystad, Netherlands: OU Press.

Just as there is no single 'feminism', and the term continues to resist pinning down, there is no single, unified feminist perspective or analysis. The recognition of overlapping identities and complex standpoints demands that we resist the essentialist implications of asserting a common, unified reading of the word. That said, some might find the account above to be too general to offer a clear account of what one might call a feminist approach to law in general, and to the law of evidence in particular. We therefore suggest some ways of describing a feminist approach to the subject:

- one that considers the effect of law on women (and men) and on their construction as defendants, witnesses, litigants, victims, judges and jurors;

- one that looks at the construction of the body of knowledge itself, its exclusions and the gendered implications of both;

- one that looks at the standpoints and reasoning processes privileged by the rules of evidence and their operation;

- one characterised by a commitment to certain 'feminist' approaches: respecting the views of those involved, attempting to avoid essentialism and over-abstraction.[15]

Perhaps one of the most fundamental challenges of feminist thinking for the law of evidence is the insistence that epistemological matters are inextricably intertwined with identity and standpoint; that there cannot be any unproblematic approach to the reception and evaluation of evidence.[16] As one commentator has observed:

> ... feminism views law – including evidence law – as partly constitutive of culture, rather than apart from it. Feminist analysis of evidence law thus focuses on the ways in which evidence law reflects, affects and instantiates patriarchal culture. Evidentiary scholarship thus becomes in part cultural criticism. Evidence law must therefore be viewed partly as a set of social practices rather than primarily as a collection of legal rules and principles. The law in action, not in theory, is the starting point for discussion.[17]

Although the title of this book refers to the law of evidence, we regard the rules of evidence (narrowly conceived by some as primarily concerned with admissibility) as inextricably intertwined with the subject of evidence in the widest sense. Thus, fact construction and assessment of evidential weight are proper matters for consideration by evidence scholars. Equally, the impact of evidential rules extends far beyond the courts in which they are applied, as

---

15 See Orenstein, A, 'Feminism and evidence', in Taylor, B, Rush, S and Munro, RJ (eds), *Feminist Jurisprudence, Women and the Law – Critical Essays, Research Agenda and Bibliography*, 1999, Littleton, Colorado: Fred B Rothman, p 507.

16 Of course, feminist scholars are by no means the only people to have made this observation.

17 Taslitz, A, 'Gender and race in evidence policy: what feminism has to offer evidence law' (1999) 28 Southwestern UL Rev 171, p 178.

they influence negotiations between litigants and cast their shadows over the procedure adopted by allegedly 'informal' tribunals.

Evidence law is ideally suited for feminist analysis 'because feminism, like evidence, is concerned with how stories are heard and how society determines credibility'.[18] Much of feminist work on evidence has, indeed, focused upon the problems that women have historically faced, particularly in the criminal context, of having their stories heard and believed.[19]

Early feminist analyses of evidence law focused primarily on rape law.[20] Feminist scholars have, for example, identified specific evidentiary rules and practices which serve to foster distrust of female victims of sexual assault.[21] As with feminist critiques of law generally, the logical starting point was where the law drew express distinctions between men and women. In the area of evidence law, those express distinctions tended to be located in the body of procedural and evidential rules applicable to the prosecution of rape and other sexual offences. Evidence law has also been criticised for variously promoting, assuming, ignoring or failing to challenge 'many of the myths about sexual assault and the underlying paradigms and discourses of gender, race and power'.[22] The laws of evidence in relation to sexual offences are of particular interest to feminist scholars, of course, because it is in such cases that the gendered assumptions of evidence law and practice are most evident. Furthermore, the legal response to sexual offences can be seen as illustrative of the law's tendency to afford greater weight to some interests than others in a way which has operated to protect male defendants at the expense of their female victims.

But not all feminist concerns about evidence arise in the context of such trials; one area of considerable concern in the 1990s was the plight of battered women who kill. Feminists turned to the rules of evidence when it became apparent that the facially neutral criminal laws of self-defence, provocation and diminished responsibility were not equally accommodating of the claims of male and female defendants. Changing the substantive law was not seen as the only, or even the best, solution, particularly in the light of concerns that domestic killings of women were perhaps too easily excused; rather, ways were sought to show judges and juries how these defences could apply not

---

18 Orenstein, A, '"My God!" A feminist critique of the excited utterance exception to the hearsay rule' (1997) 85 California L Rev 159, p 162.

19 See, eg, Scheppele, KL, 'Just the facts Ma'am: sexualised violence, evidentiary habits and the revision of truth' (1992) 37 NYLS L Rev 123.

20 See, eg, Berger, V, 'Man's trial, woman's tribulation: rape cases in the courtroom' [1977] 1 Columbia L Rev 86; Torrey, M, 'When will we be believed? Rape myths and the idea of a fair trial in rape prosecutions' (1991) 24 University of California Davis L Rev 1013.

21 Mack, K, 'Continuing barriers to women's credibility' (1993) 4 Criminal Law Forum 327.

22 Mack, K, 'An Australian perspective on feminism, race and evidence' (1999) 28 Southwestern UL Rev 367.

simply to the all-male paradigm of the bar room brawl, but also to the situation of the battered woman. The admissibility of expert testimony on Battered Woman's Syndrome has proved a vexed issue for feminist evidence scholars,[23] however, as, arguably, such evidence draws at least some of its force from the troublesome construction of women as prone to medical and psychological disorders.

More generally, feminist writers have sought to challenge a belief in the neutrality of evidence law and to expose the gender bias which is inherent in evidentiary rules and practices:

> By applying feminist method we can examine how evidence rules are gendered, that is to say, how the rules reflect the sexual power and social dynamics in a our culture, how women may be underrepresented in the evidence rules, and how women's insights may be ignored.[24]

Kit Kinports was arguably the first to explore the broader significance of feminism for evidence law in *Evidence Engendered*.[25] Writing in 1991, Kinports outlined some of the insights that feminism could bring to evidence scholarship and teaching, indicating a wide range of topics that were ripe for feminist analysis. She argued that a feminist approach to Evidence and proof would question the formal, abstract, adversarial and hierarchical nature of evidence, and would challenge specific evidentiary doctrines for failing to incorporate women's perspectives and concerns. A feminist perspective, Kinports maintained, would advocate an approach to evidence which was more contextual, more co-operative and less formal.

In recent years, a feminist approach has been applied to a range of areas of the law of evidence, including those with less 'obvious' gender implications.[26] Feminist analyses have examined the gendered assumptions and stereotypes

---

23 See Murphy, S, 'Assisting the jury in understanding victimisation: expert psychological testimony on Battered Women Syndrome and rape trauma syndrome' (1992) 25 Columbia J Law and Social Problems 277; Sheehy, E, Stubbs, J and Tolmie, J, 'Defending battered women on trial: the Battered Women Syndrome and its limitations' (1992) 16 Crim LJ 369; Posch, P, 'The negative effects of expert testimony on the Battered Woman's Syndrome' (1998) 6 Am UJ Gender & Law 485; Raitt, FE and Zeedyk, MS, *The Implicit Relation of Psychology and Law: Women and Syndrome Evidence*, 2000, London: Routledge; Downs, DA, *More Than Victims: Battered Women, The Syndrome Society and the Law*, 1996, Chicago: Chicago UP.

24 Orenstein, A, 'Apology excepted: incorporating a feminist analysis into evidence policy where you would least expect it' (1999) 28 Southwestern UL Rev 221, p 226.

25 Kinports, K, 'Evidence Engendered' (1991) Illinois UL Rev 413. Others have since followed: Hunter, R, 'Gender in evidence law: masculine norms vs feminist reforms' (1996) 19 Harv Women's LJ 127; Hunter, R and Mack, K, 'Exclusion and silence: procedure and evidence', in Naffine, N and Owens, R (eds), *Sexing the Subject of Law*, 1997, Sydney: LBC Information Services, pp 171–92; MacCrimmon, M, 'The social construction of reality and the rules of evidence' (1991) 25 British Columbia UL Rev 36; *op cit*, Taslitz, fn 17.

26 See, eg, *op cit*, Orenstein (1997), fn 18; *ibid*, Orenstein.

in evidence textbooks;[27] the gendered implications of social science evidence;[28] the use and understanding of narrative in trials;[29] the interaction of race and gender issues in evidence;[30] and the biases of judges and jurors,[31] amongst other topics. The essays in this collection similarly span a broad range of topics, just as they encompass a variety of feminist perspectives and approaches. They address questions of evidence in several different jurisdictions, and they vary in their breadth and style. We hope that readers of this collection will find its diversity stimulating and will note the recurrence of certain themes and issues in different contexts. Threads of feminist critique can be found running through these chapters, although they are woven into discussions of evidence and proof in different fora and jusrisdictions.

Donald Nicolson's chapter addresses the broadest theoretical aspects of the subject of evidence law, applying feminist critiques to the assumptions which shape fact-finding. He argues that mainstream evidence scholarship, characterised by a commitment to Enlightenment rationality and legal positivism, may be regarded as masculinist in orientation. He then offers some exploratory thoughts about the possibility of bringing to the debate about evidence the insights of feminist approaches to epistemology and ethics. Such feminist work, developed in other academic disciplines, challenges the traditional evidence scholar's assumptions of universal cognitive competence;[32] as feminists have built upon postmodern and critical insights regarding the socially constructed nature of 'reality', they have inevitably presented challenges to the view that a 'real world' of objective reality can be discovered by logical and neutral methods.[33] Nicolson's conclusion is that the incorporation of such insights into evidence scholarship may enrich it and

---

27 Althouse, A, 'The lying woman, the devious prostitute, and other stories from the evidence casebook' (1994) 88 Northwestern UL Rev 914; Althouse, A, 'Beyond King Solomon's harlots: women in evidence' (1992) 65 S California UL Rev 1265.

28 Taslitz, A, 'A feminist approach to social scientific evidence: foundations' (1998) 5 Michigan J Gender & Law 1.

29 Weiss, S, 'How we constructed "the jury": a look at narrative storytelling' (1997) 12 Berkeley Women's LJ 73.

30 Ehrenreich, N, 'OJ Simpson and the myth of gender/race conflict' (1996) 67 Colorado UL Rev 931.

31 Minow, M, 'Stripped down like a runner or enriched by experience: bias and impartiality of judges and jurors' (1992) 33 W & ML Rev 1201.

32 For a discussion of these assumptions and the challenges to them, see MacCrimmon, M, 'The social construction of reality and the rules of evidence' (1991) 25 British Columbia UL Rev 36.

33 Aviva Orenstein has coined the term 'retro-epistemology' to denote the approach of those who reject the postmodern claims concerning the role of language in shaping thought and the influence of emotional and political forces in cognitive activities. See 'Evidence in a different voice: some thoughts on Professor Jonakait's critique of a feminist approach' (1997) 4 W & MJ Women & Law 295, responding to Jonakait, RJ, '"My God!" Is this how a feminist analyzes excited utterances?' (1997) 4 W & MJ Women & Law 263.

offer the possibility of 'more just, inclusive and, perhaps, even more accurate forms of fact-finding'.

Postmodern feminist insights regarding the importance of language are not simply relevant at the level of theoretical critique, of course. Gender differences in language and communication are a potentially rich terrain for feminist analyses of evidence law. Feminist work on evidence law, as in other areas, has illustrated starkly how facially neutral rules can serve to marginalise, distort and ultimately silence women's voices within the legal process. In her chapter, Fiona Raitt explains how the hearsay rule works to the disadvantage of women by excluding that evidence which plays a crucial role in women's oral traditions. Furthermore, Raitt describes how linguistic devices and speech styles which are typically associated with adversarial examination may be inimical to women, as they 'fail to acknowledge how women use speech to communicate feelings and experiences in a different way from men'.

Modes of communication are also relevant to Kit Kinports' chapter, which examines the law relating to evidential privileges, from legal professional privilege to spousal privilege. Her comprehensive and innovative analysis of the context in which these privileges operate leads her to the conclusion that they favour certain groups and relationships in a way which is class-biased and gender-biased. According to Kinports, current rules 'privilege' interests, values and professions dominated by men, who are typically of higher socio-economic status, and fail to protect the relationships between women and their chosen confidants. Once again, feminist analysis argues that apparently neutral rules of evidence have operated in a way which fails to grant full recognition to the relational and communicative differences between the lives of men and women.

Are less formal tribunals, with freedom to depart from the strictures of technical rules of evidence, more congenial environments for the hearing of women's stories? Rosemary Hunter's chapter considers the approach to evidence in Australia's specialist anti-discrimination tribunals, which were intended to provide informal and inexpensive venues for resolution of rights claims. Her conclusions are that the absence of formal evidential rules has not made them more comfortable sites for the hearing of sexual harassment claims. Instead, the apparent informality of the tribunals has removed those protections afforded to complainants by the rules of evidence, and has created new obstacles to the receptions of women's stories.

Another Australian perspective on the subject also shows the effect of evidentiary rules outside the confines of the traditional courtroom. Kathy Mack and Sharon Roach Anleu look at the way in which evidential considerations affect the resolution of sexual assault charges without trial. The student of evidence can be forgiven for imagining that most criminal cases are heard before a judge and jury, as those are the cases which fill the pages of evidence texts and casebooks. This chapter is a reminder of the facts that most cases are dealt with either summarily or through guilty pleas, and that the rules of evidence have a powerful role to play in shaping such outcomes as well as in the conduct of jury trials. This chapter is one of several in the collection to look at questions of evidence in relation to sexual offences. As noted above, this has been a focus of feminist analysis from the earliest days of feminist evidence scholarship.[34]

Susan Easton also looks at sexual assault when she revisits an area of evidence law which has been subject to considerable feminist attention over the years: the use of sexual history evidence in rape trials.[35] In many jurisdictions, so called 'rape shield' laws have been the subject of legal and political debate,[36] and in her chapter Easton surveys the origins and history of the English provisions, while drawing upon similar debates in other jurisdictions.

Pamela Ferguson considers, in the context of sexual offence trials, the requirement of corroboration in Scots law. The required corroboration warnings which, in English law, formerly stigmatised female complainants in sexual offence cases have now been abolished, but a general requirement of corroboration still operates in Scots law. Ferguson's chapter discusses the impact of that rule upon the prosecution of sexual offences in Scotland.

The adversarial process of the common law has been criticised by feminists as reflecting male values of 'individual autonomy, competition and aggressiveness.[37] In particular, the adversarial process has been criticised for producing a trial atmosphere which is experienced as hostile and stressful by many victims and witnesses, and especially so in the context of rape and sexual assault prosecutions. One of the reasons often given for the perceived under-reporting of rape, and for the reluctance of complainants to testify, is the perception that such trials are especially likely to be conducted as an attack upon the complainant. In her chapter, Louise Ellison considers the position of complainants in such cases and recent attempts to introduce measures designed to protect complainants and other vulnerable witnesses. Through her examination of the research into the experience of witnesses, she gives

---

34 Indeed, there are examples of work on evidential and procedural aspects of rape and sexual assault law which could be described as feminist in their approach, although no explicitly feminist position is adopted by their authors: see Adler, Z, 'The relevance of sexual history evidence in rape: problems of subjective interpretation' [1985] Crim LR 769; McColgan, A, 'Common law and the relevance of sexual history evidence' [1996] OJLS 275; Temkin, J, 'Sexual history evidence – the ravishment of section 2' [1993] Crim LR 3; *op cit*, Berger, fn 20.

35 See, eg, the articles cited *ibid*.

36 Grant, Y, 'The penetration of the rape shield: *R v Seaboyer* and *R v Gayme* in the Ontario Court of Appeal' (1989–90) 3 CJWL 592; Haxton, D, 'Rape shield statutes: constitutional despite unconstitutional exclusions of evidence' [1985] Wisconsin L Rev 1219.

37 *Op cit*, Kinports, fn 25, p 425.

context to the feminist critiques of adversarialism discussed in Donald Nicolson's chapter, and offers the reader a basis for comparison of the criminal trial experience with the other fora, as discussed in the chapters by Kathy Mack and Sharon Roach Anleu and Rosemary Hunter.

Mary Childs' chapter considers different aspects of the law relating the character of the accused, beginning with the general question of whether allowing more character evidence into criminal trials would be a welcome advance to individualised and contextualised justice or a step which would operate to the disadvantage of those who are already disadvantaged or unpopular. She considers briefly the anomalies of the law with respect to cross-examination of the accused, but focuses on the area of evidence law encompassed by the term 'similar fact evidence'. She considers in particular the question of whether the Law Commission for England and Wales was correct to reject the US approach of creating a special rule to admit such evidence in respect of sexual offences.

Anne Scully has examined a controversial area of evidence law: the use of expert opinion testimony regarding Battered Woman's Syndrome in cases of domestic killings. Reviewing the case law and literature on the topic, she invites the reader to acknowledge the problems, as well as the advantages, of relying on this sort of evidence. Is the use of this type of evidence a desirable move towards the sort of contextualisation that feminists have sought, or does it present an unacceptable risk that it will contribute to the image of women as deviant and psychologically weak – the image which shaped many of the peculiarities of evidence and procedure in relation to sexual offences?

As can be seen from these brief accounts of the chapters, certain themes and issues recur: the tension between context and rules of general application; the consequences of adversarialism, both within the courtroom and outside it; the marginalising of women's voices and relational values in legal discourse; the particularly problematic shaping of the rules of evidence with respect to sexual offences; and the construction of women as psychologically troubled.

These are by no means the only areas of evidence law and theory that are suitable for feminist analysis, of course. Much work remains to be done in the study of evidence, proof and inference; the first explorations of many of these areas will undoubtedly be followed by refinement, counter-arguments and ongoing debates. We hope that this collection will inspire the reader to think about the application of such inquiries in other aspects of the subject, and to make connections between these pieces and other writings on evidence, whether explicitly feminist or not. We also hope that the reader will be encouraged to look at feminist writing on evidence and proof as part of a broader body of feminist work on law, and indeed as part of a feminist discussion about a body of social practices generally.

CHAPTER 2

GENDER, EPISTEMOLOGY AND ETHICS: FEMINIST PERSPECTIVES ON EVIDENCE THEORY

Donald Nicolson

INTRODUCTION

Evidence scholarship has traditionally suffered from all the ills that derive from legal positivism and its even more problematic child, legal formalism. Thus, until relatively recently it has concentrated almost exclusively on evidentiary rules which provide exceptions to the general notion of 'free proof'.[1] Moreover, in focusing on these exclusionary rules, evidence scholars have also suffered from what William Twining calls 'appellate court-itis'[2] and, more fundamentally, by what might be called 'black-letter syndrome'. Accordingly, they have concentrated on formal legal doctrine laid down by the superior courts rather than the day to day reality of fact-handling in the lower courts, in negotiations, pre-trial procedures, and by various other actors in the legal process, such as the police, probation officers and administrative officials.

More recently, socio-legal research has started to redress this imbalance by providing important critical insights into the process of fact-finding in law,[3] but these insights have had little impact on traditional evidence scholarship. Part of this critique has been addressed to how evidence law and practice – most notably in rape and other sexual offences cases – are premised on and reinforce sexist ideas. However, feminists have yet to extend their concerns to prevailing theoretical assumptions about the aims, methods and values of legal fact-finding. This chapter begins to fill this gap by offering a preliminary feminist critique of these assumptions. It will argue that mainstream evidence scholarship bears the traces of Enlightenment metaphysics and positivist jurisprudence, and that this ensures that fact-finding takes place in the shadow of law, with all its current male bias, and that its favoured methodologies are masculinist in orientation. In addition, it will also explore

---

1 Ie, the idea that all relevant evidence should be admissible to prove facts in issue: see Twining, W, *Rethinking Evidence: Exploratory Essays*, 1990, Oxford: Basil Blackwell, especially Chapter 6.

2 *Ibid*, p 157.

3 See the references collected in Nicolson, D, 'Facing facts: the teaching of fact construction in university law schools' (1997) 1 E & P 132, pp 139–42.

ways in which feminist approaches to epistemology and ethics may lead to more just, inclusive, and perhaps even more accurate forms of fact-finding. First, however, it is necessary to gain an idea of mainstream evidence discourse and the problems with it.

MAINSTREAM EVIDENCE DISCOURSE

For the purposes of a feminist critique, there are two important traditions in evidence discourse.[4] The central intellectual strand has been termed the 'Rationalist tradition' by William Twining, its original excavator,[5] and, more critically, 'fact positivism' by this author.[6] According to Twining, this tradition, exemplified by writers such as Bentham and Wigmore[7] and implicitly by Cross,[8] displays a 'remarkable homogeneity' in relation to the core concepts of truth, reason and justice and, hence, as to the central aims, methods and procedures of fact-finding. [9]

Along positivist lines, justice is defined narrowly as involving the application of substantive law to correct facts in terms of established legal procedures (what Twining calls 'expletive' justice). Although there are a number of other values to be protected, such as national security, civil liberties, etc, the aim of legal fact-finding and adjectival law, including evidence law, is predominantly rectitude of decisions. As regards rectitude of decisions, Enlightenment ontology[10] encourages a belief in the existence of objective reality, independent of human knowledge (a foundationalist ontology). And, in terms of Enlightenment epistemology,[11] truth is defined as knowledge which corresponds to this objective reality (the correspondence theory of truth) and as best discovered through reason, understood as the exercise of formal logic (scientific rationality).

---

4   See, also, the 'new evidence scholarship', which arose in the 1970s but has yet to have a widespread influence and is not sufficiently critical of evidence orthodoxy to warrant separate discussion. See Nicolson, D, 'Truth, reason and justice: epistemology and politics in evidence discourse' (1994) 57 MLR 726, pp 727–28. See, further, *op cit*, Twining, fn 1, pp 349–52; Jackson, J, 'Analysing the new evidence scholarship: towards a new conception of the law of evidence' (1996) 16 OJLS 309.

5   *Op cit*, Twining, fn 1, Chapter 3.

6   *Ibid*, Nicolson, particularly pp 734–40.

7   See Twining, W, *Theories of Evidence: Bentham and Wigmore*, 1985, London: Weidenfeld & Nicolson.

8   Tapper, C, *Cross and Tapper on Evidence*, 9th edn, 1999, London: Butterworths.

9   However, he also notes that there are differences between 'complacent' and 'aspirational' rationalists as to whether the Rationalist tradition's assumptions are actually upheld in practice or whether they are simply goals: *op cit*, Twining, fn 1, pp 74–76.

10 Ontology involves the study of what things are.

11 Epistemology involves the study of how we know what things are.

The second, and more pervasive, form of mainstream evidence discourse is characterised by the hard-nosed, practical and unreflective practitioner whose overwhelming concern is to win cases – through rhetoric and prejudice as much as by reason – rather than search for such a fickle mistress as truth or anything as idealistic as justice.[12] The maleness of this approach can be seen in the way that truth (like justice, virtue and beauty) is portrayed as stereotypically female: desirable, but fickle and elusive; whereas fact-finding is undertaken by practical men who inhabit the real world. Thus, when issues of truth and justice are not completely ignored, textbooks relate anecdotes in which, for instance, a judge asks counsel seeking to exclude certain facts, 'Am I not to hear the truth?', only to be told, 'No, your Lordship is to hear the evidence'.[13] The story's implicit moral is that there are many legal rules which exclude facts which the 'naive'[14] might think relevant. But another lesson is learnt: questions of truth are not questions for lawyers, but for head in the clouds philosophers, endlessly debating whether or not unobserved trees 'really' fall in the Black Forest.

I will not deal explicitly with this 'complacent fact positivism' both because it is largely unreflective and because its pervasiveness is at least partly due to the Rationalist tradition's approach to truth, reason and justice. This is not to say that the Rationalist tradition has directly inculcated indifference towards the aims and assumptions of legal fact-finding.[15] However, were there to exist a more critical theoretical tradition in evidence scholarship, complacent fact positivism might be less pervasive than it is today. Accordingly, we now turn to how feminists can contribute to such a critique.

FACT POSITIVISM AND PATRIARCHAL LAW

My critique of mainstream evidence discourse is divided into two parts. The next section looks at how the Rationalist tradition's conceptualisation of truth, reason and justice can be said to be inimical to female (or, at least, feminist) ways of knowing and morality. This section argues more specifically that its theoretical assumptions are likely to ensure that fact-finding operates 'in the shadow of the law' and that, as law's content is embedded with male values

---

12 See Nicolson, D and Webb, J, *Professional Legal Ethics: Critical Interrogations*, 1999, Oxford: OUP, Chapter 6, particularly pp 166–67.

13 Murphy, P, *A Practical Approach to Evidence*, 3rd edn, 1985, London: Blackstone, p 1. Note, however, that later editions have replaced this anecdote with a brief, but uncritical, description of the philosophical basis of fact-finding.

14 *Ibid.*

15 Most lawyers are unlikely to have been introduced to the writings of the more reflective fact positivists. Indeed, its assumptions about truth, reason and justice are probably more implicit than explicit amongst evidence scholars: see *op cit*, Twining, fn 1, p 74.

and supportive of male interests (albeit not exclusively or uniformly), the long shadow cast by law has a male form.

The starting point for the argument is that, given both its intellectual ancestry and political function, mainstream evidence discourse is best understood as a form of positivism. This 'fact positivism' is to the study and practice of fact-finding what legal positivism is to the study and practice of law. Both encourage the view that the task of lawyers and adjudicators is neutral and value-free. Both focus attention on logic, whether of rules or of proof, and away from the inherently political and partial nature of law and facts.

Positivism's influence on the Rationalist tradition can be seen in a number of important respects: the claim of rationality and the privileging of scientific rationality; the assumption that there exist objective facts 'out there', waiting to be discovered; the focus on only one type of truth, that of 'factual' truth, and only one form of justice, that of 'expletive justice'; and, finally, linked to all of these, the belief in the possibility of value-free processes of fact-finding. By analysing these assumptions in more detail and by illustrating their operation in cases involving   women charged with murder, I intend to show that fact positivism creates a form of closure that helps isolate the study and practice of fact-finding from feminist challenge.

According to fact positivism, evidential processes are aimed at discovering 'Truth',[16] understood as what actually happened in an objective sense. While the next section will examine feminist criticisms of the foundationalist epistemology behind this conception of truth, what is important here is that truth is conflated with rectitude of decision. By contrast, along with other critical theorists, feminists regard adjudicative decisions as not just about 'what happened'. They do not just rule on what can be called 'factual truth'; they actually purvey truth.

This can be illustrated by the cases of Sara Thornton and Kiranjit Ahluwalia. Both were subjected to considerable physical violence and mental abuse by husbands whom they eventually killed following provocative behaviour, yet both were convicted of murder despite pleading provocation. Both were released on appeal, having had their murder convictions reduced to manslaughter on grounds of diminished responsibility, although Sara Thornton was only successful second time around.[17] On one level, the cases purvey truths of a banal nature. Sara Thornton's trial and first appeal[18] tells us that she committed murder, whereas Kiranjit Ahluwalia's appeal[19] tells us

---

16 The capital letter is deliberate in reflecting both the Rationalist tradition's Enlightenment heritage and the foundational nature of its conceptualisation of 'Truth, Reason and Justice'.

17 *R v Thornton (No 2)* [1996] 2 All ER 1023.

18 *R v Thornton* [1992] 1 All ER 306.

19 *R v Ahluwalia* [1992] 4 All ER 889.

that she killed while suffering from diminished responsibility. However, these decisions cannot be separated from legal definitions of murder, provocation and diminished responsibility, gender stereotypes and social perceptions of violence by and against women. Provocation law, for instance, tells us that it is excusable to kill in a fit of temper immediately after being provoked (especially if a man catches his wife in the course of adultery), but not if one finally snaps through a mixture of anger, fear and frustration at years of domestic violence. In other words, the law tells us that male patterns of violence are acceptable but female patterns are not. Kiranjit Ahluwalia's case also tells us that women who passively accept years of extreme violence and adultery for the sake of their marriages and children qualify for sympathetic legal treatment. By contrast, the lesson to be learnt from Sara Thornton's trial and first appeal is that women who have a number of relationships and failed marriages, who go out to work, who drink and who are seen as aggressive deserve law's full penalty. Thus, we see that both judgments did more than just rule on factual truth; they laid down truths as to morality and gender politics.[20]

However, by concentrating on factual truth, fact positivism tends to erect a protective barrier around the gender politics contained within law. This process is reinforced by beliefs as to the best procedural method of finding factual truth and related conceptions of the lawyer's role. Thus most fact positivists seem to accept the assumption behind the current adversarial system of justice[21] that truth is best discovered 'by the opposite effect of practised and ingenious men [sic] presenting to the selection of an impartial judge the best arguments for the establishment or explanation of truth'.[22] Just as it was thought in pre-modern times that God would ensure victory to the righteous in trial by battle or ordeal, so it is assumed that adversarial battles will be won (at least usually) by those with truth on their side. Accordingly, like latter day knightly champions, lawyers are expected to act as their client's partisan in the adversarial battle. More specifically, they are *neutral* partisans – or, more pejoratively, hired guns – in being excused or even prohibited[23] from concerning themselves about the morality or politics of client ends or the means used to achieve those ends. As long as lawyers refrain from seeking

---

20 At most, sophisticated fact positivists such as Twining are ambivalent about dangerous gender stereotypes purveyed as truth by the legal system, being unsure of whether they are 'objectionable because they are inaccurate or because this is an offensive way of speaking irrespective of the accuracy of the stereotypes': Anderson, T and Twining, W, *Analysis of Evidence*, 1991, London: Weidenfeld & Nicolson, p 378.

21 But note the more critical approach of 'aspirational rationalists', such as Jerome Frank: *Courts on Trial*, Cahn, E (ed), revised edn, 1970, Princeton: Princeton UP; and see, more generally, *op cit*, Nicolson and Webb, fn 12, pp 185–88.

22 Smith, S, *Sydney Smith's Works*, Vol 11, p 19, cited in Rogers, S, 'The ethics of advocacy' (1899) 59 LQR 259, p 262.

23 See *op cit*, Nicolson and Webb, fn 12, Chapter 6 on the different positions with regard to barristers, solicitor advocates and other solicitors.

illegal ends or using tactics prohibited by law or professional rules, they are regarded as performing an inherently moral function by ensuring the adversarial system's proper working and hence the discovery of factual truth. Consequently, it is no surprise that, despite the formal constraints on prosecutorial zeal,[24] the barrister prosecuting Sara Thornton sought to portray her as a woman of loose morals, notwithstanding the irrelevance of her sexual morality to liability and his personal opinion that she did not deserve a murder conviction.[25]

The closure around law's values ensured by fact positivism's reduction of truth to factual truth and the lawyer's limited role is reinforced by the Rationalist tradition's conceptualisation of reason and justice. Its claim to 'rationality' rests upon the distinction between pre-modern methods of proof such as force of arms or ordeal and modern forms of proof based upon the use of human reason.[26] This 'reason' is conceptualised in very narrow terms as being commensurate with what is variously described as scientific rationality, formal logic, British Empiricism, etc. We shall return later to a specifically feminist critique of scientific rationality, but for now can note that the concentration on rationality helps deflect challenges to the legal status quo. By portraying legal systems as comprising coherent sets of compatible principles and adjudication as simply involving the abstract and logical application of clear law to facts, fact positivism paints a picture of law devoid of politics. This focuses attention on law's internal logic and application rather than its content and social context, thus helping to legitimise the currently sexist legal order.

This process is also furthered by the specific concentration on formal logic rather than on other forms of reasoning. Formal logic tends to be adopted by those who are content with the premises involved in a reasoning process. It encourages attention to be focused solely on their logical application rather than their content. Moreover, inductive reasoning – fact positivism's favoured form of logic – enables the concealment of one's major premises, thus suggesting that they are axiomatic and unproblematic.[27]

In any event, reason is largely an instrumentalist concept. It does not tell us what we should reason from or what we should reason to, but only how to get there.[28] However, in terms of fact positivism's holy 'Truth, Reason and

---

24 *Op cit*, Nicolson and Webb, fn 12, Chapter 8.

25 Nadel, J, *Sara Thornton: The Story of a Woman Who Killed*, 1993, London: Victor Gollancz, Chapter 7.

26 Eg, *op cit*, Twining, fn 1, pp 33, 72.

27 Graham, KW, 'There will always be an England: the instrumental ideology of evidence' (1987) 85 Michigan L Rev 1204, pp 1219–20; a point conceded by Twining, *op cit*, fn 1, p 81; *op cit*, Anderson and Twining, fn 20.

28 Simon, HA, *Reason in Human Affairs*, 1983, Oxford: Basil Blackwell, pp 7–11; Wigmore, JH, 'The problem of proof' (1913) 8 Illinois L Rev 77.

Justice' trinity, reason is aimed at ascertaining factual truth, which in turn provides the necessary conditions for the application of substantive law. Apart from elements of procedural justice, this application of substantive law to correct facts is what is meant by justice.

The resulting picture of legal fact-finding thus involves a closely controlled system in which truth, reason and justice all fall under the shadow of substantive law. Reason provides the link between facts and truth, and between truth and substantive law. However, the system is largely self-referential in that the starting points – the facts – are to a large extent selected by substantive law. Facts will only be admitted as evidence if they are relevant to the particular area(s) of substantive law raised by particular cases. The principle of relevance thus helps to filter out facts which might challenge the gendered nature of existing law. Moreover, since this principle is regarded as merely an empty conduit pipe for the application of whatever can be presented as reason,[29] the exclusion of facts which might challenge the gender (or other) politics contained in substantive law can be represented, not as a political decision, but as simply the neutral application of logic to substantive legal rules.

Thus, to return to criminal law's treatment of battered women who kill, feminists have argued that it is largely based upon standards of behaviour and morality which reflect a male perspective.[30] Given that men usually react immediately to insults and violence in a fit of anger, the provocation defence has been defined as requiring a 'sudden and temporary loss of self-control'.[31] Consequently, facts which establish a time lag or 'cooling off' period between domestic violence and killing are admitted as relevant, whereas the woman's subjection to years of physical and mental abuse by the man have often been excluded as irrelevant. Of course, as provocation law itself illustrates,[32] substantive law has to be interpreted, and is thus constantly being developed. However, such developments tend to be kept within narrow confines by legal methodology and dominant ideology.

Substantive law's influence over the facts of cases is not limited to their selection: it also helps construct them.[33] The concept of fact construction rejects the positivistic notion that there are facts out there waiting, neatly

---

29 *Op cit*, Tapper, fn 8, pp 51–52.

30 See, eg, Nicolson, D, 'Telling tales: gender discrimination, gender construction and battered women who kill' (1995) 3 FLS 185; McColgan A, 'A feminist's perspective on general defences', in Nicolson, D and Bibbings, L (eds), *Feminist Perspectives on Criminal Law*, 2000, London: Cavendish Publishing.

31 *Duffy* [1949] 1 All ER 932.

32 See *ibid*, McColgan.

33 However, fact construction is not only influenced by substantive law, but also by adjectival law: see, eg, McBarnet, D, *Conviction: Law, the State and the Construction of Justice*, 1981, London: Macmillan. However, as this is at least an implicit theme in most of the other chapters in this volume, it will not be developed here.

packaged, to be discovered and adjudicated upon in terms of law. This assumption is clearly linked to a foundationalist epistemology and a correspondence theory of truth: there can only be an objective truth if there are objective facts; true knowledge corresponds to these objective facts. As in the declaratory theory of adjudication,[34] the human and political element in adjudication is conveniently obscured, thus allowing the process of law and fact-finding to be portrayed as mechanical and capable of neutral performance.

By contrast, many theories of fact construction view 'reality' as unbounded, multi-faceted, confusing and subject to varying interpretations.[35] Following Nietzsche, one can go further and assert that instead of 'facts' there are only interpretations from specific perspectives.[36] Moreover, the only way we have of working with those things we call 'facts' is through language and other forms of discourse. As feminists have so vividly shown, language and other discourses clearly do not provide a value-free means of mechanically representing 'reality'. They are shot through with values and these values are always read into 'reality' and 'facts'. The facts in legal cases are thus constructed by the various political, moral and other discourses which are part of the language we use, including the language of law. In other words, law and fact cannot be separated because law and the discourses with which it is associated are part of the process of fact construction.[37] For example, the conclusions in *Thornton* and *Ahluwalia*[38] that, despite considerable domestic violence and provocative acts by their husbands shortly before being killed, neither woman was provoked, was not simply one of 'historical fact'.[39]

The legal construction of facts is not, however, confined to 'fact-value complexes'[40] such as provocation, intention and murder. The definitions of law, its language and underlying values also crucially influence the construction of the minutiae of cases. For instance, although difficult to ascertain, it is plausible that the law's description of any time gap between provocation and murder as a 'cooling off' rather than a 'boiling over' period

---

34 See, eg, Atiyah, PS, 'Judges and policy' (1980) 15 Israel L Rev 346, p 347.

35 Eg, *op cit*, Frank, fn 21; Jackson, B, *Law, Fact and Narrative Coherence*, 1988, Liverpool: Deborah Charles, especially Chapters 1, 3; Bennett, WL and Feldman, MS, *Reconstructing Reality in the Courtroom*, 1981, London: Tavistock Feldman; *op cit*, McBarnet, fn 33. For further references, see Cotterrell, R, *The Sociology of Law: An Introduction*, 1984, London: Butterworths, pp 222–25, 342.

36 See, eg, Nietzsche, F, *The Will to Power*, Kaufmann, W and Hollingdale, RJ (trans), 1968, New York: Random House, particularly Bk III.

37 *Ibid*, Cotterrell, p 222.

38 *R v Thornton* [1992] 1 All ER 306; *R v Ahluwalia* [1992] 4 All ER 889.

39 Cf Twining, W, 'Hot air in the redwoods: a sequel to *The Wind in the Willows*' (1988) 86 Michigan L Rev 1523, p 1545.

40 Stone, J, *Social Dimensions of Law and Society*, 1966, London: Stevens, p 737.

may influence witnesses and adjudicators to decide whether there are significant time gaps between domestic violence and killing.

The *Thornton* and *Ahluwalia* judgments provide more clear cut examples of fact construction. Given their experiences as battered women, and given the various legal categories of homicide, the defendants' actions could have been regarded as fully blameworthy (murder), morally justified (self-defence), morally excused (provocation) or medically excused (diminished responsibility). However, the male-orientation of self-defence and provocation meant that the only categories realistically available were those of rational murderer or irrational sufferer of diminished responsibility. The Court of Appeal's judgments illustrate how character depiction, plot development, the inclusion and exclusion of certain parts of the stories and the choice of language are used to construct 'the facts' so as to make them fit the chosen legal category.[41] Echoing prevailing discourses about 'appropriate femininity', in terms of which women are expected to be domesticated, passive, and demure, and are portrayed as pathologically subject to biological control,[42] and about female criminality, in terms of which female violence is seen as either the result of madness or badness,[43] Sara Thornton was constructed as a cold hearted killer and Kiranjit Ahluwalia as a helpless victim of circumstances beyond her control. These constructions were then available to be presented as justifying the labels of murder and diminished responsibility, respectively.

Fact positivism's closure around law's gendered content is reflected finally in its conceptualisation of justice as requiring no more than the rational application of substantive law to 'correct' facts. The feminist response to this formalistic concept of justice is obvious: the value of seeking factual truth is significantly reduced if the actual decision is morally or politically unacceptable. To continue the provocation example, it may have been 'true' that there was a time gap between Deepak Ahluwalia's provocation of Kiranjit and her fatal response; however, it by no means follows that it was just to reject her provocation plea.

EPISTEMOLOGY, ETHICS AND FEMINIST CRITIQUE

The problem with fact positivism's theoretical assumptions goes beyond its tendency to ensure that fact-finding takes place in the shadow of male-

---

41 *Op cit*, Nicolson, fn 30.

42 See, eg, Carlen, P and Worral, A, *Gender, Crime and Justice*, 1987, Milton Keynes: OU Press, Chapter 1.

43 See, eg, Heidensohn, F, *Women and Crime*, 1985, London: Macmillan, especially Chapter 5; Jones, A, *Women Who Kill*, 1991, London: Victor Gallancz; Bell, C and Fox, M, 'Telling stories of women who kill' (1995) 5 SLS 471.

orientated law, with a consequent reinforcing of male values and interests. Many feminists would argue that the epistemological and ethical approaches to fact-finding encouraged by fact positivism are masculinist and, hence, problematic, even if law's content was gender neutral.

As we have seen, fact positivism contains both an ontological assumption – that objective truth exists independently of human knowledge – and an epistemological assumption – humans can obtain 'true' knowledge, defined as knowledge which corresponds to that which is actually 'out there'. This in turn assumes an epistemological subject, who is able to stand above and outside his[44] historical and geographical context, and whose mind represents a mirror onto which reality is reflected. Accordingly, it can be claimed that neutral, value-free knowledge is possible through a combination of empirical observation and the use of reason.

Most feminists have avoided the esoteric ontological debate about whether an objective truth really exists – probably quite sensibly.[45] Instead, their attention has concentrated on epistemological claims about the possibility of true knowledge, the acontextual and neutral epistemological knower and the role of reason which originate in Enlightenment thought and are to be found in mainstream evidence discourse.[46] As already noted, such claims involve a foundationalist and rationalist epistemology in holding that all knowledge, whether it be in the natural or social sciences, ethics or in law, can be based on objective, rationally derived foundations.

Feminists argue that Enlightenment epistemology played an important part in the subordination of women, both by excluding their perspectives on what counts as true knowledge and more fundamentally by excluding women as epistemological subjects capable of knowledge production. Thus they argue that describing the Enlightenment as the 'Birth of Man' is correct in its literal gender specific sense. Whereas this 'Age of Reason' freed men from the epistemological (and ethical) shackles of the church and other traditional authorities, enabling them to harness Science to the yoke of Progress, women were excluded from this epistemological revolution. This was because knowledge and behaviour which is regarded (or can be presented) as rational in being controlled by the mind and as flowing logically from accepted premises is privileged, whereas women have traditionally been depicted as ruled by their hearts or even more negatively by their bodies, wombs and raging hormones. Being associated with emotion, intuition, passion, etc, rather

---

44 Enlightenment epistemology clearly assumes a male knower.
45 Thus, to deny objective truth without asserting an objective truth involves a self-referential contradiction.
46 See, eg, the essays in Nicholson, L (ed), *Feminism/Postmodernism*, 1990, London: Routledge, especially Pt I; Lennon, K and Whitford, M, *Knowing the Difference: Feminist Perspectives in Epistemology*, 1994, London: Routledge.

than 'reason', they have been disqualified as capable knowers.[47] Moreover, the Age of Reason justified women's relegation to the undervalued and uninfluential sphere of the home and to those occupations requiring their 'natural' female traits of nurturing. Consequently, politics, economics, law and other arenas of public power came to be debated in the language and experiences of men – defined as rationality.

In response, feminists argue that 'reason' and 'rationality' are not universal qualities. They are contextually specific, in that perceptions of what is rational vary historically and geographically, and politically loaded, in that the designation 'rational' usually connotes more than simply behaviour which is controlled by the intellect, but involves a value judgment as to its soundness.[48] However, having ensured women's exclusion from the public world, male perspectives could be presented simply as those of universal reason and knowledge came to bear the deep imprints of male experiences and interests.

The legitimation of this process has been significantly reinforced by the positivistic belief that knowledge obtained through reason and empirical observation using sense perception could be objective, neutral and value-free, and that as rational knowers (male) subjects could escape the distorting influences of their historical and geographical context to produce gender-neutral knowledge. This neutral and objective stance is, however, only available to those who are socially and culturally constructed as normal. As the norm has always been constructed in terms of male experiences and perspectives and, indeed, as it has always been constructed through depicting women as the Other,[49] women are again disqualified from the status of neutral and objective knowers.[50] Many feminists regard the idea of an epistemological subject capable of achieving the 'view from nowhere'[51] as simply an Enlightenment myth used to exclude the perspective of the Other – whether she be female, black, gay, etc. Yet, it is this myth, combined with the alleged objectivity and rationality of the logical/empirical approach to

---

47 See, particularly, Lloyd, G, *The Man of Reason: 'Male' and 'Female' in Western Philosophy*, 1984, London: Methuen. In the context of law, see Naffine, N, *Law and the Sexes: Explorations in Feminist Jurisprudence*, 1990, Sydney: Allen & Unwin, Chapters 1 and 2. For an example in evidence discourse, see *op cit*, Anderson and Twining, fn 20, pp 379–80.

48 On the various meanings of the term 'rational', see Kronman, AT, *Max Weber*, 1983, London: Edward Arnold, Chapter 4.

49 Indeed, it is argued that the very privileging of formal logic with its principles of strict order, and in particular the principle of the excluded middle (anything and everything must be either A or not-A), acts to force women into the role of the Other (not-A) in the definition of the norm (A, men): cf Hartsock, N, 'Foucault on power: a theory for women?', in *op cit*, Nicholson, fn 46, pp 162–63.

50 See, particularly, Braidotti, R, 'Body-images and the pornography of representation', in *op cit*, Lennon and Whitford, fn 46, p 27.

51 Nagel, T, *The View from Nowhere*, 1986, Oxford: OUP; also called the Archimedean point of view or God's eye view.

knowledge, that has so effectively disguised the male bias in the knowledge produced in the public world.

As a further strand to arguments about the intimate connection between knowledge, methodology and power, feminists have shown how male dominated discourses, such as law, have set up hierarchies of knowledges and used these to disqualify feminist challenges.[52] Given the Enlightenment's celebration of science's objectivity and liberatory potential, it is perhaps unsurprising that scientific knowledge has been given pride of place. In law, however, the knowledge purveyed by legal doctrine and the legitimation accorded to such knowledge by legal methods places legal knowledge just below if not above scientific knowledge. Nevertheless, whatever the exact ranking of the two 'big boys', the perspectives of women, feminism and 'softer' disciplines such as sociology or philosophy are disqualified as ranking too low in the hierarchy of knowledge, especially given their alleged lack of rational and objective bite.[53]

Finally, feminist ethicists have challenged the alleged gender neutrality of dominant Western conceptions of ethics.[54] These see moral subjects as completely abstracted from their social context and from gender relations. Moreover, justice and morality are constituted by the abstract, impersonal application of predetermined rules based on the intrinsic quality of moral acts (as in deontology) rather than the consequences of behaviour (as in consequentialism) and the focus of ethics is on formal equality, individual autonomy and allegedly universal rights. Having set this up as the highest form of moral reasoning, a long tradition of masculinist thought has argued that women have an inferior sense of morality; that, being ruled by their hearts rather than heads, they are unable to make proper moral judgments.[55] Moreover, while Enlightenment notions of human rights and equality were valuable in supporting the liberation of (propertied, Western and heterosexual) men, they have done little for women who were excluded not just from ethical philosophising but from moral subjecthood as well. Similarly, following the grudging extension of full moral and political subjecthood to women this century, feminists discovered that reliance on dominant ethical approaches with their focus on formal equality, individual rights and personal freedom have proved to be a mixed blessing. Thus, the equal application of gender neutral standards ignores, and in fact exacerbates, actual and

---

52 See, eg, Smart, C, *Feminism and the Power of Law*, 1989, London: Routledge, Chapter 1.

53 See, further, Yeatman, A, 'Postmodern epistemological politics and social science', in *op cit*, Lennon and Whitford, fn 46.

54 For an overview see, eg, *op cit*, Nicolson and Webb, fn 12, pp 34–36; Porter, E, *Feminist Perspectives on Ethics*, 1999, London: Longman.

55 Cf the quotes in Gilligan, C, *In a Different Voice: Psychological Theory and Women's Development*, revised edn, 1993, Cambridge, Mass: Harvard UP, Chapter 1.

constructed gender differences,[56] individual rights help to divide and buy off oppressed groups such as women[57] and the minimalist nature of deontological moral duties favour the freedom of the already empowered by only requiring moral agents to refrain from positive harm to others, rather than also helping to redress centuries of oppression.[58]

FEMINIST RECONSTRUCTIONS OF TRUTH, REASON AND JUSTICE

In response to dominant epistemological and ethical theories, feminists have proposed alternatives[59] which could be used to rethink fact positivism's conceptions of truth, reason and justice. Arguing that the very methods and assumptions of Enlightenment epistemology and ethics are masculine in nature, many feminists call for a celebration of female ways of knowing and moral thinking as equal, if not superior, to Enlightenment models.

As regards epistemology,[60] while Enlightenment approaches speak as if true knowledge can be captured by an all powerful objective knower, many feminists argue that knowledge is always produced from the partial perspective of individual knowers and, hence, the more perspectives on particular issues, the greater the approximation of knowledge to truth. Accordingly, the idea that (white, middle class, heterosexual) men can provide accurate access to truth is rejected in favour of drawing upon the experiences and perspectives of those excluded from power – women, of course, but also those from ethnic minorities, the working class, gays and lesbians, etc.

This insight led more specifically to the development of 'feminist standpoint epistemology' in terms of which the perspective of distance is rejected in favour of experience and engagement, and the (allegedly) neutral and objective perspective is rejected in favour of a gendered perspective. Indeed, some feminists argue that women's experience as the excluded and exploited Other is more inclusive and critically coherent that that of men and that the female perspective might even be able to 'subsume the partial and

---

56   See *op cit*, Nicolson, fn 4.

57   See, eg, *op cit*, Smart, fn 52, Chapter 7.

58   Cf *op cit*, Nicolson and Webb, fn 12, Chapter 2, s 3.

59   But cf early feminists who relied on Enlightenment ideas to argue that sexism was empirically untrue, irrational and unjust and that it could be eradicated by relying on Enlightenment values: see, eg, Harding, S, 'Feminism, science and anti-Enlightenment critiques', in *op cit*, Nicholson, fn 46, pp 90–94; Bartlett, KT, 'Feminist legal methods (1990) 103 Harv L Rev 829, pp 868–72.

60   The following discussion draws on *op cit*, Nicholson, fn 46; *op cit*, Lennon and Whitford, fn 46; *ibid*, Bartlett.

perverse understandings of masculine inquiry'.[61] The controversial method of 'consciousness raising', which values 'honesty over consistency, teamwork over self-sufficiency and personal narrative over abstract analysis',[62] renders more concrete the focus on the female perspective. It calls for women to explore collectively their personal experiences *qua* women in an interactive and collaborative process, enabling personal harms suffered by individual women to be revealed as collective experiences of oppression.

In addition to highlighting the importance of female perspectives on knowledge, feminists have also argued that women reason differently to men. While men tend to rely on abstract thinking, universal principles and generalisations, women, it is alleged, pay more attention to the detailed nuances of particular situations and their context. Similarly, while men regard the best way of understanding issues as involving objectivity and emotional distancing, women regard engagement, emotional involvement and personal experience as necessary for, rather than inimical to, proper understandings. Furthermore, in analysing and communicating factual information, men tend to use atomistic methods which concentrate on the logical connections between individual facts, whereas women tend to think more holistically and to understand and communicate information in the form of narratives.[63] Some feminists take this celebration of the 'feminine' by what is called 'feminist practical reasoning' one step forward and call for a celebration of those very ways of knowing – intuition, emotion and passion – used by rationalist discourse to denigrate and disqualify women and a revaluation of the everyday life practices of women, particularly in their reproductive roles, as 'complex, rational, thoughtful and important activities'.[64]

Parallel to the assertion that women have different (and possibly superior) epistemological stances to men, some feminists have claimed that women speak morality 'in a different voice'.[65] Thus it is argued that women tend to favour an 'ethics of care' which is based on connectedness, subjective emotion and responsibility for maintaining relationships; and this is sometimes supported by psychoanalytical claims[66] that men tend to see themselves as autonomous from others, whereas women see themselves as continuous with and connected to others.

---

61 Di Stefano, C, 'Dilemmas of difference: feminism, modernity and postmodernism', in *op cit*, Nicholson, fn 46, p 74.

62 *Op cit*, Bartlett, fn 59, p 864.

63 On the difference between atomism and holism, see *op cit*, Twining, fn 1, Chapter 7.

64 *Ibid*, Di Stefano, p 68, referring to McMillan, C, *Women, Reason and Nature: Some Philosophical Problems with Feminism*, 1982, Princeton, NJ: Princeton UP.

65 *Op cit*, Gilligan, fn 55.

66 Chodorow, N, *The Reproduction of Mothering: Psychoanalysis and the Sociology of Gender*, 1978, Berkeley, CA: California UP; Dinnerstein, D, *The Rocking of the Cradle and the Ruling of the World*, 1987, London: Warren.

According to Carol Gilligan, these differing perspectives translate into two different ethical perspectives. Whereas the masculine 'ethic of justice' requires that everyone should be treated equally, the 'ethic of care' demands that no one should be hurt. Whereas men tend to stand on principle and act according to people's rights irrespective of the personal consequences, women tend to be more pragmatic, being more concerned to uphold relationships and protect their loved ones from harm. Whereas the ethic of justice assumes that one can resolve moral dilemmas by abstract and universalistic moral reasoning, the ethic of care requires due attention to context and to the specific circumstances of each moral dilemma. And in resolving such dilemmas, men tend to rank ethical principles, whereas women attempt to address the concrete needs of all and to ensure that if anyone is going to be harmed it should be those who can best bear the harm. Along similar lines, Nel Noddings has argued that a morality based on rules or principles fails to capture what is distinctive and valuable about female morality. Attempting to resolve ethical dilemmas through abstract principles capable of universalisation conceals the sort of questions which need to be explored and which are an essential part of moral judgment. However, whereas Gilligan has argued that the ethic of care should be valued equally alongside the ethic of justice, Noddings has argued that it is, in fact, morally superior.[67]

The above feminist approaches to epistemology and ethics are significant in challenging Enlightenment notions of truth, reason and justice as masculinist in orientation and supportive of male interests. Moreover, in self-consciously celebrating qualities and values associated with women, they have been valuable in providing women with a sense of self-worth. However, not least for their celebration of the feminine, there are problems with what may be called 'difference feminism'.

Thus, the idea that women reason differently to men both in general and in resolving moral dilemmas has come under attack. The assertion that female ways of thinking constitute the polar opposite of masculinist epistemology is not sustainable given that all reasoning involves a mixture of abstraction and contextualisation; of general principles and specific facts.[68] Certainly, according to the Realist view of adjudication, (male) judges have always relied on a mixture of intuition, hunch and formal logic in reaching their decisions,[69] whereas research shows that, as compared with narrative and other forms of holistic reasoning, formal logic only plays a relatively minor role in the thinking of fact adjudicators when assessing arguments about facts.[70]

---

67 See Flanagan, O, *Varieties of Moral Personality: Ethics and Psychological Realism*, 1991, Cambridge, Mass: Harvard UP, Chapter 11 for the various positions taken on this issue.

68 *Op cit*, Bartlett, fn 59, pp 855–58; Thompson, J, 'Moral difference and moral epistemology', in *op cit*, Lennon and Whitford, fn 46.

69 See, eg, Frank, J, *Law and the Modern Mind*, 1949, New York: Stevens.

70 See *op cit*, Nicolson, fn 3, p 143.

Similarly, further research on moral reasoning suggests that both sexes use a mixture of care and justice perspectives.[71] At most, it can be said that women have a tendency towards seeking more facts and being concerned with the concrete circumstances relevant to moral inquiries, while men are less inclined towards a caring ethic.

But even if gender differences in epistemological and ethical thinking can be shown to exist, many feminists regard their recognition as problematic. For one thing, they ignore the many differences between women related to their different life experiences and the impact of factors such as race, class and sexual orientation. More importantly, however, speaking of a female epistemology and a female ethics ties in with the essentialist idea that women are naturally, or at least immutably, different from men. This is inherently dangerous, in that gender differences are rarely asserted without, at least, an implicit assumption of the superiority of stereotypical male values, ways of behaving and forms of thinking. Indeed, by celebrating women's qualities of intuition and caring, feminism may simply reinforce the very qualities which male ideology have claimed disqualify women from the public sphere of society and make them particularly suited to the less valued and less influential private sphere. Rather than celebrating women's natural propensity towards intuition and caring, feminists might simply be reinforcing social constructions of femaleness designed to serve male interests.[72]

The approach of difference feminism can also be criticised from a postmodernist perspective. While rejecting the rationalism of masculinist epistemology, many difference feminists retain its foundationalism and implicitly accept the notion of an autonomous subject standing outside her social context. Feminist consciousness raising, for example, appears to hold out the hope of escaping the pervasive influence of language and discourse in constructing gender and individual subjects in order to be able to reveal the authentic woman behind male constructions of femininity. However, given the dominance of difference feminism by white, middle class heterosexual woman, it is possible that consciousness raising and other feminist methods might simply replace the oppressive truths purveyed by masculinist discourse

---

71 Menkel-Meadow, C, 'Portia *redux*: another look at gender, feminism and legal ethics', in Parker, S and Sampford, C (eds), *Legal Ethics and Legal Practice*, 1995, Oxford: Clarendon, pp 28–30; and cf *op cit*, Flanagan, fn 67, pp 228–32, who argues that, if gender differences exist, it is probably because women and men face different moral dilemmas.

72 Cf the studies which reveal that African and Afro-Caribbean men also tend more towards an ethic of care than one of justice: Tronto, JC, *Moral Boundaries: A Political Argument for an Ethic of Care*, 1993, London: Routledge, pp 82–84; thus implying that a caring voice might simply be that of the subordinated, rather than that of women. Perhaps more plausible is a linkage between the ethic of justice and capitalism.

with those which ignore the perspectives and interests of black, working class and lesbian women, if not men as well.[73] There is simply no one uniform category of 'woman' upon which to ground a unified feminist epistemology. In fact, under the influence of psychoanalysis, postmodern feminists have gone beyond questioning the coherence of a female identity to argue that individual subjects do not even present a unity to themselves, never mind others. In other words, the subject is 'more like a railway junction where signifiers, discourses and messages meet or flash past than a source, origin or mirror'.[74]

Similarly, while seeing things from the perspective of oppressed rather than dominant groups might provide more valuable insights, postmodernist feminists accept that there is no such thing as an absolute and universal truth allowing one to declare female knowledge true and male knowledge false. It is obviously tempting for those confronting male hegemony to take up contrary absolutist positions. But according to postmodernism, this refuge is both illusory in that there are no absolute truths and dangerous in that challenging a foundationalist position with another foundationalist position helps maintain the idea that there are absolute truths and that it is simply a question of who has access to them. Given the intersection between truth and power in society, this will mean that most disputes over competing versions of these absolute truths will be resolved by truth following power, thus reducing the chances of successful feminist challenges to male hegemony.

The anti-foundationalism of postmodernist feminism has not, however, gone unchallenged.[75] One reason lies in the belief that postmodernism disarms the feminist critique of male oppression in that if there are no truths nothing can be declared right or wrong and we are left with a moral and political free-for-all where right is likely to follow might. Indeed, feminists have noted how men have recently attempted to deflect challenges to their discourses by asserting that all views are equally valid and that those of their

---

73 See, eg, *op cit*, Smart, fn 52, pp 79–80; Harding, S, 'Feminism, science and the anti-Enlightenment critiques', in *op cit*, Nicholson, fn 46, Chapter 4. See, more generally, Martin, B, 'Feminism, criticism and Foucault' and Welch, S, 'The truth of liberation theology: particulars of a relative sublime', in Diamond, I and Quinby, L (eds), *Feminism and Foucault: Reflections on Resistance*, 1988, Boston, Mass: Northeastern UP, especially pp 196–203; Lazreg, M, 'Women's experience and feminist epistemology: a critical neo-rationalist approach', in *op cit*, Lennon and Whitford, fn 46, especially p 52.

74 *Op cit*, Lennon and Whitford, fn 46, p 4. See, also, Young, IM, 'The ideal of community and the politics of difference', in *op cit*, Nicholson, fn 46, pp 310; Williams, C, 'Feminism, subjectivity and psychoanalysis: towards a (corpo)real knowledge', in *op cit*, Lennon and Whitford, fn 46.

75 See *op cit*, Nicholson, fn 46, especially the chapters by Di Stefano, Harding, Bordo and Hartsock; *op cit*, Lennon and Whitford, fn 46, especially Fricker's chapter.

opponents are 'just their opinion'.[76] Through their greater access to power, they are then able to maintain their hegemony in the 'free market' of ideas.

It is, however, important not to conflate anti-foundationalism with epistemological or moral relativism. The denial of absolute foundations for knowledge or morality involves an acceptance that there are no objectively valid or invalid arguments, but not that there are no strong or weak arguments.[77] Feminists do not have to claim absolute foundations in order to assert the superiority of their views. The challenge is to persuade without resorting to relativism or foundationalism, and in doing so one can equally rely on (where most appropriate) some of the ideas and methods of Enlightenment ethics and epistemology (freedom, justice, equality and reason) as well as those developed by feminists (connection, care, difference and emotion).[78]

Another concern with postmodernism is that its challenge to the concept of the subject, in general, and the idea of a natural, or at least an identifiable, female subject, in particular, comes suspiciously 'at the moment when women have just begun to remember their selves and claim an agentic subjectivity'.[79] Having achieved their own Enlightenment, white, middle class, heterosexual and Western men who form the core of the postmodernist turn, appear desirous of denying its benefits to women. Similarly, it can be argued that the absence of a notion of the female subject renders the feminist project impossible, in that one cannot speak of shared female experiences or values if one denies any unity to the category 'women' let alone the unity of individual subjects.

Admittedly, there is a danger in taking the notion of fractured subject and gender identities too far.[80] But this does not justify ignoring postmodernist criticisms of essentialism or the notion of an autonomous subject standing outside discourse. Moreover, such criticisms are not incompatible with the possibility of a feminist critique, feminist epistemologies and a feminist ethic.

As regards critique, it has to be remembered that it is largely masculine discourse which has so desperately sought to maintain binary gender

---

76 See, eg, *op cit*, Harding, fn 59, especially p 88. See, also, *op cit*, Yeatman, fn 53, p 192, arguing that recommending the 'development of non-foundationalist, intellectual "conversations" is a familiar liberal's [*sic*] attempt to get the raucous and dangerous mobs off the street by tempting some of their leaders into safely cloistered, polite conversations in civilised comfort with the decision making elite'.

77 See, eg, *op cit*, Harding, fn 59, p 100; and see, further, *op cit*, Nicolson and Webb, fn 12, p 45.

78 Cf *op cit*, Welch, fn 73.

79 Hartsock, N, 'Rethinking modernism: minority versus majority theories' (1987) 7 Cultural Critique 187, p 206 (quoted in *op cit*, Di Stefano, fn 61, p 75). See, further, *op cit*, Hartsock, fn 49.

80 Cf Harraway, D, 'A manifesto for cyborgs: science, technology and socialist feminism in the 1980s', in *op cit*, Nicholson, fn 46.

divisions in order to serve male interests.[81] When particular groups of people have been isolated for oppressive purposes, they can respond as a group without necessarily running into the essentialism trap as long as they simultaneously strive to challenge the naturalness and validity of the characteristics used both to differentiate and oppress them. As Alessandra Tannesini has argued,[82] it is essential that those to whom the concept 'women' is applied take control of how it is used in order to expose the contradictions and oppressions to which it gives rise in the hope that they might be eradicated in some non-sexist future.

Admittedly, when it comes to reconstructing new epistemologies and ethics, the idea of a specific female (and male) way of doing things becomes much more suspect in reinforcing dangerous stereotypes. At the same time, however, it is possible and probably more accurate to retain the values of feminist explorations of alternative epistemologies and ethics without claiming that they represent a peculiarly female way of doing things. Feminism is not the same as femininity. For instance, one can valorise an ethic of care, with its greater emphasis on fact-finding, context, emotions and connection, as a feminist rather than a female way of doing things,[83] if not simply a better way.[84] Similarly, according to Kathleen Lennon and Margaret Whitford:

> ... feminist epistemology is neither the specification of a female way of knowing (there is no such thing) nor simply the articulation of a feminine subjectivity which reveals itself to be diverse, contradictory and at least partially discursively constructed through patriarchal oppression. Feminist epistemology consists in attention to epistemological concerns arising out of feminist projects which prompt reflection on the nature of knowledge and our methods for attaining it.[85]

FEMINIST RECONSTRUCTIONS OF FACT-FINDING IN LAW

The preceding discussion suggests that a combination of feminism and postmodernism represents a plausible means of challenging fact positivism's epistemological and ethical assumptions. Foundationalist feminist approaches to epistemology and ethics are not only unpersuasive at a theoretical level, but

---

81 Cf *op cit*, Lennon and Whitford, fn 46, pp 13–14.

82 Tannesini, A, 'Whose language?', in *op cit*, Lennon and Whitford, fn 46, pp 213–14.

83 See *op cit*, Tronto, fn 72, who has sought to free the ethic of care from its female connotations by arguing that caring includes every one thing done to maintain, continue and repair the world so that we can live in it as well as possible (see especially p 103).

84 *Op cit*, Flanagan, fn 67, pp 202–03.

85 *Op cit*, Lennon and Whitford, fn 46, p 13.

also dangerous in potentially replicating the oppression frequently wrought by modernistic epistemologies and ethics. Conversely, the overriding political nature of feminism, and its urgency, immediacy and concrete concerns,[86] counteracts any tendency within postmodernism towards apolitical complacency, relativist pluralism, a moral free for all and a hedonistic sliding around 'in the joys of textual analysis',[87] all of which undermine the power of the feminist critique. There is no denying the difficulty of treading the tightrope between falling in one direction into a postmodernism which makes feminist critique impossible or in the other direction back into the beckoning arms of Enlightenment certainties. Yet, as Michel Foucault once perceptively said, 'My point is not that everything is bad, but that everything is dangerous ...'.[88] But, even recognising its potential dangers, I would argue that a postmodernist feminism represents the most cogent counter to the assumptions of mainstream evidence discourse and its tendency to rely on and reinforce substantive law and epistemological and ethical approaches which, if not masculinist *per se*, act to uphold male interests and values.

This raises the question as to the opportunities offered by an infusion of postmodernist/feminist approaches to epistemology and ethics into the process of fact-finding in law. With the warning that the following represents some very preliminary thoughts, a number of possibilities suggest themselves.

First, the epistemological point that truth is best achieved through hearing many voices on an issue, especially those of the oppressed, suggests a need to open up fact-finding processes to wider input in terms of both the presentation and evaluation of evidence. As regards the former, the emphasis in feminist epistemologies and ethics on finding as many facts as possible relevant to issues (and in particular their context and background) argues for a more relaxed approach to the principles of relevancy and standing, and a challenge to the current approach to assessing legal problems in terms of narrowly defined categories with little reference to their context or to the needs of the parties.[89] Feminists also challenge the status given in legal fact-finding to scientific, medical and other experts from what are regarded as reliable disciplines. Instead, they argue that, where appropriate and relevant, the knowledge of those with direct experience of issues of fact-finding may

---

86 Cf Rhodes, DL, 'Gender and professional roles' (1994) 63 Fordham L Rev 39, p 45.

87 Douzinas, C and Warrington, R, *Justice Miscarried: Ethics, Aesthetics and the Law*, 1994, London: Harvester Wheatsheaf, p 9.

88 Foucault, M, 'Afterword', in Dreyfus, H and Rabinow, P, *Michel Foucault: Beyond Structuralism and Hermeneutics*, 2nd edn, 1983, Chicago, IL: Chicago UP, p 232.

89 Menkel-Meadow, C, 'Portia in a different voice: speculations on a women's lawyering process' (1985) 1 Berkeley Women's LJ 39, p 49; Henderson, LN, 'Legality and empathy' (1987) 85 Michigan L Rev 1574; and cf Nicolson, D, 'What the law giveth, it also taketh away: gender-specific defences to criminal liability', in *op cit*, Nicolson and Bibbings, fn 30, where this approach is explored in the criminal law context.

provide an equally accurate access to 'truth'. For instance, in the sphere of domestic violence, there has been a call for greater use of experiential discourses on the reality of domestic violence rather than the pseudo-science of Battered Woman's Syndrome or post-traumatic stress disorder.[90] Indeed, a familiar feminist critique of legal trials is the way in which the voice of the expert supplants and silences that of the parties, hence denying them their authenticity and dignity.[91]

The epistemological benefits of a multiplicity of perspectives on fact-finding also raises questions about the current tendency of most factual issues to be resolved by small groups of white, middle class men, if not by single adjudicators. The case for more female judges, magistrates, and other State officials who evaluate facts is obvious and has lead to the suggestion that single judges be replaced with male-female benches.[92] Also worth considering is greater use of juries and other multi-member tribunals in order to ensure more perspectives on knowledge and more female fact-adjudicators.

Secondly, feminist perspectives on evidence might seek to build upon the recent recognition from within mainstream evidence discourse that fact-adjudicators do not reason about facts solely or even largely through an appraisal of facts in a logical and atomistic fashion, but assess facts holistically and through the form of narratives. As we have seen, the use of narrative is also said to characterise female ways of knowing and communicating. This, however, is undermined by fact that court witnesses are required to give their evidence in 'fragmentary testamentary' style – as strictly controlled responses to highly specific questions.[93] Accordingly, feminists might be expected to support changes to a more narrative based style of evidence presentation in court. Similarly, they might challenge the dominance of allegedly masculine modes of authoritative speech in court, which are marked by self-assurance, self-assertiveness and unqualified declarativeness and which result in more equivocal, hesitant, inclusive and other-orientated modes of speech being regarded as evidence of uncertainty or even confusion.[94] Even more fundamentally, the way in which court hierarchies, formalities and architecture act to intimidate and silence many courtroom participants[95] can be said to be especially problematic for women. Not only are they generally

---

90 See Nicolson, D and Sanghvi, R, 'Battered women and provocation: the implications of *R v Ahluwalia*' [1993] CLR 728, p 738.

91 *Ibid*; O'Donovan, K, 'Law's knowledge: the judge, the expert, the battered woman and her syndrome' (1993) 24 JLS 427.

92 *Op cit*, Menkel-Meadow, fn 89, p 59.

93 Jackson, B, 'Narrative models in legal proof' (1988) 1 International Journal for the Semiotics of Law 225.

94 Cf Jones, KB, 'On authority: or, why women are not entitled to speak', in *op cit*, Diamond and Quinby, fn 73, p 122.

95 See references cited in *op cit*, Nicolson, fn 3, p 142.

less accustomed to participation in public fora, but the poor acoustics of many courtrooms can be said to silence them in a more literal sense.

The intimidatory and possibly even inefficient nature of current legal proceedings can also be said to flow from their adversarial nature. As a third focus for change, feminists have long been critical of an approach to truth finding which is based on competition, dialectic argumentation and binary outcomes. The adversarial system is well known to encourage – not only in the courtroom, but throughout the legal process – exaggerated claims and various 'dirty tricks' designed to impede the emergence of truth,[96] while the assumption that truth best emerges though a struggle between equal competing parties is undermined by socio-economic realities which show that the 'haves' are likely to triumph over the 'have-nots'.[97] But, even if lawyers and litigants act with greater restraint, Carrie Menkel-Meadow argues that:

> Binary, oppositional presentation of facts in dispute is not the best way for us to learn the truth. Polarised debates distorts [sic] truth, leaves out important information, simplifies complexity and obfuscates where it should clarify. More significantly, some matters (mostly civil, but occasionally even a criminal case) are not susceptible to a binary (right/wrong, win/lose) conclusion or solution. This may be because we cannot with any degree of accuracy determine the facts, because conflicting, but legitimate, legal rights give some entitlements to both (or all) parties, or because human or emotional equities cannot be sharply divided (parental rights in child custody, for example).[98]

By contrast, feminists regard truth as best discovered through multi-faceted approaches and co-operation whereby dilemmas are turned into trilemmas or polylemmas through lateral rather than unilinear thinking,[99] and all relevant persons affected by disputes are involved in resolving them.[100] Not only will this ensure a greater source of information and hence (hopefully) more accurate fact-finding, but when all relevant parties are involved in settling a dispute the law may also be more effective in dispute *resolution* rather than where solutions are 'dictated by an outsider, won by the victor and imposed upon the loser'.[101] More fundamentally, given the courts' current 'limited remedial imaginations' in terms of which civil law remedies are largely confined to damages and injunctions, and criminal law to ascriptions of guilt,

---

96 See, eg, *op cit*, Nicolson and Webb, fn 12, Chapter 6.

97 Galanter, M, 'Why the "haves" come out ahead: speculations on the limits of legal change' (1974) 9 L & Soc Rev 95; and see, further, *op cit*, Nicolson and Webb, fn 12, Chapter 7.

98 Menkel-Meadow, C, 'The trouble with the adversary system in a post-modern, multi-cultural world' (1996) 1 J Inst Stud Leg Ethics 801, p 802.

99 Cf Gilligan's discussion of the responses of 'Amy' and 'Jake' to the Heinz Dilemma: *op cit*, fn 55.

100 See the idea of tri-partite criminal proceedings in which the victim's interests are addressed along with those of the State and defendant: *ibid*, Menkel-Meadow, p 821.

101 *Ibid*, Menkel-Meadow, p 55.

reduced guilt or innocence, feminists might argue for an even greater use of mediation and other forms of alternative dispute resolution than recently introduced by the Woolf reforms,[102] and that strategies such as victim-offender mediation should play a role in criminal cases.[103]

Watering down, if not complete abandoning, the adversarial system is likely to help bring about two further changes favoured by feminists. One is that adjudicators would be encouraged to pay more attention to the specific context and social contingencies of cases. Instead of treating legal subjects as atomistic, self-centred individuals, who somehow exist outside society, there could be a more sympathetic understanding of real-life people with their own personal histories and emotional as well as material needs.

A second consequence of moving away from an adversarial legal ethos is that it would encourage lawyers to rethink their current 'hired gun' attitude to legal representation in terms of which they seek to obtain as much as is possible (interpreted in material terms) for those clients who can afford their fees (or are fortunate to qualify for legal aid) irrespective of the morality of what clients want done or any harm that may be caused to opponents or affected others. As we have seen, an ethic of care requires moral agents to consider all those who might be harmed by prospective behaviour and to attempt to ensure that if people are going to suffer it should be those who can best bear the harm. Accordingly, lawyers might be expected to weigh their clients' interests against those of others before agreeing to zealous representation and, without necessarily abandoning their clients' interests, to attempt to address the interests and needs of all.[104] Similarly, adoption of feminist ethics would encourage lawyers to adopt less aggressive and confrontational approaches to litigation and advocacy.[105] However, a more caring approach to legal work may work to the benefit not only of opponents and third parties affected by legal cases and of the administration of justice generally, but also of clients themselves. The focus on context and relational connections would encourage lawyers to treat clients, not just as legal problems with legal solutions, but more holistically in terms of all their needs – social, emotional, and psychological, as well as material – and to

---

102 Woolf (Lord), *Access to Justice: Final Report*, 1996, London: HMSO.

103 Note that there is little support by feminists for inquisitorial proceedings, based as they are on the positivistic idea of a neutral arbiter, usually a man, scientifically investigating facts.

104 See *op cit*, Menkel-Meadow, fn 89; Cahn, NR, 'A preliminary feminist critique of legal ethics' (1990) 4 Georgetown Journal of Legal Ethics 2475; Cahn, NR, 'Styles of lawyering' (1992) 34 Hastings LJ 1039; Jack, R and Jack, DC, *Moral Vision and Professional Decisions: The Changing Values of Women and Men Lawyers*, 1989, New York: CUP; *op cit*, Rhodes, fn 86.

105 See *op cit*, Menkel-Meadow, fn 89; *ibid*, Jack and Jack, on whether female lawyers currently do adopt such an approach. Cf *op cit*, Menkel-Meadow, fn 89, p 54 on the double-bind faced by female advocates: if they act aggressively, they are denigrated as unfeminine; if they do not, they are denigrated as bad lawyers.

consider the impact on those to whom clients are relationally connected (family members, colleagues, employees, etc). Moreover, lawyers who 'enter the client's world' in order to 'understand more fully what they desire and why' are far less likely to impose solutions on clients paternalistically because of unfounded assumptions about what they want.[106]

We thus see that feminist perspectives on epistemology and ethics may improve both the quality and justice of legal fact-finding and, in particular, the atmosphere of legal proceedings, the type of cases argued and evidence heard. By allowing in more facts and issues into fact-finding, it should also challenge the closure around the values of law ensured by fact positivism's definition of truth, reason and justice. At the same time, however, Foucault's warning that 'everything is dangerous' should not be forgotten. Clearly, many of the suggested reforms to fact-finding, particularly the call for greater use of juries and the hearing of more evidence, run up against cost considerations. If anything, recent governments (irrespective of political hue) seem intent on reducing jury trials, though as the Woolf reforms show,[107] sometimes the desire to cut costs may lead to opportunities for a greater infusion of feminist methodologies into evidential processes.

At a more fundamental level, one may wonder whether some of the reforms suggested may actually impair the search for truth and justice and in particular reduce the protection afforded to female participants in the legal process. For instance, jury members might in fact place even greater reliance on gender stereotypes than judges.[108] Here, as elsewhere, one should be hesitant about making changes without a better idea, preferably obtained through empirical research, of their likely impact. At least, judges can always be exposed to gender awareness training (as happens in Australia) along similar lines to race awareness training in the UK.

It might also be argued that limiting the lawyer's hired gun role might leave clients unarmed against the State or other powerful opponents.[109] On the other hand, this is not a necessary consequence of a more morally aware approach to lawyering.[110] The legal profession as a whole can guarantee that no litigant or criminal defendant goes unrepresented, whereas an ethic of care

---

106 *Op cit*, Menkel-Meadow, fn 89, p 57. Eg, lawyers who are socialised into a competitive approach to lawyering may unthinkingly assume that battered women who kill their batterers may want them to pull out all stops to ensure an acquittal, whereas some women may feel the need for expiation through a short period of imprisonment.

107 *Op cit*, Woolf, fn 102.

108 It may also be argued that adversarial proceedings lead to the discovery of more information, but this is disputed, especially given the extent to which they encourage the concealment of information.

109 See, eg, the argument that criminal defendants are frequently let down by less than suitably zealous representation: Baldwin, J and McConville, M, *Negotiated Justice: Pressures to Plead Guilty*, 1977, London: Martin Robertson.

110 Cf *op cit*, Nicolson and Webb, fn 12, Chapter 8.

would emphasise the special need for zeal on the part of lawyers where clients are vulnerable.

A move away from the adversarial nature of legal proceedings towards mediation and other forms of alternative dispute resolution might also be said to leave female parties unprotected against more powerful opponents. Without a zealous lawyer protecting their interests and a court ensuring compliance with procedural rules of fairness, female litigants – especially in domestic disputes – might easily be steamrollered into accepting settlements harmful to them or their children or into waiving their newly gained rights.[111] One can ask, moreover, whether a move away from formal court proceedings would benefit women, given that evidential rules provide protection – admittedly insufficient – against reliance on sexist stereotypes. Finally, it can be noted that there are a number of advantages both to female participants and to feminism more generally in women having their 'day in court'. There is an important psychological and emotional benefit to obtaining a formal and public recognition of the justice of one's case, whereas feminists are able to mount more powerful campaigns around injustice which takes place in the public eye than where women come off second best in negotiation or mediation. Thus, the first appeal of Sara Thornton provided an important focus for campaigns for battered women, perhaps contributing to the more sympathetic approach in Kiranjit Ahluwalia's case a year later.[112]

At the same time, the drawbacks to feminist-inspired reforms render them dangerous rather than wrong; as requiring careful consideration before adoption rather than abandonment. In addition, as regards changes to current methods of fact-finding, what seems to be needed is not a wholesale replacement of adversarial and formal legal proceedings, but the provision of greater choice to litigants, enabling women litigants to opt for the protection and publicity of formal legal proceedings and zealous advocacy where needed or alternatively for the more consensus-building and inclusive nature of less adversarial proceedings where they are more appropriate.

At the very least, feminist perspectives on evidence provide an important input into current debates about the values and processes of fact-finding. Most importantly, they might have an impact on the attitudes of lawyers and State officials involved in fact-finding, which is perhaps as, if not more,[113] important than the exact nature of any formal reforms to evidential processes.

---

111 Cf *op cit*, Menkel-Meadow, fn 89, p 53 fn 78.

112 Cf the opening statement in the judgment, which notes that the case had 'aroused much public attention': *R v Ahluwalia* [1992] 4 All ER 889, p 891g–h.

113 See *op cit*, Menkel-Meadow, fn 89.

CHAPTER 3

RAPE AND THE ADVERSARIAL CULTURE OF THE COURTROOM

Louise Ellison

INTRODUCTION

The Home Office of England and Wales recently published a report addressing the issue of attrition in rape cases.[1] The proportion of recorded rapes resulting in a conviction has declined from 24% in 1985 to just 9%.[2] The Home Office study examined 483 incidents initially recorded as rape by the police in 1996 and followed their progress through the criminal justice system. The study found that only 6% of the cases originally recorded by the police as rape resulted in convictions for rape. A striking finding of the study was the high level of complainant withdrawal at the pre-trial stage of the criminal process. In the 31% of cases in which no further action was taken and the 25% of cases which were 'no-crimed' by the police, the most common reason was complainant withdrawal.[3] While recognising that women decide not to pursue allegations for many reasons, the report significantly accepts that the prospect of a traumatic courtroom ordeal prompts many women to withdraw: 'The high rate at which complainants withdraw and previous research ... strongly suggest that complainants feel that giving evidence in court would be a harrowing ordeal.'[4] The personal testimonies of women who have testified in rape proceedings confirm that giving evidence is often a humiliating, gruelling and ultimately unrewarding process. Many women have described their treatment in court in terms of further abuse:

> I would like to be told why you are raped again, again, again and again, because that's what they did to me. They allowed me to be raped again and again.[5]

---

1   Harris, J and Grace, S, *A Question of Evidence? Investigating and Prosecuting Rape in the 1990s*, Home Office Research Study No 196, 1999, London: Home Office.

2   *Ibid*, p ix.

3   *Ibid*, p 14. Cases where the complainant withdraws tend to be those where there is a high degree of consensual contact.

4   *Ibid*, p 48.

5   Victim Support, *Women, Rape and the Criminal Justice System*, 1996, London: Victim Support, p 39.

I had put my trust and faith in the legal system: afterwards I felt like I had been abused again but this time by the legal system itself.[6]

Explaining the treatment of rape complainants in court has formed a specific site of inquiry for feminist scholarship. Prevailing explanations have focused predominantly upon the cultural rape myths which pervade rape prosecutions,[7] the operation of discriminatory evidentiary rules,[8] sexist attitudes on the part of judges and lawyers[9] and the inadequate regulation of sexual history evidence in rape cases.[10] This chapter locates the treatment of rape complainants in the wider context of the adversarial system of trial and the essentially competitive culture of the adversarial courtroom. It argues that the adversarial system itself represents as potent a barrier to the decent treatment of rape complainants in court as do the diffuse myths and discriminatory stereotypes that continue to surround rape allegations and any ambivalence on the part of judges and lawyers to the position of the rape complainant. This chapter specifically addresses the difficulties complainants face during cross-examination and in giving direct oral evidence in open court.

CROSS-EXAMINATION TECHNIQUES

Cross-examination is commonly cited across adversarial jurisdictions as the worst aspect of giving evidence in a rape trial. In a study conducted by the UK organisation Victim Support, women described their treatment during cross-

---

6   Dublin Rape Crisis Centre, *The Legal Process and Victims of Rape*, 1998, Dublin: Dublin Rape Crisis Centre, p 150.

7   Lees, S, *Carnal Knowledge: Rape on Trial*, 1996, London: Hamish Hamilton; Taslitz, A, 'Patriarchal stories: cultural rape narratives in the courtroom' (1996) 5 S California Rev Law and Women's Studies, p 387; Temkin, J, *Rape and the Legal Process*, 1987, London: Sweet & Maxwell; Torrey, M, 'When will we be believed? Rape myths and the idea of a fair trial in rape prosecutions' (1991) 24 University of California Davis L Rev 1013.

8   The old corroboration rules and the doctrine of prompt complaint have, eg, been strongly criticised for perpetuating cultural biases that lead to the disbelief of women. See, eg, Mack, K, 'An Australian perspective on feminism, race and evidence' (1999) 28 Southwestern UL Rev, p 367.

9   See Temkin, J, 'Prosecuting and defending rape: perspectives from the Bar' (2000) 27 JLS 219.

10 See Adler, Z, *Rape on Trial*, 1987, London: Routledge and Kegan Paul; Adler, Z, 'The relevance of sexual history evidence in rape: problems of subjective interpretation' [1985] Crim LR 769; McColgan, A, 'Common law and the relevance of sexual history evidence' (1996) 16 OJLS 275; Temkin, J, 'Sexual history evidence – the ravishment of section 2' [1993] Crim LR 3.

examination as 'patronising', 'humiliating' and 'worse than the rape'.[11] Women responding to a survey conducted by Sue Lees similarly complained that they had been asked irrelevant and unfair questions during cross-examination and the majority reported feeling that they were on trial and not the defendant.[12] In a recent Australian study, conducted by Heenan and McKelvie in Victoria, almost all of the victims interviewed described feeling extremely traumatised while being cross-examined by defence counsel.[13]

Criticism of the treatment of rape complainants during cross-examination has typically focused on the use of sexual history evidence.[14] In recent years it has, however, become increasingly apparent that other aspects of cross-examination are similarly problematic for rape complainants: the wide ranging assaults upon their private lives, the hostility of defence barristers and the questioning techniques typically described by complainants as confusing and distorting.

Cross-examination as to credit

Research into the conduct of rape prosecutions has revealed the extent to which the personal lives of women are scrutinised during cross-examination.[15] Routinely, complainants are questioned extensively about their 'sexually suggestive' clothing, 'sexually provocative behaviour', their financial situation and their role as mothers. Frequently, lines of questioning will focus upon what Taslitz terms 'proxies for sluttishness':[16] past drug taking and use of alcohol and past abortions. In Heenan and McKelvie's study, many women interviewed reported being subjected to endless questioning around matters that had apparently little to do with the issues in the trial.[17] According to the researchers, complainants were routinely portrayed by defence barristers as

---

11 *Op cit*, Victim Support, fn 5. The study was based upon in-depth interviews with a small sample of rape victims who had been in contact with a local Victim Support scheme and questionnaires completed by Victim Support schemes and witness services. Of witness services who took part in the study, 41% reported that women experienced problems with the nature of questioning during cross-examination, including feeling that it was character assassination and feeling re-victimised by the defence barrister.

12 *Op cit*, Lees, fn 7.

13 Heenan, M and McKelvie, H, *Evaluation of the Crimes (Rape) Act 1991*, 1997, AG's Legislation and Policy Branch, Melbourne: Department of Justice, p 201. See, also, *Heroines of Fortitude: The Experiences of Women in Court as Victims of Sexual Assault*, 1996, Sydney: Department for Women.

14 See Easton, Chapter 9, in this volume.

15 *Op cit*, Lees, fn 7. The study was based upon the transcripts of 31 rape trials and 116 questionnaires completed by victims of rape.

16 Taslitz, AE, *Rape and the Culture of the Courtroom*, 1999, New York: New York UP, p 83.

17 *Ibid*, Heenan and McKelvie, p 250.

persons of low intelligence or of low morality who were inherently untrustworthy.[18] In one trial, Heenan and McKelvie report that a complainant was asked, during a cross-examination which lasted 11 hours, whether she had experienced post-natal depression after the birth of her baby, the history of her menstrual periods, how long she had known the man she married, whether she was living with a gay woman at the time the allegations were made and whether she was having sexual dreams around the time of the alleged assault.[19]

Feminists have further criticised defence lawyers for pursuing lines of questioning in court that reflect and perpetuate cultural myths and biases about how 'reliable' people react to and communicate traumatic events.[20] A common defence technique, for example, is to comment upon any delay between the alleged offence and a formal complaint being made by the complainant. This defence strategy appeals directly to what has been termed the 'timing myth':[21] the belief that it is 'natural' for a woman who has been sexually assaulted to complain immediately. Questioning about a lack of obvious physical injuries similarly relies on the stereotypes that govern appropriate female behaviour and ignore the fact that genuine fear for their lives prevents many women from resisting physically and sustaining severe injuries.[22]

Rape complainants are also routinely accused directly of lying during cross-examination and are confronted frequently with outlandish reasons for bringing 'false allegations'. Among the more frequently expounded motives are revenge, fantasy, embarrassment, arriving home late, emotional and psychological instability, to secure custody of children, to gain sympathy and attention, and to cover up an affair.[23] While there is no evidence that false allegations are more common for rape than for any other criminal offence, defence counsel continue to appeal during cross-examination to the pervasive myth that women lie about rape and to portray complainants as revengeful and opportunistic.

---

18 *Op cit*, Heenan and McKelvie, fn 13, p 176.

19 *Op cit*, Heenan and McKelvie, fn 13, p 215.

20 See Orenstein, A, '"My God!" A feminist critique of the excited utterance exception to the hearsay rule' (1997) 85 California L Rev 159.

21 See Stanchi, K, 'The paradox of the fresh complaint rule' (1996) 37 Boston College L Rev 441.

22 *Op cit*, Lees, fn 7, p 113.

23 See, eg, Williams, G, *Proof of Guilt*, 1958, London: Stevens, p 159.

Bullying tactics

The often intimidating manner in which cross-examination is conducted has been identified as a further source of difficulty for rape complainants. Women interviewed in the Victim Support survey, for example, accused defence barristers of being unduly aggressive.[24] In Heenan and McKelvie's study, the women interviewed described defence counsel as 'frightening', 'aggressive' and 'belligerent' and often felt that the defence barrister was waging a personal attack against them.[25] As one woman complained: 'Oh ... he was antagonistic, he was offensive, theatrical ... he didn't treat me with any respect.'[26] The intimidation of complainants is achieved not only through tone of voice and physical gesture but also through the deployment of various discursive devices. These include repeating the same question many times, pretending not to hear the answers, sudden contrasts of very gentle then very aggressive questioning, repeatedly demanding precise recollection of seemingly obscure facts, asking questions in rapid succession and pre-emptive interruption.[27] Other strategies observed in a recent study by the Dublin Rape Crisis Centre included insensitive, repeated questioning and deliberately misrepresenting parts of a complainant's testimony.[28] One woman interviewed in the study stated, 'The basic strategy of the accused's lawyer was to confuse me, to the point where I was blocking out everything and just concentrating on the questions that he was asking me. He kept harassing me in a subtle way, he kept trying to trip me up'.[29] Many women have expressed frustration at the coercive questioning techniques employed by defence barristers during cross-examination and report feeling manipulated in the witness box:[30]

> I didn't like him at all ... I'd try and explain it in my own way and he'd say sort of like 'but no what I'm asking is ... just say yes or no' ... he only let me explain so much and then he'd cut me off ... like he just wanted to hear what he wanted to hear ... and he never really gave me a chance to say what I wanted to say.[31]

---

24 *Op cit*, Victim Support, fn 5, p 56.

25 *Op cit*, Heenan and McKelvie, fn 13, p 201.

26 *Op cit*, Heenan and McKelvie, fn 13, p 202.

27 See Chambers, G and Millar, A, 'Proving sexual assault: prosecuting the offender or persecuting the victim?', in Carlen, P and Worral, A (eds), *Gender, Crime and Justice*, 1987, Milton Keynes: OU Press, p 71; *op cit*, Taslitz, fn 16, p 93.

28 *Op cit*, Dublin Rape Crisis Centre, fn 6, p 126.

29 *Op cit*, Dublin Rape Crisis Centre, fn 6, p 127. As Matoesian has remarked, 'much like the physical act of rape, where the ... [victim] is relatively powerless in the face of male aggression and brute strength, so she is similarly passive and limited in response to the ... [defence counsel's] influence during questioning ...': Matoesian, G, *Reproducing Rape – Domination through Talk in the Courtroom*, 1993, Cambridge: Polity, p 150.

30 *Op cit*, Lees, fn 7, p 31.

31 *Op cit*, Dublin Rape Crisis Centre, fn 6, p 202.

Heenan and McKelvie report that many of the women interviewed described feeling 'silenced' during cross-examination by defence counsel's frequent interruptions and instructions to give yes or no answers.[32] A number of women claimed that their words were 'twisted', and felt that they were prevented from responding to questions in more detail: '[It was] horrible ... every time I tried [to describe what happened] he interrupted me.'[33]

Improper and degrading cross-examination adds unnecessarily to the trauma of testifying in rape cases and is likely to have a deleterious impact upon the ability of complainants to give their best evidence in court. Moreover, the techniques typically employed by defence barristers during cross-examination undoubtedly deter some women from coming forward and reporting offences or cause others to withdraw after making an initial complaint. As McEwan observes: 'There is little incentive for rape victims to come forward when the system which is supposed to protect the public from crime serves them up in court like laboratory specimens on a microscope slide.'[34] In seeking to explain the treatment of rape complainants in court there has been a tendency within rape literature to examine rape cases in isolation and to focus upon those factors peculiar to rape trials: specifically, the use of sexual history evidence and the cultural myths and stereotypes which surround rape prosecutions. These explanations, however, provide only a partial analysis of the problems facing rape complainants. As McBarnet explains, 'these stereotypes tell us *how* rape victims are degraded in court but they do not tell us *why*, nor indeed why degradation in court is an experience not confined to victims of rape alone'.[35] The answers to these questions, it is submitted, lie in the inherently combative nature of adversarial advocacy and the inadequate regulation of cross-examination generally in criminal trials.

---

32 *Op cit*, Heenan and McKelvie, fn 13, p 244.

33 *Op cit*, Heenan and McKelvie, fn 13, p 202. Advocacy manuals have for many years cautioned advocates to exercise special care when examining women in court. Strick (Strick, A, *Injustice for All*, 1996, New York: Barricade, p 42) says: 'A female witness is evasive in her answers by nature ... She is not a natural born reasoner, is not logical, but relies almost exclusively upon intuition.' Women have been accused of 'using every weapon in their armoury' during cross-examination, including 'smiles, coquetry, shrugs, sauciness, tears and the ability to faint at a convenient and dramatic time': Linton, N, 'The witness and cross-examination' (1965) X Berkeley J Soc 7. Du Cann (Du Cann, R, *The Art of the Advocate*, 1993, London: Penguin, p 108) describes how some women become blatantly flirtatious in the witness box while others become unnecessarily shy: '... all are unnatural to a greater or lesser extent because they are suspicious.' Levy suggests that an extra degree of control is required when questioning women, as women 'are generally more verbal and more ready to elaborate on their answers' and 'experienced counsel who have cross-examined women over the years cannot help but conclude that they can be the most difficult and dangerous of witnesses': Levy, E, *Examination of Witnesses in Criminal Cases*, 1991, Totonto: Carswell, p 236.

34 McEwan, J, 'Documentary hearsay evidence – refuge for the vulnerable witness?' [1989] Crim LR 642.

35 McBarnet, D, 'Victim in the witness box – confronting victimology's stereotype' (1983) 7 Contemporary Crises 293.

Adversarial advocacy

The culture of the adversarial courtroom is essentially combative and competitive. This is evidenced in advocacy manuals in which criminal trials are referred to routinely as fights[36] and battles[37] and cross-examination is compared to a physical fight between advocate and witness. In advocacy texts, references to 'verbal pugilism',[38] 'forensic duels' and 'verbal combat'[39] are commonplace and lawyers are described alternately as 'warriors', 'generals', and 'gladiators',[40] who 'butcher', 'break'[41] and 'destroy' opposing witnesses.[42] As Thornburg notes:

> War provides a rich source domain for trial metaphors, providing words for process and participants and communicating the message that a hostile and competitive attitude is an important characteristic of the adversary system.[43]

Sporting metaphors are similarly employed to capture the competitiveness of adversarial proceedings. Judges are, for example, referred to as umpires or referees, the parties as 'winners' or 'losers', and the courtroom as the 'playing field'.[44]

The 'macho adversarialism'[45] of courtroom culture partly underlies the treatment of rape complainants in court. Principally, the adversarial nature of proceedings encourages advocates to engage in tactics designed to intimidate, humiliate and confuse; tactical gains are to be made from antagonising and embarrassing opposing witnesses in court. Cross-examination is thus often directed at unsettling a witness, 'hoping to rattle them so that they will be

---

36 'The conduct of a trial at law is in many respects comparable with the conduct of a military operation. Going to law is a great deal like going to war.' (Napley, D, *The Technique of Persuasion*, 1991, London: Sweet & Maxwell, p 74.)

37 'The centrepiece of the adversary system is the oral trial and everything that goes before it is a preparation for the battlefield.' (Devlin, P, *The Judge*, 1979, Oxford: OUP, p 54.)

38 *Ibid*, p 58.

39 'Resort to the law is a form of civilised warfare, the advocate the modern representative of the medieval champion.' (*Op cit*, Du Cann, fn 33, p 61.)

40 'Parties arm themselves, draw battle lines, offer or refuse quarter, plan pre-emptive strikes, joust, cross swords, undertake frontal assaults, win by attrition, seek total annihilation of their enemies, marshal forces, attack and sandbag their opponents. They deliver blows, attack flanks, kill, fire opening salvos, skirmish and cry craven.' (Thornburg, E, 'Metaphors matter: how images of battle, sports and sex shape the adversary system' (1995) 10 Wisconsin Women's LJ 13.)

41 Wellman, FL, *The Art of Cross-Examination*, 4th edn, 1997, New York: Simon & Schuster, p 39.

42 Evans, K, *Golden Rules of Advocacy*, 1993, London: Blackstone, p 97.

43 Thornburg has argued that the metaphors of litigation as a sporting contest or a battle foster unacceptable actions and attitudes: *ibid*, Thornburg, p 237.

44 'In our system the judge presides somewhat like a referee on the football field, blowing his whistle from time to time for an infringement but not actually kicking the ball himself save in very limited or exceptional circumstances.' (*Op cit*, Du Cann, fn 33, p 3.)

45 *Op cit*, Taslitz, fn 16, p 154.

unable to effectively present their evidence, or at least will appear less credible and competent in the jury's eyes'.[46] As Taslitz notes:

> The incentives of the adversary system are such that it is hard to expect defence counsel to cross-examine rape victims in ways that clarify rather than obfuscate. Defence counsel will continue to use metaphoric word choice, rapid-fire questioning, unsupportable innuendo, known objectionable matter, insult and confusion. No matter what the change in evidence codes or the high-minded calls for civility, defence counsel will zealously do whatever works.[47]

These same strategic incentives encourage, if not compel,[48] advocates to exploit prevailing cultural biases, including rape myths and gender stereotypes.[49]

The view that improper cross-examination is essentially a product of compelling systemic pressures is supported by evidence that witnesses other than rape complainants are subject to similar defence strategies in court. Brereton, for example, conducted a comparative study of rape trials and assault trials and found that complainants of assault were just as likely to be subjected to attacks upon their character and credibility.[50] According to Brereton, defence counsel relied primarily 'on a limited number of generic 'tried and true' cross-examination strategies which were adapted to fit the particular factual circumstances of the case'.[51] Rock similarly reports that wounding allegations would be put to prosecution witnesses 'as a matter of course' during cross-examination and many witnesses felt harassed, intimidated and bullied by defence counsel.[52] Such research confirms the need for a wider analysis of cross-examination in rape trials that explores the deeper structural and strategic imperatives of the adversarial trial process.

Inadequacy of existing constraints

The principal mechanisms for regulating cross-examination in criminal trials are the trial judge's common law duty to restrain unnecessary, improper or

---

46 Kinports, K, 'Evidence engendered' (1991) Illinois UL Rev 427.

47 *Op cit*, Taslitz, fn 16, p 117. According to Taslitz, cross-examination is governed by male adversarial rules and women 'unaccustomed to verbal combat and courtroom language games' are disadvantaged as a result (p 9). See, generally, Raitt, Chapter 4, in this volume.

48 'A lawyer who fails to appeal to race or gender bias will start to lose cases if biased appeals work with juries ... To survive, the lawyer will have to incorporate bias into trial strategies and arguments.' (*Op cit*, Taslitz, fn 16, p 106.)

49 See Yaroshefsky, E, 'Balancing victim's rights and vigorous advocacy for the defendant' (1989) Annual Survey of American Law 152.

50 Brereton, D, 'How different are rape trials? A comparison of the cross-examination of complainants in rape and assault trials' (1997) 37 Br J Crim 242.

51 *Ibid*, p 243.

52 See Rock, P, *The Social World of the English Crown Court*, 1993, Oxford: Clarendon, p 174.

oppressive questions and the Bar's Code of Conduct. The experience of rape complainants in court is attributable, in part, to the inadequacy of these restrictions.

Code of Conduct of the Bar of England and Wales

Advocates are subject to a professional code of conduct which lays down guidelines for the conduct of cross-examination. According to the *Code of Conduct of the Bar of England and Wales*, for example, a practising barrister must not 'make statements or ask questions which are merely scandalous or intended or calculated only to vilify, insult or annoy either a witness or some other person'.[53] Research into the conduct of rape trials, however, suggests that the code of conduct does little to curtail improper cross-examination. Lees, for example, reports that, in the rape cases she monitored, the code was routinely breached by defence counsel and there was no intervention by either prosecution counsel or the trial judge on these occasions.[54] Research into the experiences of other categories of witness indicate that the code is equally ineffective in other trial contexts.[55]

Interviews with legal practitioners suggest a perceived conflict between any ethical duty to protect complainants or witnesses and the defence lawyer's duty to 'promote and protect fearlessly and by all proper and lawful means his lay client's best interests'.[56] In interviews conducted by Rock, for example, barristers explained that professional effectiveness demanded indifference on the part of counsel to the welfare of witnesses: '... to become overly nice about a witness's feelings would impair performance and betray a client.'[57] It was taken for granted by counsel that cross-examination would be an uncomfortable, if not painful, experience for many witnesses. As one lawyer interviewed admitted: 'It's a dreadful business. We do have to be brutal.'[58] Similarly, in interviews conducted by Brown *et al* with Scottish legal

---

53 General Council of the Bar of England and Wales, *Code of Conduct of the Bar of England and Wales*, 1991, London: Bar Council, Pt VI, para 610(e). The code also states that a barrister 'must not suggest that a witness or other person is guilty of fraud or misconduct or attribute to another person the crime or conduct of which his lay client is accused unless such allegations go to a matter in issue (including the credibility of the witness) which is material to his lay client's case and which appears to him to be supported by reasonable grounds' (para 610(h)). On the proper bounds of cross-examination as to credit, the code is particularly vague: 'No clearer rule can be laid down than this, that he is entitled to test the evidence given by each individual witness and to argue that the evidence taken as a whole is insufficient to amount to proof that the defendant is guilty of the offence charged. Further than this he ought not to go.' (Annex H, para 13.5.)

54 *Op cit*, Lees, fn 7, p 249.

55 *Op cit*, Rock, fn 52.

56 *Ibid*, General Council of the Bar, para 203(a).

57 *Op cit*, Rock, fn 52, p 174.

58 *Op cit*, Rock, fn 52, p 174.

practitioners, one advocate confessed, 'You try and get away with anything which you think that the jury will use in assessing the credibility of the complainer or the credibility of your client'.[59] Defence lawyers freely admitted that they would do whatever they could to suggest that a complainant in a rape trial was of 'easy virtue' precisely because they believed that juries were swayed by such trial tactics.[60] Temkin recently interviewed barristers highly experienced in rape trials and reports that those interviewed were clear that their approach was 'robust to the point of ruthlessness'.[61] One female counsel interviewed admitted that when she was defending it was 'no holds barred'. Temkin concludes that the barristers who participated in the study appeared 'blissfully unconstrained by notions of ethics. Their duty was to their client'. This readiness to assume that nothing should stand in the way of a 'full and fearless defence' effectively robs the Code, it is submitted, of its capacity to control the behaviour of defence barristers during cross-examination.[62]

Role of trial judge

Trial judges are under a common law duty to restrain unnecessary questioning[63] and to ensure that cross-examination is not conducted in an unfair or oppressive manner.[64] Research into the conduct of rape trials suggests that trial judges rarely exercise this discretion to protect complainants from improper assaults upon their characters and from bullying or offensive questioning. Some feminists have attributed this reluctance to intervene to an overwhelmingly male judiciary which is 'woefully ignorant and prejudiced about rape and sexual assault'.[65] Research, however, suggests that judicial intervention during cross-examination in other trial contexts is similarly infrequent. The trial judge, in fact, exercises his or her discretion within tight structural constraints and this underlies the failure to protect both rape complainants and other witnesses from irrelevant and inappropriate questioning.[66] In an adversarial system, the principle of party autonomy dictates that responsibility for presenting the evidence lies with the parties and the trial judge is consigned to the role of impartial umpire. Judicial passivity is encouraged, as it is assumed to preserve the appearance of

---

59   Op cit, Rock, fn 52, p 108.

60   Brown, B, Burman, M and Jamieson, L, Sex Crimes on Trial: The Use of Sexual Evidence in Scottish Courts, 1993, Edinburgh: Edinburgh UP, p 206.

61   Temkin, J, 'Rape in court' (1998) The Guardian, 27 October, p 17.

62   See Blake, M and Ashworth, A, 'Some ethical issues in prosecuting and defending criminal cases' [1998] Crim LR 1, pp 16–34.

63   See Mechanical and General Inventions Co Ltd and Lehwess v Austin and Austin Motor Co Ltd [1935] AC 346; Kalia [1975] Crim LR 181.

64   The principles which govern a trial judge's discretion to disallow cross-examination to credit are set out in Hobbs v Tinling [1929] 2 KB 151.

65   Op cit, Lees, fn 7, p 248.

66   See Ellison, L, 'Cross-examination in rape trials' [1998] Crim LR 605, pp 606–15.

fairness in criminal proceedings.[67] Accordingly, excessive or inappropriate judicial intervention can be the ground for a successful appeal.[68] The Court of Appeal underlined the limits of judicial intervention and the dangers of overstepping the boundaries in *R v Sharp*:

> A judge should not intervene, when cross-examination is being conducted by competent counsel, save to clarify matters which he did not understand or thought that the jury might not have understood ... If the judge's interventions and criticisms of counsel are unnecessary and unjustified, this can result in the quashing of the conviction on the ground of a material irregularity in the trial.[69]

Fear of appearing partisan and of compromising the ability of counsel to present his or her version of events renders judicial discretion an ineffective constraint on inappropriate cross-examination.

GIVING EVIDENCE IN COURT

The principle of orality is a foundation of the adversarial process and it dictates, with limited exceptions, that witnesses give direct oral testimony in open court. Many of the problems experienced by complainants of sexual offences stem directly from this insistence upon live oral evidence. Interviews with rape complainants have, for example, revealed that testifying before a courtroom of strangers is extremely difficult and a source of considerable embarrassment for rape complainants.[70] Women have described 'having to speak loudly about such intimate questions as one of the worst aspects of taking a case to court'.[71] The experience of one woman interviewed by the UK organisation Victim Support is typical:

> [I was] paralysed by everybody – all their friends and family – staring and looking at me. It shouldn't have been so bad if they hadn't been in the room when I gave evidence, that should not have been allowed. They were laughing and calling me a liar. No one told them to shut up.[72]

---

67 'It is always open to the judge to probe, but the tradition is strong that he is an arbiter and not an inquisitor and that the coming to the aid of a party in distress might impair his impartiality.' (*Op cit*, Devlin, fn 37, p 62.)

68 See *R v Rabbitt* (1931) 23 Cr App R 112; *R v Hirock and Others* [1970] 1 QB 67; *R v Hamilton* [1969] Crim LR 486.

69 (1994) 98 Cr App R 144. In *R v Gunning* [1980] Crim LR 592, the Court of Appeal held that: '... when a judge's interventions were on such a scale as to deprive the accused of the chance, to which he was entitled under the adversarial system, of developing his evidence under the lead and guidance of defending counsel, the trial must be regarded as a mistrial even in the absence of an allegation that the judge's questioning was hostile to the accused.' See, also, *R v Perks* [1973] Crim LR 388.

70 See, eg, *op cit*, Victim Support, fn 5, p 16.

71 Lees, S, 'Judicial rape' (1993) 16 Women's Studies International Forum, p 26.

72 *Op cit*, Victim Support, fn 5, p 28.

Women also experience problems having to face the defendant and his supporters whilst giving evidence.[73] In response to the Victim Support survey, 47% of witness services contacted reported that women felt fearful of facing the defendant and his supporters.[74] One woman interviewed in the study stated, 'I was absolutely terrified, I had never been to court before in my life. I was very scared about the fact that I would have to look at him again, to see his face'.[75] In Heenan and McKelvie's recent study, the victims interviewed felt 'distressed', 'terrified' and 'unsafe' being close to the defendant. One woman interviewed explained how the accused's presence had affected her performance in court: 'I felt very distressed and uncomfortable. I was terrified before I went in there 'cos I knew he'd be in there, and yes it did [make it harder to give evidence].'[76] The reliance on live oral evidence in adversarial proceedings also exposes rape complainants to the formality of the courtroom which many reportedly find intimidating. Complainants are further forced to endure months of waiting for a court appearance and frequent distressing delays.

While most adversarial jurisdictions have now introduced procedures to mitigate the stress of testifying for child witnesses through the use of screens, CCTV and video-recorded testimony there has been a notable reluctance to extend these measures to adults victims of sexual violence. Deeply embedded assumptions of the adversarial process have militated against even basic protection for rape complainants, despite overwhelming evidence that, for them, testifying in open court is often a traumatic ordeal. Adversarial theory assumes that a physical confrontation between accused and accuser has instrumental benefits: the reliability of testimony is allegedly enhanced and accurate fact determination is promoted. As a result, complainants are generally required to confront defendants in court.[77] Furthermore, confrontation advocates have in recent years increasingly argued that a face to face encounter has an intrinsic value beyond testing the probative value of evidence. The procedural right to confront and challenge, it is claimed, has an important role to play in preserving the dignity of criminal defendants and maximising their participation in the trial process.[78] The use of screens, CCTV and video-recorded testimony by adult witnesses is thus presented as an

---

73 *Op cit*, Victim Support, fn 5, p 15.

74 *Op cit*, Victim Support, fn 5, p 16.

75 *Op cit*, Victim Support, fn 5, p 45.

76 *Op cit*, Heenan and McKelvie, fn 13, p 105.

77 The right of a defendant to challenge and confront the witnesses against him does not, however, require witnesses to give direct oral evidence in court in the physical presence of the accused. The interests of a defendant are met when questioning is conducted at a pre-trial hearing where only the defendant's lawyer is present. See, eg, *Kostovski v Netherlands* (1992) 14 EHRR 396.

78 Massaro, T, 'The dignity value of face to face confrontations' (1988) 40 Florida UL Rev 863.

unwarranted infringement upon the confrontation rights of criminal defendants.[79] The reluctance to extend protective measures to adult victims of sexual violence may also be explained in terms of the faith traditionally placed in demeanour evidence and the supposed ability of jurors and judges to discern sincerity or deception from a witness's behaviour in the witness box. Screens and CCTV, it is feared, may interfere with a jury's assessment of important non-verbal clues. Adult rape complainants have been denied protection on the basis of these assumptions and yet there is no persuasive evidence that physical confrontation increases witness reliability[80] or that witness demeanour is a reliable indicator of veracity. There is, in fact, a body of behavioural research that suggests that observation of demeanour diminishes rather than enhances the accuracy of credibility judgments and that the stress involved in physically confronting a defendant is likely to inhibit a witness's coherence, confidence and ability to recall facts.[81]

Recent developments

In 1998, the Home Office published the report of an interdepartmental working group on the treatment of vulnerable and intimidated witnesses within the criminal justice system.[82] The report, *Speaking Up For Justice*, proposed a range of measures aimed at lessening the ordeal of children and vulnerable adult witnesses at each stage of the criminal process including measures aimed specifically at reducing the trauma associated with a courtroom appearance. The Working Group accepted that current courtroom practices were adversely affecting the ability of certain adult witnesses, including complainants in rape cases, to give their best evidence. The recommendations of the Home Office Working Group have been largely implemented in the Youth Justice and Criminal Evidence Act (YJCEA) 1999.[83]

The Act introduces a range of special measures available to eligible witnesses. Witnesses may be eligible for assistance on grounds of age or

---

79 See Friedman, R, 'Thoughts from across the water on hearsay and confrontation' [1998] Crim LR 697. The confrontation rights of defendants must, however, be weighed against the competing interests of any witness or complainant. In *Doorson*, the European Court of Human Rights stated that the 'principles of a fair trial also require that in appropriate cases, the interests of the defence are balanced against those of witnesses or victims called upon to testify'. *Doorson v The Netherlands* (1996) 22 EHRR 330. See, also, *Van Mechelen v The Netherlands* (1997) 25 EHRR 547.

80 See Law Commission, *Evidence in Criminal Proceedings: Hearsay and Related Topics*, Consultation Paper No 138, 1995, London: HMSO.

81 See Wellborn, OG, 'Demeanour' (1991) 76 Cornell L Rev 1104.

82 Home Office, *Speaking Up For Justice: Report of the Interdepartmental Working Group on the Treatment of Vulnerable or Intimidated Witnesses in the Criminal Justice System*, 1998, London: Home Office.

83 The Act received royal assent on 27 July 1999.

incapacity[84] or alternatively, on grounds of fear or distress about testifying.[85] Under s 16, a witness is eligible for special measures to help them giving evidence in criminal proceedings if they are under 17 years old; or they suffer from a mental disorder, or have a mental impairment or learning disability that the court considers significant enough to affect the quality of their evidence; or they suffer from a physical disorder, that the court considers likely to affect the quality of their evidence.[86] Under s 17, a witness is eligible for special measures if the court is satisfied that the witness is likely to suffer fear or distress in giving evidence to an extent that is expected to affect its quality.[87] There is a presumption that complainants of sexual offences[88] will benefit from a special measures direction. Section 17(4) provides that complainants of sexual offences will be considered eligible unless they inform the court that they do not want to be eligible.[89]

Where a party is eligible for special measures, the court must determine whether any of the special measures available to the witness would be likely to improve the quality of the evidence given by the witness. If this test is satisfied, the court must then determine which of those measures (or combination of them) would be likely to maximise, so far as practicable, the quality of such evidence. The court must consider any views expressed by the witness and whether the measure might tend to inhibit such evidence being effectively tested by a party to the defence.[90] The range of special measures potentially available to adult rape complainants includes the use of screens[91] and the ability to give evidence through a live television link.[92] Section 25 of

---

84   YJCEA 1999, s 16.

85   *Ibid*, s 17.

86   The 'quality' of a witness's evidence refers to its quality in terms of completeness, coherence and accuracy; and 'coherence' refers to a witness' ability in giving evidence to give answers which address the questions put to the witness and can be understood both individually and collectively: *ibid*, s 16(5).

87   The court must take into account, in particular, the nature and alleged circumstances of the offence to which the proceedings relate; the age of the witness; the social and cultural background and ethnic origins of the witness; the domestic and employment circumstances of the witness; any religious beliefs or political opinions of the witness; and any behaviour towards the witness on the part of the accused or members of the family or associates of the accused or any other person who is likely to be an accused or a witness in the proceedings. The court must also consider any views expressed by the witness: *ibid*, s 17(3).

88   Defined by *ibid*, s 62.

89   Where a party is eligible for special measures, any party to the proceedings may apply for a 'special measures direction' or the court may raise the issue of its own motion: *ibid*, s 19(1).

90   *Ibid*, s 19(3).

91   *Ibid*, s 23. The screen must not prevent the witness from being able to see, and be seen by, the judge, legal representatives and the jury.

92   *Ibid*, s 24.

the Act allows the courtroom to be cleared of people who do not need to be present while a rape complainant gives evidence.[93]

One of the more far-reaching provisions concerns the use of pre-trial video-recorded interviews. Section 27 provides that a special measures direction may provide for a video-recorded interview to be admitted as a witness's evidence-in-chief.[94] Where the court has already allowed a video-recording to be admitted as the witness's main evidence, s 28 provides that the witness may be cross-examined before trial and the cross-examination recorded on video for use at trial.[95] These measures are, however, to be available only to children and adult witnesses with a significant impairment of intelligence or other mental or physical disorder.[96]

While the special measures contained within the YJCEA 1999 are to be welcomed, the protection they afford rape complainants has, disappointingly, been constrained by a continuing attachment to the primacy of oral evidence and conventional adversarial methods.[97] Adult rape complainants are to benefit from the availability of screens and CCTV but they are to be denied the protection inherent in the use of video-recorded evidence.[98] Generally, adult rape complainants will still be required to give live oral evidence in criminal proceedings, albeit via a TV link. Complainants will thus have to endure lengthy delays which, as Lees notes, put 'unnecessary pressure on women who have to relive the experience so long afterwards, and have sometimes been subjected to intimidation in the meantime'.[99]

There is also a risk, as a recent Australian study demonstrates, that a commitment to traditional adversarial values and methods may yet limit the impact of the reforms.

---

93 This measure is only available in a case involving a sexual offence or when the court is persuaded that someone has tried to intimidate, or is likely to intimidate, the witness. The direction may not exclude the accused, legal representatives acting in the proceedings or any interpreter or other person appointed to assist the witness. Under the YJCEA 1999, s 26, a direction may provide for the removal of wigs and gowns by judges and legal representatives.

94 The court may subsequently direct that a video recording to be excluded or edited if the interests of justice so require: *ibid,* s 27(2).

95 As with video-recorded evidence-in-chief, a video recording of cross-examination may afterwards be excluded if necessary in the interests of justice.

96 YJCEA 1999, s 28, para 8.49. When the new legislation was being considered in parliament, it was suggested that initial estimates were that some 900 witnesses a year would be involved in pre-recorded cross-examination. See Bates, P, 'The Youth Justice and Criminal Evidence Act – the evidence of children and vulnerable adults' (1999) 11(3) CFLQ 289.

97 See Ellison, L, 'The protection of vulnerable witnesses in court: an Anglo-Dutch comparison' (1999) 3 E & P 29.

98 The primary advantages of pre-trial video-recorded evidence are that the complainant may thereafter undergo therapy without fear that this will undermine her credibility as a witness and that the stress of waiting for a court appearance is substantially reduced.

99 *Op cit,* Lees, fn 7, p 106.

The Crimes (Rape) Act 1991

In Victoria, the Crimes (Sexual Offences) Act 1991 introduced a number of provisions permitting the use of alternative arrangements for giving evidence in certain cases involving children and complainants with an intellectual disability.[100] The Crimes (Rape) Act 1991 extended the use of these provisions for the first time to adult victims of sexual offences.[101] The protective measures available include permitting evidence to be given via CCTV, the use of screens, and permitting only persons specified by the court to be present while the witness is giving evidence.[102] In 1997, the Victorian Department of Justice published an evaluative study of the reforms introduced in the Crimes (Rape) Act 1991.[103] The evaluation endeavoured to look at the extent to which the alternative arrangements for giving evidence are used during rape proceedings and also explored the range of perceptions held by legal practitioners and judges with respect to using the arrangements. Heenan and McKelvie report that, despite the reforms, giving evidence continues to be a harrowing and often traumatic experience for many complainants. The broad intentions of the new legislation were often confounded by the assumptions held by legal practitioners and members of the bench with respect to who ought to use the arrangements, under what circumstances they should be used, and what effect they will have on jurors' decision making. The study found that the extent to which the alternative arrangements for giving evidence are used remains extremely limited, especially for adult victims.[104] Few applications, for example, were made by practitioners for adult complainants to use CCTV or screens and judges rarely exercised their own discretion to order that the arrangements be used.[105]

Interviews with judges and barristers revealed that a significant number were unconvinced of the need for measures such as CCTV.[106] One lawyer interviewed stated, 'I mean where is the threat? That person is not going to jump out of the dock and attack you, that person is removed by 30, 40, 50 feet

---

100 Crimes (Sexual Offences) Act 1991, s 37C.

101 In these cases, the court must be satisfied that, without alternative arrangements being made, the witness is likely, in giving evidence, to suffer severe emotional trauma or to be so intimidated or stressed as to be severely disadvantaged as a witness.

102 In cases where alternative arrangements are used at the trial proceedings, the judge must warn the jury not to draw any inference adverse to the defendant, or to give the evidence any greater or lesser weight because of the making those arrangements: YJCEA 1999, s 32.

103 *Op cit*, Heenan and McKelvie, fn 13.

104 Just over 25% of complainants who gave evidence at trial used an alternative arrangement.

105 *Op cit*, Heenan and McKelvie, fn 13, p 109.

106 Obviously, not all complainants will want to use CCTV. A small number of victims spoke of it being 'empowering' for them to describe what had happened in the accused's presence: *op cit*, Heenan and McKelvie, fn 13, p 114.

of the room.'[107] One complainant who had directly asked the prosecutor whether she could use CCTV was told that there was no real need, given that 'she ha[d]n't been brutalised'.[108] Defence lawyers interviewed voiced strong objections to the use of alternative arrangements in rape cases and complained that the use of measures such as screens and CCTV were an unwarranted infringement of the confrontation rights of criminal defendants. The basic principle that an accused should be able to face his accuser should not, they maintained, be undermined: 'The court is a public place and if people are to make allegations which are publicly prosecuted they should make them publicly, not behind some screen or veil or anything else ... it's fundamentally unfair.'[109] Furthermore, interviewees were particularly concerned about the potential prejudicial effect that might result for an accused. It was feared that a jury would infer the guilt of the accused if special arrangements had to be made to accommodate the complainant's fear of being in the same room as him. Some defence barristers expressed the view that the use of CCTV could compromise their ability to cross-examine effectively: 'I'm very concerned about it because it takes away from me a weapon that I can use for my client – in other words, eye contact, or sort of 'getting down to it' a little bit.'[110]

The Victoria study also found a reluctance on the part of prosecutors to make applications for complainants to make use of alternative arrangements even in cases where the complainant herself felt that she would be disadvantaged as a witness or be severely traumatised if she was made to give evidence in the presence of the accused.[111] Heenan and McKelvie report that there was a strong assumption held by many practitioners and members of the bench that CCTV somehow lessened the emotional impact of the victim's evidence, and therefore made her seem less real or believable. Strategic disincentives therefore militated against the use of facilities such as CCTV:

> I just think that when juries see ... the whole person they relate to them as a human being. People watch so much television these days, they see a complainant on the TV and it has a displacement effect, whereas the accused is sitting in front of them as a real live person. I just feel that it doesn't help.[112]

In England and Wales, similar views are reported in the Home Office Study which states that Crown Prosecution Service lawyers, judges and barristers did not see CCTV as a good idea in the general run of cases. According to the report, it was felt that a complainant can have a more positive impact on the

---

107 *Op cit*, Heenan and McKelvie, fn 13, p 73.

108 *Op cit*, Heenan and McKelvie, fn 13, p 112.

109 *Op cit*, Heenan and McKelvie, fn 13, p 74.

110 *Op cit*, Heenan and McKelvie, fn 13.

111 *Op cit*, Heenan and McKelvie, fn 13, p 114.

112 *Op cit*, Heenan and McKelvie, fn 13, p 76.

jury by giving evidence in person.[113] Despite the reservations expressed by prosecuting barristers, there is no empirical evidence to support these assumptions.

The 'subversion and circumvention of rape law reform is often presented as evidence of entrenched patriarchy and misogyny within our legal culture'.[114] As the above discussion has sought to make clear, the strategic incentives of the adversarial process and an unwillingness to depart from conventional adversarial methods represent equally effective obstacles to improving the position of rape complainants in court.

CONCLUSION

The criminal justice system has been accused of demonstrating an 'unremitting harshness' towards complainants in rape cases;[115] their treatment in court has been described as a second violation or as judicial rape. Feminists have criticised various aspects of rape trials: their quasi-pornographic nature,[116] evidentiary rules which serve to undermine the credibility of complainants, the use of sexual history evidence and the support and promotion of cultural rape myths in court. In focusing upon conventional trial methods and the combative, competitive culture of criminal proceedings, this chapter has sought to demonstrate that the most significant and potentially obstinate barrier to fairer rape trials is the adversarial process itself.

As some feminist writers have speculated, a trial process created by women might be quite different from the traditional adversary model.[117] Drawing upon Gilligan's theory of male and female reasoning, women, it is suggested, may favour a more co-operative, less competitive judicial system, one which does not impede 'the expression of concern for the person on the other side'.[118] Within a feminist model of litigation, Menkel-Meadow

---

113 *Op cit*, Home Office, fn 82, p 48.

114 Bronitt, S, 'The rules of recent complaint: rape myths and the legal construction of the "reasonable" rape victim', in Easteal, P (ed), *Balancing the Scales: Rape Law Reform and Australian Culture*, 1998, Sydney: Federation, p 42.

115 Barnett, H, *Introduction to Feminist Jusriprudence*, 1998, London: Cavendish Publishing, p 274.

116 See Smart, C, 'Law's power, the sexed body, and feminist discourse' (1990) 17 JLS 194; Lees, S, *Ruling Passions: Sexual Violence, Reputation and the Law*, 1997, Buckingham: OU Press, p 78.

117 See *op cit*, Kinports, fn 46, p 428; Menkel-Meadow, C, 'The trouble with the adversary system in a postmodern, multi-cultural world' (1996) 1 J Inst Stud Leg Ethics 49; Menkel-Meadow, C, 'Portia in a different voice: speculations on a women's lawyering process' (1985) 1 Berkeley Women's LJ 39.

118 Gilligan, C, *In a Different Voice: Psychological Theory and Women's Development*, 1982, Cambridge, Mass: Harvard UP, p 135.

contends, an ethic of care and responsibility for others may supplant the 'macho ethic of the courtroom battle'.[119] Accordingly, trial advocacy would more closely resemble a 'conversation' with the fact-finder rather than a 'war-like system of communication between disputants'.[120] Trials would be less intimidating for all participants and the kinds of tactics deployed by defence lawyers to confuse, harass and humiliate witnesses would not be tolerated.[121]

The feminist ideal of a more co-operative, less confrontational, trial process is however, unlikely to achieved 'without massive restructuring of the adversary system'.[122] In the short term, therefore, as Kinports notes, the ideal must give way to a more pragmatic approach and feminists should seek to mitigate the worst excesses of the adversarial process.[123] As this chapter has suggested, short term measures which would improve the treatment of rape complainants within the criminal trial process include removing complainants from the courtroom through extension of the video evidence provisions of the YJCEA 1999 to adult rape complainants. At the same time, a fresh debate must take place within the legal profession, re-examining and redefining the ethical boundaries of vigorous advocacy.

---

119 *Op cit*, Menkel-Meadow (1985), fn 117, p 53.

120 *Op cit*, Menkel-Meadow (1985), fn 117, p 55.

121 It has been suggested that women trial lawyers practising within the adversarial process are less comfortable with the hostility and combativeness that characterises legal proceedings. See Freyer, J, 'Women litigators in search of a care-orientated judicial system' (1995) 4 Am UJ Gender & Law 199; Oh, C, 'Questioning the cultural and gender-based assumptions of the adversary system' (1992) 7 Berkeley Women's LJ 125.

122 *Op cit*, Kinports, fn 46, p 428.

123 *Op cit*, Kinports, fn 46, p 456.

CHAPTER 4

GENDER BIAS IN THE HEARSAY RULE[1]

Fiona E Raitt

This chapter explores the role of speech and communication in the hearsay rule of evidence. It does so by arguing that the hearsay rule – a rule of apparently universal application and irrelevant to gender – masks a hidden gender bias that works to the disadvantage of women. This disadvantage particularly manifests itself in the courtroom where female complainants in criminal cases may be unable to draw on the testimony of confidantes to enhance their credibility or to provide corroborative support of crucial facts, because such testimony would be regarded as hearsay.

What is meant here by 'gender bias'? I have borrowed the model adopted by sex discrimination legislation in the US and Europe, namely that a bias is considered to exist if the effect of the application of the rule is directly or indirectly to discriminate against one sex. As Fredman explains, 'the concept of indirect discrimination addresses situations in which equal treatment leads to unequal results'.[2] It may well be that some of the arguments that follow in this chapter demonstrate a problem that is applicable to both men and women. However, if it can be shown that the problem proportionately discriminates against women more than men, then the feminist spectre of a gender bias will have been raised. It is my argument that this is precisely the effect of the hearsay rule, owing to gender differences in the use of language.

GENDER BIAS WITHIN LAW

There is now a well established feminist jurisprudence highlighting the gendered nature of law,[3] and within that, feminist critiques of specific areas of the law, including contract, criminal law, legal method, employment, family

---

1 I am grateful to Pamela Ferguson, Suzanne Zeedyk and the editors of this volume for comments on earlier drafts. I am indebted to Beverley Brown for helping me to organise my ideas.

2 Fredman, S, *Women and the Law*, 1997, Oxford: Clarendon, p 240.

3 Eg, O'Donovan, K, *Sexual Divisions in Law*, 1985, London: Weidenfeld & Nicolson; Smart, C, *Feminism and the Power of Law*, 1989, London: Routledge; MacKinnon, C, *Toward a Feminist Theory of the State*, 1989, Cambridge, Mass: Harvard UP; and the other texts in the *Feminist Perspectives* series, especially Bottomley, A (ed), *Feminist Perspectives on the Foundational Subjects of Law*, 1996, London: Cavendish Publishing.

law, medical law and property.[4] Catharine MacKinnon has characterised law generally as androcentric and male normative. Her characterisation is all-embracing – no aspects of substantive or procedural law escape its effect:

> ... the State appears most relentless in imposing the male point of view when it comes closest to achieving its highest formal criterion of distanced aperspectivity. When it is most ruthlessly neutral, it is most male; when it is most sex blind, it is most blind to the sex of the standard being applied. When it most closely conforms to precedent, to 'facts', to legislative intent it most closely enforces socially male norms ... [5]

Although the corpus of the law of evidence has received relatively little feminist analysis,[6] there is no reason to suppose that this area of law should be immune from the biases shown in other areas. Indeed, in her review of various North American task force reports set up to examine gender issues in the courts, Mack noted that several of these reports identified disadvantages suffered by female litigants and witnesses and documented 'the disparity in credibility and respect accorded men and women' which 'directly affect[ed] the outcome of legal proceedings'.[7] Certain specific rules of evidence have attracted substantial criticism from feminists. These include the rules relating to previous sexual history evidence of a complainant in rape and other sexual offences,[8] credibility of female victims (especially girls) and the use and extent of expert evidence of Battered Woman's Syndrome in cases involving battered women who kill violent partners.[9] This chapter examines one rule that appears to have escaped significant attention – the hearsay rule.[10]

---

4   See, in regard to these specific areas – contract: Frug, MJ, *Postmodern Legal Feminism*, 1992, London: Routledge; criminal: Lacey, N, 'Unspeakable subjects: sexuality, integrity and criminal law' (1997) 8(2) Women: A Cultural Review 143; legal method: *op cit*, Smart, fn 3; employment: *op cit*, Fredman, fn 2; family: O'Donovan, K, *Family Law Matters*, 1993, London: Pluto; medical: Sheldon, S and Thomson, M, *Feminist Perspectives on Health Care Law*, 1998, London: Cavendish Publishing; property: Green, K, 'Thinking land law differently' (1995) FLS 131.

5   *Op cit*, MacKinnon, fn 3, p 248.

6   Notable exceptions are Kinports, K, 'Evidence engendered' (1991) Illinois UL Rev 413; Mack, K, 'Continuing barriers to women's credibility: a feminist perspective on the proof process' (1993) 4 Criminal Law Forum 327; and Hunter, R, 'Gender in evidence: masculine norms vs feminist reforms' (1996) 19 Harv Women's LJ, p 127.

7   *Ibid*, Mack, p 332.

8   See, eg, Adler, Z, *Rape on Trial*, 1987, London: Routledge and Kegan Paul; Brown, B, Burman, M and Jamieson, L, *Sex Crimes on Trial*, 1993, Edinburgh: Edinburgh UP; Kelly, L, *Surviving Sexual Violence*, 1988, Cambridge: Polity; Lees, S, *Carnal Knowledge: Rape on Trial*, 1996, London: Hamish Hamilton; Temkin, J, *Rape and the Legal Process*, 1987, London: Sweet & Maxwell.

9   Fox, M, 'Legal responses to "battered women who kill"', in Bridgeman, J and Millns, S (eds), *Law and Body Politics*, 1995, Aldershot: Dartmouth; McColgan, A, 'In defence of battered women who kill' (1993) 13 OJLS 508; Nicolson, D, 'Telling tales: gender discrimination, gender construction, and battered women who kill' (1995) 3 FLS 185; O'Donovan, K, 'Defences for battered women who kill' (1991) 18 JLS 219; Wells, C, 'Battered Women Syndrome and defences to homicide: where now?' (1994) 14 LS 266.

10 But see Orenstein, A, '"My God!" A feminist critique of the excited utterance exception to the hearsay rule' (1997) 85 California L Rev 159.

THE PROOF PROCESS AND THE HEARSAY RULE

The proof process in both civil and criminal law is intended to elicit facts and to determine the 'truth'. Traditional theories of evidence assume the objective and value-free nature of the fact-finding process, although these theories have been critiqued for failing to acknowledge the 'inherently political and partial nature of law and facts'.[11] According to the traditional theoretical model, facts are proven through the application of a body of rules designed to govern admissibility of evidence. The law ideally seeks production of 'best evidence' provided by witnesses giving oral testimony under oath in open court. Oral testimony is the single most important form of evidence in the proof process.[12]

The hearsay rule states that an assertion 'other than one made by a person while giving oral evidence in the proceedings is inadmissible as evidence of any fact stated'.[13] Hearsay evidence is excluded because it is regarded as unreliable and therefore not 'best evidence'. By this it is meant that the maker of the original statement is not physically present in court to testify as to the accuracy of the statement, and as such there is non-compliance with the general rule that only best evidence is admissible. In common law jurisdictions that adopt an adversarial approach, hearsay evidence is generally *in*admissible in criminal proceedings, while in civil proceedings it tends to be admissible, albeit accorded limited weight.[14] In this chapter, discussion of the hearsay rule is primarily concerned with criminal proceedings, for it is there that the rule continues to have most impact. The chapter focuses on oral evidence, for although hearsay evidence can extend to documentary evidence, it predominantly pertains to the spoken word.

The effect of the hearsay rule is to exclude evidence intended to prove the *content* of prior statements, but not to exclude its *occurrence*. Various explanations have been proposed as to the reason for the development of the rule. The classic justifications for rejecting hearsay evidence were given by Lord Normand in the 1952 case of *Teper v R*:

> [It] is not the best evidence and it is not delivered on oath. The truthfulness and accuracy of the person whose words are spoken to by another witness cannot be tested by cross-examination, and the light which his demeanour would throw on his testimony is lost.[15]

---

11 Nicolson, D, 'Truth, reason and justice: epistemology and politics in evidence discourse' (1994) 57 MLR 726.

12 Rembar, C, *The Law of the Land*, 1989, New York: Simon & Schuster.

13 Tapper, C, *Cross and Tapper on Evidence*, 8th edn, 1995, London: Butterworths, p 46.

14 The position is different in some civil law systems, eg, France, Germany and The Netherlands, where hearsay is also permitted in criminal proceedings.

15 [1952] AC 480, p 486.

Cogent objections have been offered to each of these justifications embodied within Lord Normand's opinion. The objections reflect three main themes. First, the argument that hearsay is not best evidence is countered by the fact that it is already admitted in many civil cases and in the many exceptions to the rule in criminal cases. The court addresses any concerns over reliability of 'second hand' evidence through varying the degree of weight it attaches to the evidence in question. Thus, evidence given on commission, or by video-recording, or as a dying declaration (each of which is recognised as an exception to the hearsay rule) may well not carry as much weight as if it had been delivered in person. Nonetheless, such evidence is admitted because it generally adds something to the proof process, and because it may be the best *available* evidence.[16]

Secondly, the argument that hearsay evidence lacks the solemnity of the oath in underlining to a witness the seriousness of testimony in court is no longer convincing. In an increasingly secular Western world, the significance of the oath, with its dependency on a belief in religious retribution, is rapidly diminishing, and retaining the offence of perjury for those who lie in the witness box would arguably be just as effective. Thirdly, the argument that hearsay should be excluded because it prevents effective cross-examination or observation of demeanour, merit the same response as the first point, namely that of the weight attaching to such evidence. If the consequence of being unable to interrogate a witness about hearsay testimony is that the particular witness cannot provide a meaningful answer, or is forced to dissemble or remains silent in response to searching questions, then the cross-examination has been effective. The point will have been made – the witness cannot say, because his or her knowledge is limited.

Most recently, the relevance of the hearsay rule in the modern law of criminal evidence has been subject to detailed consideration by the Law Commissions of both Scotland and England.[17] They concluded that the state of the law was not defensible. There is a large and amorphous group of statutory and common law exceptions. Judicial discretion plays a significant part in determining the admissibility of hearsay, resulting in a body of case law that is conflicting and inconsistent and thus difficult to reconcile. Statutory reform has already occurred in relation to Scotland through the Criminal Procedure (Scotland) Act 1995 and has been recommended for England. It is not the purpose of this chapter to examine closely the content of

---

16 This is the basis for much of the statutory reform of the hearsay rule that has taken place in Scots law. See the Criminal Procedure (Scotland) Act 1995, s 259.

17 Law Commission, *Criminal Law – Evidence in Criminal Proceedings: Hearsay and Related Topics*, Consultation Paper No 138, 1995, London: HMSO; Law Commission, *Evidence in Criminal Proceedings: Hearsay and Related Topics*, Report No 245, Cm 3670, 1997, London: HMSO; , Scottish Law Commission, *Hearsay Evidence in Criminal Proceedings*, Report No 149, 1995, Edinburgh: Scottish Law Commission.

these Law Commission Reports.[18] Rather, it is intended to focus on the ways the rule impacts on gender issues.

On the face of it, the hearsay rule presents as one of universal application. Nowhere in the detailed deliberations of either Commission is there any suggestion that in either the operation or the effect of the hearsay rule are there any aspects which are discriminatory or have a gendered bias. Unlike other rules of evidence such as sexual history evidence and the recent complaint doctrine which obviously discriminate against women, the hearsay rule appears gender neutral. However, I argue here that the hearsay rule does indeed work disproportionately against women's interests. Women are placed at a material disadvantage arising out of linguistic differences in communication patterns between men and women, and also in the language of professional discourse used within the courtroom.

GENDER DIFFERENCES IN LANGUAGE AND COMMUNICATION

It has been frequently observed that women and men communicate differently.[19] Women appear to conduct much of their personal relations through the conversations they have with family members and friends, and research has repeatedly established that women are more likely than men to have intimate confidantes.[20] Women's interactions with women friends function primarily on a face to face basis, in contrast to men's interactions with male friends, which are mostly side by side.[21] In other words, women seek friends with whom they can be at ease, confide in and make disclosures to in a safe setting: 'someone to trust'; whereas men seek friends with whom to undertake activities: 'someone to go out with'.[22]

---

18 But for thoughtful responses to the Consultation Paper and the Report, respectively, both expressing disappointment over the recommendations, see Zuckerman, A, 'Law Commission's Consultation Paper No 138 on Hearsay: (1) the futility of hearsay' (1996) Crim L Rev 4; Spencer, J, 'Hearsay reform: a bridge not far enough?' [1996] Crim LR 29.

19 Tannen, D, *You Just Don't Understand*, 1990, New York: Ballantine.

20 Eg Chodorow, N, *The Reproduction of Mothering: Psychoanalysis and the Sociology of Gender*, 1978, Berkeley, CA: California UP; Cochrane, R, 'Preface', in Siann, G, *Gender, Sex and Sexuality*, 1994, London: Taylor and Francis; Duck, S, *Friends, for Life*, 1983, Hemel Hempstead: Harvester Wheatsheaf; Illich, I, *Gender*, 1993, London: Marion Boyars; O'Connor, P, *Friendships Between Women: A Critical Review*, 1992, Hemel Hempstead: Harvester Wheatsheaf; Rubin, L, *Just Friends: The Role of Friendship in our Lives*, 1985, New York: Harper and Row; Sherrod, D, 'The influence of gender on same-sex friendships', in Hendrick, C (ed), *Close Relationships*, 1989, Newbury Park, California: Sage.

21 Bell, R, *Worlds of Friendship*, 1991, London: Sage; Derlega, V and Winstead, B (eds), *Friendship and Social Interaction*, 1986, New York: Springer; Komarovsky, M, *Blue Collar Marriage*, 1967, New York: Vintage.

22 Helgeson, V, Shaver, P and Dyer, M, 'Prototypes of intimacy and distance in same-sex and opposite sex relationships' (1987) 4 Journal of Social and Personal Relationships 195.

If women's friendships are characterised by 'intimacy, mutual self-disclosure and a focus on talk' it has been suggested that in contrast, men's friendships are characterised by 'sociability, a lack of self-disclosure, and a focus on activity'.[23] Men appear to have little tradition of intimate conversation.[24] They tend to use speech functionally, to convey information, rather than to describe and discuss emotions. Johnson and Aries found that men's interactions with friends are directed towards activities and 'light conversation' such that 'their abilities to articulate personal concerns and to engage close friends in the solving of personal problems are probably diminished'.[25] On the other hand, talk was found to be 'the substance of women's friendship'.[26] In her study of 4,500 women, Hite found that the overwhelming majority of both married and single women had their deepest emotional relationship with a woman friend, and that they were much more likely to share intimacies with a woman than with a man, including their male partner.[27]

Undoubtedly, there are dangers in placing too much emphasis on gender differences in language and communication. For example, Crawford has argued that it can lead us to characterise a distinctive female style of speech as inferior, and thus suggest an essentialist view of language.[28] However, it is possible to acknowledge linguistic differences without representing women's style as deficient. In the context of the law of evidence, difficulties arise because the hearsay rule is assumed to operate universally and with neutrality. The rule presupposes that the exclusion of certain forms of communication will affect men and women equally. If it is accepted that there are gender differences in conversation and communication styles, the assumption of gender neutrality in the operation of the hearsay rule is immediately challenged, and it becomes possible to see how women are disadvantaged. The present hearsay rule overlooks the particular significance that women accord to their conversations, a significance that is infused with symbolism about the personal and political power reflected in these

---

23 Coates, J, 'Women's friendships, women's talk', in Wodak, R, *Gender and Discourse*, 1997, London: Sage, p 245. See, also, Lakoff, R, *Language and Woman's Place*, 1975, New York: Harper and Row; Gilligan, C, *In a Different Voice: Psychology Theory and Women's Development*, 1982, Cambridge, Mass: Harvard UP.

24 Pleck, J, 'Man to man: is brotherhood possible?', in Glazer-Malbin, N, *Old Family, New Family*, 1975, New York: Van Nostrand.

25 Johnson, F and Aries, E, 'Conversational patterns among same-sex pairs of late-adolescent close friends' (1983) 142 J Genetic Psychology 225.

26 Johnson, F and Aries, E, 'The talk of women's friends' (1983) 6 Women's Studies International Forum 353.

27 Hite, S, *Women as Revolutionary Agents of Change (The Hite Reports: Sexuality, Love and Emotion)*, 1993, London: Sceptre.

28 Crawford, M, *Talking Difference: On Gender and Language*, 1995, London: Sage.

communications.[29] The family members and friends who are fulfilling the listening role will often have been carefully selected to receive this information, and considerable trust is placed in these recipients, for the information conveyed may be of a highly personal and sensitive nature.

Yet, because such information is deemed by the hearsay rule to be 'second hand', its significance and potential value are disregarded. It is not available to corroborate the testimony of the complainant. Ideally, for the Crown to obtain a conviction, the essential elements of the crime will be corroborated, for even though English law no longer insists upon corroboration in criminal cases, corroborative evidence is still *desirable* to put the issue of sufficiency of evidence beyond contest. In those jurisdictions that retain a corroboration rule, such as Scotland, the need for testimony in support of the complainant is often vital. The types of crimes that typically involve women and female children are crimes of sexual or physical violence that tend to occur in private.[30] There will rarely be any eyewitnesses to such crimes to provide corroborative testimony. Equally, there may be no tangible corroborative evidence such as cuts, bruises or the existence of a weapon. Nonetheless, despite the absence of visible external injury, a woman may be highly intimidated or even in fear of her life because she is being stalked or receiving threatening telephone calls.

In many rape cases the lack of independent external evidence may be compounded by suggestions that the woman victim consented to sexual intercourse. Even where there is 'forensic or medical evidence which might be corroborative of physical violence or force and hence lack of consent [it] is often open to multiple interpretation and is rarely firm or conclusive'.[31] In contrast to the position concerning women, the kind of crimes involving male victims, such as theft, assaults, vandalism and public disorder offences occur in public places where there is a greater opportunity for the presence of witnesses, and thus independent corroboration. The need to resort to hearsay evidence in such public crimes involving men is therefore much reduced. The exclusion of hearsay evidence in sex crimes where there may be little else available to the prosecution to support the complainant's testimony therefore impacts on women disproportionately. If the hearsay rule were to be relaxed to allow words spoken by victims to confidantes to be repeated in court as evidence of the truth of the events recounted, that could compensate for the corroborative obstacles presented by crimes of sexual violence.

---

29 A symbolism encapsulated in the 1970s feminist slogan, 'the personal is political'. For wider discussion, see Heinzelman, S and Wiseman, S (eds), *Representing Women: Law, Literature and Feminism*, 1994, Durham, NC: Duke UP.

30 Koss, M, Gidyez, C and Wisniewski, N, 'The scope of rape: incidence and prevalence of sexual aggression and victimization in a national sample of higher education students' (1987) 55 J Consulting and Clinical Psychology 162; *op cit*, Kelly, fn 8; Edwards, S, *Sex and Gender in the Legal Process*, 1996, London: Blackstone.

31 Chambers, G and Millar, A, *Prosecuting Sexual Assault*, 1986, Edinburgh: Scottish Office Central Research Unit, p 95.

An illustration of how the hearsay rule affects women's communications can be seen in the example of a female adult survivor of child sexual abuse whose recovery leads her to join an incest survivors' group. If she subsequently gains the courage to report the abuse to the authorities and a prosecution ensues, none of the content of what she has previously disclosed to her group will be competent as evidence of the truth of her allegations, due to the operation of the hearsay rule. Since women are invariably more comfortable making disclosures of early child sexual abuse to another survivor, disclosures that may not be made until years after the event,[32] the effect of the hearsay rule is to devalue both the significance of the disclosure and the relationship of trust.

However, were she to make similar disclosures to an 'official' or 'professional' authority, such as a GP, psychologist or psychiatrist, the position is different. The strict application of the hearsay rule is often relaxed to permit opinion testimony from a professional source, such as medical personnel, as disclosures to a professional person are accorded an enhanced status. They will probably have been recorded in writing, in a public work environment and often with the specific objective of gathering information to keep records for subsequent use. Thus, an expert witness called to speak on behalf of such a party has some freedom to introduce facts, presented as opinion, that if adduced from the non-expert would be deemed inadmissible as hearsay.

Although an expert's opinion testimony is supposed to be drawn solely from facts that are admissible in evidence, Roberts has pointed out that the hearsay rule is especially susceptible to technical breaches by experts tendering psychiatric or psychological opinion evidence.[33] In such cases, frequently all an expert has to rely on is information given to him or her previously by the complainant. While Roberts is critical of the laxity with which the rule is applied in these instances, I would argue that such laxity demonstrates the justification for permitting confidantes to give evidence in support of complainants' testimony. Although it is frequently argued that at least expert evidence has the merit of neutrality and objectivity,[34] that point fails to acknowledge the criticisms of expert 'bias'.[35]

---

32 Hall, L and Lloyd, S, *Surviving Child Sexual Abuse*, 1989, Lewes: Falmer.

33 Roberts, P, 'Expert evidence in Canadian criminal proceedings', in Reece, H (ed), *Law and Science*, 1998, Oxford: OUP.

34 Eg Kenny, A, 'The expert in court' (1983) 99 LQR 197.

35 The expert as the purveyor of rational and superior knowledge is highly contested in critical, feminist and postmodern theory. See, eg, O'Donovan, K, 'Law's knowledge: the judge, the expert, the battered woman, and her syndrome' (1993) 20 JLS 427. For a broader discussion of the role of experts in the behavioural sciences, see Raitt, FE and Zeedyk, MS, *The Implicit Relation of Psychology and Law: Women and Syndrome Evidence*, 2000, London: Routledge.

Women undoubtedly use speech to make sensitive disclosures to another woman, and in particular a close friend, colleague or family member. In regard to sexual assault, Scottish research has confirmed that:

> ... complainers require, more than other complainers, access to specialist advice, support and assistance ... The assumption was made that family and friends would provide the necessary support. In many cases this was so, and some complainers had no desire to talk to other people.[36]

Implicit in this finding is the acknowledgment that complainers will disclose details of their assault to these confidantes, placing the latter in a unique position to offer testimony in court. Female patterns of speech are therefore naturally suited to intimate disclosures such as a sexual assault. Yet the repetition of this type of disclosure by the recipient confidante for the purpose of proving the intrinsic truth of the complaint is precisely the type of statement prohibited by the hearsay rule.

If women were permitted to call upon those in whom they had confided to testify on matters deemed under the present evidential regime to be hearsay testimony, some contribution might be made towards the wider challenge to the normative rules that regulate case construction. The construction and selection of narratives in a trial is thus a choice – it is not that there is an unequivocal 'truth' out there waiting to be discovered – and part of exercising that choice is the exclusion of evidence that does not fit neatly into predetermined categories. The types of narratives acceptable to law have been neither chosen nor influenced by women, and they are frequently disrespectful of and hostile to women's individuality. The problem is neatly demonstrated in the cases of battered women who kill their abusers. British cases such as *Ahluwalia*,[37] *Thornton*[38] and North American cases such as *State v Wanrow*[39] and *R v Lavallee*[40] provide prime examples of the inadequacy of orthodox male norms for women's experiences. In these cases, fact construction from the perspective of both the prosecution and the defence had to be undertaken within the parameters of existing criminal defences. The standard defences that might have been available to battered women who kill – namely, self-defence, provocation, necessity or justification – were originally designed with men in mind, and have proven manifestly unsuitable for battered women's circumstances. The stories of these women were for the most part excluded from the courtroom by a combination of these defences

36 Chambers, G and Millar, A, *Investigating Sexual Assault*, 1983, Edinburgh: Scottish Office Central Research Unit, p 134.
37 *R v Ahluwalia* [1992] 4 All ER 889.
38 *R v Thornton* [1992] 1 All ER 306; *R v Thornton (No 2)* [1996] 2 All ER 1023.
39 *State v Wanrow* 88 Wash 2d 221, 559 P 2d 548 (1977).
40 *R v Lavallee* [1990] 1 SCR 852.

and the rules of evidence. Such contextualising accounts of their abuse that were admitted were offered not by the woman herself but by experts.[41]

GENDER AND THE LANGUAGE OF THE COURTROOM

The hearsay rule also disadvantages women in relation to the formalities of the language used in the courtroom. Both the content of 'legalspeak' and the structures of legal discourse are the antithesis of women's pattern of communication, with its preference for shared intimacies and contextualisation. It is inevitable that legal discourse reflects male experience. For centuries, women were explicitly excluded from the legal process. For much of this century, women were not regarded as legal persons.[42] It is only in the last few decades that women were permitted to enrol in law school and gain admission to the legal profession.[43] It is even more recently that they have begun to have their experiences recognised in the modification of a fundamental legal concept such as 'the reasonable man', now adjusted in some instances to take account of the actions of 'the reasonable woman'.[44] Their influence on the contemporary feminising of legal method and process is fractured and of unpredictable status. At the level of testimony within the courtroom, women's evidence is shaped and constrained by (masculinist) rules of evidence and the rigid lawyering codes of examination-in-chief and cross-examination, neither of which acknowledges even the possibility of distinctive female subjectivities or experiences.

Court practitioners are trained to control the witness in order to minimise rambling and unfocused answers. The objective of the exercise is to extract evidence according to a strict predetermined brief. The art of cross-examination is often to obtain monosyllabic answers, through counsel's monitoring and manipulation of the responses, keeping a tight rein on the witness.[45] As Stone explains:

> The advocate initiates and controls the process. His [sic] purpose is what determines the course which cross-examination takes. The advocate's overall purpose is to present his case in a persuasive way, so that the court will believe it, or so that, at least, the court will not accept his opponent's case ... A cross-

---

41 A large body of literature has emerged on this subject. See references in *op cit*, fn 9.

42 See discussion of the 'person cases' in Sedley, S (Sir), 'Law and public life', in Nolan (Lord) and Sedley, S (Sir) (eds), *The Making and Remaking of the British Constitution*, 1995, London: Blackstone.

43 McGlynn, C, *The Woman Lawyer*, 1998, London: Butterworths.

44 Though whether such adjustment is merely semantic is open to debate.

45 Ehrlich, S and King, R, 'Consensual sex or sexual harassment: negotiating meaning', in Bergvall, V, Bing, J and Freed, A (eds), *Re-Thinking Language and Gender Research: Theory and Practice*, 1996, London: Addison Wesley Longman, p 166.

examiner questions a witness, but, as a rule, he is not really seeking information ... It is accepted practice that a cross-examiner will try to elicit only statements which support his case.[46]

The recommended style of advocacy requires the lawyer to be subtly dominant: not overtly bullying, but sufficiently aggressive and competitive to win the case in what is, ultimately, an adversarial system that rewards point scoring and the exploitation of weaknesses in the opponent's case.

An aggressive and competitive style may be inimical to women. It has been suggested by Coates, in a study involving speech styles of men and women in law, medicine and education, that 'women ... maintain a more co-operative discourse style rather than adopting the more adversarial style that is typically used and valued in these professions'.[47] Such behavioural descriptors could undoubtedly be criticised for their essentialist and reductionist dimensions, for it appears that even when men believe that they are acting co-operatively, they are nonetheless perceived by others as continuing to behave competitively.[48] Of course, some women lawyers may act just as aggressively and competitively as their male counterparts, but it is unclear whether they adopt masculine norms because that is how they have been trained, or because of some other reason, such as a belief that the masculine style is the one most likely to succeed. At present, however, the adjudication process within the courtroom gives neither lawyers (of either gender) or witnesses little choice but to try to conform to the standards traditionally associated with men.

The impression a witness makes in the witness box is crucial to the credibility and reliability that will be attached to his or her evidence by the trier of fact. Studies carried out in a wide variety of settings have shown that the form and style of speech used by a speaker can influence the extent to which the content of that speech is acceptable to others.[49] Within the courtroom, various studies have shown how the type of speech deployed can impact on the credibility and reliability of a witness. Two important linguistic patterns emerge. First, speech is either 'powerful' or 'powerless', and the more powerful the speech the more likely it is to enhance credibility. Powerful speech is given coherently, with confidence, and without hesitation or stuttering. In contrast, powerless speech is punctuated with hesitancies, such

---

46   Stone, M, *Proof of Fact in Criminal Trials*, 1984, Edinburgh: Green.

47   Coates, J, 'Language, gender and career', in Mills, S (ed), *Language and Gender: Interdisciplinary Perspectives*, 1995, London: Longman.

48   Sweeney, L, 'The competitive negotiator' (1992) J Law Society of Scotland 49; see, also, Menkel-Meadow, C, 'Portia in a different voice: speculations on a woman's lawyering process' (1985) 1 Berkeley Women's LJ 39.

49   O'Barr, W and Atkins, B, '"Women's language" or "powerless language"'', in McConnell-Ginet, S, Borker, R and Furman, N (eds), *Women and Language in Literature and Society*, 1980, New York: Praeger; Conley, J, O'Barr, W and Lind, E, 'The power of language: presentational style in the courtroom' (1978) Duke LJ 1375.

as 'um', 'ah' and 'eh'; with indecisive comments, such as 'sort of', 'I suppose so' and 'maybe'; and with disjointed fillers, such as 'you know' and 'well'. As Conley *et al* have noted, powerful speech typically emanates from 'well-educated, white-collar men and expert witnesses of both sexes', while powerless speech is associated with witnesses of lower social status – the poor, the uneducated and women.[50]

The second influential linguistic pattern identified by linguistic researchers relates to the delivery of testimony. Delivery will be either in a narrative or fragmented form. Powerful speech will be delivered in an articulate narrative style of testimony, while fragmented speech is powerless. A narrative style emerges when a witness is permitted to speak in 'freestyle', responding to questioning with long answers that tell a structured story. This is the opposite of fragmented testimony, when closed questions are used to constrict the witness's answers to 'yes' or 'no' or to specific and limited facts, such as might be elicited from the question, 'When did you arrive at work?' or 'Did you drive or walk to work that day?'.

Fragmented testimony is most often used when a lawyer particularly needs to control the witness, keep them strictly to the point and/or prevent them from digressing. Conley *et al* have argued that fragmented testimony results in less convincing testimony for a jury, whereas narrative testimony, as the embodiment of powerful speech, is perceived as enhancing the credibility of a witness. This is in part because jurors interpret a lawyer's willingness to allow a witness to narrate in freestyle as reflecting that lawyer's confidence in the competence of the witness.[51]

It is of course most often in cross-examination that a lawyer will wish to exert control over a witness. It will be especially effective for defence lawyers to deploy advocacy techniques that produce powerless and fragmented speech against a female complainant whose credibility they wish to undermine, that is, in sexual offences. This is when a woman will be at her most vulnerable to aggressive cross-examination and thus most likely to produce fragmented, weak and unconvincing testimony. In these circumstances, even if a woman wanted to give her testimony in a narrative form she is likely to be prevented from doing so, which can leave her feeling her story has been decontextualised and distorted. The effect is intentional. Most legal texts and manuals written about the art of successful cross-examination stress the need to pose questions of the witness in order to influence and shape the response s/he is able to give. Both the questions asked and the manner in which they are asked are designed to elicit a particular response. Lees has reported that women complainants in rape cases commonly claimed 'they were not allowed to explain fully what had

---

50   *Op cit*, Conley *et al*, fn 49, pp 1380–81.
51   *Op cit*, Conley *et al*, fn 49, pp 1386–87.

happened to them, or how they *felt* during the rape'. Instead, in the courtroom, 'most women were confined to answering questions briefly, and often to simply answering yes or no'. Moreover, despite the legislation that is intended to prevent gratuitous exploration of previous sexual history, 'the large majority of women ... complained of being treated unsympathetically and being asked irrelevant and unfair questions'.[52]

In such cases, permitting hearsay evidence from a confidante regarding a woman's account of her experience of events surrounding the alleged rape and her feelings could reinforce the woman's narrative in court and help to counter attacks from defence lawyers. For, as Wood and Rennie's study showed, there are a variety of reasons why women are often reluctant to characterise attacks by acquaintances as rape, and will instead defer to a more anodyne formulation proposed by others, such that the rape becomes 'sexual assault, sexual misunderstanding, harassment, confusion, whatever ...'[53] This dilution of terminology and its attendant ambiguity will be seized upon by defence lawyers who, in cross-examination, will exploit the woman's uncertainty as well as infer blameworthiness.

The reluctance of victims to report offences and the confusion they experience in articulating their experience is not confined to women or to sexual offences. Victims and other witnesses involved in all sorts of crimes also report feeling humiliated, degraded and frustrated by the process of cross-examination from which it is reasonable to conclude that they do not feel their authentic voice was heard or respected.[54] This is inevitable in a system where lawyers are trained to examine witnesses through rigorous questioning designed solely 'to construct a destructive examination which undermines [the] opponent's case ... asking the kinds of questions which will discredit the witness or the witness's evidence'.[55] Furthermore, the level of hostility confronting women complainants in crimes of sexual violence is not imagined, for it has been acknowledged by the barristers who adopt such tactics. In a recent study of barristers' ethics in the courtroom, Temkin found the strategy selected by barristers when defending alleged rapists was to be 'robust to the point of ruthlessness', with one barrister asserting that when she was defending 'it's no holds barred'. Temkin concluded that defence efforts were mainly directed at discrediting the complainant, and as a result 'the facts were regarded as of relatively minor significance'.[56]

---

52 *Op cit*, Lees, fn 8, p 31. Emphasis in original.

53 Wood, L and Rennie, H, 'Formulating rape: the discursive construction of victims and villains' (1994) 5(1) Discourse and Society 125, p 145.

54 McEwan, J, 'Documentary hearsay evidence – refuge for the vulnerable witness?' [1989] Crim LR 629, p 642; Raine, J and Smith, R, *The Victim/Witness in Court Project: Report of Research Programme*, 1991, London: NAVSS; Rock, P, *The Social World of the English Crown Court*, 1993, Oxford: Clarendon.

55 Jones, P, *Lawyer's Skills*, 1997, London: Blackstone, p 225.

56 Temkin, J, 'Rape in court' (1998) *The Guardian*, 27 October, p 17.

Within the courtroom, O'Barr has shown the significance of 'form' in regulating speech and how prescribing that 'form' controls and constrains the 'facts' that are allowed to emerge and be proven.[57] Thus, the rules of evidence and procedure create and sustain a framework for extracting, sifting and ordering the words of a witness, in the main discouraging narrative. Matoesian, too, has explored courtroom speech and argues that it operates as a system of domination. In his study of transcripts of rape trials, Matoesian found that 'patriarchy as an *abstract structure* of domination is instantiated by or tracked into the *mediate organizational structure* of courtroom talk'.[58] According to Matoesian, this structure of courtroom talk imposes a 'patriarchal logic of sexual rationality' on the participants in the trial, of whom it is the woman victim who is most disadvantaged. Matoesian's analysis of trial transcripts shows how stylised use of language, repetition of particular phrases and subtle ellipses could conspire 'to hyperaccentuate the inconsistency or irony in the victim's account' and thus to undermine her credibility.[59] This process is pursued in the name of objectivity, relevancy and admissibility. Generally witnesses are discouraged from discussing feelings as this is likely to be characterised as subjective and irrelevant.

The entire advocacy process encourages a highly stylised linguistic product, and extracts testimony from women of a type that they frequently regard as alien to their actual experiences.[60] Women suffer from traditional advocacy techniques because these techniques fail to acknowledge how women use speech to communicate feelings and experiences in a different way from men. This failure, coupled with the disadvantage resulting from the hearsay rule that precludes bringing certain testimony into the courtroom, could be ameliorated through reform of the hearsay rule.

REFORM OF THE HEARSAY RULE: EXTENDING THE CATEGORIES OF EXCEPTIONS

The negative experiences of bias within the judicial system that women have recounted must be remedied. If we fail to remove bias, we undermine one of the declared key aims of the criminal justice system, namely, the successful prosecution of crime. Securing this aim is dependent on both the co-operation

---

57 O'Barr, W, 'Asking the right questions about language and power', in Kramarae, C, Schulz, M and O'Barr, W (eds), *Language and Power*, 1984, London: Sage.

58 Matoesian, G, *Reproducing Rape – Domination Through Talk in the Courtroom*, 1993, Cambridge: Polity, p 33.

59 Matoesian, G, 'Language, law and society: policy implications of the Kennedy Smith rape trial' (1995) 29 Law & Soc Rev 669, p 681.

60 Ellison, L, 'Cross-examination in rape trials' [1998] Crim LR 605.

of witnesses and the production of the best available evidence. As regards the co-operation of witnesses, it is incumbent on those involved in the system to ensure that everything possible is done to protect these witnesses and minimise further trauma induced by the trial process. The system is fundamentally flawed if women who have appeared as complainants frequently regret that they ever made the original complaint.[61] Government working parties established to review the position of witnesses have recognised this.[62] The remit of the Scottish group, which mirrored that of the English group, included the need to consider how 'to encourage [vulnerable] witnesses to give evidence of crime and to enable them to give best evidence in court'.[63]

As regards the production of best available evidence, reform must be directed at women's perception that they have no voice, or that the account attributed to them in court is not their own. A witness whose testimony is suppressed or distorted is not able to proffer good quality evidence. As the Scottish Law Commission observed in its *Report on Hearsay Evidence in Criminal Proceedings* recommending a relaxation of the hearsay rule: '[t]he giving of evidence should not be a test of memory, and still less should it be a cause of acute emotional distress, if that can be prevented by rational means.'[64]

It is apparent from women's complaints that they often do experience something akin to 'acute emotional distress' in the witness box and are unable to recount their story in a satisfactory manner.[65] As has been suggested several times throughout this chapter, one reformative measure would be to admit statements that have been articulated to a third party on an earlier occasion, and to admit it not just as proof of the fact it was made, but also as truth of the content of that statement. Such evidence is presently designated secondary hearsay and inadmissible, and, disappointingly, the prospect of according it admissibility was rejected recently by the Law Commission as likely to lead to the production in court of much irrelevant material that would simply distract the trier of fact.[66] However, the proposal is not as radical a departure from principle or practice as it may at first glance appear, when considered in the wider context of existing exceptions to the hearsay rule and the rationale to the retention of the rule.

---

61 Victim Support, *Women, Rape and the Criminal Justice System*, 1996, London: Victim Support.

62 In England, an Inter-Departmental Working Group published *Speaking Up for Justice: Report of the Interdepartmental Working Group on the Treatment of Vulnerable or Intimidated Witnesses in the Criminal Justice System*, 1998, London: Home Office. In Scotland, a similar working group published *Towards a Just Conclusion – Vulnerable and Intimidated Witnesses in Scottish Criminal and Civil Cases*, 1998, Edinburgh: Scottish Office.

63 *Ibid*, Scottish Office.

64 *Op cit*, Scottish Law Commission, fn 17, para 7.15.

65 *Op cit*, Lees, fn 8.

66 *Op cit*, Law Commission (1997), fn 17, para 10.30.

There are a number of exceptions to the hearsay rule that confirm that the law does recognise the significance of speech, and by implication, a gender difference. Since the law has accommodated the continued survival of these exceptions, there is clearly scope for further extensions to these excepted categories. At least three common law exceptions offer particular support to the arguments set out in this chapter: *res gestae* evidence; *de recenti* evidence (equivalent to the English doctrine of recent complaint); and distress as corroboration. Where any one of these is invoked, witnesses to whom the complaint was made are permitted to give evidence of what the complainant said to them. In so doing, these witnesses in effect repeat what they were told by the complainant, thus enhancing her credibility.

It has long been accepted that, where words are uttered in the heat of the moment, and form part of the *res gestae* of events, they can be repeated in court as evidence of their intrinsic truth. Provided there is no motive to concoct or fabricate the words, it is assumed that the element of spontaneity will act as a barrier to falsified testimony.[67] A second hearsay exception is that categorised in English law as the doctrine of recent complaint and in Scots law as *de recenti* evidence. The distinction between *res gestae* and recent complaint or *de recenti* evidence is often a fine one, but in the case of the latter the words uttered are not necessarily integral to the commission of the offence. Instead they are words uttered at the first opportunity the victim has to make an assertion.[68]

In each jurisdiction, the recent complaint or *de recenti* exception permits the use of prior consistent statements of complaint by a witness in sexual offences. Such statements are not normally admissible, but are permitted in cases of sexual violence to rebut the suggestion that the witness might now be fabricating the allegation.[69] The doctrine holds that, in sexual offences, there is an assumption that a victim will make a verbal report of the incident at the earliest opportunity, and a failure to do so may lead to negative inferences being drawn regarding the veracity of the complaint.[70] The origins of this doctrine have been well documented and exposed in feminist theory as grounded in the mythology of the mendacious and unreliable female whose testimony must be evaluated by psychiatric experts before admission to the courtroom as reliable.[71] The assumptions that early reporting would inevitably follow physical or sexual assault have been consistently discredited by research that has shown that a constellation of reactions follow sexual

---

67 *Op cit*, Tapper, fn 13, p 547.

68 *Morton v HM Advocate* 1938 JC 50.

69 *Op cit*, Tapper, fn 13, p 273.

70 For a recent illustration of the doctrine and its effect, see the Privy Council decision in *White v R* [1999] 1 Cr App R 153.

71 A mythology that owes much to Wigmore's assertion that 'No judge should ever let a sex offence charge go to the jury unless the female complainant's social history and mental make-up have been examined and testified to by a qualified physician': Wigmore, JH, *Wigmore on Evidence*, 1937, Boston, Mass: Little, Brown, Vol IIIA, para 924a.

assault including, shock, numbness, disbelief, fear, anxiety and humiliation.[72] In the aftermath of an assault, reporting it to the authorities may be the last imperative on a woman's mind.[73]

Thirdly, though to a lesser extent, the Scottish doctrine of distress as corroboration influences the hearsay rule.[74] The doctrine permits a witness to speak of the emotional state of a complainant following a traumatic incident, a state that is frequently accompanied by, but is not necessarily articulated in, words. Although the doctrine is often referred to as 'distress as corroboration' or 'corroboration by distress', recent cases have affirmed that the corroboration offered by the distress is in practice limited to the bolstering of credibility. For the distress to function as corroboration of the essential facts of the crime, it has to be specifically and exclusively linked to the *actus reus*, a requirement that is extremely hard to fulfil.[75] Where evidence is admitted *de recenti*, or as distress as corroboration, the law implicitly acknowledges the impulse for victims of sexually traumatic incidents to make disclosures of these incidents to close friends, thus strengthening the argument for admitting the subsequent 'hearsay' testimony from these confidantes.

Although the Law Commission has recently recommended relaxing the hearsay rule, their recommendation is restricted to the admissibility of a witness's previous consistent statements only in very specific circumstances. These are:

(a)   the rebuttal of an allegation of recent invention;

(b)   prior identification of a person, object or place; and

(c)   recent complaint in crimes other than sexual offences.

While the Commission has taken the relatively progressive step of recommending that, in these specific circumstances, the previous statement 'be admissible as evidence of the facts stated, and not merely to bolster the credibility of the witness's oral evidence',[76] the proposals have been attacked by one of their own consultants, Professor John Spencer, as 'unduly timid'.[77] As Spencer ironically observes, the Law Commission's recommendation to continue to exclude the majority of previous statements makes everything turn on what is said at the trial by the witness, and 'it requires us to accept two remarkable scientific propositions: first, that memory improves with time; and secondly, that stress enhances a person's powers of recall'.[78] Spencer's

---

72   See, eg, Burgess, A and Holmstrom, L, 'Rape trauma syndrome' (1974) 131 Am J Psychiatry 981.

73   *Op cit*, Temkin, fn 8.

74   Discussed in more depth by Easton, Chapter 9, in this volume.

75   See *Smith v Lees* 1997 SCCR 139 and *Fox v HM Advocate* 1998 SLT 335.

76   *Op cit*, Law Commission (1997), fn 17, paras 10.35–10.38.

77   *Op cit*, Spencer, fn 18.

78   *Op cit*, Spencer, fn 18.

argument is, in my view, very persuasive and echoes what has been argued here in regard to the significance of confidante testimony.

However, I would go further in criticising the limitations of the Commission's recommendations, for they do not address the bias identified in this chapter. For example, the proposed new rule would not extend to the confidante of a complainant who was too traumatised to speak of an assault for some days, weeks or months after the assault, for there is no 'recency' in such a complaint. Given the particular characteristics of women's speech and the circumstances about which they frequently make disclosures, admitting testimony from a confidante in all types of cases involving violence or perceived violence would be a justifiable extension of the hearsay rule. Such hearsay testimony should be admitted not only to bolster the credibility of the complainant, but also to establish the truth of the assertion. After all, the efficacy of the proposal to admit hearsay testimony from a confidante assumes the presence in court of both the complainer and the confidante. They would obviously therefore be available for cross-examination, when their demeanour could be observed and appropriate conclusions as to testimonial weight could be drawn. Thus, the most persuasive objection to admitting hearsay evidence, that the hearsay evidence emanates from an absent source that cannot be tested, is removed. The physical presence of a confidante would provide a greater degree of moral support for the complainant and reduce her sense of isolation. Of course, it might be argued that admitting hearsay from a confidante is of limited value to women, since it will be equally subject to attack in cross-examination, but it cannot place women in a worse position than that in which they currently find themselves. Pending a more radical overhaul of the legal process, the potential of any change must be explored. Substantial inroads have already been made to the hearsay rule and more have been recommended, so further incursions of the type proposed here are difficult to resist if we wish to eliminate bias.

CONCLUSION

In summary, this chapter set out to explore the gender bias in the hearsay rule and to consider ways to remedy that inequity. The nature of the crimes in which women tend to be victims increases their vulnerability in the courtroom, as does their style of communication and the adversarial techniques of cross-examination which unite to discount women's testimony. In such circumstances, admitting hearsay evidence of a woman's previous statements through the medium of a confidante could supplement her account. It could do so by offering a perspective of the facts more compatible with her experience of what actually occurred, than that extracted from her under cross-examination. If the trier of fact was permitted to hear from a confidante about the content, tone, and emotional impact of conversations between the complainant and the confidante, that could serve to contextualise the complainant's experience and allow her voice to be heard in an alternative narrative. This would be a welcome and overdue step, for as currently constituted, the explicit effect of the rules of evidence is to deny the complainant's experience.

CHAPTER 5

THE 'PRIVILEGE' IN THE PRIVILEGE DOCTRINE: A FEMINIST ANALYSIS OF THE EVIDENTIARY PRIVILEGES FOR CONFIDENTIAL COMMUNICATIONS[1]

Kit Kinports

The rules that grant certain relationships an evidentiary privilege have been called a 'unique aspect of evidence law'[2] because they contravene the traditional common law principle that 'the public has a right to every man's evidence'.[3] They have been criticised on the grounds that 'rather than facilitating the illumination of the truth, they shut out the light'.[4] They have also been defended as 'important protectors of individual privacy in modern society'.[5] And they recently received a good deal of public attention in the US, as President Bill Clinton and other executive branch officials asserted various privileges in response to testimony sought by Independent Counsel Kenneth Starr.[6] But they have not been subjected to a feminist critique.[7]

This paper is intended to fill that gap and to analyse the law governing evidentiary privileges from a feminist perspective. Focusing primarily on the rules in effect in the US, I will examine with a feminist lens both the more fundamental question whether any evidentiary privileges ought to exist at all,

---

1   I am indebted to Emily Neufeld Grant for her valuable research assistance in connection with this paper.

2   Mueller, C and Kirkpatrick, L, *Modern Evidence: Doctrine and Practice*, 1995, Boston, Mass: Little, Brown, p 427.

3   *Cobbett's Parliamentary History of England*, 1812, London: TC Hansard, Vol 12, p 693 (speech of Lord Chancellor Hardwicke in the House of Lords, 25 May 1742).

4   Strong, J (ed), *McCormick on Evidence*, 1992, St Paul: West, § 72, p 269.

5   Krattenmaker, T, 'Testimonial privileges in federal courts: an alternative to the proposed federal rules of evidence' (1973) 62 Georgetown LJ 61, p 86.

6   See, eg, *Swidler and Berlin v US* 524 US 399 (1998) (applying the attorney-client privilege to notes taken by an attorney at a meeting where the Deputy White House Counsel was seeking legal representation, and refusing to create an exception to the privilege simply because the client subsequently died and the notes were relevant to a criminal proceeding); *In re Lindsey* 158 F 3d 1263, p 1273 (DC Cir 1998) (refusing to permit the Deputy White House Counsel to claim the attorney-client privilege with respect to information communicated to him by the President that was relevant to possible criminal violations because of '[t]he obligation of a government lawyer to uphold the public trust'); *In re Sealed Case* 148 F 3d 1073 (DC Cir 1998) (rejecting a privilege claim asserted by Secret Service agents assigned to protect the President); *stay denied sub nom Rubin v United States* 524 US 1301, p 1302 (1998) (*per* Rehnquist CJ, noting that the court of appeals' opinion seemed 'cogent and correct').

7   I sketched out some preliminary thoughts on this topic in Kinports, K, 'Evidence engendered' (1991) Illinois UL Rev 413, pp 440–42.

and then the more specific question as to which relationships ought to be accorded a privilege. Although my analysis of the more fundamental question leads to somewhat equivocal results, I conclude with respect to the second question that the privilege doctrine has not been applied in a gender or class neutral manner.

SHOULD THE LAW OF EVIDENCE RECOGNISE ANY PRIVILEGES?

> If there's one thing that women find unsatisfactory about guys ... [,] it is that guys do not communicate enough.
>
> We have some good friends, Buzz and Libby, whom we see about twice a year. When we get together, Beth and Libby always wind up in a conversation, lasting several days, during which they discuss virtually every significant event that has occurred in their lives and the lives of those they care about, sharing their innermost feelings, analyzing and probing, inevitably coming to a deeper understanding of each other and a strengthening of a cherished friendship. Whereas Buzz and I watch the playoffs.
>
> I don't mean to suggest that all we talk about is sports. We also discuss, openly and without shame, what kind of pizza we need to order. We have a fine time together, but we don't have heavy conversations, and sometimes, after the visit is over, I'm surprised to learn – from Beth, who learned it from Libby – that there has recently been some new wrinkle in Buzz's life, such as that he now has an artificial leg.[8]

As this humorous column suggests, the doctrine of evidentiary privileges appears to be consistent with feminist ideals in some respects. To the extent that the privilege rules are based – as some commentators have asserted[9] – on the humanistic goal of protecting certain private relationships, they seem in keeping with the value that women tend to place on relationships, interdependence, and connection and responsibility to others.[10]

On the other hand, the utilitarian rationale for the privilege doctrine adopted by most courts – that privileges are necessary to encourage communication in the context of confidential relationships[11] – is more

---

8 Barry, D, 'Hey, guys, I'm talking to you' (1992) *Chicago Tribune Magazine*, 21 June, p 27.

9 *Op cit*, Krattenmaker, fn 5, p 90 (commenting that '[t]estimonial privileges, through fostering this control [over information about oneself], help to provide a context for the development of personal autonomy, emotional release, self-evaluation, and limited and protected communication'); Louisell, D, 'Confidentiality, conformity and confusion: privileges in federal court today' (1956) 31 Tulane L Rev 100, pp 110–11 (associating privileges with 'a right to be let alone, a right to unfettered freedom, in certain narrowly prescribed relationships, from the state's coercive or supervisory powers').

10 See, generally, Gilligan, C, *In a Different Voice: Psychological Theory and Women's Development*, 1982, Cambridge, Mass: Harvard UP.

11 *Op cit*, Strong, fn 4, p 270. The utilitarian rationale is associated with Wigmore, whose views are described below, p 82.

consistent with male values. As numerous studies have found, it is men who typically are more reluctant to discuss their feelings and other intimate topics, whereas women tend to be more open in their relationships.[12] Perhaps because men are socialised or expected to be tough, independent, unemotional, and unexpressive, they may view expressions of emotion and discussions of feelings as evidence of weakness – whereas women are socialised or expected to be nurturing, emotional, and understanding.[13] Or perhaps the explanation is that women place a higher value on self-disclosure and enjoy intimate conversations more so than men.[14] Whatever the reason, studies conducted in the US, Great Britain and Europe have found that women are more open and disclose more intimate information than men.[15] Moreover, these findings hold true regardless of the age of the subjects,[16] and they have been consistently replicated over the past 30 years.[17]

Accordingly, the privilege rules can be seen as geared primarily towards men, who might need some assurance that their words will remain confidential before they are willing to discuss intimate topics. Women, on the other hand, may be more likely to communicate independent of the evidentiary safeguard that the privilege rules supply, and therefore privileges may not serve their interests as fully as they serve the interests of men.

Whether or not creating the privilege doctrine in the first instance is consistent with feminist goals and ideals, it is clear that the actual evolution of the doctrine – specifically, the determination of which relationships are accorded an evidentiary privilege – has not been gender neutral. The following section turns to that issue.

---

12 Derlega, V, Metts, S, Petronio, S and Margulis, S, *Self-Disclosure*, 1993, Newbury Park, CA: Sage, pp 44–64; Duck, S, *Understanding Relationships*, 1991, New York: Guilford, p 81; Dindia, K and Allen, M, 'Sex differences in self-disclosure: a meta-analysis' (1992) 112 Psych Bulletin 106 (analysis of 205 other studies conducted between 1958 and 1989 involving more than 23,000 subjects found differences in self-disclosure between men and women, although the differences were not as large as some others had suggested); Dolgin, K and Minowa, N, 'Gender differences in self-presentation: a comparison of the roles of flatteringness and intimacy in self-disclosure to friends' (1997) 36 Sex Roles 371; Reisman, J, 'Intimacy in same-sex friendships' (1990) 23 Sex Roles 65, pp 74–76; Winstead, B, 'Sex differences in same-sex friendships', in Derlega, V and Winstead, B (eds), *Friendship and Social Interaction*, 1986, New York: Springer, Chapter 5.

13 *Ibid*, Derlega *et al*, pp 44–45, 49, 56–57; *ibid*, Dolgin *et al*, p 312.

14 *Ibid*, Derlega *et al*, p 55–56.

15 *Ibid*, Duck, p 81. This is not to say, however, that there are no differences between different races and ethnic groups. The studies conducted to date have not sufficiently explored the effect of those variables. See *ibid*, Dindia and Allen, p 109.

16 Dolgin, K, Meyer, L and Schwartz, J, 'Effects of gender, target's gender, topic, and self-esteem on disclosure to best and middling friends' (1991) 25 Sex Roles 311, pp 311–12.

17 *Ibid*, Dindia and Allen, p 114 (finding, however, that the size of the differential has decreased somewhat in that period).

WHICH RELATIONSHIPS SHOULD BE PRIVILEGED?

> In a society with egalitarian pretensions, the creation and justification of a privilege to refuse to respond to a judicial inquiry is essentially a political question; that is, it is an allocation of power as between the various components of the society.[18]

> A poor man's only privilege is perjury.[19]

In a frequently quoted passage, Wigmore asserted that 'four fundamental conditions' must be satisfied in order to justify the creation of an evidentiary privilege.[20] Wigmore summarised those four conditions as follows:

(a) The communications must originate in a *confidence* that they will not be disclosed.

(b) This element of *confidentiality must be essential* to the full and satisfactory maintenance of the relation between the parties.

(c) The *relation* must be one which in the opinion of the community ought to be sedulously *fostered*.

(d) The *injury* that would inure to the relation by the disclosure of the communications must be *greater than the benefit* thereby gained for the correct disposal of litigation.[21]

Although originally set forth several decades ago, Wigmore's framework continues to influence the development of the privilege doctrine today.[22]

A similar – and also frequently cited – standard for determining the scope of evidentiary privileges is the balancing test adopted by the US Supreme Court. Under that test, as described in *Trammel v United States*, an evidentiary privilege is justified only if it 'promotes sufficiently important interests to outweigh the need for probative evidence'.[23] The court explained: 'Testimonial exclusionary rules and privileges ... must be strictly construed

---

18   Wright, C and Graham, K, *Federal Practice and Procedure*, 1980, St Paul, Minn: West, § 5422, pp 673–74.

19   'Developments in the law – privileged communications' (1985) 98 Harvard L Rev 1450 (quoting anon).

20   McNaughton, J (ed), *Wigmore on Evidence*, 1961, Boston, Mass: Little, Brown, § 2285, p 527.

21   *Ibid*.

22   For a few examples of the many court opinions relying on Wigmore's analysis, see *In re Grand Jury* 103 F 3d 1140, p 1152 (3d Cir 1997); *Allred v State* 554 P 2d 411, p 417 (Alaska 1976); *State v Jackson* 687 A 2d 485, p 487 (Conn 1997). In fact, the Supreme Court of Canada has given the Canadian courts discretion to recognise privileges on a case by case basis in those circumstances that satisfy Wigmore's conditions: *Slavutych v Baker* [1976] 1 SCR 254, pp 260–62.

23   *Trammel v US* 445 US 40, p 50 (1980).

and accepted "only to the very limited extent that permitting a refusal to testify or excluding relevant evidence has a public good transcending the normally predominant principle of utilizing all rational means for ascertaining truth".'[24]

Unfortunately, however, the courts have never applied either Wigmore's four conditions or the Supreme Court's balancing test in a gender and class neutral way. In many cases, the courts cite Wigmore or the Supreme Court, and then conclude – without any real analysis[25] – that the asserted privilege either does or does not meet the particular standard they are applying. Even where the courts engage in some analysis, they cannot avoid making the value judgments that are implicit in both tests. For example, what relationships are valued so highly that it can be said society wants to 'sedulously foster' them within the terms of Wigmore's third condition? Which 'public goods' are precious enough to 'transcend' (in the Supreme Court's words) the usual presumption that the fact-finder should hear all relevant evidence? Moreover, both Wigmore's fourth condition and the Supreme Court's test require a balancing of competing interests that inescapably calls for a value judgment on the part of the decision maker.[26]

Not surprisingly, those who make these value judgments – the predominantly male legislatures and judiciary[27] – do so in a way that mirrors their own values. As a result, the law of privileges as applied has tended to favour the professions that are dominated by men and that serve a wealthier clientele. Although this bias has subsided somewhat in recent years as privileges have been recognised for more professionals, the law of privileges still 'privileges' men, particularly those of higher socio-economic status. In elaborating on this point, I will examine the privilege rules governing the legal profession, the clergy, health care professionals, mental health professionals, and spouses.

---

24 *Trammel v US* 445 US 40, p 50 (1980), quoting *Elkins v US* 364 US 206, p 234 (1960) (Frankfurter J dissenting).

25 See, eg, *Phillips v Alabama Department of Pensions and Security* 394 So 2d 51, p 54 (Ala Civ App 1981) (declining to recognise privilege for social workers); *State v Lassai* 366 So 2d 1389, p 1391 (La 1978) (denying privilege to director of counselling).

26 Wigmore himself acknowledged that his fourth condition is 'open to [some] dispute' with respect to even the attorney-client privilege and the marital privilege. See *op cit*, McNaughton, fn 20, § 2286, p 528.

27 In the federal system, the privilege rules are established by the courts (see below, fn 67), whereas they are determined for the most part by the legislatures in the States. See *op cit*, Mueller and Kirkpatrick, fn 2, p 432. While women constitute 51% of the population in the US, they make up only 22.3% of the State legislatures, 9% of the US Senate and 12.9% of the US House of Representatives – and those figures are at an all time high. See Verhovek, S, 'Record for women in Washington legislature' (1999) *New York Times*, 4 February, p 18. Moreover, only 9% of all judges in the US are women. See Babcock, B, 'Feminist lawyers' (1998) 50 Stanford L Rev 1168, pp 1703–04.

The legal profession

The attorney-client privilege is the oldest privilege. It dates back to the late 16th century, during the reign of Elizabeth I, and apparently has been accepted as long as witnesses have been testifying in jury trials, 'commend[ing] itself at the very outset as a natural exception to the then novel right of testimonial compulsion'.[28] The privilege was originally intended to protect the 'the oath and the honor of the attorney' rather than the client.[29] At that time, attorneys were, of course, only men,[30] and the privilege was sometimes characterised as protecting 'honor among gentlemen'.[31] In fact, the courts of that era apparently endorsed the theory that 'the law should respect the honorable obligations of gentlemen, [and] often accorded deference to *any* gentleman who had promised confidentiality'.[32]

This view had fallen out of favour by the late 1700s, but the attorney-client privilege found support in a new theory – that the privilege is necessary to encourage clients to communicate all relevant information to their attorneys.[33] Although there have been occasional voices questioning this assumption,[34] it continues to be well accepted today. As the Supreme Court explained in *Upjohn Co v United States*, the attorney-client privilege 'encourage[s] full and frank communication between attorneys and their clients and thereby promote[s] broader public interests in the observance of law and administration of justice'.[35]

---

28 *Op cit*, McNaughton, fn 20, § 2290, p 543.

29 *Op cit*, McNaughton, fn 20, § 2290, p 543.

30 Gilbert, G, *The Law of Evidence*, 1754, Dublin: A Strahan, p 98 (summarising the attorney-client privilege by referring to 'A Man retained as Attorney, Counsel, or Sollicitor').

31 *Op cit*, McNaughton, fn 20, § 2286, p 530.

32 *Op cit*, 'Developments', fn 19, p 1495. Emphasis added.

33 *Op cit*, McNaughton, fn 20, § 2290, p 543.

34 Bentham, J, *Rationale of Judicial Evidence*, 1827, London: Hunt and Clarke, Vol 5, p 304 (arguing that the only 'mischief' in discouraging clients from confiding in their attorneys is that 'a guilty person will not in general be able to derive quite so much assistance from his law adviser, in the way of concerting a false defence'); Zacharias, F, 'Rethinking confidentiality' (1989) 74 Iowa L Rev 351, pp 354, 382, 386 (citing empirical studies indicating that some clients are unaware of the privilege and are nevertheless equally willing to confide in their attorneys, and pointing out that strict confidentiality 'may conflict with society's interests'). See, also, *In re Lindsey* 158 F 3d 1263, p 1278 (DC Cir 1998) (commenting that '[o]nly a certain conceit among those admitted to the bar could explain why legal advice should be on a higher plane than advice about policy, or politics, or why a President's conversation with the most junior lawyer in the White House Counsel's office is deserving of more protection from disclosure in a grand jury investigation than a President's discussions with his Vice President or a Cabinet Secretary').

35 *Upjohn Co v US* 449 US 383, p 389 (1981); see, also, *Trammel v US* 445 US 40, p 51 (1980) (noting that the privilege 'rests on the need for the advocate and counselor to know all that relates to the client's reasons for seeking representation if the professional mission is to be carried out').

But even this shift in rationale did not undermine the notion that the privilege was meant to protect a profession dominated by men. One State supreme court described the importance of open lines of communication between attorney and client in these terms: 'An order of men, honorable, enlightened, learned in the law, and skilled in legal procedure, is essential to the beneficent administration of justice.'[36] Moreover, the interests of the client that received new emphasis under the revised justification for the privilege seemed to revolve around businesses, land ownership, and other activities restricted at that time to men. As one attorney put it in arguing on behalf of the privilege in the mid 18th century:

My lord, formerly persons appeared in court themselves; but as business multiplied and became more intricate, and titles more perplexed, both the distance of places, and the multiplicity of business, made it absolutely necessary that there should be a set of people who should stand in the place of the suitors, and these persons are called attornies ... [I]t would be destructive to all business, if attornies were to disclose the business of their clients. In many cases men hold their estates without titles; in others, by such titles, that if their deeds could be got out of their hands, they must lose their fortunes ... Now, if an attorney was to be examined in every case, what man would trust an attorney with the secret of his estate ...?[37]

Even today, when women have entered the legal profession in substantial numbers,[38] the attorney-client privilege as applied tends to favour those of higher socio-economic status, who are more likely to be men.[39] The privilege attaches only to those with a licence to practise law.[40] Thus, it does not protect

---

36 *Wade v Ridley* 32 A 975, p 976 (Me 1895).

37 Mr Recorder (counsel for the defendant) arguing for the privilege in *Annesley v Earl of Anglesea* 17 Howells State Trials 1139, pp 1224–25 (Ex 1743).

38 Berger, M and Robinson, K, 'Gender bias in the American Bar Association Journal: impact on the legal profession' (1998) 13 Wisconsin Women's LJ 75, p 78, n 21 (noting that 26% of US lawyers were women in 1997).

39 There is still a wage gap between working women and men. See Robinson-Jacobs, K, 'When it comes to pay, it's still a man's world' (1998) *Los Angeles Times*, 23 April, p D1 (noting that women in the US typically earn 74% of men's earnings). Women are also more likely to be in poverty. See Nice, J and Trubek, L, *Cases and Materials on Poverty Law: Theory and Practice*, 1997, St Paul: West, p 9 (observing that almost one-third of families headed by women lived below the poverty line in 1995, and more than half of all poor families were headed by women). In addition, women tend to have fewer savings and lower pensions. See Mechtenberg, D, 'Women need to plan for financial future' (1998) *Denver Post*, 17 May, p L6 (finding that women start saving later and save only about half of what men save); Moseley-Braun, C, 'Women's retirement security' (1996) 4 Elder LJ 493 (describing gender disparity in pensions).

40 *Op cit*, McNaughton, fn 20, § 2300, p 580 (concluding that '[t]here is no ground for encouraging the relation of client and legal adviser except when the adviser is one who has been formally admitted to the office of attorney or counselor'). See, eg, *Moorhead v Lane* 125 FRD 680, p 686 (CD Ill 1989) (finding privilege inapplicable to an individual who had a law degree but was not a licensed member of the State Bar). The privilege has been applied in a few cases, however, where clients reasonably believed that they had consulted a licensed attorney. See Stone, S and Taylor, T, *Testimonial Privileges*, 1993, Colorado Springs, CO: Shepard's/McGraw-Hill, § 1.17, pp 44–45.

conversations with an accountant – assuming the accountant is not assisting a lawyer provide legal services[41] – even though it is often difficult to distinguish the advice given by tax lawyers and accountants, aside from the fact that attorneys tend to charge higher fees and therefore attract clients with greater assets.[42] Some State legislatures have recently enacted privilege statutes protecting accountants, but they are still in a minority,[43] and there is no comparable privilege in the federal system.[44] Moreover, the majority of accountants have traditionally been men,[45] and clients seeking advice from accountants by definition have at least some income.

Even more important, clients without the financial resources to hire an attorney are often left without a privilege in a world where the availability of free legal services is rapidly diminishing. For example, the Supreme Court acknowledged in *Johnson v Avery* that 'the high percentage of [prisoners] who are totally or functionally illiterate, whose educational attainments are slight, and whose intelligence is limited', combined with the unavailability of appointed counsel for those wishing to file habeas petitions, meant that '[i]n the case of all except those who are able to help themselves – usually a few old hands or exceptionally gifted prisoners – the prisoner is, in effect, denied access to the courts unless ... help [from jailhouse lawyers] is available'.[46] Nevertheless, the courts have routinely held that the attorney-client privilege

---

41 *Op cit*, Mueller and Kirkpatrick, fn 2, p 646.

42 Katsoris, C, 'Confidential communications – the accountants' dilemma' (1966) 35 Fordham L Rev 51, p 66 (quoting American Bar Association statement of principles as acknowledging that 'questions of law and accounting have sometimes been inextricably intermingled' in the field of income tax, so that 'there has been some doubt as to where the functions of one profession end and those of the other begin'); Anon, 'How do lawyers stack up against other professionals?' (1994) *American Lawyer*, September, p 56 (commenting on the disparity in fees charged by attorneys and accountants).

43 *Op cit*, Stone and Taylor, fn 40, § 3.04, p 7; pp 128–29 (Supp 1999) (citing 18 statutes).

44 *Couch v US* 409 US 322, p 335 (1973) (reasoning that 'there can be little expectation of privacy where records are handed to an accountant, knowing that mandatory disclosure of much of the information therein is required in an income tax return'); see, also, *US v Arthur Young and Co* 465 US 805, pp 817–18 (1984) (relying on *Couch* and distinguishing 'the private attorney's role as the client's ... loyal representative whose duty it is to present the client's case in the most favorable possible light' from an 'independent certified public accountant, [who] assumes a public responsibility transcending any employment relationship with the client' and therefore must 'maintain total independence from the client at all times').

45 In 1974, only 24% of accountants in the US were women, although women began comprising half of the profession in 1990. See Miller, T, 'Women surge into accounting' (1996) *Accounting Today*, 16 December, p 20.

46 *Johnson v Avery* 393 US 483, pp 487, 488 (1969) (striking down prison regulation that prohibited inmates from helping each other prepare habeas petitions).

does not apply to jailhouse lawyers.[47] Similarly, when one State supreme court decided to allow lay representation of employees in administrative hearings involving personnel matters on the grounds that union representatives have some expertise in this area and the 'economic fact[s] of life' foreclose employees from hiring attorneys, the court made it clear that the attorney-client privilege did not apply because '[t]he lay representative is not an attorney'.[48] Likewise, the attorney-client privilege generally does not extend to discussions that *pro se* plaintiffs have with one another,[49] to communications with law students who are providing *pro bono* services,[50] or presumably to battered women's conversations with domestic violence advocates[51] – even if these individuals are providing legal services to those who do not have access to a licensed attorney.

Members of the clergy

Another of the oldest testimonial privileges protects the clergy-communicant relationship. Originally recognised in 16th century England to protect the confidentiality of the confessional, the privilege was abandoned with the Reformation and the Church of England's rejection of Roman Catholicism.[52] Nevertheless, other European countries continued to adhere to the clergy-communicant privilege, and it was first endorsed in the US by a New York court in 1813.[53] During the middle of the 19th century, the privilege began to reappear in English law.[54]

---

47 *Op cit*, Stone and Taylor, fn 40, § 1.17, p 45 and n 157. One State Supreme Court even refused to extend the privilege to a prisoner who was 'assigned to the law library to help other prisoners with their legal problems by writing letters, preparing pleadings, and otherwise giving them whatever advice he could': *State v Spell* 399 So 2d 551, p 556 (La 1981). But compare *State v Melendez* 834 P 2d 154, pp 157–59 (Ariz 1992) (applying the privilege where a prisoner was told he had the right to be represented by another inmate in prison disciplinary hearings but was not warned about the absence of a privilege).

48 *Hunt v Maricopa County Employees Merit System Commission* 619 P 2d 1036, p 1040 (Ariz 1980). But compare *Welfare Rights Organization v Crisan* 661 P 2d 1073 (Cal 1983) (interpreting a State statute affording welfare recipients a right to representation by attorneys or laypersons in administrative proceedings to extend the attorney-client privilege to lay representatives).

49 *Moorhead v Lane* 125 FRD 680, p 687 (CD Ill 1989).

50 *Op cit*, McNaughton, fn 20, § 2300, p 581 (noting that this is true, 'however much legal skill [the student] may possess in comparison with some of those who are within' the legal profession).

51 For a discussion of the separate statutory privilege enacted for these counsellors in some States, see below, fn 115, and accompanying text.

52 *Op cit*, Stone and Taylor, fn 40, § 6.01, pp 2–3.

53 *Op cit*, 'Developments', fn 19, pp 1555–56.

54 *Op cit*, Stone and Taylor, fn 40, § 6.01, p 3. The privilege is not recognised in Canada, however, *R v Gruenke* [1991] 3 SCR 263, except as a matter of statute in two provinces. See Sopinka, J, Lederman, S and Bryant, A, *The Law of Evidence in Canada*, 1992, Toronto: Butterworths, pp 694–700.

The clergy-communicant privilege is now well established in the US, having been adopted in every State.[55] The modern rationale for this privilege is the importance of recognising 'the human need to disclose to a spiritual counsellor, in total and absolute confidence, what are believed to be flawed acts or thoughts and to receive priestly consolation and guidance in return'.[56] Despite this lofty ideal, the privilege has not been applied in a gender or class neutral way.

First, in some jurisdictions, this privilege – unlike that protecting the attorney-client relationship[57] – is not held by the communicant (the equivalent of the client in this context), but instead by the clergy,[58] who tend to be predominantly male in most established religions.[59] Moreover, whether or not a particular jurisdiction puts the privilege in the hands of the communicant or the clergy, it is much less likely to protect conversations with nuns, even when they are engaged in the same type of spiritual counselling that a priest or minister might provide. In *In re Murtha*, for example, the court justified its refusal to extend the privilege to a nun on the grounds that she 'did not conduct any type of religious services ... nor did she carry on any of the religious functions of a priest, such as hearing confessions or giving absolution'.[60] What the court failed to recognise is that nuns who provide spiritual counselling and advice 'do ... in fact perform a number of priestly functions which are recognised by the Catholic Church'.[61]

Likewise, other courts have rejected privilege claims where the person consulted was not a member of the clergy in the traditional sense – even where the communicant's access to more established members of the clergy was limited. In *State v Buss*, for example, the court refused to extend the

---

55 *Op cit*, Stone and Taylor, fn 40, § 6.02, p 3.

56 *Trammel v US* 445 US 40, p 51 (1980).

57 *Op cit*, Stone and Taylor, fn 40, § 1.18, p 48.

58 Sippel, J, 'Priest-penitent privilege statutes: dual protection in the confessional' (1994) 43 Catholic UL Rev 1127, p 1135 (listing 11 State statutes that put the privilege in the hands of the clergy).

59 Dorgan, C (ed), *Statistical Handbook of Working America*, 1995, Detroit, Mich: Gale Research, p 50 (indicating that only 11.4% of the clergy in the US are women).

60 279 A 2d 889, p 892 (NJ Super Ct App Div 1971).

61 *Eckmann v Board of Education* 106 FRD 70, pp 72–73 (ED Mo 1985) (also reasoning that 'a spiritual director is a recognized office in the Catholic Church, and is considered to be a form of ministry of the Gospel by the Church', and that, 'since Vatican II, the Church has allowed sisters to engage in religious and spiritual direction, in giving retreats and in administering Holy Communion'); see, also, *Blough v Food Lion Inc* 142 FRD 622, p 625 (ED Va 1992) (applying the privilege to a former nun who was a counsellor at a multi-denominational, non-profit counselling service operated by several churches because she was 'an accredited practitioner in the Roman Catholic Church' and was giving 'spiritual counsel and advice'), *vacated and remanded on other grounds*, 1993 US App Lexis 21725 (4th Cir Aug 25, 1993). See, generally, Campbell, S, 'Catholic sisters, irregularly ordained women and the clergy-penitent privilege' (1976) 9 University of California Davis L Rev 523 (advocating that the privilege be extended to nuns).

privilege to 'a non-ordained "family minister"' who was acting as 'an assistant to a priest' and helping 'carry out the work of the [Catholic] Church' in an area where there was a shortage of priests.[62] The court reasoned that 'non-ordained church counselors' are not members of the clergy and that the defendant's statements were not a '"confession ... in the course of discipline enjoined by the church"' because the family minister 'did not administer the Catholic sacrament of confession in the narrow, ecclesiastical sense'.[63]

In addition to limiting the persons deemed to be members of the clergy, some courts have restricted the types of communications protected by the privilege in a way that reflects class bias. Traditionally, the privilege applied only to communications *required* by the tenets of a religion, and the privilege statutes in some States continue to contain such language.[64] If strictly construed, this restriction would limit the privilege to communications like those made by Roman Catholics during confession and would deny any privilege whatsoever to members of many other faiths.[65]

Even States that follow the modern trend and apply the privilege more broadly still confine it to cases where members of the clergy are consulted in their professional capacity. Some courts have interpreted this limitation to require that the communicant be seeking religious or spiritual counselling and therefore to exclude confidential communications made for purposes of receiving secular counselling, such as marriage counselling.[66] What these

---

62 *State v Buss* 887 P 2d 920, p 922 (Wash Ct App 1995).

63 *Ibid* (quoting the State's privilege statute). See, also, *Rutledge v State* 525 NE 2d 326, pp 327, 328 (Ind 1988) (holding that the privilege did not protect a confession a prisoner made to a member of the Gideons International Organization, who 'periodically visited jails to talk with inmates about the Bible and being forgiven for their sins' and who 'present[ed] to prisoners a plan of salvation but [did] not encourage them to make confessions'); *State v Hereford* 518 So 2d 515, p 516 (La Ct App 1987) (denying the privilege to a self-ordained minister who was incarcerated with the defendant, and reasoning that '[s]imply because [he] studied the Bible and took it upon himself to give religious guidance to others does not make him a clergyman').

64 *Op cit*, Stone and Taylor, fn 40, § 6.10, p 21; § 6.12, p 26.

65 Such a narrow interpretation therefore raises constitutional concerns under the establishment clause of the First Amendment. See *In re Grand Jury Investigation* 918 F 2d 374, pp 384–85 and n 14, p 387, n 21 (3d Cir 1990); *Scott v Hammock* 870 P 2d 947, p 954 (Utah 1994).

66 *Op cit*, Stone and Taylor, fn 40, § 6.11, pp 23–25. For illustrative cases, see *Simrin v Simrin* 43 Cal Rptr 376, pp 378–79 (Dist Ct App 1965) (ruling that the privilege does not apply to 'communications made to a religious or spiritual advisor acting as a marriage counselor'); *Commonwealth v Stewart* 690 A 2d 195, p 200 (Pa 1997) (holding that the privilege extends only to confidences disclosed to a member of the clergy 'in his or her capacity as confessor or spiritual advisor' and, therefore, does not include confidential communications 'even for counseling or solace ... unless motivated by spiritual or penitential considerations'); *Commonwealth v Patterson* 572 A 2d 1258, p 1265 (Pa Super Ct 1990) (refusing to apply the privilege to a defendant's conversations with a minister because 'there was no evidence that Reverend Dickson was acting in any capacity other than that of counselor' and, therefore, 'the [defendant's] statements were not motivated by religious considerations or in order to seek the forgiveness of God' and 'were not made to Reverend Dickson in the course of his duties as a minister'); *State v Buss* 887 P 2d 920, p 924 (Wash Ct App 1995) (holding that the privilege does not extend to 'counseling or family ministry', even if there is 'a public policy basis for protecting a broader variety of ministry-related confidential relationships').

courts fail to recognise is that members of the clergy are often trained to provide marriage counselling and treat personality problems, and '[m]atters of this kind fall readily into the realm of the spirit'.[67] Moreover, it is not evident that any principled line can be drawn between religious and secular counselling,[68] and attempting to do so creates a 'class and cultural bias' in jurisdictions that recognise a privilege for psychotherapists by denying protection to those who cannot afford to pay a therapist for counselling or who simply prefer to turn to their priest or minister.[69]

Health care professionals

Somewhat less well accepted is the privilege protecting confidential communications between doctor and patient. Historically, there was no such

---

67 Rules of Evidence for United States Courts and Magistrates, 56 FRD 183, p 248 (1972) (Advisory Committee's Note to Proposed Federal Rule of Evidence 506) (explaining why the proposed clergy-communicant privilege included 'all confidential communications with a clergyman in his professional character as spiritual adviser'). See, also, *In re Verplank* 329 F Supp 433, p 435 (CD Calif 1971) (extending the privilege to draft counselling given by a Presbyterian minister who served as a college chaplain and who also had responsibility for draft counselling services provided by the college, because '[d]ecisions as to the positions that a draft registrant will adopt in his relationships with the selective service laws and regulations often involve very deep and intimate spiritual and moral considerations'); *Rivers v Rivers* 354 SE 2d 784, pp 787, 788 (SC 1987) (applying the privilege to marriage counselling conducted by a Methodist minister on the grounds that '[d]ecisions that a husband or a wife makes concerning his or her marriage can, and often do, involve spiritual and moral considerations' and that the church, by making marriage counselling one function of a Methodist minister, 'made marriage counseling a practice of the church').

The Advisory Committee that drafted the Federal Rules of Evidence endorsed a number of privileges, including one protecting members of the clergy. But these proposals met with more criticism than any of the Advisory Committee's other proposed rules, creating 'an intense public controversy'. Krattenmaker, T, 'Interpersonal testimonial privileges under the Federal Rules of Evidence: a suggested approach' (1976) 64 Georgetown LJ 613, p 638. Ultimately, Congress rejected the Advisory Committee's approach, 'mainly because of the intense lobbying of protected groups', *op cit*, 'Developments', fn 19, p 1494. Instead, Congress enacted Federal Rule of Evidence 501, which does not expressly create any privileges, but provides that the law of privileges 'shall be governed by the principles of the common law as they may be interpreted by the courts of the US in the light of reason and experience'. For further discussion of the history underlying this rule, see *ibid*, Krattenmaker, pp 635–46; *op cit*, Mueller and Kirkpatrick, fn 2, pp 435–38.

68 Mitchell, M, 'Must clergy tell? Child abuse reporting requirements versus the clergy privilege and free exercise of religion' (1987) 71 Minnesota L Rev 723, pp 748–49 (noting that '[a] typical counseling session will be an unpredictable, often emotional, welter of several types of communication'). See, also, *Rivers v Rivers* 354 SE 2d 784, p 788 (SC 1987) (commenting on 'the practical difficulty in distinguishing between the counseling [the plaintiff] received from [a minister] as a therapist and between the counseling she received from him as a clergyman').

69 *Op cit*, 'Developments', fn 19, p 1562. See, also, *op cit*, Krattenmaker, fn 5, p 69 (arguing that no distinction should be drawn between clergy and other personal counsellors, who offer 'equally important and helpful sources of confidential counseling'). For a discussion of the psychotherapist privilege, see below, text accompanying fns 94–118.

privilege in England,[70] and even today the UK and common law provinces in Canada do not recognise a doctor-patient privilege.[71] The Advisory Committee that drafted the Federal Rules of Evidence did not endorse the doctor-patient privilege,[72] and as a general rule, the federal courts do not accept it.[73]

In 1828, however, the New York legislature became the first to create a doctor-patient privilege in the US,[74] and today the privilege has been widely, though not universally, incorporated in State statutes.[75] Advocates of the doctor-patient privilege believe that it encourages patients to communicate fully with their doctors. As an early New York decision explained, '[t]o open the door to the disclosure of secrets revealed on the sick bed, or when consulting a physician, would destroy confidence between the physician and patient, and ... might tend very much to prevent the advantages and benefits which flow from this confidential relationship'.[76]

But just as the common law may have been more reluctant to accept the doctor-patient privilege than the attorney-client privilege because doctors were 'of somewhat lower social class' than lawyers in English society,[77] so today even those jurisdictions that have adopted the doctor-patient privilege tend to confine it to health care workers of the highest professional status – those with MD degrees. A few State statutes protect other medical personnel –

---

70 *Op cit*, McNaughton, fn 20, § 2380, pp 818–19.

71 Howard, M, Crane, P and Hochberg, D, *Phipson on Evidence*, 1990, London: Sweet & Maxwell, § 20–13, pp 501–02; *op cit*, Sopinka *et al*, fn 54, pp 712–17.

72 *Op cit*, Rules of Evidence for United States Courts and Magistrates, fn 67, pp 241–42 (Advisory Committee's Note to Proposed Federal Rule of Evidence 504) (reasoning that 'the exceptions which have been found necessary in order to obtain information required by the public interest or to avoid fraud are so numerous as to leave little if any basis for the privilege').

73 See, eg, *Whalen v Roe* 429 US 589, p 602, n 28 (1977) (noting that '[t]he physician-patient evidentiary privilege is unknown to the common law'); *Patterson v Caterpillar Inc* 70 F 3d 503, pp 506–07 (7th Cir 1995); *Gilbreath v Guadalupe Hospital Foundation, Inc* 5 F 3d 785, p 791 (5th Cir 1993).

74 *Op cit*, 'Developments', fn 19, p 1460.

75 *Op cit*, Stone and Taylor, fn 40, § 7.01, pp 31–37 (Supp 1999) (citing statutes from 42 States plus the District of Columbia).

76 *Edington v Mutual Life Insurance Co* 67 NY 185, p 194 (1876). But see *op cit*, McNaughton, fn 20, § 2380a, p 829 (criticising the privilege on the grounds that information communicated to a doctor is rarely confidential 'in any real sense', and that '[p]eople would not be deterred from seeking medical help because of the possibility of disclosure in court').

77 *Allred v State* 554 P 2d 411, p 414, n 4 (Alaska 1976). Perhaps a simpler explanation is that judges are lawyers and, therefore, 'the significance of the attorney-client relationship is more readily apparent to the courts'. See *op cit*, Stone and Taylor, fn 40, § 7.02, p 9. See, also, *op cit*, Bentham, fn 34, p 302 (observing that 'English judges have taken care to exempt the professional members of the partnership from so unpleasant an obligation as that of rendering service to justice').

nurses,[78] physicians' assistants,[79] dentists,[80] pharmacists,[81] speech pathologists,[82] physical therapists,[83] osteopaths,[84] podiatrists,[85] naturopaths,[86] optometrists,[87] and chiropractors[88] – but they are in the clear minority. In the majority of States, where the privilege statutes do not expressly encompass these other groups, the courts are likely to rule that confidential communications made to them are not protected,[89] unless they were acting as a physician's agent and therefore come under the umbrella of the doctor-patient privilege.[90]

As applied, therefore, the privilege tends to afford greater protection to health care professionals with more education and greater status, and those

---

78 *Op cit*, Stone and Taylor, fn 40, § 7.01, pp 31–37 (Supp 1999) (citing 11 State statutes).

79 *Op cit*, Stone and Taylor, fn 40, § 7.01, pp 31–37 (Supp 1999) (citing one statute).

80 *Op cit*, Stone and Taylor, fn 40, § 7.01, pp 31–37 (Supp 1999) (citing 10 statutes).

81 *Op cit*, Stone and Taylor, fn 40, § 7.01, pp 31–37 (Supp 1999) (citing two statutes).

82 *Op cit*, Stone and Taylor, fn 40, § 7.01, pp 31–37 (Supp 1999) (citing two statutes).

83 *Op cit*, Stone and Taylor, fn 40, § 7.01, pp 31–37 (Supp 1999) (citing one statute).

84 *Op cit*, Stone and Taylor, fn 40, § 7.01, pp 31–37 (Supp 1999) (citing four statutes).

85 *Op cit*, Stone and Taylor, fn 40, § 7.01, pp 31–37 (Supp 1999) (citing four statutes).

86 *Op cit*, Stone and Taylor, fn 40, § 7.01, pp 31–37 (Supp 1999) (citing one statute).

87 *Op cit*, Stone and Taylor, fn 40, § 7.01, pp 31–37 (Supp 1999) (citing four statutes).

88 *Op cit*, Stone and Taylor, fn 40, § 7.01, pp 31–37 (Supp 1999) (citing eight statutes). In addition, the privilege statutes in six States are drafted in general terms that could reach more broadly, privileging, eg, health care providers or practitioners. See *op cit*, Stone and Taylor, fn 40, § 7.01, pp 31–37 (Supp 1999).

89 *Op cit*, 'Developments', fn 19, p 1534 (noting that courts usually restrict the privilege to doctors unless the statute contains more expansive language). For illustrative cases, see *Medical-Express Inc v Tarpley* 629 So 2d 331, p 332 (La 1993) (denying privilege to ambulance technicians and nurses because the State's privilege statute is limited to 'physicians'); *Robinson v Meca* 632 NYS 2d 728, p 730 (App Div 1995) (rejecting privilege for optometrists on the grounds that 'the practice of optometry is distinct from the practice of medicine'); *In re Polen* 670 NE 2d 572, p 574 (Ohio Ct App 1996) (denying privilege to chiropractors because the privilege statute extends only to medical doctors, osteopaths, podiatrists and dentists); *Buchanan v Mayfield* 925 SW 2d 135, pp 137–38 (Tex Ct App 1996) (refusing to apply privilege to dentists); *State v Ross* 947 P 2d 1290, pp 1292–93 (Wash Ct App 1997) (denying privilege to paramedics and rejecting defendant's argument that paramedics are 'highly trained and act as physician extenders'). But compare *Lococo v XL Disposal Corp* 717 NE 2d 823, pp 827–28 (Ill Ct App 1999) (extending privilege to paramedics, though finding an exception applicable in that case); *State v Jaggers* 506 NE 2d 832, p 833 (Ind Ct App 1987) (applying privilege to chiropractors); *Kessler v Troum* 392 A 2d 662, p 664 (NJ Super Ct Law Div 1978) (interpreting physician-patient privilege statute to apply to dentists because they are 'authorised to practice medicine'); *People v Hanf* 611 NYS 2d 85, p 86 (County Ct 1994) (concluding that emergency medical technicians are persons authorised to practice medicine because they act as doctors' agents and at doctors' direction).

90 See, eg, *Darnell v State* 674 NE 2d 19, p 22 (Ind Ct App 1996) (rejecting privilege for nurses unless they are acting 'under the direct supervision of a physician'); *State v Cahoon* 799 P 2d 1191, pp 1193–94 (Wash Ct App 1990) (refusing to protect statements made to emergency medical technicians outside the presence of a physician). But see *State v McKinnon* 525 NE 2d 821, p 823 (Ohio Ct App 1987) (rejecting even the agency theory for nurses).

individuals tend to be male.[91] Communications with health care workers of lesser status are much less likely to be covered by the privilege, even if the patient was disclosing the same sort of information typically conveyed to doctors and for the same purposes. There does not seem to be any principled distinction between the confidences conveyed to a physician and those communicated, for example, to a nurse or an emergency medical technician – especially in emergency situations or in areas with scarce medical resources, where access to doctors is limited. As Wigmore noted decades ago, '[t]he real support for the privilege seems to be mainly the weight of professional medical opinion pressing upon the legislature'.[92] And it is doctors who are much more likely to have the financial resources and status necessary to attract the attention of the legislators and judges voting to create evidentiary privileges.[93]

Mental health professionals

Although the privilege for psychotherapists did not exist at common law[94] and is still not recognised in the UK or Canada,[95] it seems even more well accepted in the US today than the doctor-patient privilege. The Advisory Committee that drafted the Federal Rules of Evidence supported the privilege[96] (despite their refusal to endorse the doctor-patient privilege),[97] the Supreme Court adopted it for the federal courts in *Jaffee v Redmond*,[98] and every State has some form of psychotherapist privilege.[99] As the Supreme Court explained in *Jaffee*:

> Effective psychotherapy ... depends upon an atmosphere of confidence and trust in which the patient is willing to make a frank and complete disclosure of facts, emotions, memories, and fears. Because of the sensitive nature of the problems for which individuals consult psychotherapists, disclosure of confidential communications made during counselling sessions may cause embarrassment or disgrace. For this reason, the mere possibility of disclosure

---

91 In the US, only 21.8% of doctors and 10.5% of dentists are women, compared to 38.1% of pharmacists, 72.5% of physical therapists, 91.8% of speech therapists and 94.4% of nurses. See *op cit*, Dorgan, fn 59, pp 39–40.

92 *Op cit*, McNaughton, fn 20, § 2380a, p 831.

93 McAllister, B, 'Pressure's up to $100 million a month' (1998) *Washington Post*, 12 March, p A13 (reporting that the American Medical Association spent $8.6 million lobbying the Federal Government during the first half of 1997, more than any other organisation or corporation).

94 *Op cit*, 'Developments', fn 19, p 1539.

95 *Op cit*, Howard *et al*, fn 71, § 20–13, p 501; *op cit*, Sopinka *et al*, fn 54, pp 713–15.

96 Proposed Federal Rule of Evidence 504, *op cit*, Rules of Evidence for United States Courts and Magistrates, fn 67, pp 240–41.

97 See above, fn 72 and accompanying text.

98 518 US 1 (1996) (interpreting Federal Rule of Evidence 501, which is described above, fn 67).

99 518 US 1, p 12 and n 11 (1996).

may impede development of the confidential relationship necessary for successful treatment.[100]

Though the psychotherapist–patient privilege is well accepted in theory, there has been a good deal of controversy surrounding its scope and, in particular, which mental health professionals it covers. The Advisory Committee that drafted the Federal Rules of Evidence defined 'psychotherapists' to include only medical doctors and those 'licensed or certified as a psychologist under the laws of any state'.[101] The Supreme Court rejected this approach in *Jaffee*, holding that confidential conversations with licensed social workers are entitled to the same protection in federal court as conversations with psychiatrists and psychologists.[102] Although the majority of States now extend the privilege to psychologists[103] and at least certain social workers,[104] and about half the States protect marriage[105] and/or other counsellors,[106] these extensions are relatively recent phenomena.[107] Moreover, such privileges are not universally recognised, and the courts generally refuse to accord any privilege to mental health professionals who are not specifically enumerated in the State's privilege statute.[108] Even those States that have given the privilege a more expansive scope often have certain prerequisites,

---

100 518 US 1, p 10 (1996). But see Shuman, D and Weiner, M, 'The privilege study: an empirical examination of the psychotherapist-patient privilege' (1982) 60 North Carolina L Rev 893, pp 918–26 (summarising the results of various surveys showing that Texas' therapist privilege did not encourage more people to seek treatment or make fuller disclosures to their therapists).

101 Proposed Federal Rule of Evidence 504(a)(2), *op cit*, Rules of Evidence for United States Courts and Magistrates, fn 67, p 240.

102 *Jaffee v Redmond* 518 US 1, pp 15–17 (1996).

103 *Op cit*, Stone and Taylor, fn 40, § 7.01, pp 31–37 (Supp 1999) (citing statutes from 40 States and the District of Columbia that expressly cover psychologists, plus eight others that apply to psychotherapists and thus presumably include psychologists).

104 *Op cit*, Stone and Taylor, fn 40, § 7.01, pp 31–37 (Supp 1999) (citing statutes from 41 States and the District of Columbia that expressly protect social workers).

105 *Op cit*, Stone and Taylor, fn 40, § 7.01, pp 31–37 (Supp 1999) (citing statutes from 25 States and the District of Columbia that expressly protect marriage counsellors).

106 *Op cit*, Stone and Taylor, fn 40, § 7.01, pp 31–37 (Supp 1999) (citing statutes from 32 States that expressly protect, eg, licensed professional counsellors or mental health counsellors).

107 Note, 'Functional overlap between the lawyer and other professionals: its implications for the privileged communications doctrine' (1962) 71 Yale LJ 1226, pp 1252–53 (noting that, as of 1962, no States protected social workers or marriage counsellors, and only 11 protected psychologists).

108 *Op cit*, 'Developments', fn 19, p 1540. For illustrative cases, see *Wiles v Wiles* 448 SE 2d 681, p 684 (Ga 1994) (defining 'psychiatrist' to include only 'medical doctors who spend a significant amount of time diagnosing and treating mental illness', and not all physicians who are consulted about a psychological problem); *State v Lassai* 366 So 2d 1389, p 1391 (La 1978) (denying privilege to the director of counselling at a drug treatment centre, and apparently finding irrelevant the argument that she was 'in the same position' as a physician or social worker); *State v Sandberg* 392 NW 2d 298, pp 304–05 (Minn Ct App 1986) (denying privilege to a crisis intake worker at a mental health centre because she was not a physician, psychologist or registered nurse), *aff'd in part and rev'd in part on other grounds*, 406 NW 2d 506 (Minn 1987); *State v Clark* 570 NW 2d 195, pp 203–04 (ND 1997) (defining 'psychotherapist' to include only medical doctors and licensed psychologists, and therefore excluding social workers).

requiring, for example, that the mental health professional have attained a specific educational level[109] or obtained a licence[110] in order to qualify for the privilege.

This hierarchical approach to the privilege for mental health professionals undermines the principles underlying the privilege, and does so in a gendered and class biased way. The professions most likely to be covered by the privilege are those that tend to be more heavily dominated by men[111] and that treat clients of higher socio-economic status. Although Justice Scalia's dissenting opinion in *Jaffee* argued against extending the psychotherapist privilege to social workers on the grounds that they do not have the same 'greatly heightened degree of skill' as psychiatrists or psychologists and have not received training 'comparable in its rigor (or indeed in the precision of its subject)',[112] a social worker often functions as a 'poor man's psychiatrist'.[113] Particularly in an era of scarce government funding for mental health services, public mental health facilities do not have the luxury of relying exclusively on psychiatrists and psychologists.[114] Similarly, women who are victims of violence often seek counselling from rape crisis or domestic violence

---

109 *State v Howland* 658 P 2d 194, p 199 (Ariz Ct App 1982) (reading statute to require that psychologists have a doctorate degree and therefore denying privilege to a psychologist with a master's degree in psychology); 225 Illinois Compiled Statutes 20/9 (1998) (requiring that social workers have a masters degree).

110 *State v Edwards* 918 SW 2d 841, p 844 (Mo Ct App 1996) (interpreting statute to deny privilege to unlicensed therapist); *State v Gotfrey* 598 P 2d 1325, pp 1327–28 (Utah 1979) (reading privilege statute to exclude unlicensed clinical psychologist). See, also, *op cit*, Rules of Evidence for United States Courts and Magistrates, fn 67, p 243 (Advisory Committee's Note to Proposed Federal Rule of Evidence 504) (explaining that the proposed privilege for psychologists – unlike that for psychiatrists, attorneys, and members of the clergy – did not apply when an individual reasonably believed that the person she was consulting was a licensed psychologist because of 'the number of persons, other than psychiatrists, purporting to render psychotherapeutic aid and the variety of their theories').

111 Only about one-quarter of psychiatrists in the US are women. See Herman, R, 'The growing presence of women in psychiatry' (1991) *Washington Post*, 1 October, p Z9 (putting the figure at 24%). Moreover, PhD psychologists have traditionally been men. See Hendrix, K, 'When women turn to matters of the mind' (1992) *Los Angeles Times*, 19 April, p E1 (noting that, while 58% of those receiving doctorates in psychology in 1990 were women, only 20% of the doctorates awarded in 1968 went to women). By contrast, women tend to dominate the social work profession. See Fishman, K, 'Therapy for children' (1991) *The Atlantic*, June, p 47 (observing that 68% of social workers were women in 1990).

112 *Jaffee v Redmond* 518 US 1, p 29 (1996) (Scalia J dissenting).

113 Comment, 'Underprivileged communications: extension of the psychotherapist-patient privilege to patients of psychiatric social workers' (1973) 61 California L Rev 1050.

114 *State v Gotfrey* 598 P 2d 1325, p 1329 (Utah 1979) (Stewart J concurring in part and dissenting in part) (noting that the effect of requiring that psychologists be licensed was 'to make an invidious discrimination in the quality of psychological services available to a person who can afford to consult a private practitioner and the quality of service which lesser advantaged persons may receive when seeking the same services from a government sponsored institution', whose employees were exempt from the licensing requirement); *ibid*, Comment, pp 1050–51.

counsellors.[115] A child might well find that a teacher or school counsellor is the most accessible source of mental health service.[116] And people often confide in their hairdressers and bartenders, yet no jurisdiction extends a privilege to these communications.[117]

I am not necessarily endorsing the creation of a privilege for hairdressers and bartenders, but there is little justification for limiting the privilege to mental health professionals with MD or PhD degrees. Other mental health professionals – social workers and counsellors – may not have the social status or educational background of a psychiatrist or psychologist, but they provide identical counselling services for the same sorts of problems, and usually at a reduced cost that makes them more accessible to lower-income individuals.[118]

Spouses

The spousal privilege is the second oldest privilege, dating back to the late 1600s and predated only by the attorney-client privilege.[119] In its original form, the privilege acted to prevent a wife from testifying against her husband. Although the precise source of this adverse testimony privilege is subject to some debate, it is clear that it was rooted in gender biased notions about the marital relationship. Some trace the adverse testimony privilege to the old common law rule disqualifying a wife from testifying either for or

---

115 Though a number of State legislatures have extended a privilege to domestic violence and/or rape crisis counsellors in recent years, not all States have done so. See *op cit*, Stone and Taylor, fn 40, § 7.01, pp 31–37 (Supp 1999) (citing statutes from 18 States and the District of Columbia that protect some type of victim counsellors). In addition, some States have granted only a qualified privilege to such counsellors. See Warren, E, 'She's gotta have it now: a qualified rape crisis counselor-victim privilege' (1995) 17 Cardozo L Rev 141, pp 146–48.

116 Such conversations would be protected in only a minority of States. See *op cit*, Stone and Taylor, fn 40, § 7.01, pp 31–37 (Supp 1999) (citing statutes from 15 States that privilege communications with school psychologists or counsellors, only four of which apply to teachers).

117 *Jaffee v Redmond* 518 US 1, p 22 (1996) (Scalia J dissenting) (commenting that '[f]or most of history, men and women have worked out their difficulties by talking to, *inter alia*, parents, siblings, best friends and bartenders – none of whom was awarded a privilege against testifying in court').

118 *Jaffee v Redmond* 518 US 1, p 16 (1996) (observing that a social worker's 'clients often include the poor and those of modest means who could not afford the assistance of a psychiatrist or psychologist, but whose counseling sessions serve the same public goals'); *op cit*, 'Developments', fn 19, pp 1550–51 (noting the 'functional overlap' between psychotherapists and other counsellors, who treat the same problems and therefore have the same need for trust and confidentiality); Spencer, G, 'Cuomo proposes Bill to replace "Son of Sam" law' (1992) New York LJ, 24 March, p 1 (quoting Governor's comment in proposing privilege for rape crisis counsellors that '[s]urvivors of sexual assault who take advantage of the services offered by rape crisis centers, which are usually free, deserve the same protections given to other therapeutic relationships').

119 *Op cit*, McNaughton, fn 20, § 2333, p 644.

against her husband.[120] The spousal disqualification rule was in turn based on two aspects of medieval jurisprudence: 'first, the rule that an accused was not permitted to testify in his own behalf because of his interest in the proceeding; second, the concept that husband and wife were one, and that since the woman had no recognized separate legal existence, the husband was that one'.[121]

Others, most notably Wigmore, believe that the adverse testimony privilege developed independently of the spousal disqualification rule, in recognition of the husband's role as master of the household. Wigmore explained:

> [A] natural repugnance was felt (especially in those days of closer family unity and more rigid paternal authority) to condemning a man by admitting to the witness stand against him those who lived under his roof, shared the secrets of his domestic life, depended on him for sustenance and were almost numbered among his chattels. In a day when the offense of petit treason by a wife or a servant – violence to the head of the household – was still recognized, it would seem unconscionable that the law itself should abet (as it were) a testimonial betrayal which came close enough to petit treason, and should virtually permit a wife to cause her husband's death.[122]

Although the notions that a woman forfeits her legal status as a person when she marries and that the husband is the master of the household are no longer accepted today, the adverse testimony privilege was endorsed by the Advisory Committee that drafted the Federal Rules of Evidence,[123] and is still in force in the federal courts[124] and almost two-thirds of the States.[125] It is

---

120 *Trammel v US* 445 US 40, p 44 (1980). The spousal disqualification rule is still in effect in a few States. See *op cit*, Stone and Taylor, fn 40, § 5.02, p 3 and n 4 (citing five statutes).

121 *Ibid.* See, also, Blackstone, W, *Commentaries on the Laws of England*, 1809, London: Strahan, Bk 1, p 441. ('By marriage, the husband and wife are one person in law: that is, the very being or legal existence of the woman is suspended during the marriage, or at least is incorporated and consolidated into that of the husband.')

122 *Op cit*, McNaughton, fn 20, § 2227, p 212. See, also, *op cit*, Gilbert, fn 30, p 96 (noting that, without the adverse testimony privilege, 'Wives [would be able] to destroy the Interest of their Husbands, and the Peace of Families could not easily be maintained').

123 Proposed Federal Rule of Evidence 505, *op cit*, Rules of Evidence for United States Courts and Magistrates, fn 67, pp 244–45.

124 *Trammel v US*, 445 US 40 (1980).

125 *Op cit*, Stone and Taylor, fn 40, § 5.02, p 2. In many States, however, the adverse testimony privilege applies only in criminal cases. See *op cit*, Stone and Taylor, fn 40, § 5.02, pp 3–4 and nn 4, 8 and 13. Moreover, there is some disagreement as to which spouse holds the privilege – whether the testifying spouse can waive it and agree to testify against the defendant spouse. See, eg, *Trammel v US* 445 US 40, p 53 (1980) (overruling prior precedent and putting the privilege solely in the hands of the testifying spouse). See, also, Chiss, M, 'Troubling degrees of authority: the continuing pursuit of unequal marital roles' (1993) 12 Law and Inequality J 225, p 252 (arguing that vesting the privilege in the (usually male) defendant 'continue[s] implicitly to regard husbands as more responsible and rational').

currently justified on the grounds that allowing one spouse to testify against the other would be detrimental to 'the harmony and sanctity of the marriage relationship'.[126] Even though the sexist bases for the privilege have now been rejected and the privilege is stated in gender neutral terms, it is still used primarily to protect husbands from adverse testimony provided by their wives.[127]

A second marital privilege – more analogous to the professional privileges discussed above – protects confidential communications between spouses. The confidential communications privilege was not explicitly recognised until the middle of the 19th century, in part because the adverse testimony privilege made the question of the admissibility of marital confidences moot in most cases.[128] Although the Advisory Committee that drafted the Federal Rules of Evidence did not endorse this privilege,[129] it is in effect in the federal courts[130] and virtually every State.[131] Like the other privileges described above, it is justified by the importance of protecting the confidentiality of certain relationships: admitting confidential spousal communications into evidence, it is said, 'would tend to destroy that bond of mutual confidence and unquestioning trust that is essential to the peace and happiness of this most sacred of all domestic relations'.[132]

---

126 *Trammel v US* 445 US 40, p 44 (1980). But see *op cit*, Bentham, fn 34, p 340 (maintaining that the effect of the marital privilege is to 'secure to every man ... a safe accomplice' and to 'make every man's house his castle [and] convert that castle into a den of thieves'); *op cit*, McNaughton, fn 20, § 2228, p 216 (arguing that, because of 'the multifold circumstances of life that contribute to cause marital dissension, the liability to give unfavorable testimony appears as only a casual and minor one, not to be exaggerated into a foundation for so important a rule').

127 Lempert, R, 'A right to every woman's evidence' (1981) 66 Iowa L Rev 725, p 727 (noting that only a handful of the hundreds of cases he had seen, dating back to the mid-17th century, involved a husband testifying against his wife); *op cit*, 'Developments', fn 19, p 1587 and n 170 (estimating that, 90% of the time, the adverse testimony privilege is used to prevent a wife from testifying against her husband).

128 *Op cit*, McNaughton, fn 20, § 2333, p 645.

129 *Op cit*, Rules of Evidence for United States Courts and Magistrates, fn 67, p 246 (Advisory Committee's Note to Proposed Federal Rule of Evidence 505) (thinking it unlikely that 'marital conduct will be affected by a privilege for confidential communications of whose existence the parties in all likelihood are unaware', and distinguishing other privileges because they involve 'a professional person who can be expected to inform the other of the existence of the privilege' and because those other relationships, unlike marriage, are 'essentially and almost exclusively verbal in nature'). The unpopularity of the Advisory Committee's stance on this privilege is one of the reasons why its proposed privilege rules were ultimately rejected by Congress. See *op cit*, Mueller and Kirkpatrick, fn 2, p 610.

130 *Trammel v US* 445 US 40, p 45, n 5 (1980) (citing *Wolfle v US* 291 US 7 (1934) and *Blau v US* 340 US 332 (1951)).

131 *Op cit*, Mueller and Kirkpatrick, fn 2, p 610.

132 *State ex rel Barker v McAuley* 51 Tenn (4 Heisk) 424, p 433 (1871). But compare Hutchins, R and Slesinger, D, 'Some observations on the law of evidence: family relations' (1929) 13 Minnesota L Rev 675, pp 681–82 (arguing that abolition of the privilege would not significantly affect the extent to which spouses confide in one another).

Both forms of spousal privilege – the adverse testimony privilege and the confidential communications privilege – are limited to couples who are legally married. Thus, they do not apply to cohabiting couples, even to those who have been living together for years,[133] are raising children together,[134] and believe that they are legally married.[135] Likewise, the marital privileges do not protect other intimate relationships, such as gay and lesbian couples or best friends.

Wigmore justified such limitations on the grounds that the policies underlying the privileges do not apply to a non-marital relationship because 'the relation is not one in which the law wishes to foster confidence'.[136] Likewise, one State supreme court spoke in terms of limiting the privilege 'to those whose relationships are worthy of protection'.[137] But rather than viewing the marital privilege as a 'privilege' that must be earned,[138] it seems more faithful to the rationale underlying the privilege to recognise that it acknowledges the human need for an intimate partner in whom to confide. Given the reality that 'confidentiality, sexuality, and intimacy arise in many kinds of relationship[s]', the privilege rules should 'respect each individual's choice of an intimate relationship, instead of singling out any particular relationship for preferential treatment'.[139]

---

133 See, eg, *US v Acker* 52 F 3d 509, pp 514–15 (4th Cir 1995) (refusing to apply either privilege to a couple who had lived together for 25 years in a State that did not recognise common law marriages); *State v Hankins* 642 SW 2d 606, pp 611–12 (Mo 1982) (denying both privileges where the couple had been living together for six years, they had a child together and the woman sometimes used the man's name).

134 See, eg, *State v Williams* 688 So 2d 1277, pp 1280–81 (La Ct App 1997) (denying both privileges to a couple who lived together and had three children together, on the grounds that the State did not recognise common law marriages, even though it did give full faith and credit to common law marriages entered into in other States); *People v Suarez* 560 NYS 2d 68, p 70 (Sup Ct 1990) (denying the confidential communications privilege to a couple who had lived together for several years and had several children together, though admitting that 'there are non-formalized relationships where the parties have a bond of intimacy similar to or greater than that between married couples' and, therefore, '[c]ogent arguments may be made for a privilege to apply to relationships between gay partners, roommates, friends, co-workers or other family members').

135 See, eg, *US v Hamilton* 19 F 3d 350, p 354 (7th Cir 1994) (refusing to apply the confidential communications privilege even though the defendant thought that he was legally married to a woman who had never divorced her former husband); *Phillips v State* 701 SW 2d 875, pp 892–94 (Tex Crim App 1985) (refusing to apply the adverse testimony privilege where the defendant lived with a woman who used his name and who believed that she had a common law marriage with him, but who had never been divorced from her first husband).

136 *Op cit*, McNaughton, fn 20, § 2335, p 647.

137 *State v Watkins* 614 P 2d 835, p 840 (Ariz 1980) (upholding the constitutionality of the policy restricting marital privileges to those who are 'formally married').

138 *US v Acker* 52 F 3d 509, p 515 (4th Cir 1995) (arguing that 'reason dictates that, before the courts extend a marital privilege to benefit a defendant, the defendant must have assumed both the privileges and responsibilities of a valid marriage under the law').

139 *Op cit*, 'Developments', fn 19, pp 1563, 1590.

Moreover, limiting the privilege to the traditional marital relationship 'tend[s] to legitimize the male-dominated institution of marriage',[140] privileging relationships that are often characterised by gender inequities in terms of both power and resources.[141] As one commentator observed, 'the law's conception of marital unity historically has been premised on married women's economic, social, and physical subordination to their husbands'.[142] Furthermore, the traditional justification for the marital privileges – that marriage is 'the best solace of human existence'[143] – may be more apt from the husband's point of view. Research suggests that women are more frequently the recipients of disclosures of personal information[144] and that women tend to value same-sex friendships more so than do men.[145] Thus, while men may be more likely to choose their wives as their primary confidants, women may be more likely to confide in other women than in their husbands.[146] As a result, limiting the spousal privileges to the traditional marital relationship better serves the interests of men.[147]

Another consequence of the formal marriage requirement is that the overwhelming majority of jurisdictions have refused to extend either form of

---

140 *Op cit*, 'Developments', fn 19, p 1591.

141 Baer, J, *Women in American Law: The Struggle Toward Equality from the New Deal to the Present*, 1993, New York: Holmes and Meier, Vol 2, pp 128–29 (noting that 'the amount of power a spouse has bears a direct relationship to the extent of his or her contribution to the family's income' and 'contemporary law cannot, and has not, removed the asymmetry of marriage'); Blumstein, P and Schwartz, P, *American Couples*, 1983, New York: William Morrow, p 55 (observing that 'wage disparities between men and women are related to the disparity of power within marriage'); Heyn, D, *Marriage Shock: The Transformation of Women into Wives*, 1997, New York: Dell, p 11 (chronicling the changes in personality, goals, mental health and appearance that married women experience, and concluding that 'it is men who are thriving in marriage, now as always').

142 *Op cit*, Chiss, fn 125, p 265.

143 *Stein v Bowman* 38 US (13 Pet) 209, p 223 (1839).

144 *Op cit*, Dolgin *et al*, fn 16, p 312; *op cit*, Winstead, fn 12, p 93.

145 Buhrke, R and Fuqua, D, 'Sex differences in same- and cross-sex supportive relationships' (1987) 17 Sex Roles 339, pp 350–51 (finding that women describe their same-sex relationships as being closer than men do, whereas men describe their cross-sex relationships as being closer than women do); *op cit*, Reisman, fn 12, pp 67, 78–79 (noting that women are more likely than men to be able to name a close friend other than their spouse); Veniegas, R and Peplau, L, 'Power and the quality of same-sex friendships' (1997) 21 Psychology of Women Quarterly 279; *op cit*, Winstead, fn 12, pp 83–87.

146 *Ibid*, Buhrke and Fuqua, pp 348–49 (finding that both men and women are more likely to seek out women for support); *op cit*, Dolgin *et al*, fn 16, p 326 (finding that 'female-female best friend pairs disclose more to each other than do other friendship dyads'); *op cit*, Dolgin and Minowa, fn 12, p 371; Levinson, S, 'Testimonial privileges and the preferences of friendship' (1984) Duke LJ 631, pp 649–50 and n 57.

147 For other commentary endorsing an expansion of the marital privilege, see *op cit*, Krattenmaker, fn 5, p 94 (advocating 'a general, qualified privilege for confidential communications that pass between individuals intimately related or in a position of close personal trust'); *ibid*, Levinson, pp 654–56 (suggesting that everyone should receive a certain number of 'privilege tickets' to allocate as they choose); *op cit*, 'Developments', fn 19, p 1591 (proposing that a presumptive privilege be created for cohabiting couples and that judges be allowed to extend a privilege in other cases to relationships that are proven to have sufficient indicia of intimacy).

privilege to family members other than spouses[148] – despite the fact that a number of other countries recognise a privilege for other family members.[149] For example, American courts have raised a number of objections to a parent-child privilege: that confidentiality is not 'essential to a successful parent-child relationship', given that children are unlikely to be aware of the privilege and '[b]onds other than shared secrets typically hold the parent-child relationship together';[150] that 'the existence or nonexistence of a parent-child privilege is probably one of the least important considerations in any child's decision as to whether to reveal some indiscretion, legal or illegal, to a parent';[151] that any '[h]arm [that] may inure to the relationship between an adult child and a parent when the parent disclosed the adult child's confidences [will] vary depending on the closeness of the particular family';[152] and that any benefits achieved by creating such a privilege 'must yield to the real damage that a parent-child privilege would inflict upon the truth-seeking function of legal proceedings'.[153] But each of these criticisms can also be levelled at the marital

---

148 *In re Grand Jury* 103 F 3d 1140, pp 1147–48 (3d Cir 1997) (citing a number of federal and State precedents); *In re Grand Jury Proceedings of John Doe v US* 842 F 2d 244 (10th Cir 1988) (forcing 15 year old to testify against his mother and other members of his family); *People v Sanders* 457 NE 2d 1241, p 1245 (Ill 1983) (declining to recognise privilege for confidential communications between parents and children); *State v Willoughby* 532 A 2d 1020, pp 1021–23 (Me 1987) (refusing to recognise intra-family testimonial privilege and, therefore, affirming criminal contempt convictions of parents and sister who refused to testify against adult defendant); *Three Juveniles v Commonwealth* 455 NE 2d 1203 (Mass 1983) (holding that minor children living at home had no privilege to refuse to testify against their father); *In re Inquest Proceedings* 676 A 2d 790 (Vt 1996) (declining to recognise privilege to protect parents from testifying against their 25 year old son); *State v Maxon* 756 P 2d 1297, pp 1301–02 (Wash 1988) (refusing to extend privilege to confidential communications made to defendant's parents).

149 Covey, J, 'Making form follow function: considerations in creating and applying a statutory parent-child privilege' (1990) Illinois UL Rev 879, p 883 (noting that a broader privilege exists in France, Germany, Sweden and other civil law countries in Western Europe).

150 *State v Maxon* 756 P 2d 1297, pp 1301–02 (Wash 1988).

151 *In re Grand Jury* 103 F 3d 1140, p 1153 (3d Cir 1997).

152 *In re Inquest Proceedings* 676 A 2d 790, p 793 (Vt 1996).

153 *State v Maxon* 756 P 2d 1297, p 1302 (Wash 1988); see, also, *In re Grand Jury* 103 F 3d 1140, p 1153 (3d Cir 1997); *In re Inquest Proceedings* 676 A 2d 790, p 793 (Vt 1996), p 793. A few courts have drawn a distinction between minor and adult children, indicating at least a willingness to consider a privilege for confidences disclosed to a parent by a minor child. See *In re Erato*, 2 F 3d 11, p 16 (2d Cir 1993) (leaving open an adverse testimony privilege with respect to minor children and commenting that, in such cases, 'the argument would be available that compelling a parent to inculpate a minor child risks a strain on the family relationship that might impair the mother's ability to provide parental guidance during the child's formative years'); *Three Juveniles v Commonwealth* 455 NE 2d 1203, p 1206 (Mass 1983) (leaving open a confidential communications privilege between parent and child, noting that 'there is limited support for a testimonial privilege to protect confidential communications from child to parent'); *In re Inquest Proceedings* 676 A 2d 790, p 794 (Vt 1996) (declining to decide 'whether a parent's interest in protecting a minor or incompetent child's confidential communications or conduct could ever outweigh the public interest in the criminal fact-finding process'). Compare *People v Hilligas* 670 NYS 2d 744, pp 746–47 (Sup Ct 1998) (rejecting *People v Fitzgerald*, which is described below, fn 155, and limiting privilege to minor children).

privilege.[154] Moreover, forcing parents and children to testify against each other, and refusing to respect the confidences communicated between them, ignores 'basic human instincts to protect the members of one's family, even from the State', which the law ought to protect.[155] And finally, recognising a privilege for the marital relationship, but not the parent-child relationship, devalues the interests of women by failing to acknowledge that women attach greater importance to their relationships with their children than do men, at times valuing them more than their relationships with their husbands.[156]

---

154 See above, fns 126, 129 and 132 (citing similar arguments made by critics of the marital privilege). See, also, *In re Grand Jury Proceedings, Unemancipated Minor Child* 949 F Supp 1487, p 1494 (ED Wash 1996) (finding 'no meaningful distinction between the policy reasons behind the marital communications privilege and those behind a parent-child privilege'); *In re Agosto* 553 F Supp 1298, pp 1303, 1325 (D Nev 1983) (analogising marital relationship to parent-child relationship).

155 *Three Juveniles v Commonwealth* 455 NE 2d 1203, p 1209 (Mass 1983) (O'Connor J dissenting). A handful of authorities have agreed and have created a privilege for at least some family members. See *In re Grand Jury Proceedings, Unemancipated Minor Child* 949 F Supp 1487, p 1494 (ED Wash 1996) (advocating some form of parent-child privilege on the grounds that 'reason and experience dictate that parents and children share a unique relationship, in which the ability to communicate in confidence without the fear of betrayal will often be the very foundation of the relationship'); *In re Agosto* 553 F Supp 1298, pp 1325–29 (D Nev 1983) (holding that both privileges apply in cases where children and parents are asked to testify against each other); *In re Application of A and M* 403 NYS 2d 375, p 380 (App Div 1978) (recognising privilege for confidential communications made by minor child to parent because 'the thought of the State forcing a mother and father to reveal their child's alleged misdeeds, as confessed to them in private, to provide the basis for criminal charges is shocking to our sense of decency, fairness and propriety' and 'the interest of society in protecting and nurturing the parent-child relationship is of such overwhelming significance that the State's interest in fact-finding must give way'); *People v Fitzgerald* 422 NYS 2d 309, pp 313–14 (Westchester County Ct 1979) (refusing to limit the privilege to minor children, and instead protecting confidential communication made to father by 23 year old son who did not live at home, because '[t]he parent-child relationship of mutual trust, respect and confidence ... is one that should be and must be fostered throughout the life of the parties' and, 'in many cases, the closeness of the family unit may well increase as the child becomes an adult'); Idaho Code § 9-203(7) (1998) (protecting confidences communicated by minor children to parents); Mass Ann Laws Ch 233, § 20 (1998) (applying adverse testimony privilege to minor children living at home with their parents); Minn Stat § 595.02(1)(j) (1998) (extending confidential communications privilege to confidences disclosed by minor child to parent).

Likewise, a number of commentators have endorsed a broader privilege for family members. See, eg, Watts, W, 'The parent-child privileges: hardly a new or revolutionary concept' (1987) 28 William and Mary L Rev 583 (proposing a privilege for minor children and their parents); *op cit*, 'Developments', fn 19, p 1591 (advocating a presumptive privilege for immediate family members); *op cit*, Covey, fn 149, (endorsing a parent-child privilege); Note, 'Parent-child loyalty and testimonial privilege' (1987) 100 Harv L Rev 910.

156 Becker, M, 'Maternal feelings: myth, taboo, and child custody' (1992) 1 S California Rev Law and Women's Studies 133, pp 147 and 152 (citing a number of studies indicating that, even in egalitarian relationships, women tend to be more emotionally involved with their children and feel more strongly about them than do men, and concluding that 'the mother's relationship with the child has a primacy of meaning with respect to the child without parallel for the father, [for whom] the primary and emotionally more intense relationship is likely to be with the mother').

CONCLUSION

Although the concept of evidentiary privileges is arguably consistent with feminist ideals, especially if privileges are created to serve the humanistic goal of protecting certain fundamental relationships, the doctrine as it has evolved has tended to 'privilege' the interests, values, and professions dominated by men, particularly men of higher socio-economic status. The predominantly male judges and legislators who define the privilege rules have acted to protect their own values and interests, and those of 'powerful groups seeking the prestige and convenience of a professionally based privilege'.[157] It may be true, as some have argued, that recognising additional privileges would create troublesome line-drawing issues[158] and thus undermine the judicial system's legitimate interest in ensuring that the fact-finder hear all relevant evidence. But what these 'slippery slope' arguments fail to acknowledge is that the law of privileges has always engaged in line-drawing – as it must, once the decision is made to create some evidentiary privileges. The privilege doctrine is not flawed simply because it draws lines, but because it does so in a gender and class biased manner, favouring certain groups and relationships that cannot be distinguished on any principled basis from others that are not protected by an evidentiary privilege.

---

157 *Op cit*, Strong, fn 4, § 75, p 282. For illustrations of this phenomenon, see *op cit*, Wigmore, fn 20, § 2286, pp 536–37 (quoting American Bar Association Committee report opposing the creation of 'any new privileges for secrecy of communications in any occupation', including accountants and social workers); Capra, D, 'Communications with psychotherapists and social workers' (1996) New York LJ, 12 July, p 3 (noting that 14 amicus briefs were filed by various organisations representing psychiatrists and social workers when the Supreme Court considered the psychotherapist privilege in *Jaffee v Redmond* 518 US 1 (1996)); *op cit*, Krattenmaker, fn 67, p 641 and n 196 (listing the various interest groups that appeared before Congress in order to urge the creation of a privilege for their members when Congress was considering the proposed Federal Rules of Evidence).

158 *State v Watkins* 614 P 2d 835, p 840 (Ariz 1980) (refusing to extend the marital privilege to couples who are not legally married, in part because of '[t]he administrative difficulty of defining and determining which relationships are to be considered *de facto* marriages, rather than casual alliances'); *People v Sanders* 457 NE 2d 1241, p 1245 (Ill 1983) (declining to recognise privilege for confidential communications between parents and children, in part because 'it would be impossible to contain [such a privilege] logically from spreading to conversations with other relatives in whom a person might normally confide, or even to close friends').

CHAPTER 6

EVIDENTIARY HARASSMENT: THE USE OF THE RULES OF EVIDENCE IN AN INFORMAL TRIBUNAL

Rosemary Hunter

Feminist critiques of the rules of evidence have noted their tendency to confine, distort or simply to silence women's stories.[1] What happens, then, in a regime in which the rules of evidence are relaxed? This chapter investigates the hearing process in a tribunal not bound by the rules of evidence, which determines cases concerning alleged discrimination and sexual harassment. In sexual harassment cases, complainants attempt to tell stories of unwelcome and invasive behaviour that is often unwitnessed, frequently prolonged, and always embarrassing and humiliating to recount. Relative informality and the absence of traditional evidentiary restrictions might be thought to enhance the ability of women who have been targets of sexual harassment to tell their stories and to have them believed. Tribunal observations in a number of sexual harassment cases, however, demonstrated that respondents' counsel used the rules of evidence (or their absence) tactically to obstruct the hearing process. Comparisons with recent studies of rape trials reveal disturbing similarities, if not a more abusive process for complainants.

THE HEARING PROCESS

Anti-discrimination legislation in Australia exists at both federal and State levels. State legislation prohibits discrimination on a wide range of grounds,[2] while the federal legislation deals only with racial, sex and disability discrimination. Sexual harassment is covered at both levels, usually by means of a specific prohibition of particular behaviour or behaviours defined as 'sexual harassment'.[3] The legislation at both levels also covers a wide range of

---

1   See, eg, MacCrimmon, M, 'The social construction of reality and the rules of evidence' (1991) 25 British Columbia UL Rev 36; Scheppele, KL, 'Just the facts ma'am: sexualised violence, evidentiary habits and the revision of truth' (1992) 37 NYLS L Rev 123; Scheppele, KL, 'Manners of imagining the real' (1994) 19 Law & Soc Inq 995; Hunter, R, 'Gender in evidence: masculine norms vs feminist reforms' (1996) 19 Harv Women's LJ 127; Hunter, R and Mack, K, 'Exclusion and silence: procedure and evidence', in Naffine, N and Owens, R (eds), *Sexing the Subject of Law*, 1997, Sydney: LBC, pp 171–92.

2   Including race; colour; descent; national or ethnic origin; sex; marital status; pregnancy; parental status; family responsibilities; physical, intellectual or psychiatric disability; sexuality; transgender status; age; trade union membership; industrial activity; political belief or activity; and religion.

3   See below, fn 15.

areas, including employment, education, the provision of goods and services, and accommodation,[4] although the majority of complaints are made in the area of employment.[5]

In addition, most of the Australian anti-discrimination statutes establish their own procedural regimes, generally consisting of a complaint handling agency charged with receiving and attempting to conciliate complaints, and a specialist tribunal to hear and determine complaints that have not been able to be resolved by conciliation.[6] The great majority of complaints are resolved prior to hearing (whether by means of withdrawal or conciliated settlement).[7] This is particularly true of sexual harassment complaints, where there are strong incentives on both sides to avoid public ventilation of the matter, and effective methods developed by complaint handling agencies for the conciliation of sexual harassment disputes. Desire to avoid the hearing process itself, particularly lengthy cross-examination, may also play a role in encouraging complainants to settle in sexual harassment cases.[8]

---

4   The full list of areas variously covered is: employment; partnerships; qualifying bodies; professional, trade or business organisations; associations; trade unions; employment agencies; education; provision of goods, services and facilities; accommodation; access to premises, places and vehicles; disposal of land; clubs; community service organisations; local government; sport; and the administration of Commonwealth and State laws and programmes.

5   Eg, of the 1,785 formal complaints received during 1997–98 under the federal Racial Discrimination Act 1975, Sex Discrimination Act 1984 and Disability Discrimination Act 1992, 53% were in the area of employment. The highest proportion of employment complaints (81%) was made under the Sex Discrimination Act 1984: Human Rights and Equal Opportunities Commission (HREOC), *Annual Report 1997–98*, 1998, Sydney: HREOC, pp 24, 29, 32.

6   More recently, specialist anti-discrimination tribunals in Victoria and New South Wales have been amalgamated with specialist tribunals established under other legislation to form general tribunals adjudicating across a range of areas (eg, town planning, tenancy disputes, guardianship matters, small claims, review of administrative decisions and anti-discrimination cases), although specialist anti-discrimination divisions remain within each tribunal structure. At federal level, the specialist tribunal has been abolished and its functions transferred to a generalist court, although this was partly for constitutional reasons which rendered the tribunal's decisions unenforceable. See *Brandy v HREOC* (1995) 183 CLR 245.

7   Eg, of complaints under the three federal Acts finalised in 1997–98 that were found to have substance, 73% were either withdrawn or conciliated. *Ibid*, HREOC, pp 23, 28, 31. See, also, Thornton, M, 'Equivocations of conciliation: the resolution of discrimination complaints in Australia' (1989) 52 MLR 733; Hunter, R and Leonard, A, *The Outcomes of Conciliation in Sex Discrimination Cases*, Working Paper No 8, 1995, Centre for Employment and Labour Relations Law, University of Melbourne; Devereux, A, 'Human rights by agreement? A case study of the Human Rights and Equal Opportunity Commission's use of conciliation' (1996) 7 Aust Dispute Res J 280.

8   Of the five lawyers interviewed, only one mentioned this as an incentive to settle: Ms Mandy Chambers (solicitor), interviewed 31 October 1997. Other interviewees tended to consider that what was likely to occur at a hearing was far from the complainant's mind during the conciliation process. A research project currently being undertaken by the author and others will investigate in more detail the reasons why complainants choose to settle or pursue their cases to hearing.

If a matter is referred for hearing, however, parties are faced with a somewhat ambivalent process. The original intention of specialist anti-discrimination tribunals was to provide informal, low-cost fora for the adjudication of rights, with the ability to hear directly from parties without the need for legal representation. For example, the tribunal to be discussed here, the Victorian Anti-Discrimination Tribunal, was constituted for hearings by three members drawn from a panel of members, only one of whom (the President or Deputy President) was required to be legally qualified.[9] Lawyers or other representatives were only permitted by leave of the tribunal,[10] and while the tribunal had power to make orders for costs, it would only do so in exceptional circumstances. As a general rule, each party bore their own costs.[11] The tribunal was bound to 'act fairly and according to the substantial merits of the case', but was not bound by the rules of evidence 'or by practices and procedures applicable to courts of record'.[12] Tribunal decisions strictly did not have precedential value, although in practice the tribunal followed its own previous interpretations of the legislation. Tribunal decisions on points of law were relatively rare, however. The tribunal was more usually called upon to resolve factual disputes and to determine whether the facts as found fell within the statutory prohibitions of discrimination.

Despite legislative encouragement to adopt more relaxed procedures, anti-discrimination tribunals have experienced a persistent pull towards formality, arising from their structural position in the legal hierarchy and the pervasive influence of adversarialism.[13] Although the Anti-Discrimination Tribunal, for example, was required only to act fairly and could receive whatever evidence in whatever form it determined, it was also subject to appeal on questions of law to the Supreme Court of Victoria. Grounds for appeal could include the weight given to particular evidence, or whether the conclusions drawn from the evidence were reasonably open to the tribunal. The possibility (or threat) of an appeal, together with the sometimes contemptuous attitude evinced by

---

9   Equal Opportunity Act 1995 (Vic), s 182. All members other than the President were part time, and were appointed by the State government for fixed terms from fields considered relevant to the tribunal's work, eg, law, social work, academia, equal opportunity practice, ethnic affairs. Some members were also appointed to other State tribunals. The discussion here is framed in the past tense, since, as noted in fn 6, the tribunal has subsequently become the Anti-Discrimination List of the Victorian Civil and Administrative Tribunal, whose procedures differ in some respects from those of the former tribunal. The membership of the List is substantially the same as that of the former tribunal, although some new members have been added.

10   *Ibid*, s 144.

11   *Ibid*, s 138; *Sinnappan v State of Victoria: Decision on Remedy* (1994) EOC 92-658.

12   *Ibid*, ss 141, 142.

13   See Thornton, M, *The Liberal Promise: Anti-Discrimination Legislation in Australia*, 1990, Melbourne: OUP, Chapter VI.

superior courts towards the decisions of such tribunals,[14] acted as strong constraints on the tribunal's freedom of movement, forcing it to operate within accepted boundaries in order to render its decisions 'safe', or relatively appeal-proof, in the interests of the parties. Moreover, despite the presence of lay tribunal members and the requirement for leave for parties to be legally represented, the personnel in control of the tribunal's processes were mostly lawyers, and those processes had been shaped in ways with which lawyers are most familiar. Parties with access to and the means to afford legal representation for a tribunal hearing routinely sought leave to be represented, and that leave was routinely granted, even if the other side was unrepresented. The tribunal's procedure was adversarial, with parties bearing sole responsibility for the presentation of their cases to a (generally) passive bench, each side presenting their case in turn, and evidence being led and witnesses cross-examined in accordance with adversarial norms. The tribunal's hearing rooms were laid out very much like a court, with a raised bench for the tribunal facing a bar table and witness box. Formal rules regarding the burden and standard of proof were applied, with complainants required to establish each alleged act of discrimination or sexual harassment on the balance of probabilities.[15]

Within this structure, the notion that the tribunal was not bound by the rules of evidence, except to the extent it determined,[16] appeared anomalous and provided fruitful ground for exploitation. The potential for exploitation was realised in one of the very first cases heard by an anti-discrimination

---

14 Examples are too numerous to list, but appeals against tribunal decisions are very frequently successful. For an early comment on this phenomenon, see Adams, W, 'The judiciary and anti-discrimination law' (1986) 11 Legal Service Bulletin 247. See, also, *op cit*, Thornton, fn 13; Hunter, R, 'Sex discrimination legislation and Australian legal culture', in Thacker, A (ed), *Women and the Law: Judicial Attitudes as they Impact on Women*, 1998, Geelong: Deakin UP, pp 73–74. For a contrary view, see Bailey, P and Devereux, A, 'The operation of anti-discrimination laws in Australia', in Kinley, D (ed), *Human Rights in Australian Law*, 1998, Sydney: Federation, p 310.

15 Due to legislative amendments, the requirements for establishing sexual harassment in employment varied, according to the date that the harassment was alleged to have occurred. For acts occurring prior to 1 January 1996, complainants had to show that their employer or supervisor (as defined) had made it reasonably clear to them that their career prospects or working conditions were contingent upon their acceptance of sexual advances or toleration of persistent sexual suggestions or innuendo from the employer or supervisor; or that the employer or supervisor had knowingly permitted them to be harassed with sexual advances or importuned or harassed with persistent sexual suggestions or innuendo by a fellow worker, whilst acting in the course of their employment: Equal Opportunity Act 1984 (Vic), s 20(1); Equal Opportunity Act 1995 (Vic), s 218. On 1 January 1996, the previous definition of 'sexual harassment' was replaced by a broader definition, which required the complainant to prove that the employer or anyone employed by the employer had made an unwelcome sexual advance, or an unwelcome request for sexual favours, or engaged in other unwelcome conduct of a sexual nature, in circumstances in which a reasonable person, having regard to all the circumstances, would have anticipated that the complainant would be offended, humiliated or intimidated: Equal Opportunity Act 1995 (Vic), s 85.

16 Equal Opportunity Act 1995 (Vic), s 142(1).

tribunal, *Harrison v Watson*,[17] in which an academic claimed she had been denied promotion on the ground of her sex. The absence of the rules of evidence enabled the respondent to introduce a great deal of irrelevant and hearsay evidence impugning the complainant's character, which both humiliated the complainant and considerably extended the length of the hearing.[18] The Victorian Anti-Discrimination Tribunal, perhaps in order to avoid such behaviour, asserted that its general practice was to 'apply the rules of evidence by analogy' (presumably by analogy with ordinary civil proceedings). But counsel would frequently test that principle and force the tribunal to make point by point rulings. For example, counsel for one party would ask a question or seek to introduce a piece of evidence in reliance on the provision that the strict rules of evidence did not apply. Counsel for the other party would then object, and require the tribunal to rule first on whether it would entertain the objection, and if so, on the objection itself. Moreover, the tribunal tended to take evidentiary objections very seriously, sometimes allowing lengthy argument on the point, and frequently adjourning to consider the submissions, and consult evidence texts and superior court rulings on the issue, before making its decision.

Bailey and Devereux have claimed that the exemption of anti-discrimination tribunals from the strict rule of evidence

> serves less to create a very free process in the tribunals than it does to avoid the ability to take and pursue excessively technical points about evidentiary rules. Because there is always an appeal on a point of law to a court, the tribunals tend to be careful to apply the main rules of evidence, while avoiding lengthy discussions on fine issues. This seems a useful position, and probably results in quicker hearings and a greater possibility of reasonably well informed parties being able to represent themselves.[19]

This was emphatically *not* the case in my observations of sexual harassment cases heard by the Victorian Anti-Discrimination Tribunal. Rather, counsel continuously used evidential objections to challenge the tribunal's authority, harass witnesses, intimidate or distract opposing counsel, prolong the time taken to hear the case, and prevent the admission of contextual information that would help to make sense of the complainant's story.

THE RESEARCH MATERIAL

My research on sexual harassment cases formed part of a larger study of 'women's experience in court', investigating the ways women's stories of

---

17 (1979) unreported, 19 June, NSW Anti-Discrimination Board.

18 Thornton, M, 'Board's first decision' (1979) 4 Legal Service Bulletin 180.

19 *Op cit*, Bailey and Devereux, fn 14, p 315.

violence and harassment are heard and responded to in a variety of civil court settings.[20] The research involved interviews with lawyers, support workers and women litigants, together with extensive court observations. In relation to sexual harassment proceedings, I formally interviewed five lawyers – three barristers and two solicitors, although two of the barristers had also acted for sexual harassment complainants as solicitors before going to the Bar – and observed eight cases over a period of two years, 1996–97. These observations included informal conversations, initiated by themselves, with three of the complainants.

At the beginning of the study period, the tribunal had been hearing very few sexual harassment cases, with almost all complaints being resolved by conciliation or settling prior to hearing (including at the door of the court, as I witnessed at least twice when I arrived to observe hearings that did not ultimately commence). Only two sexual harassment cases were heard during 1996.[21] During 1997, however, a total of seven sexual harassment cases proceeded to hearing.[22] This was partly as a result of legislative changes which introduced two new procedural elements: the ability for respondents, as a preliminary matter, to apply to the tribunal to have the complaint struck out,[23] and the ability for either party to apply to have the complaint 'expedited', that is, fast tracked through the conciliation process to hearing.[24] Two of the cases observed were strike-out applications, and a further two were expedited. During the period in which observations took place, therefore, the tribunal had had little exposure to sexual harassment cases. This fact, plus a number of recent new appointments to the tribunal, meant that most tribunal members were hearing stories about the dynamics of harassment for the first time.

---

20 The other types of matters included in the research were domestic violence protection orders in the magistrates' court and cases involving family violence (mostly children's matters) in the Family Court. See Hunter, R, 'Litigants in person in contested cases in the Family Court' (1998) 12 AJFL 171; Hunter, R and Stubbs, J, 'Model laws or missed opportunity?' (1999) 24 Alt LJ 12; Hunter, R, 'Having her day in court? Violence, legal remedies and consent', in Breckenridge, J and Laing, L (eds), *Challenging Silence: Innovative Responses to Sexual and Domestic Violence*, 1999, Sydney: Allen & Unwin, pp 59–68.

21 Although the total number of hearings in 1996 is difficult to determine (due to reporting based on financial rather than calendar years, and multiple counting of cases involving multiple parties), a rough estimate may be gained from the fact that the tribunal issued 48 decisions during 1996.

22 In the same year, the tribunal issued a total of 81 decisions, hence sexual harassment cases made up a higher proportion of the tribunal's work than in the previous year, although still quite a small proportion overall. A similar proportion was found in 1998 (12 decisions concerning sexual harassment out of a total 142 decisions).

23 Equal Opportunity Act 1995 (Vic), s 109.

24 *Ibid*, ss 119–24.

Of the nine cases heard overall during the two year period, three (one strike out and two hearings) involved male complainants, while the remaining six had female complainants. This does not represent the typical gender breakdown of sexual harassment complainants, but resulted from an unusual 'rush' of complaints by men proceeding to hearing. In general, the overwhelming majority of sexual harassment complaints are made by women.[25] Five of the cases concerned small business respondents, three concerned public sector organisations, and one concerned a large private company. In one of the cases the respondent did not appear, and this was one of the three cases in which the complainant was fully successful. The two strike-out applications were heard by the President (a woman) alone. The remaining cases were heard by panels of three members: five involving two female members and one male member, and two involving three female members. In five of the cases the presiding member was a woman (the President or a Deputy President), while the other two cases were presided over by a male Deputy President. Interviewees had varying views on the significance of the sex of tribunal members. One thought that having women on the tribunal made female complainants feel much more comfortable,[26] while another noted that in her experience, tribunal members' understanding of sexual harassment was not correlated with their sex.[27] The features and outcomes of the nine sexual harassment cases heard during the research period are set out in the table below.

---

25 Eg, in the 1996–97 financial year, the Victorian EOC received 395 complaints of sexual harassment, 350 of which (89%) were lodged by women: EOC (Vic), *Annual Report 1996–97*, 1997, Melbourne: Victorian Government, pp 15–16.

26 Ms Mandy Chambers (solicitor), interviewed 31 October 1997.

27 Dr Jocelynne Scutt (barrister), interviewed 20 October 1997.

Anti-Discrimination Tribunal sexual harassment cases 1996–97

Case name	Tribunal composition	Nature of case	Expedited?	Complainant sex	Respondents	Length of hearing	Outcome
Keaney	President (F)	Strike out	n/a	Female	Male colleague, public sector agency	40 minutes	Wholly struck out
Isaacs	President (F)	Strike out	n/a	Male	Female employer, small business	1 hour	Partly struck out[1]
Murphy	President (F), two members (F, M)	Hearing	No	Female	Male employer, small business	5 days	Upheld in part[2]
Gray	Deputy President (F), two members (F, M)	Hearing	Yes	Female	Male supervisor, government department	45 days	Upheld

Notes

1 The remaining elements of the complaint were subsequently dismissed after a three day hearing: *Isaacs v Sosnowski t/a QA Industrial Chemicals* (1998) unreported, 17 November, Victorian Civil and Administrative Tribunal, Anti-Discrimination List.

2 The complainant's subsequent appeal against the decision was unsuccessful: *Murphy v Colorific Lithographics Pty Ltd* (1997)unreported, 11 April, Supreme Court of Victoria.

Case name	Tribunal composition	Nature of case	Expedited?	Complainant sex	Respondents	Length of hearing	Outcome
Case 5	President (F), two members (F, M)	Hearing	No	Female	Male supervisor, private company	11 days	Settled
Russo	President (F), two members (F)	Hearing	Yes	Male	Female employer, small business	9 days	Dismissed
Simms	President (F), two members (F)	Hearing	No	Female	Male employer, small business	1 hour (undefended)	Upheld
Wilson	Deputy President (M), two members (F)	Hearing	No	Male	Female employer, small business	9 days	Dismissed[3]
McKenna	Deputy President (M), two members (F)	Hearing	No	Female	Male colleague, public sector agency	18 days	Upheld[4]

Notes

3 The complainant's subsequent appeal against the decision was unsuccessful: *Wilson v Phoenix Contracting Services Pty Ltd* [1998] VSC 81.

4 The respondent's subsequent appeal against the decision ran for a further six days in the Supreme Court, but was unsuccessful: *State of Victoria v McKenna* [1999] VSC 310.

A notable feature of the cases that went to hearing is their considerable length. Of the six defended hearings, the shortest was five days, while the longest ran for 45 days. Moreover, none of these hearings was continuous. Since most tribunal members were part time, hearing dates were scheduled according to their availability. *Murphy v Colorific*,[28] for example, was heard for one day in April 1996 and was then completed over four days in July. *Russo v Petracca*,[29] one of the expedited cases, commenced in June 1997 but was adjourned until August due to the complainant's ill health. After six hearing days in August, it finally concluded over a further two days in October. Case 5 was heard during seven days in July to August 1997 and a further four days in September, at which point only the complainant and two of her witnesses had given evidence. Owing to the unavailability of one of the respondent's counsel and the complainant's advanced stage of pregnancy, the case was then adjourned until February 1998; however, it settled before coming back on for hearing. *Gray v State of Victoria*[30] had 26 hearing days over the course of the entire year of 1997. It commenced at the end of January and resumed for four days in April, four days in May, three days in June, one day in September, one day in November, and nine days in December, at which point the complainant's case was completed. The respondent's case then continued for a further 19 hearing days in January, February and May 1998, followed by written submissions finalised in September 1998.

The reasons for the extraordinary length of these hearings varied. For example, the 18 days taken for *McKenna v State of Victoria*[31] was largely due to the calling of a total of 52 witnesses, and *Gray* also involved a considerable number of witnesses (approximately 30). *Murphy, Russo, Wilson v Phoenix Consulting*[32] and *Gray* each involved a number of alleged incidents of sexual harassment, and *Gray* and *McKenna* involved additional complaints of sex discrimination and victimisation, with each alleged incident being examined in great detail. *Gray*, for example, included 17 alleged incidents of sexual harassment and sex discrimination, a further 16 alleged incidents of sex discrimination and victimisation, and six separate incidents of alleged victimisation. Stanley and Wise have noted the importance of confronting 'small, mundane and accumulating' incidents of sexual harassment, and of naming 'the "dripping tap" behaviours, events and situations as sexual harassment',[33] but the attempt to establish 'dripping tap'-type harassment at a

---

28 *Murphy v Colorific Lithographics Pty Ltd and Hevey* (1996) unreported, 22 August, Anti-Discrimination Tribunal.

29 (1997) unreported, 20 November, Anti-Discrimination Tribunal.

30 *Gray v State of Victoria and Pettman* [1999] VCAT 33.

31 *McKenna v State of Victoria (Victoria Police), Mansfield, Fyfe and Arnold* (1998) EOC 92-927.

32 *Wilson v Phoenix Consulting Services Pty Ltd and Haig* (1998) EOC 92-936.

33 Wise, S and Stanley, L, *Georgie Porgie: Sexual Harassment in Everyday Life*, 1987, London: Pandora, p 114 (emphasis in original).

hearing can be a lengthy and painful process. On the other hand, the alleged incidents of sexual harassment in *Russo* were paid scant attention by the respondent's barrister, who focused his questioning almost entirely on the attempt to establish that the complainant's motive for bringing the complaint was to obtain money to pay off extensive gambling debts.

More generally, sexual harassment cases that proceed to hearing tend to be extremely hard fought. Both employers and individual respondents are keen to establish their personal or organisational innocence, while complainants seek vindication of their grievances in a context in which the tribunal is their last opportunity to have their story believed. The tribunal in *Gray* commented on the extraordinary length of the hearing in that case, which it attributed largely to the parties' inability to produce a statement of agreed facts. Rather, every factual allegation, or its correct interpretation, had been disputed.[34] The problem is compounded by the general application in sexual harassment cases of the so called *Briginshaw* standard of proof, which holds that the seriousness of the allegations, and/or the gravity of the consequences flowing from a particular finding, require the trier of fact to be more positively satisfied that the events occurred than it would need to be on some lesser matter.[35] This has the effect of elevating the standard of proof closer to 'beyond reasonable doubt'.

Nevertheless, the length of the cases is disproportionate compared to other proceedings, both civil and criminal. The eight contested family law cases observed for my study, for example, ran for an average of only three and a half days, with most involving a number of alleged incidents going to a party's parenting ability, several witnesses, and in four of the cases, an unrepresented party, which tended to prolong the hearing.[36] In the criminal area, a recent report found that rape complainants in Victorian courts spend an average of three hours in the witness box, and noted an earlier study which found that rape complainants spend on average at least twice as much time in

---

34 *Gray v State of Victoria* [1999] VCAT 33, p 5.

35 *Briginshaw v Briginshaw* (1938) 60 CLR 336, pp 361–62, *per* Dixon J. The ruling is routinely applied in sexual harassment cases, as noted by Tyler, D and Easteal, P, 'The credibility gap' (1998) 23 Alt LJ 211, and by my interviewee, Ms Melinda Richards (barrister), interviewed 15 October 1997. See, eg, *Gray v Ritossa* (1994) EOC 92-635; *Murphy v Colorific* (1997) unreported, 22 January, Anti-Discrimination Tribunal; *Russo v Petracca* (1997) unreported, 20 November, Anti-Discrimination Tribunal; *McKenna v State of Victoria* (1998) EOC 92-927, pp 78,163, 78,164; *State of Victoria v McKenna* [1999] VSC 310, pp 11–12. The use of the *Briginshaw* standard has occasionally been criticised, eg, by Commissioner Rayner in *Patterson v Hookey* (1996) unreported, 9 December, HREOC. It was directly challenged by the complainant's counsel in *Gray*, but the tribunal proceeded to apply the *Briginshaw* test in its decision: *Gray v State of Victoria* [1999] VCAT 33, p 5.

36 Data gathered from a large sample of Family Court cases in May to June 1998 indicated that the average length of contested hearings in the Family Court is around 1.5 days: Hunter, R, *Family Law Case Profiles*, 1999, Sydney: Justice Research Centre, p 158.

the witness box giving evidence as complainants in non-sexual assault cases.[37] Yet the sexual harassment complainants in the five contested hearings observed spent an average of more than four days in the witness box.

A direct comparison was provided by Case 5, in which the complainant's allegations against her supervisor had previously been the subject of a rape trial in the county court, in which the supervisor was acquitted. During the trial, the complainant had been in the witness box for three out of a total of five days, whereas in her sexual harassment case she was in the witness box for eight out of a total of 11 days before the case was adjourned and then settled. Each of the sexual harassment complainants was represented by a barrister, incurring costs of approximately $1,000 per day of hearing,[38] in a jurisdiction in which, regardless of the outcome, each party was normally expected to bear their own costs.[39] To a considerable extent, then, the length of the hearings may be attributed to attrition tactics engaged in by counsel for the respondent(s), combined with the tribunal's failure to exercise control over such tactics.[40] Means of holding up proceedings included, as noted earlier, frequent challenges to the admission of evidence, forcing the tribunal continually to consider and make rulings on evidentiary points. The strategic use of evidentiary issues in four of the cases will now be examined in greater detail. Notably, these four cases involved both male and female complainants, but were all presided over by a woman.

---

37 Heenan, M and McKelvie, H, *The Crimes (Rape) Act 1991: An Evaluation Report*, 1997, Melbourne: Victorian Department of Justice, pp 206–07, 245. A similar finding of an average of three hours in the witness box for victims, out of an average four days for sexual assault trials, was made by a contemporaneous NSW report: NSW Department for Women, *Heroines of Fortitude: The Experiences of Women in Court as Victims of Sexual Assault – Summary Report*, 1996, Sydney: Department for Women, p 9.

38 Estimates made by two interviewees: Ms Melanie Young (barrister), interviewed 22 October 1997, and Ms Mandy Chambers (solicitor), interviewed 31 October 1997.

39 See, eg, *Murphy v Colorific: Reasons for Decision as to Costs*, Anti-Discrimination Tribunal, 22 January 1997 (unreported). Of the cases observed, only the complainant in *Simms* was awarded costs, owing to the unreasonable conduct of the respondents in effectively ignoring and seeking to evade the tribunal proceedings: *Simms v Datagap and Giamirra*, Anti-Discrimination Tribunal, 2 May 1997. The complainants' applications for costs in *Gray* and *McKenna* were still in the process of determination at the time of writing. However, two respondents were awarded costs, in *Wilson* and in *Isaacs*, on the grounds that the complaints were so completely lacking in substance they should not have been brought: *Wilson v Phoenix Contracting* (1998) EOC 92-936, pp 78,234–35; *Isaacs v Sosnowski t/a QA Industrial Chemicals* (1998) unreported, 9 December, Victorian Civil and Administrative Tribunal, Anti-Discrimination List.

40 This point was made by four of the five interviewees.

STRATEGIC USES OF THE RULES OF EVIDENCE

Objections as a form of intimidation and harassment

A frequent deployment of the rules of evidence was in the making of trivial objections, for example, to the relevance of a question, in order to put an opponent off their stride and/or to harass a witness. While game playing between barristers is a traditional element of advocacy,[41] it was pushed to extremes in the sexual harassment cases, and subject to almost no limits by the tribunal. It was facilitated in two of the four cases discussed (*Russo* and Case 5) by the fact that the complainant's barrister was very junior, while the respondents were represented by senior and experienced counsel (in *Russo*, a QC). In fact, in only two of the cases observed (*Murphy* and *Wilson*) was the complainant's barrister more senior than the respondent's.

In Case 5, for example, the respondents' barristers (the employer and the individual respondent were separately represented) were barely interrupted at all during their lengthy, repetitive, and at times abusive cross-examination of the complainant. Yet they both attacked the complainant's barrister with the utmost vigour during his re-examination, objecting to almost every question on the basis that it was not relevant, not proper for re-examination, not an accurate reflection of what was said earlier, or that the evidence should have been elicited during evidence-in-chief. The complainant's barrister was labouring under a particular disability since he had only come into the case on day eight of the hearing, towards the end of the complainant's cross-examination, after her first barrister withdrew from the case. Thus, he had had no control over what had gone before and did not know his way around the transcript, yet his opponents insisted on holding him to the strictest letter of the rules. After about an hour of this barrage, the President intervened to note that the tribunal's duty to act fairly might best be served by allowing matters to be raised in re-examination that might not be strictly within its usual ambit, and then allowing the respondents an opportunity for further cross-examination if necessary. Re-examination then proceeded, and at the end of it, the employer's barrister asked only one question by way of further cross-examination.

The same continual interruptions occurred while the complainant's barrister took other witnesses through their evidence-in-chief, with the employer's barrister objecting to almost every question on the basis that his opponent was leading or that the matter raised was not relevant. At one point the tribunal made it clear that it wanted to hear what the witness had to say in

---

41 See, eg, Hunter, R and McKelvie, H, *Equality of Opportunity for Women at the Victorian Bar*, 1998, Melbourne: Victorian Bar Council, pp 136–38.

a coherent manner, and the objections died down, but soon afterwards, the tribunal entertained 15 minutes of argument on the relevance of another question, and the employer's barrister continued arguing with the President after she made a further ruling on relevance. At several points the employer's barrister asked that the witness be sent from the room during evidentiary argument. The first witness was asked to leave the room at least four times; the second witness was sent out, recalled, then sent out again at least eight times in the course of an hour and a half. It was clearly unnecessary for her to be excluded during the hearing of all objections, and this form of harassment left her obviously upset and barely coherent, seriously undermining her ability to corroborate the complainant's story.

The *Gray* case contained many similar examples of interruptions to fluster the complainant and her barrister: objections to leading questions, non-responsive answers, and the complainant looking at a piece of paper without having been given leave to refer to her notes, and allegations that the complainant's barrister was prompting her, giving evidence from the Bar table, and making speeches. A particular issue in this case was that the complainant was alleging a 'pattern and practice' of sexually harassing behaviour by her supervisor over a period of time, with the incidents set out in her written particulars being a non-exhaustive list of examples of what had occurred. On the other hand, the respondents (again, the institutional and individual respondents were represented separately) insisted that every alleged incident ought to be particularised, detailed and dated, otherwise they would be taken by surprise and unable to defend the case adequately.[42] After the respondents objected vigorously to the complainant mentioning an alleged occurrence that was not included in her particulars, the tribunal decided that the complainant should provide a list of further particulars, detailing every incident to be relied upon, but the respondents then objected that the complainant should not be allowed this opportunity but should be held to the list originally provided. While the complainant ultimately 'won' this point, the wider issue of how a story of persistent harassment can be told, and the tribunal's ability to hear that story in a way different from the criminal courts, was completely obscured from view.

To its credit, the tribunal did seek to address the complainant's argument in its decision, acknowledging that an accumulation of minor incidents of a sexual nature which made her feel uncomfortable had 'created a climate causing her anxiety and apprehension to a greater degree than each alone would have caused', and noting the two common elements in all of the incidents: that the individual respondent was in a position of power and authority over the complainant, and it was understandable in the

---

42 For discussion of the way in which legal procedures atomise and decontextualise incidents, with a particularly adverse impact on women's stories of gendered injuries, see *op cit*, Hunter and Mack, fn 1, pp 175–77, and references cited therein.

circumstances that she had not confronted the respondent about his behaviour.[43] But this was only after each of the incidents had been enumerated and individually tested against the statutory definitions, in the process of which about half of the alleged incidents were found not to constitute sexual harassment or sex discrimination. This does little to overcome the evidentiary difficulties faced by complainants in 'dripping tap' harassment cases, since a complainant who sought to rely on a limited list of representative incidents, and thereby to restrict the scope of the proceedings and their exposure to lengthy cross-examination and time wasting, would run the risk of failing to prove their case altogether.

It should be noted that it was not only female complainants who were subjected to continual objections and intimidation by respondents' barristers. The gender politics of sexual harassment are such that men alleging they have been sexually harassed are culturally 'feminised' by virtue of their complainant status. This point was made quite openly by the complainant's barrister in *Wilson*. The complainant was very well dressed, upper middle class, and formerly a highly paid executive. In his opening statement, his barrister noted that the complainant had previously experienced divorce, bankruptcy, and the serious illness of a child, but had never thought of himself as a victim until experiencing the alleged sexual harassment at the hands of his former employer. As this acknowledgment of perceived victim status indicates, sexual harassment complainants of either sex are placed in a position of abjection, which renders them vulnerable to further harassment in the witness box.

Hearsay

The tribunal's attitude to hearsay evidence was a matter of some confusion. One of my interviewees thought that the tribunal generally excluded hearsay evidence,[44] although in my observation such evidence was generally allowed in, but with an invitation for closing submissions to address the weight that should be given to it. Occasionally, however, the tribunal would decide to apply the rules of evidence and exclude a piece of hearsay evidence. For example, in *Murphy*, it spent half an hour hearing objections to the admission of a letter from one of the complainant's witnesses who was said to be unavailable to attend the tribunal. During the course of this argument the complainant's barrister put his instructing solicitor into the witness box and led evidence regarding the writer's unavailability, but the tribunal decided it had insufficient evidence and refused to admit the letter. Owing to the tribunal's inconsistent approach, it was always worth it for a barrister to make

---

43 *Gray v State of Victoria* [1999] VCAT 33, p 22.

44 Ms Mandy Chambers (solicitor), interviewed 31 October 1997.

a hearsay objection. Indeed, another interviewee considered that the tribunal took hearsay objections far too seriously, as part of its general over-responsiveness to barristerial bullying.[45]

Another avenue for hearsay objections opened up in *Gray* when, in order to try to curb the length of the hearing, the tribunal directed that witnesses should provide written statements by way of evidence-in-chief, allowing only minimal oral evidence before proceeding to cross-examination. Consequently, however, as each witness was called, the respondents' barristers would object to large parts of their statements, mostly on the grounds of hearsay and relevance. Eventually, the tribunal asked to hear all objections to all remaining witness statements at once, a process which consumed the best part of a day. Thus, the time that might have been saved by dispensing with evidence-in-chief was more than made up by objections, responses, replies, the tribunal adjourning to consider the matter, and making its rulings on each impugned paragraph of the statements.

Similar fact evidence

Similar fact or propensity evidence is often sought to be relied upon in sexual harassment cases due to the particular nature of the behaviour – it is likely to have been unwitnessed, but it is also not uncommon to find that the perpetrator has treated others in the same way. Thus, if evidence can be produced from another of the harasser's targets about his treatment of her, this lends credibility to the complainant's story. One interviewee noted that she had not struck any problems in calling such evidence;[46] however, the complainants in *Gray* and Case 5 did strike problems.

In *Gray*, the evidence of several of the complainant's witnesses concerned alleged incidents in which the individual respondent had made sexual remarks or engaged in other unwelcome behaviour of a sexual nature towards them. The respondents argued against the admission of this evidence on several grounds: that it was generally inadmissible by analogy with criminal proceedings, that the evidence was not of a sufficiently similar nature to the complainant's allegations to render it admissible even if some restricted admission was allowed, and that admitting the evidence would dramatically expand the scope of a case which was already far too broad. The legal argument, deliberation and ruling on this matter took up two and a half days. Since the tribunal decided to admit the evidence, the respondents also sought, and obtained, a lengthy adjournment of the case to consider the implications of the ruling (that is, to decide whether to appeal against it), and to obtain

---

45   Ms Melinda Richards (barrister), interviewed 15 October 1997.
46   Ms Mandy Chambers (solicitor), interviewed 31 October 1997.

instructions and prepare responses to the witness statements. Thus, again, the complainant's 'victory' on this point came at the price of considerably prolonging the proceedings.

In Case 5, when the introduction of similar fact evidence supporting the complainant's claims was again objected to, the tribunal referred to its previous ruling in *Gray* for the proposition that, since it was engaged in civil rather than criminal proceedings, it would be primarily concerned with the relevance of evidence, rather than whether its prejudicial effect outweighed its probative value.[47] However, it then proceeded to rule out the evidence in question. The complainant was alleging that the individual respondent had taken her to a private part of the work premises and sexually assaulted her. The witness alleged that the individual respondent had several times taken her to the same area of the premises to talk to her in private. The tribunal decided that this evidence was not sufficiently similar to the complainant's allegations to render it relevant, a decision which appeared to collapse relevance into the criminal standard for admission of similar fact evidence. It certainly did not clarify the tribunal's approach to similar fact evidence, and there is likely to be further argument over the admission of such evidence in subsequent cases.

Expert/medical evidence

Expert evidence might be called in several contexts in a sexual harassment case. In *Gray*, for example, the complainant's barrister wished to call an expert to give evidence about appropriate sexual harassment training programmes and grievance procedures within organisations, in order to help establish the institutional respondent's vicarious liability, for failing to take 'reasonable precautions' to prevent the harassment from occurring.[48] After argument and deliberation on the admissibility of this evidence taking up almost a whole day, the tribunal decided to apply the rule that opinion evidence going to the ultimate issue in the case should not be admitted.

Most usually, however, expert medical and/or psychological evidence is called to establish the injury caused to the complainant by the harassment, in order to found a substantial claim for damages for pain and suffering. In part, this practice has been compelled by the very low benchmarks initially set by anti-discrimination tribunals in awarding general damages to successful

---

47 Note, however, that the ruling on similar fact evidence in *Gray* has not been published by the tribunal.

48 Equal Opportunity Act 1995 (Vic), s 103: an employer is not vicariously liable for a contravention of the Act by an employee if the employer proves, on the balance of probabilities, that the employer took reasonable precautions to prevent the employee contravening the Act.

sexual harassment complainants.[49] This form of injury to women, while no longer invisible, still tends to be considered as fairly minor or trivial. Two interviewees noted the need to call specific evidence of psychological trauma in order to obtain a decent damages award,[50] although one observed that having the complainant examined by a psychiatrist is also an expensive process.[51]

The introduction of expert medical/psychological evidence may become a costly strategy for the complainant in other ways, as well. One way in which respondents have countered this kind of evidence is to challenge the causal link between the complainant's diagnosed psychological condition and the alleged harassment,[52] and to suggest alternative causes, providing the opportunity for intrusive examination of the complainant's personal life. In *Murphy*, for example, the complainant called evidence from a treating counsellor, her GP, and a consultant psychologist and psychiatrist, to show very significant psychological consequences of the harassment, variously diagnosed as chronic adjustment disorder or post-traumatic stress disorder, which had rendered her unfit for work and reliant on sickness benefits for almost two years. In seeking to show that this disorder had been caused by something other than sexual harassment, the respondent's barrister cross-examined in detail on the complainant's relationship with her boyfriend and parents, and her counselling and medical history, including discussion of intimate and entirely irrelevant medical details which the complainant found acutely embarrassing. Another interviewee confirmed the experience of respondents calling for a complainant's medical records as a means of

---

49 For the first 10 years of reported sexual harassment cases (1984–94), general damages in successful cases tended to fall within the range of $2,000–$7,000 (approx £750–£2,500), with only rare exceptions. Eg, *Orr v Liva Tool and Diemakers Pty Ltd* (1985) EOC 92-126 (first reported successful case, Equal Opportunity Act 1984 (Vic): $1,000); *Boyle v Ishan Ozden* (1986) EOC 92-165 (first successful case under the federal Sex Discrimination Act 1984: $2,200); *Aldridge v Booth* (1986) EOC 92-177 ($7,000); *Hill v Guilfoyle* (1988) EOC 92-233 ($2,500); *A v Caboolture Shire Council* (1992) EOC 92-403 ($3,000); *Ritossa v Gray* (1992) EOC 92-452 ($7,000); *Krepp v Valcic t/a Capel Bakery* (1993) EOC 92-520 (Western Australia: $4,000); *McLaren v Zucco* (1994) EOC 92-650 ($4,000). The exceptions were either described as particularly serious or egregious cases (eg, *Hill v Water Resources Commission* (1985) EOC 92-127 ($27,500); *Horne v Press Clough Joint Venture* (1994) EOC 92-591 ($12,000)), or involved proof of substantial psychological injury to the complainant (eg, *Bevacqua v Klinkert* (1993) EOC 92-515 ($50,000)).

50 Ms Melinda Richards (barrister), interviewed 15 October 1997; Ms Mandy Chambers (solicitor), interviewed 31 October 1997. For a striking illustration of this point, see *Brown v Lemeki and the Government of Papua New Guinea, Rees v Lemeki and the Government of Papua New Guinea* and *Johnston v Lemeki and the Government of Papua New Guinea* (1997) unreported, 27 May, HREOC. Two women who had been persistently sexually harassed and stalked by a foreign diplomat produced evidence of their psychological injuries and were each awarded $10,000. The diplomat's driver also made a complaint of having been exposed to the harassing behaviour of his employer, which made him feel angry, helpless and guilty for not being able to protect the two women, and was awarded the same amount of damages, without any specific evidence!

51 Ms Melinda Richards (barrister), interviewed 15 October 1997.

52 Ms Melinda Richards (barrister), interviewed 15 October 1997.

intimidation, to discourage her from pursuing her case or from calling medical evidence, or using the material disclosed to harass the complainant in the witness box.[53]

In *Gray*, the respondents not only sought to subpoena the complainant's counselling records, they also sought (on the fourth day of preliminary jurisdictional and procedural argument) to have the complainant examined by their own medical expert, in accordance with the provisions of the Supreme Court Rules of Civil Procedure. As the complainant's counsel pointed out in response, the tribunal was in no way bound by the Rules of Civil Procedure. She also urged the tribunal that if it was going to make an order for the complainant to be medically examined, it should order that the respondents produce a female medical practitioner for the complainant to attend, arguing that the provision of a female practitioner was absolutely vital in a sexual harassment case. The respondents strenuously objected to this proposition, citing the general rule that the defence could choose any appropriate practitioner to conduct the examination. The complainant's barrister replied that many established rules were not appropriate in the Anti-Discrimination Tribunal, but there had been insufficient recognition of this point in the past.

After yet another adjournment, the tribunal ordered that the respondents should be allowed to examine the complainant medically. It refused to make an order in the terms sought by the complainant's barrister, but 'given the circumstances', strongly recommended that an appropriate female practitioner be selected. The respondents ignored this recommendation. The complainant then decided not to call the psychological evidence and removed the counsellor from her list of witnesses, so as not to be exposed to the further trauma of a medical examination by the respondents' male expert. This matter became the subject of further manoeuvring later in the case, as the complainant's barrister attempted to get in some evidence of the complainant's psychological state without subjecting her client to open season on her records, and the respondents' counsel objected at length at every turn.

Lack of protection

Ironically, while the rules of evidence were used to prevent complainants from giving their accounts of sexual harassment in a full and coherent way, complainants were also deprived of some of the evidentiary protections for primary witnesses that have been introduced by recent reforms. For example, in Case 5, the complainant's sexual history was exposed and explored in a way that would now be prohibited in a rape trial.[54] It was made 'relevant' by the respondent's contention about the complainant's motive for bringing the

---

53   Dr Jocelynne Scutt (barrister), interviewed 20 October 1997.
54   Evidence Act 1958 (Vic), s 37A.

complaint (allegedly in retaliation for the supervisor's disciplining of another worker with whom the complainant had a sexual relationship). Similarly, the tribunal would have a discretion whether to observe the newly enacted privilege for counselling records in sexual assault cases,[55] and would no doubt be urged by the respondent's counsel that it should not apply this particular rule of evidence.

Moreover, it appears that alleged incidents of sexual harassment were dissected in greater and more painful detail than would have been the case in a rape trial. This point was explicitly made by the complainant in Case 5, and was also clearly evident in *Gray*, when the positions and actions of hands, legs, bodies, clothing and furniture were dissected during cross-examination to the minutest degree. While these two cases might be seen as extremes, they illustrate just how far the tribunal could stray from its mandate to 'act fairly and according to the substantial merits of the case'.

It was a persistent theme of my interviews, too, that the tribunal was not assertive enough with the barristers appearing before it, and let them get away with bullying and delaying tactics, to the disadvantage of complainants, rather than setting clear ground rules.[56] At the time of the interviews the tribunal had always had a female President, and was only just beginning to sit occasionally headed by a male Deputy President. The sex of the presiding officer was undoubtedly a factor in barristers' attitudes towards the tribunal, particularly when the barrister was a male QC or otherwise enjoyed considerable seniority, and the woman presiding over the tribunal was a more junior practitioner and/or less experienced in advocacy. This was particularly evident in *Russo* and Case 5, when barristers for the respondent turned on intense displays of charm and bluster respectively, in order to manipulate or terrorise the tribunal. The *Wilson* case provided something of a contrast in this respect. It, too, involved a robust contest between the barristers for each side, but the tribunal, headed by a man, dealt with objections efficiently and decisively, focusing on the actual issues and keeping the case moving.

Conclusion

The legislative definition and prohibition of sexual harassment represented, as Catherine MacKinnon observed, a breakthrough in the legal recognition of women's experience.[57] Unfortunately, while the substantive law may have begun to incorporate women's perspectives, the procedures by which that law

---

55   Evidence (Confidential Communications) Act 1998 (Vic).

56   Ms Melanie Young (barrister), interviewed 22 October 1997; Ms Mandy Chambers (solicitor), interviewed 31 October 1997; Ms Melinda Richards (barrister), interviewed 15 October 1997.

57   MacKinnon, C, *Feminism Unmodified: Discourses on Life and Law*, 1987, Cambridge, Mass: Harvard UP, p 103.

is supposed to be given effect remain selectively deaf to women's stories. Dispensing with the rules of evidence is no answer. As the experience of the Victorian Anti-Discrimination tribunal demonstrates, this simply provides opportunities for the exploitation of uncertainty, the creation of delay, intrusive and abusive questioning under the guise of 'relevance', and removal of such protections as the rules of evidence can provide to complainants.

A more firm and consistent approach by the tribunal would overcome some of these problems. This need not mean that the tribunal should always be presided over by a man. Rather, female Presidents and Deputy Presidents need to be empowered against the tactics of senior male barristers by having a clear conception of how and why the rules of evidence will be applied in any given proceedings. Laying down ground rules, and a rationale for them, which could be articulated by the tribunal and consistently referred to by the tribunal members and barristers alike, would help to quell some of the objections and time wasting behaviour observed.

The rationale for the evidential rules adopted should relate to the nature of the proceedings.[58] Thus, for example, relevance could be established as the basic principle for admission, and relevant hearsay, similar fact and expert evidence could be admitted but be subject to closing submissions on the weight to be attached to such evidence. Given that the tribunal alone is the trier of fact, exclusionary rules designed to ensure that juries do not make decisions on the basis of unsound evidence should have little role to play.[59] This approach would also have the advantage of enabling parties and their witnesses to tell their stories in a complete and coherent way. Other questions on the admission of evidence should be decided by reference to the substantive cause of action. So sexual harassment complainants should, by analogy, be protected from the admission of sexual history evidence or counselling records. Evidence as to the complainant's purported vindictive or vexatious motives for bringing the proceedings should also be disallowed as irrelevant. The focus should remain on whether or not the events alleged as sexual harassment did or did not occur – which the complainant must prove on the balance of probabilities. In addition, the tribunal should limit the

---

58   See Taslitz, A, 'Gender and race in evidence policy: what feminism has to offer evidence law' (1999) 28 Southwestern UL Rev 171, p 197.

59   See, eg, Eser, A, 'Collection and evaluation of evidence in comparative perspective' (1997) 31 Israel L Rev 429; Twining, W, 'Freedom of proof and the reform of criminal evidence' (1997) 31 Israel L Rev 439; van Kessel, G, 'A summary of Mirjan R Damaska's *Evidence Law Adrift*' (1997–98) 49 Hastings LJ 359. Each of these writers argues that exclusionary rules of evidence are necessary where the jury is the trier of fact, but are unnecessary when this is not the case. Van Kessel articulates two further rationales for exclusionary rules of evidence – the temporal concentration of proceedings and party control over the gathering and presentation of evidence – but these rationales do not vitiate the proposal made here. The need to focus the issues and avoid surprise can be achieved by outlines of argument filed before the case begins, and the need to give the opposing party a means to challenge evidence can be achieved by means of (limited) cross-examination and closing submissions.

detailed exploration of matters which cause distress and embarrassment to complainants and do not assist the tribunal to make its determination.

These proposals take up Taslitz' suggestion that standards of admissibility might vary according to the social ends to be served – an approach he identifies specifically as feminist, since it involves attention to the consequences of evidential rules and practices for society as a whole, rather than for any group or individual.[60] In other words, if the social aim of the legislation is to eliminate sexual harassment and provide compensation for those who are unlawfully harassed, the evidential rules applied in sexual harassment proceedings should further that aim. Ideally, too, we need refashioned rules of evidence to facilitate understanding of experiences of sexual harassment, such as persistent behaviour and psychological injury. For example, judicial notice could be taken of the fact that sexual harassment is often repeated, and that it causes significant psychological trauma. This would assist the process of proof in 'pattern and practice' cases, discourage respondents from fishing for alternative explanations for the complainant's psychological injury, and take the notion of rules of evidence designed for the substantive action one step further. Fundamentally, the role of all anti-discrimination tribunals must include the setting of clear evidential parameters, in order to ensure the treatment of all parties with dignity and respect.

---

60 *Op cit*, Taslitz, fn 58, p 215.

CHAPTER 7

RESOLUTION WITHOUT TRIAL, EVIDENCE LAW AND THE CONSTRUCTION OF THE SEXUAL ASSAULT VICTIM[1]

Kathy Mack and Sharyn Roach Anleu

INTRODUCTION

The conventional function of evidence law is to control the information which can be received by a court, the form(s) in which information is presented and the use(s) to which information is put. However, the power of evidence law reaches beyond the confines of the adversary trial, as recognised by recent evidence scholarship which considers 'the way information is processed by all participants throughout the litigation process and not just during adjudication.'[2] Specifically, evidence law influences resolutions without trial in direct practical ways and more subtly as part of law's general constitutive power. By controlling what is accepted as proof, evidential regimes reflect *and* construct the social and cultural context in which they function.[3] In this sense, evidence law, whether operating within or beyond the trial, is a manifestation of the epistemological power of the legal system to determine what counts as knowledge.[4]

We recognise that analysing evidence law and its impact on sexual assault trials has been an important project for feminist legal scholars, and that much has been learned from this work.[5] However, an analysis of the role of evidence law in the prosecution of sexual assault, and the resolution of such charges without trial, is still capable of revealing more about the epistemological power of evidence law in particular and its interaction with other discourses of power.

---

1   Our thanks to Rosemary Hunter and Andrew Ligertwood for helpful comments and to Jan Sidford for her valuable research and editorial assistance.

2   Jackson, J, 'Analysing the new evidence scholarship: towards a new conception of the law of evidence' (1996) 16 OJLS 309, p 317.

3   Taslitz, A, 'Gender and race in feminine evidence policy: what feminism has to offer evidence law' (1999) 28 Southwestern UL Rev 171, pp 179–87; Hunt, A, *Explorations in Law and Society: Toward a Constitutive Theory of Law*, 1993, New York: Routledge.

4   Davies, M, *Asking the Law Question*, 1994, Sydney: LBC, pp 175–76, 225–26.

5   Temkin, J, *Rape and the Legal Process*, 1987, London: Sweet & Maxwell; Torrey, M, 'When will we be believed? Rape myths and the idea of a fair trial in rape prosecutions' (1991) 24 University of California Davis L Rev 1013; Schafran, L, 'Writing and reading about rape: a primer' (1993) 66 St John's L Rev 979; Stewart, M, Dobbin, S and Gatowski, S, '"Real rapes" and "real victims": the shared reliance on common cultural definitions of rape' (1996) 4 FLS 159.

In Australia, as in many other jurisdictions, the evidentiary regime in rape trials (including rules relating to 'prompt' complaints, corroboration, and cross-examination, especially cross-examination about sexual history) depended upon and reinforced many false beliefs about women and sexual assault.[6] Legislation has attempted to change these regimes,[7] in part reflecting a liberal feminist belief that changing laws would alleviate at least some of the harms women experienced within the trial itself and would generate wider understanding about women and sexual assault.[8] More recent research has identified the limitations of liberal beliefs and the reforms they created.[9] Projects on sexing law[10] and the emphasis on literal and metaphorical embodiment[11] have led to a better understanding of the dynamic process of law's role in constituting and constructing society as well as inscribing social power on individuals.[12]

This paper examines the resolution of sexual assault charges without trial. The process of discussion and agreement as to charge and plea exposes a particular instance of the power of evidence law outside the adversary trial.

Concerns about plea bargaining in sexual assault cases have been raised in some empirical research in Australia. For example, Jenny Bargen and Elaine Fishwick report that:

> A number of respondents to our survey questioned the relevance of plea-bargaining as an appropriate mechanism in sexual assault proceedings. Although there is no research material available on plea-bargaining[,] respondents to our survey repeatedly called for the practice to be stopped, which indicates its use is widespread and inappropriate.[13]

How does plea negotiation operate in sexual assault cases, and how do evidence law and its reforms impact on the resolution of sexual assault charges without trial? To answer these questions, we first consider the low conviction rates in sexual assault cases, and note the failure to implement fully reforms to evidence law which it was hoped would improve trial outcomes.

---

6   See, generally, Easteal, P (ed), *Balancing the Scales: Rape, Law Reform and Australian Culture* 1998, Sydney: Federation, especially Chapters 4–7, 9–11.

7   *Ibid*.

8   '... demands for law reform have been grounded in liberalism.' (Mason, G, 'Reforming the law of rape: incursions into the masculinist sanctum', in Kirkby, D (ed), *Sex, Power and Justice*, 1995, Melbourne: OUP, p 52, cited in *ibid*, Easteal, p 209.)

9   Heath, M and Naffine, N, 'Men's needs and women's desires: feminist dilemmas about rape law reform' (1994) 3 Aus Fem LJ 30.

10 Lacey, N, 'On the subject of sexing the subject', in Owens, R and Naffine, N (eds), *Sexing the Subject of Law*, 1997, Sydney: LBC, Chapter 4.

11 Naffine, N, 'The body bag', in *ibid*, Owens and Naffine.

12 Smart, C, *Feminism and the Power of Law* 1989, London: Routledge.

13 Bargen, J and Fishwick, E, *Sexual Assault Law Reform: A National Perspective*, 1995, Canberra: Office of the Status of Women.

Next, we draw on a research project conducted in Australia[14] which examines the resolution of criminal charges by a guilty plea after discussions between prosecution and defence legal representatives, leading to a plea agreement.[15] This research identifies likely trial outcome as the most important factor in both prosecution and defence decision making, and the sentence discount as an important factor influencing defence counsel to advise an accused to plead guilty. We then consider the interaction among these factors in sexual assault cases. We conclude that the limited impact of evidence reforms at trial, and the continued vitality of rape myths, also affect resolution without trial in several ways. Prosecution and defence identification of an appropriate resolution in light of likely trial outcome accepts and reiterates the false beliefs about women and sexual assault which operate in the trial. The analysis used to justify a reduction in sentence for a guilty plea also depends on a particular stereotypical construction of a victim of sexual assault. Thus, it appears that evidence law, whether deployed formally in the criminal trial or indirectly in plea bargaining discussions, promotes, assumes, depends on, ignores or fails to challenge many of the myths about sexual assault and the underlying discourses of gender and power.[16]

A REASONABLE PROSPECT OF CONVICTION?

As most criminal justice professionals know, a formal jury trial of criminal charges is relatively rare. Over 90% of criminal matters in Australia are

---

14 Mack, K and Anleu, S, *Pleading Guilty: Issues and Practices*, 1995, Melbourne: Australian Institute of Judicial Administration. We would like to thank the AIJA for its support of the research project and to note that parts of the text of this paper are drawn directly from the report.

15 Our research into guilty pleas in Australia involved in-depth, semi-structured interviews with judges, police prosecutors, Director of Public Prosecutions staff and defence practitioners (solicitors and barristers). This project included 55 interviews, with a total of 64 interviewees, 52 men and 12 women, in all Australian States. We inquired about present practices and sought views about problems, possible changes and improvements. We also reviewed relevant judicial decisions, legislation, policy and practice statements, published reports and academic writing from Australia and overseas, to form a basis for evaluating Australian practices and attitudes. None of the questions in our focused interview protocol were directly about sexual assault cases, though sexual assault was raised as an unsolicited example of one or another aspect of plea discussions by at least 18 of our interviewees.

We recognise the epistemological issue of the potential gap which may exist between what people say they do and what actually happens. By choosing interviewees from different jurisdictions and from different categories of participants, we elicited information from multiple standpoints, which enables us to draw some general conclusions about Australian practice.

16 See *op cit*, Temkin, fn 5; *op cit*, Torrey, fn 5; *op cit*, Schafran, fn 5.

resolved summarily,[17] and most charges in all jurisdictions are resolved without trial, usually by a guilty plea.[18] The guilty plea is, in a sense, the usual outcome of a criminal charge. However, the picture is somewhat different for sexual assault charges.

Conviction rates

Conviction rates for sexual assault in Australia are relatively low, whether by guilty plea or after trial. For example, in South Australia, during the period from 1981 to 1991, the 'percentage of defendants charged with rape who were convicted as charged fell from 39% to just under 11%'.[19] In 1991, only 4% of offences reported resulted in a finding of 'guilty as charged'.[20] In Victoria, a

---

17 Eg, in calendar year 1997, 97% of the criminal cases in South Australia were heard in the magistrates' court: Office of Crime Statistics, *Crime and Justice in South Australia 1997 – Police, Adult Courts and Corrections*, 1998, Adelaide: AG's Department, Tables 3.1 and 4.7. In 1997, 35,491 criminal cases were finalised in the South Australian magistrates' court, while 1,123 criminal cases were finalised in the higher courts (990 in the district court and 133 in the Supreme Court): Office of Crime Statistics, pp 4, 6. Similar patterns exist in other Australian States: see Findlay, M, Odgers, S and Yeo, S, *Australian Criminal Justice*, 2nd edn, 1999, Melbourne: OUP, p 134.

18 In the South Australian magistrates' courts, of the 35,491 cases finalised in 1997, 57.2% (20,310) pleaded guilty, and a further 0.2% (67) pleaded guilty after the commencement of the trial. In the higher courts, of the total of 1,123 persons charged, 44.3% (497) pleaded guilty to the major offence as charged and a further 7.4% (83) pleaded guilty to another offence; and 2% (23) pleaded guilty after the commencement of the trial. In a further 286 cases (25.4% of the total) the prosecution dropped the major charges: *ibid*, Office of Crime Statistics, Tables 3.35 and 4.1. National comparisons for higher courts show that, in South Australia in 1995, 43.5% of the total cases (1,582) were finalised via a guilty plea; 65.2% of the 4,313 defendants in New South Wales pleaded guilty and 67.4% of the 1,700 defendants in Victoria entered guilty pleas: Australian Bureau of Statistics, *1995: Australian Criminal Courts*, 1997, Canberra: Australian Bureau of Statistics, Table 5).

New South Wales statistics show that 66.5% of persons charged in local court appearances and 62.4% charged in higher courts were sentenced after entering a guilty plea: New South Wales Bureau of Crime Statistics and Research, *New South Wales Criminal Court Statistics 1993*, 1994, Sydney: NSW Bureau of Crime Statistics and Research, pp 11, 65. In the Queensland superior courts, approximately 80% of criminal matters end in a guilty plea: Criminal Justice Commission, Research and Co-Ordination Division, *Evaluation of Brisbane Central Committals Project*, 1996, Brisbane: Criminal Justice Commission, p 39.

Patterns in the UK appear to be similar. About two-thirds of defendants in the Crown Court plead guilty, though there is some variation over time (63% in 1994, 68.7% in 1997) and considerable variation between circuits. See Henham, R, 'Bargain justice or justice denied? Sentence discounts and the criminal process' (1999) 62 MLR 515, pp 517, 524, citing *Judicial Statistics, Annual Report 1994*, Cm 2891, 1995, London: HMSO, p 66; *Judicial Statistics, Annual Report 1996*, Cm 1736, 1997, London: HMSO, Ch 6, and *Judicial Statistics, Annual Report 1997*, Cm 3980, 1998, London: HMSO, Table 6.8.

19 *Op cit*, Heath and Naffine, fn 9, p 48.

20 *Op cit*, Heath and Naffine, fn 9, p 49.

similar filtering takes place, though the drop out rate is different at different stages.[21] Charges are laid in about 40% of cases where rape is reported. About 70–80% of those will be filtered out between charging and prosecution, and less than 44% of cases prosecuted will result in conviction. In 1993–94, in Victoria, of 1,093 rape charges laid, 249 proceeded to prosecution, and 74 were convicted either by a guilty plea or after trial.[22] In a New South Wales study, of the sexual assault matters which went to trial, there was an overall conviction rate of 31%.[23] For cases in which the complainant was an Aboriginal woman, the conviction rate at trial was 25%, and there was a much lower rate of guilty pleas.[24]

Research in Victoria specifically examined non-trial outcomes, including guilty pleas.[25] The accused pleaded guilty to rape in 21% of the cases studied, and to a less serious sexual or non-sexual offence after one or more rape charges had been withdrawn in 25.5% of cases.[26] Of those who pleaded guilty to rape, 72% pleaded guilty to a lesser number of charges and 66.7% did so after negotiations to have charges changed or reduced in number.[27] Over a third (37.7%) of those who pleaded guilty first indicated their intention to do so at committal, 40% did so between committal and trial and 15% entered a guilty plea at or during the trial.[28]

Research in New South Wales covering the period 1988–1993 indicates that the accused pleaded guilty to some sort of sexual assault charge, including lesser offences such as indecent assault, in 26–33% of cases.[29] However, when the principal charge is considered, guilty pleas were entered in 22% of offences studied. About 40% entered a plea of guilty at or immediately after committal,

---

21 In Victoria, the police are the 'key filters in the prosecution process', with the result that convictions at trial may be more frequent than expected. See Brereton, D, '"Real rape", law reform and the role of research: the evolution of the Victorian Crimes (Rape) Act 1991' (1994) 27 A and NZ J Crim 74, p 83; Brereton, D, 'How different are rape trials?' (1997) 37 Br J Crim 242, pp 249–50.

22 Heenan, M and McKelvie, H, *Evaluation of the Crimes (Rape) Act 1991*, 1997, Melbourne: Department of Justice, pp 13–14. See, also, Heenan, M, 'Sex crimes and the criminal justice system' (1997) 9 Aus Fem LJ 90, p 91. In Australia, police lay initial charges and handle cases though committal or preliminary examination. Professional, legally trained prosecutors – the office of Director of Public Prosecutions – generally only become directly responsible for prosecution once the case is committed for a jury trial.

23 Department for Women, *Heroines of Fortitude: The Experiences of Women in Court as Victims of Sexual Assault*, 1996, Sydney: Department for Women, p 76.

24 *Ibid*, p 75.

25 *Ibid*, Heenan and McKelvie, Chapter 6.

26 *Ibid*, Heenan and McKelvie, pp 171–72, 174. 'Rape offence' is defined to mean rape, attempted rape and assault with intent to rape: p 171, fn 138.

27 *Ibid*, pp 171–72.

28 *Ibid*, pp 171–72.

29 *Ibid*, Department for Women, fn 23, pp 65–66.

another one-third at sentence indication and 24% pleaded guilty at or during the trial.

In 1997, defendants facing sexual assault charges in the South Australian higher courts were the least likely to plead guilty as charged. Of the 585 persons facing sexual offence charges, 30.8% pleaded guilty as charged compared with 34.5% of those facing offences against the person charges; 53.5% of those defending robbery and extortion charges and 73.9% of those facing drugs charges. Defendants facing sexual assault charges are also the group most likely to be acquitted. Of those facing sexual offences charges, 23.3% were acquitted, compared with 10.1% of those facing assault charges, 3.9% of those facing robbery charges and 2.6% of those facing drug offences charges.[30]

Statistics for England and Wales also suggest that guilty plea rates are lowest for sexual assault cases 'ranging from as low as 39% in rape cases to a high of 93% in drug possession cases'.[31]

The filtering process which prevents sexual assault reports from leading to conviction is complex,[32] involving many participants and factors. We argue that the low conviction rate after trial and the low guilty plea rate relate to the failure of evidence law reforms and the continued reliance on inaccurate and demeaning constructions of women and sexual violence.

Failure of evidence law reform at trial

Analysis of sexual assault trials and appellate cases in Australia demonstrates that reform of evidence laws which were intended to protect women from unwarranted attacks on their credibility at trial are not being used appropriately. The application of these reforms shows the persistence of negative beliefs about and constructions of women generally and rape victims in particular.[33]

---

30 *Op cit*, Office of Crime Statistics, fn 17, pp 61–64 and Fig 31.

31 *Op cit*, Henham, fn 18, pp 516–17, citing *Criminal Statistics, England and Wales 1996*, Cm 3764, 1997, London: HMSO, Table 7E, p 159; and Flood-Page, C and Mackie, A, *Sentencing Practice: An Examination of Decisions in Magistrates' Courts and the Crown Courts in the Mid-1990s*, Home Office Research Study No 180, 1998, London: HMSO, Figure 8.17, p 89.

32 *Op cit*, Heath and Naffine, fn 9, pp 45–50.

33 *Op cit*, Department for Women, fn 23; *op cit*, Heenan and McKelvie, fn 22; *op cit*, Easteal, fn 6. In *Heroines*, researchers listened to all sound recorded sexual assault matters [150 cases] occurring in a one year period from 1995–96 in the district court of NSW. These cases occurred throughout NSW and represented all cases where the accused person was charged with aggravated sexual assault, sexual assault, assault with intent to have sexual intercourse and attempting any of these offences. In Victoria, Heenan and McKelvie analysed all the 1992 and half the 1993 prosecutions under the Crimes (Rape) Act 1991. They also conducted extensive interviews with legal practitioners, judges and victims/survivors and analysed a sample of judges' instructions to juries. Easteal presents an in-depth legal analysis of all rape law reforms in Australia since the 1970s, including substantive, evidence and procedural law.

Evidence of prior sexual activity was raised without the legally required application to the court in 30% of the trials studied in Victoria,[34] 35% in New South Wales,[35] and 38% in Tasmania.[36] Even where an application is made, the tests prescribed by the legislation may not be applied by the court or they may be applied without any real analysis.[37] Courts which continue to admit sexual history support a social and legal construction of a woman's consent, which, once given to a particular sexual partner, is difficult to withdraw effectively.

Application of the changed evidentiary rules governing recent complaint still constructs truth as established by immediacy and denies the experience of women for whom delay may well be the norm. In evidence law, for a woman who has been raped, truth is demonstrated by immediate complaint; delay indicates fabrication.[38] In most Australian jurisdictions, Parliament has attempted to change this construction of truth by requiring the trial judge to point out to the jury that there may be 'good reasons' for delay.[39] Of the trials studied in New South Wales, the statutory direction about good reasons for delay was given in only half of the cases where it was apparently required.[40] When given, the impact of the positive statutory direction was sometimes weakened by comments emphasising that a delayed complaint could also indicate a lack of credibility. Such negative comments are now permitted, and sometimes required, by the Australian High Court, when needed to 'restore a balance of fairness'.[41]

Continued judicial corroboration warnings maintain an image of women as lacking the capacity for truthfulness about sexual assault, while having a special ability to conceal untruth, an image which resonates with wider fears about false rape claims. Judicial instructions which require a clearer manifestation of consent are seen as inconsistent with conventions of male dominance and female submission in heterosexual sex. Especially harsh treatment of Aboriginal women speaking of sexual assault shows the capacity

---

34 *Op cit*, Heenan and McKelvie, fn 22, p 153.

35 *Op cit*, Department for Women, fn 23, p 230.

36 Henning, T, *Sexual Reputation and Sexual Experience Evidence in Tasmanian Proceedings Relating to Sexual Offences*, 1996, Hobart: Tasmania UP, pp 24–28.

37 Henning, T and Bronitt, S, 'Rape victims on trial: regulating the use and abuse of sexual history evidence', in *op cit*, Easteal, fn 6, p 90.

38 Hunter, R and Mack, K, 'Exclusion and silence: procedure and evidence', in *op cit*, Owens and Naffine, fn 10, p 180.

39 See Crimes Act 1958 (Vic), s 61(1)(b); Crimes Act 1900 (NSW), s 405B; Criminal Code (Tas), s 371A; Evidence Act 1906 (WA), s 36BD; Sexual Offences (Evidence and Procedure) Act 1994 (NT), s 4; Evidence Act 1971 (ACT), s 76C; Evidence Act 1929 (SA), s 34i(6).

40 *Op cit*, Department for Women, fn 23, p 219.

41 *Crofts* (1996) 88 A Crim R 232, p 251.

of evidence law to allow racist and sexist stereotypes to operate in the adversary trial.[42]

Thus, in a sexual assault case, conviction at trial cannot be regarded as a likely outcome, in part because of the failure of evidence reform, so that rape myths continue to operate within the trial.

How does this interact with plea discussions and guilty pleas in sexual assault cases?

GUILTY PLEAS IN SEXUAL ASSAULT CASES

The prosecutor

In Australia, the essential criterion in a prosecutor's decision whether to maintain a prosecution or to reduce charges is that of a 'reasonable prospect of conviction'.[43] Against a background of failure of evidence law reform at trial, and the continued impact of rape myths, the 'reasonable prospect of conviction' criterion will often appear to justify a withdrawal or a reduction of charges in many sexual assault cases. For example, the prosecutor's assessment of likelihood of conviction includes consideration of the 'credibility of witnesses and their likely impression on the arbiter of fact'.[44] The South Australian policy expands on this point by raising questions such as 'Does it appear the witness is exaggerating ... or is either hostile or friendly to the accused or may be otherwise unreliable?' 'Has a witness a motive for telling less than the whole truth?' 'What sort of impression is the witness likely to make: How is the witness likely to stand up to cross-examination?' 'Is there anything which causes suspicion that a false story may have been concocted?'[45]

However, a significant factor in assessing witness credibility at trial is the persistence of inaccurate stereotypes about rape and rape victims which impact on the trial. An investigation of the processes whereby prosecutors decide to reject sexual assault cases shows that they are most likely to reject a case where the assault differs significantly from the so called 'classic rape'

---

42 Mack, K, 'An Australian perspective on feminism, race and evidence' (1999) 28 Southwestern UL Rev 367, and sources cited therein.

43 Commonwealth Director of Public Prosecutions, *Prosecution Policy of the Commonwealth*: www.nla.gov.au/dpp/prospol.html, paras 2.4, 2.5; Director of Public Prosecutions (SA), *Statement of Prosecution Policy and Guidelines*, July 1999, Adelaide: DPP, p 7.

44 *Ibid*, Commonwealth Director of Public Prosecutions, para 2.6; *ibid*, Director of Public Prosecutions (SA), p 7.

45 *Ibid*, Director of Public Prosecutions (SA), p 8.

situation, regardless of whether they themselves believe the victim and agree that rape occurred. Prosecutors assess the evidence and the victim's credibility in light of a hypothetical trial and estimate the jury's likelihood of convicting the defendant. In processing sexual assault cases, prosecutors develop typifications of sexual assault crimes and allegations that deviate from these typifications are generally not pursued.[46] Thus, when assessing sexual assault cases and deciding whether or not to seek a negotiated guilty plea, prosecutors anticipate the nature of any possible trial, rely on their knowledge of juries and common sense notions of heterosexual relations and persistent myths about rape. When the victim's accounts of the rape are inconsistent, notwithstanding 'normal inconsistencies' that are explainable because the victim is upset or confused after the assault, or when the victim's account deviates from prosecutors' typifications of rape-relevant behaviour, then the likelihood of case rejection increases.[47]

Victorian research suggests several factors which lead prosecutors to accept guilty pleas to offences other than rape.[48] Cases involving younger complainants, a complainant who had a relationship with the accused, who changed stories about the assault or who did not suffer identifiable physical injuries were more likely to result in a guilty plea to a non-rape offence, as were cases where the complainant was reluctant to give evidence. When the accused pleaded guilty to a non-rape offence, the median age of the complainant was 14, compared to a median age of 20 when the accused pleaded guilty to rape. Most interesting is the observation that '44.6% of the accused who successfully negotiated a plea to an offence other than rape had made full admissions to rape offences in their interviews with the police'.[49]

Reforms to evidence law could provide protection for women testifying about sexual assault. However, substantial commitment from the prosecutor is necessary to implement these laws, both at trial and in evaluating sexual assault charges for prosecution. If prosecutors do not demand full enforcement at trial of evidentiary laws which challenge stereotypes about rape, such stereotypes will also have a negative impact on decision making in determining when there is a reasonable prospect of conviction to initiate or maintain a sexual assault charge. If charges are reduced or withdrawn, these invalid constructions of women and sexual assault which are a staple of the criminal trial are not challenged, so false beliefs about sexual violence continue. Thus, the unlikelihood of conviction becomes a self-fulfilling

---

46 Frohmann, L, 'Discrediting victims' allegations of sexual assault: prosecutorial accounts of case rejections' (1991) 38 Social Problems 213, pp 213–19. See, also, Frohmann, L, 'Convictability and discordant locales: reproducing race, class and gender ideologies in prosecutorial decision making' (1997) 31 Law & Soc Rev 531, pp 531–37.

47 *Ibid*, Frohmann (1991), pp 216–18. See, also, *op cit*, Stewart *et al*, fn 5.

48 *Op cit*, Heenan and McKelvie, fn 22, pp 175–77.

49 *Op cit*, Heenan and McKelvie, fn 22, pp 175–77.

prophecy and the protection of the law is denied to those who are targets of sexual assault.[50]

The defence

In our research, we found that the primary factor which motivates a guilty plea is the strength of the prosecution case, so that the likely outcome of a trial is the conviction of an accused who has actually committed an offence. If the prosecution case is strong and conviction is certain, a plea of guilty is regarded as the wisest course for prosecution and defence.[51] This was the reason most frequently given in our interviews. A legal aid solicitor indicates that:

> First of all, there is the strength of the prosecution case. In many cases we tend to find that the client is probably guilty of something, although not necessarily the charge that they have been charged with and experience, certainly in New South Wales, has shown that where police are left to charge the person with offences they will always pick the most serious criminal charge rather than what's the most appropriate charge. We tend to find ... that most of our clients have done something, and as a result of that we can then negotiate what is the appropriate charge. ... People are very keen to get matters over and done with, I think it's also fair to say.

Our research showed that defence counsel's advice to plead guilty is perhaps the most significant factor in determining when and whether an accused pleads guilty to a criminal charge, a view which other researchers confirm:

> The defendant, who is likely to be confused and unfamiliar with the intricacies and routines of the court, is in a weak position to question or reject the advice that is offered. Indeed, he [sic] will in most cases be foolish to do so. Most defendants, it seems, are relieved and happy to entrust the case to their legal advisers and to follow whatever advice they are given.[52]

Advice to plead guilty is based on defence counsel's assessment of the likelihood of conviction. Emmelman shows that defence lawyers assess the

---

50 A similar problem may arise for prosecutors where the victims of crime are Aboriginal or non-English speaking, or young or otherwise socially disadvantaged. Because of difficulties they may face in giving clear testimony, or as a result of direct prejudice, a jury may be less likely to believe these persons. If their testimony is a significant element in the prosecution case, conviction may be less likely. However, the effect of choosing not to pursue such a case is to deny the full protection of the law to people who are already among the most vulnerable.

51 Farr, K, 'Administration and justice: maintaining balance through an institutionalised plea negotiation process' (1984) 22 Criminology 291, p 307; JUSTICE, *Negotiated Justice: A Closer Look at the Implications of Plea Bargains*, 1993, London: JUSTICE, p 6; Schulhofer, S, 'A wake-up call from the plea-bargaining trenches' (1994) 19 Law & Soc Inq 135, p 141; Lynch, D, 'The impropriety of plea agreements: a tale of two counties' (1994) 19 Law & Soc Inq 115, p 118.

52 McConville, M and Baldwin, J, *Courts, Prosecution and Conviction*, 1981, Oxford: Clarendon, p 13.

strength of evidence *'through a tacit, taken-for-granted process* that *emulates trial proceedings'*.[53] This process is founded on their implicit understanding of the evidence and its likely reception in a trial process; it is a general and primarily unspoken understanding of evidence.

Rape convictions are regarded as unlikely, for a number of reasons. The victim is perceived as unlikely to testify, given the distress she will experience. As the law of evidence requires oral testimony from a witness who is physically present in the court room,[54] the victim's absence will result in a withdrawal of charges or an acquittal. If the case goes to trial, the jury may be regarded as unlikely to convict as they may be influenced by various myths about 'real' rape and 'real' rape victims.[55] Information about drinking, drug use, sex outside marriage and prior social acquaintance between the defendant and victim will cause jurors to blame the victim, whether the defence is claiming there was consent or that there was no sexual intercourse.[56]

These factors suggest that a defence lawyer will rarely recommend that an accused plead guilty to any sexual assault, certainly not to the most serious charge and especially not at an early stage, when it is unclear whether the victim will actually give evidence. One judge in our study suggests that it is 'a fairly common occurrence, that the accused will wait and see what he can do, whether the victim does turn up pre-hearing'.

However, there are factors which defence lawyers recognise as indicating that a guilty plea may be preferable to a trial. If a conviction results from a trial where a 'real' or 'ideal' victim gives credible evidence in spite of substantial personal distress, the sentence for the accused may be much worse. One defence lawyer explains:

> In a serious assault situation if the person pleads guilty the victim doesn't give evidence and a judge would have the victim's declaration – or in a rape situation, any sort of matter – whereas if he pleads not guilty, then the judge will hear the victim give evidence ... and if that victim comes across in a persuasive manner and speaks of the injury that they sustained or the trauma that they have experienced and ongoing, then that's going to have a greater

---

53 Emmelmann, D, 'Gauging the strength of evidence prior to plea bargaining: the interpretive procedures of court-appointed defense attorneys' (1998) Law & Soc Inq 927, p 928 (emphasis in original). See, also, Emmelmann, D, 'Trial by plea bargain: case settlement as a product of recursive decision making' (1996) 30 Law & Soc Rev 335.

54 Palmer, A, *Principles of Evidence*, 1998, Sydney: Cavendish Publishing, pp 25–26. Note that the law does permit exceptions for special classes of witness (pp 30–35).

55 *Op cit*, Torrey, fn 5; Henning, T, 'The impact of evidence and procedure upon victims', paper given at the Second Annual Evidence Teachers' Conference, February 1999, Sydney; Bronitt, S, 'The rules of recent complaint: rape myths and the legal construction of the "reasonable" rape victim', in *op cit*, Easteal, fn 6; *op cit*, Temkin, fn 5. See, also, *op cit*, Schafran, fn 5; *op cit*, Stewart *et al*, fn 5.

56 LaFree, G, *Rape and Criminal Justice: The Social Construction of Sexual Assault*, 1989, Belmont, CA: Wadsworth, p 226–28.

impact on a judge than if a judge just reads a statement from the victim ... and that may well then influence the judge as to what the penalty is.

Victorian research suggests that, even where there is a plea to a rape offence, about two-thirds of these pleas are to fewer or altered charges.[57] Whether the accused made a full admission to the police is a significant factor. Of accused who plead guilty to at least one rape offence, 53.7% had made such admissions, compared to 6.7% of those who went to trial.[58] A third of those who plead guilty were unknown to the complainant, whereas only 8.6% of accused who went to trial were complete strangers. Interestingly, neither the presence of physical injuries nor prior convictions appeared to influence the likelihood of a guilty plea to a rape offence, though injuries which required medical attention were slightly more likely to be present when the accused plead guilty to a rape offence.

It appears that the stereotypes and myths which have been so damaging at trial, and which reform of evidence law has attempted to ameliorate, are still operating powerfully in the plea discussion process. Though the formal reach of evidence law reform is limited, the artificial construction of truth and credibility created and reinforced by evidence law and its applications at trial still operates, in spite of its inconsistency with the lived experience of those who have suffered sexual assault.

The sentence discount and plea negotiations in sexual assault cases

The other major factor which appears to affect plea negotiations is the offer of a discount on sentence in return for a plea of guilty.[59] The discount rewards the accused for saving money and time which would otherwise be used in a trial and, to some extent, for sparing the victim and witnesses the burden of testimony. Courts and defence counsel believe that the availability of such a benefit, if substantial, can be used to encourage guilty defendants to admit their guilt without trial, and that a greater discount for pleas at an early stage will motivate earlier pleas from those who might otherwise plead guilty on the day of trial.[60] It is also a significant factor in the conduct of defence counsel when persuading a client to plead guilty.[61]

---

57   *Op cit*, Heenan and McKelvie, fn 22, p 172.

58   *Op cit*, Heenan and McKelvie, fn 22, p 173.

59   Mack, K and Roach Anleu, S, 'Sentence discount for a guilty plea: time for a new look' (1997) 1 Flinders J Law Reform 123; Willis, J, 'New wine in old bottles: the sentencing discount for pleading guilty' (1995) 13 Law in Context 39.

60   There is some doubt as to whether the accused is actually significantly motivated by such considerations: see *ibid*, Mack and Roach Anleu; *ibid*, Willis.

61   Coates, R, 'What are the problems from the defendant's perspective?', in Australian Institute for Judicial Administration, *Reform of Court Rules and Procedures in Criminal Cases* (collection of papers presented at AIJA Conference, Brisbane, 3–4 July 1998), 1998, Carlton, Vic: AIJA, p 48.

The discount for a guilty plea is not automatic, nor is it fixed in amount. Several factors may affect the discount.[62] Legislation and case law indicate that an early plea will generally attract a more substantial discount than a late plea.[63] Avoiding a lengthy trial is also a significant factor, as is the nature of the offence, especially where there is concern for a victim.[64] A judge gave a summary:

> ... it's terribly difficult to categorise because there are a number of factors that you'd take into account because they vary from case to case, but I suppose the major ones are the strength of the Crown case in the face of which the plea of guilty is entered; the stage at which the plea of guilty is entered, if it's done at the last moment, then it really isn't worth any particular discount at all; whether or not it indicates genuine contrition; the resources or anxiety in the case of sexual assaults that might be alleviated or saved through the plea of guilty. Those, I suppose spring to mind as the primary four, but there would be a number of others as well.

The discount is not lost because the guilty plea is entered to charges less serious than those originally filed, whether or not there was a real risk of conviction on the more serious charge, or whether the change was a result of plea discussions.[65] A plea when the proof is slight generates a bigger discount when compared with a defendant facing certain conviction whose only merit is saving time,[66] and there may be no discount if the crime is very serious.[67]

A criminal defence lawyer suggested that discounts are more likely to occur after a plea of guilty to sexual offences. She commented that:

> It really comes down to the early plea [which] seems to get some [discount], and your sexual offences, the argument is that, the fact that you've relieved the complainant of a significant amount of stress by entering a plea early is seen as legitimately justifying a discount. Because you have a defendant where there's

---

62 *Op cit*, Henham, fn 18.

63 Legislation: Sentencing Act 1995 (NT), s 5(2)(j); Crimes Act 1900 (NSW), s 439; Sentencing Act 1991 (Vic), s 5(2)(e); Criminal Code Act Compilation Act 1913 (WA), s 19b(1)(b); Penalties and Sentences Act 1992 (Qld), s 13. In the UK, Criminal Justice and Public Order Act 1994, s 48.

Cases: *Winchester* (1992) 58 A Crim R 345; *Harradine* (1992) 164 LSJS 382; *Slater* (1984) 36 SASR 524; *Holder* [1983] 3 NSWLR 245.

For recommendations of a precise statement of graded discounts, see *Reducing Delays in Criminal Cases: Pegasus Taskforce Report*, 1992, Melbourne: AG's Department, pp 24–25; *Report of the Royal Commission on Criminal Justice*, 1993, London: HMSO, pp 111–12, para 47; Seabrook, S, *The Efficient Disposal of Business in the Crown Court*, 1992, London: General Council of the Bar, para 512; Wright, EW, 'Victoria's approach to reducing criminal case delays: specific initiative', 1989, AIJA Eighth Annual Conference, p 42.

64 *Shannon* (1979) 21 SASR 442; *Courtney-Smith (No 2)* (1990) 48 A Crim R 49, p 71; *Nicholls* (1991) 53 A Crim R 455.

65 *Morton* [1986] VR 863, p 867; *Simpson* (1993) 68 A Crim R 439; *Giakas* [1988] VR 973 p 978.

66 *Shannon* (1979) 21 SASR 442, p 453: 'A plea of guilty is not ... a matter of mitigation where it result[s] ... only from recognition of the inevitable.'

67 *Higgins v Fricker* (1992) 63 A Crim R 473, p 479 .

probably a real chance of being acquitted ... [for example,] the rape case where there may not be eye witnesses [other than the complainant/victim]. I suppose he's giving up a chance of being acquitted and she's gaining the security of knowing that she doesn't have to worry about going to trial. So in that case it seems to be accepted as a significant discount.

Other interviews confirmed these factors. As one barrister commented:

I think generally it's [the timing of the plea] the most important factor. I think also the length of the trial or the proposed trial is a matter of significance in the saving of obviously the court's time and trouble. The nature of the case, if it's for instance a case involving negotiations between a paedophile, or a rape case. ... You can save them [the victims] a lot of trauma ...

The strength of the case is also a factor which affects the discount in a rape case. As noted in the quote above, the recognition that the accused is giving up a chance of acquittal is seen as supporting a discount. However, a case where the evidence is perceived as strong will not attract a substantial discount. A defence lawyer comments that 'a rape case where the evidence is overwhelming is not going to attract ... the same sort of discount as a case where ... there are mitigating circumstances in relation to personal matters in relation to the accused'. Note the reiteration of the belief that a relationship between the accused and the witness is seen as weakening the case, in spite of evidence law reform prohibiting or limiting use of sexual history evidence. A judge stated that 'the father who's looking at uncorroborated evidence of sexual crimes from his daughter who pleads expressly to avoid embarrassment would get quite a substantial discount'. Again, note here the emphasis on corroboration as a significant factor in assessing the case, even though evidence law reform emphasises the lack of any requirement of corroboration.

Discounts may be reduced or denied altogether where a guilty plea is only a late recognition of the inevitability of conviction.[68] This may also be true in a sexual assault case, as indicated by one interviewee, who commented that:

... some judges take the view when ... an accused comes along now and pleads guilty on the day, they can't give him [sic] any great discount ... after having the victim – if it had been a girl in a sexual matter – go through the trauma of preparing herself mentally for trial.

A prosecutor put it this way: '... the person who jumps up on a rape charge on their first appearance in court and says "Look, I feel awful, I don't want to put anyone to any trouble. I'll plead guilty" ... They are given ... a recognised discount.' Of course, this person is relatively rare in practice.[69]

---

68 *Shannon* (1979) 21 SASR 442.
69 See text accompanying fns 22–29.

New South Wales research confirms that a plea of guilty in a sexual assault cases in advance of the trial will result in a discount.[70] Judicial comments at sentencing emphasised that the discount recognised the avoidance of distress and humiliation for the victim and that, because the conviction rate is low, the accused has given up a possibility of acquittal. It appears that the particular charge to which the accused pleads guilty is also significant. Victorian research indicates that 'accused who pleaded guilty to at least one count of rape were likely to receive a heavier sentence than those who were found guilty of rape by a jury.' It is suggested that because those 'who pleaded guilty to rape were more likely to be strangers to the victim/survivor, and that the victims were more likely to have sustained physical injuries that required medical treatment', judges were more likely to regard heavier penalties as appropriate.[71] UK research also reflects the complexity of factors which judges consider. On the one hand, it is suggested that guilty pleas to indecent assault which were originally charged as rape may attract a smaller discount because they are serious offences.[72] However, average sentences for those who pleaded guilty to rape was 3.9 years, whereas those who were convicted after a plea of not guilty averaged a sentence of 8.1 years.[73] This suggests a discount of nearly 50% for a guilty plea to rape, though of course there are many factors which affect sentences in rape cases.

The sentence discount is a significant factor on which defence lawyers rely to persuade their clients that a guilty plea is the wisest course. Mike McConville points out that where a sentence discount for a guilty plea is available, conventional ethics now require strong pressure from the defence lawyer to persuade the defendant to plead guilty.[74] As the discount in a sexual assault case can be quite substantial, compared to the sentence the accused would receive after trial, counsel are under a duty to point this benefit out 'in the strongest terms'.[75] Richard Coates, former Chair of National Legal Aid (Australia), candidly commented that a clear benefit to the client, such as an additional sentence discount for an early plea, may also be an effective way to ensure that overworked criminal defence lawyers are motivated to prepare properly and meet their professional obligations.[76] If judges do not give a clear discount for early pleas 'it will not be possible to get defence lawyers to continue to encourage their clients [who will ultimately plead guilty] to enter a plea at committal'.[77]

---

70 *Op cit*, Department for Women, fn 23, pp 291–92.
71 *Op cit*, Heenan and McKelvie, fn 22, pp 248–49.
72 *Op cit*, Henham, fn 18, p 516.
73 *Op cit*, Henham, fn 18, p 517, citing *op cit*, Flood-Page and Mackie, fn 31.
74 McConville, M, 'Plea bargaining: ethics and politics' (1998) 25 JLS 562.
75 *R v Turner* [1970] 2 QB 321.
76 Personal comment from Mr Coates, Brisbane, 3 July 1998, confirmed by fax 12 October 1998.
77 *Op cit*, Coates, fn 61, p 48.

The construction of the victim

Our interviews consistently confirmed one powerful image – the distressed victim, fearing the trauma of trial – so that a negotiated outcome, as early as possible, was invariably constructed as better for the victim, and of course as better for the defendant and for the judicial system. This was mentioned by all categories of interviewees: defence lawyers, prosecutors and, most frequently, by judges. One judge stated:

> ... someone who pleads the night they're picked up on a rape, says 'I did it. I plead guilty to it. Now get me to the judge as soon as you can', deserves a much bigger discount than the person who [pleads], on the morning of the hearing, the woman having had to give evidence at committal and put through the whole thing. All the anxiety, standing there terrified of the court and faced with these people ...

Another judge pointed out that 'if he pleaded guilty to rape, it [an early plea] might be worth something because you can give him credit for not bringing the party along ...'.

A second image that emerged, though less often and more implicitly, was the image of the 'real' or 'ideal' rape victim.[78] According to Terese Henning, the ideal victim is a conservatively dressed woman who sustained serious injuries from an attacker who was a stranger and who used a weapon. She was visibly distressed at the time of the attack and complained to the first person she saw after the attack. She was also manifestly distressed at the trial.[79] She was not under the influence of drugs or alcohol and she was not engaging in 'risky' behaviour, such as inviting a man into her home.[80] She also displayed some resistance.[81] This is precisely the image evidence law reform has attempted to eradicate.[82] Indeed, this dominant image affects rape victims' preparations before testifying in a rape trial. Some research shows that victims are not completely intimidated by the legal process but actively initiate preparations for the scheduled court event. Their preparations were affected by their capacity to conform with cultural stereotypes of rape victims, to manage themselves in an adversarial, legal environment; and to accommodate the potential emotional effects of participating in the trial process. Through these activities, victims aimed to present themselves to judges and juries as credible victims. Those who prepared the least had previous experience with the legal system and their cases conformed most

---

78 *Op cit*, Schafran, fn 5; *op cit*, Torrey, fn 5; *op cit*, Stewart *et al*, fn 5.

79 *Op cit*, Henning, fn 55; *op cit*, Torrey, fn 5.

80 *Op cit*, Stewart *et al*, fn 5.

81 Jamieson, L, 'The social construction of consent revisited', in Adkins, L and Merchant, V, *Sexualising the Social: Power and the Organisation of Sexuality*, 1996, London: Macmillan, pp 55–73.

82 *Op cit*, Torrey, fn 5, p 1041.

closely with classic rape scenarios while those who reported the greatest level of self-preparation had little knowledge of the trial process and had been assaulted by men they knew or had not reported the incident immediately.[83]

Perhaps the most vivid example of the 'ideal' victim ideology is reflected in the comments of a judge:

> If you've got a very grave crime, even a very early plea of guilty would not attract the same discount because of the gravity of the crime ... A middle aged woman walking her dog in the morning was hit over the head with a large rock by a youth passing by and her face was all smashed in. She was left to die. He came back an hour later and then raped her while she was torn and bleeding ... Eventually she was found and fortunately she survived and she was very badly injured. Now he pleaded guilty at an early stage, but the community outrage about the crime was so much that you really couldn't give much of a discount for the early plea of guilty.

Certainly, this victim suffered enormously, but that does not deny the reality of rape and the suffering it causes to other women in less 'ideal' circumstances.

CONCLUSION

There is powerful interaction among the failure of evidentiary law reform at the trial level; prosecution and defence analysis of likely trial process and outcome which necessarily incorporates a consideration of evidentiary issues at trial; the sentence discount which also reflects the likelihood of conviction; the construction of the victim in these processes; and a general system of resolution without trial. This interaction is a clear example of John Jackson's point that 'evidence should be viewed ... as a much more problematic process involving an interaction between what is found or presented with the background and experience of the fact investigator or fact finder'.[84]

The failure of evidence reform in sexual assault trials has several consequences. The victim's distress at trial has not been alleviated by evidentiary reform, at least not as much as was hoped. Trials can still be bad experiences for victims. Images of the 'ideal' rape victim have not been eradicated from the trial, so that convictions in rape cases where the victim is not 'ideal' continue to be difficult to achieve. This ideology of the ideal rape victim is reflected in our interviewees' comments, as well as in other empirical research. These images affect the assessment of the likely trial result and so control the outcome of plea negotiations. Thus, a resolution without trial, even

---

83 Konradi, A, 'Preparing to testify: rape survivors negotiating the criminal justice process' (1996) 10 Gender and Society 404, pp 424–29.

84 *Op cit*, Jackson, fn 2, p 324.

if it means withdrawing the charges, is constructed as better for everyone. Her distress at having to go to trial is alleviated, and the risk that a trial may result in an acquittal, which may be emotionally devastating for her, is avoided. A resolution which results in a guilty plea, even to a much lesser charge and/or accompanied by a minimal sentence, provides the same benefits of trial avoidance, with some vindication for her. To encourage the accused to plead guilty, and to reward him for his generosity to her in pleading guilty to a charge in which he might have a chance of acquittal, he will possibly receive a lesser charge than his conduct actually merits and certainly a lesser sentence.

This presents a real dilemma for a victim of sexual assault. She can choose to give evidence and suffer the distress and humiliation of the trial process. Alternatively, she can acquiesce in a plea agreement, allegedly for her benefit, which results in the reward to the accused of a lesser sentence.[85]

Abolishing particular evidence laws which specifically disadvantage women's testimony in a sexual assault trial is certainly progress. However, it is clear that the effectiveness of these reforms at trial has been limited. Worse, a system where very few cases actually get to trial, and where the reforms are undermined within those trials which do occur, creates an even greater space for police, lawyers and judges to apply their own misconceptions, which further undermine and nullify the positive impact which law reform should have. It is 'now thoroughly documented ... that the legal profession is not applying the reformed laws of sexual offences' and that 'popular sexist myths ... are part of the culture of the legal profession'.[86] Invisibility and informality of plea negotiations and resolution without trial can conceal injustice.[87] Both prosecution and defence need to be aware of the sometimes subtle and indirect ways attitudes about women, men and sexual assault impact on decision making, powerfully reinforcing wider social patterns of disadvantage. Their own perceptions about who is credible (and who the jury

---

85 *Op cit*, Department for Women, fn 23, p 293.

86 Rush, P and Young, A, 'A crime of consequence and a failure of legal imagination: the sexual offences of the model criminal code' (1997) 9 Aus Fem LJ 100, pp 121–22. Feminist reformers have focused on gender and racial awareness training for police, judges, lawyers and law students. Such education programs are underway in Australia and in other jurisdictions such as Canada, the US and New Zealand: Mack, K, 'Gender awareness in Australian courts: violence against women' (1995) 5 Crim Law Forum 788; Mahoney, K, 'International strategies to implement equality rights for women: overcoming gender bias in the courts' (1993) 1 Aus Fem LJ 115.

87 For a general review of the advantages and disadvantages of plea negotiations, see *op cit*, Mack and Anleu, fn 14, pp 7–12; Bishop, J, *Prosecution Without Trial*, 1989, Sydney: Butterworths, pp 4, 184; Byrne, P, 'Plea bargaining' (1988) 62 ALJ 799, pp 799–800; Clark, P, 'The public prosecutor and plea bargaining' (1986) 60 ALJ 199 pp 199–200, 208–10; Sallmann, P, *Report on Criminal Trials* 1985, Melbourne: AIJA, pp 136–37; and Wundersitz, J, Naffine, N and Gale, F, 'The production of guilt in the juvenile justice system: the pressures to "plead"' (1991) 30 Howard J of Crim Justice 192, p 197 (on the Children's Court).

will regard as credible) will inevitably impact on their assessment of the likely outcome of a sexual assault trial.[88]

This 'subversion and circumvention of rape law reform is often presented as evidence of entrenched patriarchy and misogyny within our legal culture'.[89] However, the legal culture's attitudes must be located within a wider entrenched social acceptance of these beliefs, which are reflected and reinforced by actors at every stage in the legal system. Anne Edwards and Melanie Heenan argue that the fundamental obstacle is not:

> ... the law and the criminal justice system, but ... the cultural beliefs and power relationships of patriarchal society which shape the social and sexual expectations and practices of men and women and the moral and social interpretations and evaluations of situations where rape is alleged.[90]

Regina Graycar has commented that, through the process of judging, judges 'create' or construct women's lives.[91] A similar effect is created within the process of plea discussions, where the police, the prosecution and the defence combine to reconstitute the events and to reconstruct the participants in a way which:

> ... perpetuates long-established sexist assumptions about women, and their unreliability and deceitfulness as witnesses, that recent legislative reforms are specifically intended to exclude from the trial process.[92]

Thus, the reiteration of sexist (or racist) images in plea discussions is more complex than may first appear. When a sexual assault case is discussed and a resolution agreed to, the behaviour of the complainant is evaluated in accordance with legal and social norms which are proclaimed by the law to be 'common sense' about prompt complaint, corroboration and previous sexual conduct. However, these meanings are not part of the 'common sense' of many women who have experienced sexual assault.[93] When the law repeatedly deploys this alleged 'ordinary human experience', it demonstrates a persistent failure to accommodate the reality of women's experience of sexual abuse.[94]

An adequate explanation for the failure of evidentiary law reform in sexual assault cases must recognise the power of legal discourse. Carol Smart warns that:

---

88 *Op cit*, Bronitt, fn 55, pp 42–43; *op cit*, Rush and Young, fn 86, pp 101, 120–22.

89 *Op cit*, Bronitt, fn 55, p 42.

90 Edwards, A and Heenan, M, 'Rape trials in Victoria: gender, socio-cultural factors and justice' (1994) 27 A & NZ J Crim 213.

91 See Graycar, R, 'The gender of judgments', in Thornton, M (ed), *Public and Private: Feminist Legal Debates*, 1995, Adelaide: OUP, p 267.

92 *Ibid*, Edwards and Heenan, p 225.

93 van de Zandt, P, 'Heroines of fortitude', in *op cit*, Easteal, fn 6, p 138.

94 *Op cit*, Hunter and Mack, fn 38, pp 181–83.

Feminist reform efforts are inevitably co-opted by legal knowledge and legal victories, so that no matter how radical they appear, such reforms actually extend the power of law. Ironically, using law to undercut dimensions of oppression serves to reinforce the dominance of law. Law remains one of the most powerful discourses; it invalidates other kinds of knowledge, especially feminism, or selectively incorporates those which most easily fit into its predefined categories.[95]

The idea that law is a powerful constitutive discourse does not lead inevitably to the conclusion that all feminist law reform must fail. Understanding the power of law also suggests that, if this immense power can be redirected, it can generate different constructions of women, of men, of sex. Challenging this intersection between the legal culture and wider social cultures requires recognising the constitutive function of evidence law and understanding that evidence law does not operate only in the criminal trial but works at all stages of the criminal justice process. Simon Bronitt argues that the 'most effective way to displace the discriminatory stereotypes which continue to dominate rape trials [and the plea discussion process] is to generate an alternative narrative ... which is both empirically and normatively sound'.[96]

One place in which this alternative narrative can be generated is in the criminal trial itself, which can have a powerful educative and even transformative function. One of the researchers in the New South Wales study tells us:

> I got a true sense of the power of a judge in a sexual assault case – not from hearing countless comments that infuriated me, but from hearing a few comments from judges which were wonderfully wise, empowering and affirming for the woman complainant ...
>
> This judge said the woman complainant was a 'heroine of fortitude'[97] and said it was 'a tribute to the human spirit that she has survived' ... And then I realised just how powerful these people are. During the research, I also felt uplifted by the many comments made by judges about women's lives, their feelings and their difficulties.[98]

We must seriously honour the courage of women who have reported their experience of sexual assault by resisting the temptation to accept inappropriate resolutions without trial, which reinforce the very constructions of women and men which are acted out in sexual assault. At the very least, prosecutors must consult with each woman who may testify about sexual

---

95 Smart, C, 'Law's power, the sexed body, and feminist discourse' (1990) 17 JLS 194, p 196.

96 *Op cit*, Bronitt, fn 55, p 57.

97 The NSW report takes its title from this statement by Madgwick J, (1994) District Court Case No 94/41/1/0177, Wollongong (unreported).

98 *Op cit*, van de Zandt, fn 93, p 137.

assault to find out whether she does indeed prefer a resolution without trial. Heenan and McKelvie report that in some cases, the victim's desire not to continue is a significant factor in the prosecution's decision to withdraw charges. However, in other cases, they report considerable distress from some complainants whose cases did not go to trial.[99] Victorian research suggests that such consultations were generally undertaken, though some victims were strongly dissatisfied with the process and the outcome.[100] While there is clearly an obligation on prosecutors to make an independent decision about the likelihood of conviction and whether to accept a negotiated outcome, there should also be an obligation to provide victims the greatest support the evidence laws allow and to indicate this support.

Prosecutors must be sensitive to all these circumstances and weigh the decision to maintain or withdraw prosecution with special care. Maintaining prosecution may be necessary to emphasise the seriousness and wrongfulness of sexual assault, to provide adequate deterrence, and to combat myths about sexual assault in the community. Prosecution guidelines state that a decision to prosecute must not be influenced by 'race ... sex ... national origin'.[101] This is surely an admirable goal. However, in Australia today, these qualities inevitably do have an impact on the prospect of conviction. Recognising this impact is an essential part of the prosecutor's responsibility. Ignoring this social reality can maintain or even aggravate wider social inequalities. Perhaps a better statement of the principle which should guide prosecutors is from an American judge: '... prosecutors have an affirmative duty to make sure that racial and national origin *bias*, as well as gender *bias and prejudice*, do not enter into their charging decisions [and] their plea bargaining decisions.'[102] Canada's Martin Report emphasised the same point: 'Racism, sexism, and other forms of discrimination have no place in the administration of criminal justice.'[103]

Adequate support is needed for trials which can empower and heal, in part by insisting that evidentiary law reform be implemented, not undermined. Rather than using the terror of trials as an excuse to withdraw or

---

99   *Op cit*, Heenan and McKelvie, fn 22, Chapter 6.

100 *Op cit*, Heenan and McKelvie, fn 22, pp 181–83.

101 *Op cit*, Commonwealth Director of Public Prosecutions, fn 43, para 2.13(a); *op cit*, Director of Public Prosecutions (SA), fn 43, p 11; Western Australian Statement of Prosecution Policy and Guidelines, s 32(a).

102 Burnett, AL, 'Permeation of race, national origin, and gender issues from initial law enforcement contact through sentencing: the need for sensitivity, equalitarianism and vigilance in the criminal justice system' (1994) 31 Am Crim LR 1153, p 1169 (emphasis added).

103 AG's Advisory Committee, *Charge Screening, Disclosure, and Resolution Discussions*, 1993, Ontario: AG's Advisory Committee, p 91.

reduce charges, the remedy must be to improve the pre-trial and trial experience. A properly conducted sexual assault trial, rather than a negotiated outcome, can be an important component in reconstructing both evidence law and the wider society.

CHAPTER 8

CORROBORATION AND SEXUAL ASSAULTS IN SCOTS LAW

*Pamela R Ferguson**

INTRODUCTION

Sexual assaults are generally more difficult to prove than most other crimes. Statistics produced by the Scottish Executive show that in respect of all crimes and offences, 88% of persons called before the criminal courts in Scotland in 1998 were convicted of, or pleaded guilty to, at least one charge.[1] A verdict of 'not guilty' following trial was recorded in only 3% of cases, with a further 1% receiving a 'not proven' verdict.[2] This is in contrast to the position in relation to sexual assaults, in which 71% were convicted, 15% were found 'not guilty', and a further 8% were 'not proven'.[3] One reason for this lower conviction rate lies in the difficulty of finding corroborated evidence in substantiating allegations of sexual assault. This chapter considers the corroboration requirement in Scots law in relation to rape and other sexual offences, and also describes developments in the use of 'corroboration by distress'. While the focus is mainly on Scotland, reference is made to English law for comparative purposes.

THE SUBSTANTIVE LAW

Before the evidentiary aspects can be discussed, a short description of the substantive law is required, and the differences between English and Scots law will be highlighted briefly. The Sexual Offences Act 1956 now defines rape in

---

* My thanks are due to Fiona Raitt for her many helpful comments on earlier versions of this chapter.

1 Criminal Proceedings in Scottish Courts, CrJ/1999/8, December 1999, Table 4. In a further 9% of cases, the charges were deserted, or the accused's plea of 'not guilty' was accepted by the Crown. The figure for deserted cases/not guilty plea accepted for sexual assaults was 7%.

2 The 'not proven' verdict is a verdict of acquittal. It does not allow the accused to be prosecuted at a later date for the same crime, and is technically the same as a verdict of 'not guilty'.

3 There is no separate category of 'rape'. The term 'sexual assault' includes rape, assault with intent to rape, and indecent assault.

English law to include non-consensual anal intercourse thereby making this, at least linguistically, a 'gender neutral' crime so far as its victims are concerned.[4] Scots law continues to distinguish rape of a female from buggery of a male or female. Rape in Scots law is defined as carnal knowledge of a female person by a male person, obtained by overcoming her will.[5] 'Carnal knowledge' is limited in this context to penetration of the vagina by the penis. Oral or anal penetration is regarded as sexual assault, but not rape. The emphasis on the 'overcoming of the will' in the Scots definition means that intercourse with a woman who is in a state of extreme intoxication may not be rape in Scotland (unlike in England).[6] This is on the basis that a complainer who is very drunk has no will to overcome, hence cannot be raped.[7] Instead,

> ... to take advantage in this way of a drunken woman, whose intoxication is solely due to her own voluntary actions, and who is, as a consequence, in no condition to refuse or resist, constitutes the crime of indecent assault.[8]

Sexual intercourse with a sleeping woman is not rape, for the same reason.[9] Such indecent assaults are given the rather euphemistic term 'clandestine injury to women'.[10] As Edwards has written:

> Whilst women are in the main the victims, the domain of sexual assault has been nevertheless largely defined by men, and masculinist legal definitions have circumscribed what conduct constitutes sexual assault for legal purposes.[11]

In Scots law, whether a woman has been 'raped' or not is viewed from the perspective of the perpetrator rather than the victim. The fact that a man has had sexual intercourse with a woman without her consent does not determine the legal classification of the incident. If the woman was extremely intoxicated at the time of the intercourse, one must inquire whether she took the drink voluntarily, or whether the accused plied her with drink. In either case, the

---

4   Sexual Offences Act 1956, s 1, as amended by the Criminal Justice and Public Order Act 1994, s 142. See, also, Rumney, P and Morgan-Taylor, M, 'Recognizing the male rape victim: gender neutrality and the law of rape' (1997) 26 Anglo-Am L Rev, pp 198–234, 330–56. For an argument that rape is now 'gender neutral' only in a linguistic sense, see Hunter, RC, 'Gender in evidence: masculine norms vs feminist reforms' (1996) 19 Harv Women's LJ 128.

5   English cases have made it clear that rape is not defined in that jurisdiction as intercourse 'against her will', but rather is intercourse without consent – see *R v Camplin* [1845] 1 Den 89; *R v Fletcher* [1859] Bell CC 63; *R v Olugboja* (1981) 73 Cr App R 344.

6   *R v Larter and Castleton* [1995] Crim LR 75.

7   See *HM Advocate v Logan* 1935 JC 100. English law uses the term 'complainant', and Scots law 'complainer'. The latter term has been used for consistency throughout this chapter, since it deals mainly with Scots law.

8   *Sweeney v X* 1982 SCCR 509, p 523.

9   *Charles Sweenie* (1858) 3 Irv 109; *Fox v HM Advocate* 1998 SCCR 115.

10   *Charles Sweenie* (1858) 3 Irv 109.

11   Edwards, SSM, *Sex and Gender in the Legal Process*, 1996, London: Blackstone, p 322.

woman may be equally intoxicated and equally abused, and may feel that she has been raped, but only in the latter situation is she regarded as having been raped in the eyes of the law. Attacks by feminist writers on the definitions of sexual assaults in other jurisdictions apply with equal force to Scots law definitions.[12] The focus of this chapter is not, however, on the substantive law but on an evidentiary aspect, namely, the requirement in Scots law for corroborated evidence.[13]

CORROBORATION

English law

In relation to English law it has been stated that:

> Until recently, requirements for corroboration played an important part in the law of evidence in criminal cases. But ... almost nothing remains of this once major common law rule ... the general rule is that any judgment or conviction may be based on the uncorroborated evidence of a single witness or on uncorroborated evidence of any other kind.[14]

Although a finding of corroboration was not a prerequisite for conviction, until 1994 a corroboration warning was required in cases involving alleged sexual offences[15] and an English jury may yet be warned of the perils of convicting an accused person on the basis of a complainant's uncorroborated testimony.[16] While this warning applied to sexual offences other than rape, including those with male victims, the approach of the courts prior to 1994 is epitomised by the oft-quoted words of Salmon LJ in *R v Henry*:[17]

---

12 See, eg, Lees, S, *Carnal Knowledge: Rape on Trial*, 1996, London: Penguin; Temkin, J, *Rape and the Legal Process*, 1987, London: Sweet & Maxwell; Adler, Z, *Rape on Trial*, 1987, London: Routledge.

13 For a comparison of the substantive law of rape in Scotland and England, see Ferguson, PR, 'Controversial aspects of the law of rape: an Anglo-Scottish comparison', in Hunter, R (ed), *Justice and Crime: Essays in Honour of The Right Honourable The Lord Emslie*, 1993, Edinburgh: T & T Clark. A detailed discussion of the Scots law of evidence is outside the scope of the present paper, but see Field, D and Raitt, F, *Evidence*, 1996, Edinburgh: Green; MacPhail, I, *Evidence*, 1987, Edinburgh: Law Society of Scotland; Sheldon, D, *Evidence: Cases and Materials*, 1996, Edinburgh: Green.

14 Murphy, P, *Murphy on Evidence*, 6th edn, 1997, London: Blackstone, pp 505–06. See, also, Tapper, C, *Cross and Tapper on Evidence*, 8th edn, 1995, London: Butterworths, pp 255–56.

15 See Criminal Justice and Public Order Act 1994, s 32(1)(b).

16 More than half of the States in the US continue to allow a corroboration warning to be given in rape cases – see Mack, K, 'Continuing barriers to women's credibility: a feminist perspective on the proof process' (1993) 4 Criminal Law Forum 327, p 339.

17 (1968) 53 Cr App R 150.

[H]uman experience has shown that in these courts girls and women do sometimes tell an entirely false story which is very easy to fabricate, but extremely difficult to refute. Such stories are fabricated for all sorts of reasons, which I need not now enumerate, and sometimes for no reason at all.[18]

In *R v Makanjuolo*,[19] the Court of Appeal made it clear that there remains a discretion to warn the jury of the dangers of relying on uncorroborated testimony in such cases, if the judge thinks it necessary to do so. While emphasising that the mere fact that the witness is a complainant in a case of alleged sexual assault is not sufficient for the warning to be given, Lord Taylor also stressed that the Court of Appeal would be '... slow to interfere with the exercise of discretion by a trial judge who has the advantage of assessing the manner of a witness's evidence as well as its content'.[20]

Scots law

The situation in Scotland is altogether different. For the vast majority of crimes in Scots law, corroborative evidence is an essential requirement.[21] According to Baron Hume, one of the 'Institutional Writers':

... no one shall in any case be convicted on the testimony of a single witness. No matter how trivial the offence, and how high so ever the credit and character of the witness, still our law is averse to rely on his single word, in any inquiry which may affect the person, liberty, or fame of his neighbour; and rather than run the risk of such an error, a risk which does not hold when there is a concurrence of testimonies, it is willing that the guilty should escape.[22]

Although the reference to the need for 'a concurrence of testimonies' suggests that the prosecution would have to lead evidence from at least two witnesses, what was really required was evidence from two independent sources. While this could be provided by testimony from two eye-witnesses, it could equally consist of any two from a range of other evidence, including 'real evidence', forensic evidence, admission by the accused, and circumstantial evidence. As Hume himself stated:

It would not ... be a reasonable thing, nor is it our law, that the want of a second witness to the fact cannot be supplied by the other circumstances of the

---

18   (1968) 53 Cr App R 150, p 153.

19   [1995] 2 Cr App R 469.

20   *Ibid*, p 472.

21   For a description of the corroboration requirement in general, see Gordon, GH, 'At the mouth of two witnesses: some comments on corroboration', in *op cit*, Hunter, fn 13, p 33.

22   Hume, D, *Commentaries on the Law of Scotland Respecting Crimes*, Bell, R (ed), 4th edn, 1844 (reprinted 1986), Vol 2, p 383. The works of the 'institutional writers' such as Hume are regarded as authoritative; Hume has been referred to as '*the* source of the non-statutory law' in Scotland (Christie, M, *Breach of the Peace*, 1990, Edinburgh: Butterworths, p 1; emphasis in original).

case. If one man swear that he saw the pannel [the accused] stab the deceased, and others confirm his testimony with circumstances, such as the pannel's sudden flight from the spot, the blood on his clothes, the bloody instrument found in his possession, his confession on being taken, or the like; certainly these are as good, nay better even than a second testimony to the act of stabbing.[23]

In the case of *Lockwood v Walker*,[24] Lord Justice-Clerk Macdonald stated:

No doubt our law does not require that every fact in a case shall be proved by two witnesses, but it most certainly does require that every *crucial fact* shall be so proved, or proved where there is only one witness by corroborative facts and circumstances proved, or by corroborative documentary evidence.[25]

The Crown can establish many facts in a criminal case without providing corroborated evidence, but the fundamental or 'crucial' facts, often referred to as the *facta probanda*, require to be proved in this manner. The Crown requires

... to corroborate not only the identification of the accused as the person who committed the crime but also the fact that the crime itself had been committed, since that fact is a crucial fact.[26]

In practice, therefore, the prosecution must produce evidence from two separate sources to establish that

(a) a crime was committed; and

(b) the accused was the perpetrator.

In the case of *Morton v HM Advocate*,[27] it was stated:

This rule has provided an invaluable safeguard in the practice of our criminal courts against unjust conviction, and it is a rule from which the courts ought not to sanction any departure.[28]

The Lord Justice-Clerk also reaffirmed that it was the 'conjunction of *separate and independent* testimonies, each incriminating, that makes corroboration'.[29]

Morton was decided in 1938. Whether the corroboration requirement remains as strong today is debatable. While it has often been claimed that the

---

23 *Op cit*, Hume, fn 22, p 384. See, also, Alison's *Practice of the Criminal Law*, 1833, Edinburgh: W Blackwood, p 551: 'The evidence of a single witness, how clear and conclusive soever, is not sufficient to warrant a conviction; but the evidence of one witness is sufficient, if it is supported by a train of circumstances.'

24 *Lockwood v Walker* 1910 SC (J) 3; 1910 6 Adam 124; 1909 2 SLT 400.

25 *Lockwood v Walker* 1910 SC (J) 3, p 5. Emphasis added.

26 *Smith v Lees* 1997 SCCR 139, p 145.

27 *Morton v HM Advocate* 1938 JC 50.

28 *Ibid*, p 55, *per* Aitchison LJC. See, also, Burnett, J, *A Treatise on Various Branches of the Criminal Law in Scotland*, 1811, Edinburgh: G Ramage, p 518; *Smith v Lees*, 1997 SCCR 139, p 142.

29 *Ibid*. Emphasis added.

notorious miscarriages of justice which occurred in England (such as that of the Birmingham Six, Guildford Four, Maguire Seven, Judith Ward and the like) would not have occurred in Scotland because of the need for corroborated evidence,[30] it may be argued that this requirement has, in reality, been whittled down to a rather minimal one. In relation to confession evidence, the need for corroboration means that, in theory, an extra-judicial admission by an accused person is not enough to secure a conviction. In reality, however, Scots law allows for what is called the 'self-corroborating' confession. This means that where the accused's confession contains information that only the perpetrator of the crime would know, then the confession requires no additional evidence to support it. Confessions have been treated as being self-corroborating where the information contained therein was not new information, known only to the perpetrator, but rather consisted of details about the crime which were not in the public domain. Such information could have been known by the police. Although this provides a safeguard against those persons who 'confess' to crimes which they have not in fact committed,[31] it does nothing to safeguard against the possibility that the police have fabricated the confession, or coerced the accused into writing it.[32]

The corroboration requirement has been weakened in other areas too, notably in relation to identification evidence, such that the High Court itself has stated that 'where one starts with an emphatic positive identification by one witness then very little else is required'.[33] Gordon has concluded:

> The requirements of corroboration ... are fairly weak ... It is not the law that an accused cannot be convicted unless there is evidence from two sources each of which 'points to guilt', or evidence from two sources 'implicating' him, in the once-classic definition in *Morton*.[34]

He later states:

> All that is required is evidence from one source, together with some independent evidence giving some support to that source. Once that is present,

---

30 For a description of these cases, see Ashworth, A, *The Criminal Process*, 1994, Oxford: Clarendon, pp 10–12.

31 For an example of a false confession, fabricated by the accused himself, see *Boyle v HM Advocate* 1976 SLT 126.

32 For a detailed critique of the self-corroborating confession, see Gordon, G, 'At the mouth of two witnesses: some comments on corroboration', in *op cit*, Hunter, fn 13.

33 *Ralston v HM Advocate* 1987 SCCR 467. See, also, *Nelson v HM Advocate* 1988 SCCR 536, in which a positive identification by one witness was corroborated by the fact that a second witness picked out the accused at an identification parade on the basis that he was of the same build as the perpetrator. A recent case is *Adams v HM Advocate* 1999 SCCR 188, in which the witness said at an identity parade that the accused 'resembled' the robber, but could not elaborate on this.

34 *Fox v HM Advocate* 1998 SCCR 115, p 150.

there is sufficient evidence in law and the case should go to the jury for them to decide whether the evidence is weighty enough to convince them of guilt.[35]

CORROBORATION AND SEXUAL OFFENCES

At the heart of the corroboration requirement is a belief that

(a) witnesses may lie; or

(b) they may be mistaken in their evidence.

In relation to the act of intercourse without her consent, a complainer is most unlikely to be 'mistaken' about this, hence it is a fear of fabricated allegations which is said to justify the requirement for corroboration.[36] Since the biblical story of Potiphar's wife, it has been widely believed that women frequently make false allegations of rape.[37] As against this, it is commonly believed that the Scottish 'not proven' verdict is resorted to in preference to 'not guilty' where a complainer's testimony is in fact believed, but there is insufficient corroboration of her evidence for a verdict of guilty. This is supported by recent statistics: in relation to crimes and offences generally, 22% of all acquittals in 1998 were verdicts of 'not proven', but the equivalent figure for sexual assaults was considerably higher, at 35%.[38] Empirical studies have also shown that the belief that women commonly make false allegations of rape is an unfounded one.[39] Any evidentiary rules that impose higher hurdles of proof in rape cases therefore discriminate against rape complainers for no sound reason. It is accordingly unacceptable for a legal system to require corroboration in relation to some offences only, such as rape or sexual offences. Likewise, a system which provides for a 'corroboration warning' in respect of the testimony of certain *witnesses* must demonstrate that there is something intrinsically different, intrinsically 'less trustworthy' about the testimony of that class or classes of witness. Again, given the lack of evidence of increased fabrication of testimony in sexual offences, a corroboration warning, which applies to such complainers only, would be unacceptable.

The problem with corroboration in Scots law appears to be an altogether different one. It does not, in theory, treat female testimony differently from

---

35 *Fox v HM Advocate* 1998 SCCR 115.

36 She could, of course, be mistaken as to the identity of the accused as the perpetrator. In the vast majority of cases, however, the accused does not deny that he had intercourse with the complainer, hence identity is rarely at issue.

37 Genesis 39.

38 Criminal Proceedings in Scottish Courts, CrJ/1999/8, December 1999, Table 4.

39 Mack cites an empirical study which found that 1.6% of rape allegations were false, as opposed to 2.6% of stolen car complaints: *op cit*, Mack, fn 16, p 336. See, also, *op cit*, Lees, fn 12, pp 124–27.

that given by male witnesses, nor discriminate against rape complainers or victims of sexual assault, *per se*. Yet it remains the case that, contrary to Hale's oft-quoted description, rape is an allegation which is difficult to make, and *more difficult to prove* than other crimes.[40]

A recent textbook on sexual offences in English law states that 'the basic rules of evidence apply to sexual offences as they do to any other criminal allegation',[41] and the position in Scots law is similar; whether an accused person is charged with murder, assault, robbery, theft, or rape, the requirement for corroboration applies. However, as Hunter has argued:

> Since most adult sexual offenses – for which charges are brought – are committed against women, we can begin to see a gendered slant to the rules of evidence.[42]

Although the need for corroborated evidence in Scots law is not peculiar to rape cases, it does make successful prosecution of such cases more difficult than other crimes. Rape is a crime that is commonly committed in private, hence eye witnesses are rare.[43] In rape cases, the *facta probanda* or crucial facts are:

(a) penetration of the complainer's vagina,

(b) by the accused's penis,

(c) forcibly, and

(d) against the complainer's will.[44]

With the advent of DNA profiling, establishing (a) and (b) is generally less of a problem than hitherto. A more difficult problem lies in establishing that the accused had intercourse with the complainer 'against her will'.

Where the complainer alleges that she was raped and the accused maintains that she was a willing participant, corroboration of the former's testimony may be found by evidence of the forceful nature of the intercourse. Hence the Crown may rely on the complainer's physical injuries, such as cuts and bruises, to corroborate her account. It is not uncommon for an accused to allege that minor bruising can be explained by the fact that this was part of rough, but consensual, sex. The more severe the injuries, the greater the

---

40 Hale contended that rape was an accusation 'easy to be made and hard to be proved, and harder to be defended by the party accused, tho' never so innocent': Hale, M (Sir), *The History of the Pleas of the Crown* (1736), 1971, London: Professional, p 634.

41 Hill, B and Fletcher-Rogers, K, *Sexually Related Offences*, 1997, London: Sweet & Maxwell, p 19.

42 Hunter, RC, 'Gender in evidence: masculine norms vs feminist reforms' (1996) 19 Harv Women's LJ 127, p 128.

43 Hunter's article focuses on 'private relations' which she describes as 'events that usually occur without witnesses, often in a domestic setting, and often between intimates'. She suggests that '[t]his element of privacy is an important factor in understanding why the rules of evidence have difficulty dealing with cases involving sexual behavior or violence against women': *ibid*, p 129.

44 *Smith v Lees* 1997 SCCR 139, p 144. It was stated that '[t]hese four fundamental facts require to be established by corroborated evidence'.

prospect of convincing a jury that she was not a willing participant. This, of course, has limitations. If the accused has managed to overcome the complainer's will by use of threats, there may be no distinctive physical injuries. Hence, where an assailant threatened to use a knife, or succeeded in intimidating the complainer into submission by sheer physical presence, there may be no visible injuries to corroborate her version of events. As Edwards has demonstrated, convictions in England are less common if no, or minimal, violence is apparent.[45] She also quotes Mike Tyson's comment to his appeal lawyers: 'If I had all my weight on her [the complainer] she'd have been black and blue, but she had no bruises. If she had no bruises then it couldn't have happened the way she said it happened'.[46]

In both Scotland and England the forensic process attempts to secure physical evidence to support the woman's version of events. A recent textbook on sexual offences describes this process as follows:

> Physical examination should take place as soon as possible and *certainly* before the victim has bathed. He or she will be asked to undress on a clean sheet of paper. Clothing may be required for forensic examination and he or she will be examined for injuries, bruises, scratches, bite marks, etc.[47]

No mention is made of the fact that feelings of being 'unclean' or 'dirty' lead many victims to clean themselves up before they go to the police. Indeed, the violation causes some women to scrub themselves for a prolonged period.[48] Although this is not helpful, from a forensic/evidentiary point of view, the use of the word 'certainly' in the above paragraph (rather than, say, 'ideally' or 'if at all possible') might suggest to the reader that it would be unreasonable for a complainer to have washed before contacting the police, thus denying a woman's common reaction that washing is essential to try to counter the feelings of violation.

A lack of bruises, scratches, or bite marks may weaken the prosecution case in England, since a jury may be less likely to believe a complainer who cannot provide physical injuries to support her testimony. In Scotland this does more than weaken the case; a lack of physical injuries may prove fatal to the prosecution. As a matter of law, the trial judge may direct the jury to acquit on the basis that there is nothing to corroborate the complainer's testimony.[49]

---

45 *Op cit*, Edwards, fn 11, p 337.

46 *Op cit*, Edwards, fn 11, p 337.

47 *Op cit*, Hill and Fletcher-Rogers, fn 41, p 5. Emphasis added.

48 See the accounts of complainants in *op cit*, Lees, fn 12, pp 19, 45.

49 See *Robertson v HM Advocate* 1998 SCCR 390, in which the accused was charged with attempted rape and convicted of assault with attempt to ravish – an alternative verdict which was suggested to the jury as a possibility by the trial judge. The complainer's evidence was that she had been raped, but the Crown libelled attempted rape because there was no corroboration of the complainer's evidence in respect of the penetration.

This runs counter to police advice that to avoid greater physical injury, women should not attempt to resist the attack.

CORROBORATION BY DISTRESS

Since it is often so difficult in rape cases to find corroborative evidence in support of a complainer's testimony, the Crown have attempted to use evidence from third parties as to the complainer's distress after the intercourse to corroborate her account that she was not a willing participant.[50] These developments started with the case of *Yates v HM Advocate*,[51] in which the appellant was charged with raping a 16 year old girl by using threats. According to the indictment, the accused 'did assault [the complainer] ... present a knife ... at her throat, threaten to cut her throat, place an arm round her, hold said knife ... against her body ... [etc]'.[52] The appellant's evidence was that the girl had initially consented to intercourse but near the end began to suggest that she did not want the intercourse to continue. The complainer had gone home immediately after the intercourse and arrived there within a few minutes. Several witnesses saw her at that time and gave evidence that she was in a dramatically shocked condition. The accused admitted that intercourse had taken place, hence 'her evidence that he had had sexual intercourse with her was corroborated by his evidence to a similar effect'.[53] Importantly, the court stated that 'a jury can infer from evidence of the complainer's distress *that she did not consent* to intercourse and that force must have been used'.[54]

Yates appealed against his conviction, arguing that there was no corroboration of the complainer's evidence that a knife had been used, and that the indictment ought to have been amended by deletion of all references to the knife. Although this would not have affected his guilt of the rape charge, it would have had an impact on his sentence.[55] The High Court held however, that while the use of force was a crucial fact (as previously described) requiring corroborated evidence, the use of the knife was not itself

---

50 For a description of the English law approach to distress as corroboration, see Davidson, FP, 'Corroboration in distress' (1997) 2 Scottish Law and Practice Quarterly 30. Davidson's paper also describes the Scottish position, prior to the case of *Smith v Lees* 1997 SCCR 139.

51 *Yates v HM Advocate* 1977 SLT (Notes) 42.

52 This charge was recounted in the later case of *Smith v Lees* 1997 SCCR 139, p 147, but not in the actual reports of the case of *Yates* (*ibid*).

53 *Smith v Lees* 1997 SCCR 139, p 148.

54 *Ibid*. Emphasis added.

55 The Scottish Court does not operate according to official sentencing guidelines. The maximum sentence for rape is life imprisonment.

a crucial fact, hence corroboration of the complainer's evidence as to the knife was not required.

Yates was applied in a number of later cases, including *Gracey*,[56] *Stephen* ,[57] *Moore*[58] and *Cannon*.[59] In each of these cases the accused admitted that he had had sexual intercourse with the complainer, and evidence of the complainer's distress thereafter was relied upon by the Crown only to support the woman's testimony that the accused had forced her to have sexual intercourse with him. In *Gracey* it was emphasised that distress could only provide corroboration if the jury were satisfied that the distress was genuine and was due to the alleged incident. In *Cannon*, the intercourse occurred at about 10 pm, and the complainer was seen some 12 hours later by a family friend. The complainer had seen no one in the intervening period, apart from her very young children. The testimony of the friend as to the complainer's distress at that time was held to be capable of corroborating the complainer's own testimony. Significantly, the court accepted that: '... the distress was observed at the first opportunity for it to be seen after the event.'[60]

The time interval in the case of *Moore* was similar to that in *Cannon*; however, in *Moore*, the complainer had been in contact with other people during that time, but they had not perceived her as distressed. The Appeal Court took the view that in light of this, corroboration of the complainer's testimony could not be supplied by evidence of her later distress. Echoing the words used in *Morton*, Lord Hope stated:

> What matters is not the time interval as such but whether the shocked condition or the distress of the complainer was caused by the rape. Only then can it be said that it provides *separate and independent testimony* to corroborate what she herself has said in her evidence.[61]

The use of a complainer's distress as corroboration was extended to non-sexual crimes in the cases of *Bennett v HM Advocate*[62] and *Horne v HM Advocate*[63] in relation to assault and robbery, and abduction, respectively. There had been some disquiet in academic circles that the principle of 'corroboration by distress' had been stretched quite far by this line of cases. For instance, in commenting on the case of *Cannon*, Gordon had noted that the case 'carries the application of the concept of corroboration by distress quite a

---

56 1987 JC 45; 1987 SLT 749; 1987 SCCR 260.

57 1987 SCCR 570.

58 1990 JC 371; 1991 SLT 278; 1990 SCCR 586.

59 1992 JC 138; 1992 SLT 709; 1992 SCCR 505.

60 1992 SCCR 505, p 511, *per* Lord Hope.

61 1990 JC 371, p 377. Emphasis added.

62 1989 SCCR 608.

63 1991 SCCR 248.

long way'.[64] In some cases, the Crown attempted to use a complainer's distress to provide corroboration for the physical aspects of the offence – the penetration in rape cases or the assault itself – rather than to corroborate the complainer's testimony that what took place occurred by overcoming her will/without consent. In *Begg v Tudhope*,[65] the accused appealed against his conviction of two charges of indecent assault against school pupils. The '*Moorov* doctrine', a doctrine based on similar fact evidence, had been applied by the trial judge in *Begg*, such that the evidence of one pupil about one assault was used to corroborate that of the other pupil in respect of the second assault.[66] The doctrine is used where the accused displays a pattern of conduct, and the incidents in question are closely related in time and place. Lord Stott observed, albeit *obiter*, in the *Begg* case, 'I have no doubt that evidence of an offence of the type alleged may be corroborated by evidence of the girl's condition immediately after',[67] thus suggesting that distress itself could corroborate the complainer's testimony that she had been indecently assaulted. Lord Stott's approach was followed in the case of *McLellan v HM Advocate*,[68] in which the accused was convicted of using lewd, indecent and libidinous practices towards an eight year old girl. The Crown led evidence of the incident from the girl herself and sought to rely on the testimony of the girl's mother that her daughter was in a state of distress shortly after the alleged incident. The judge had instructed the jury that this could amount to corroboration of the girl's account, but the accused's conviction was quashed on appeal. The girl's evidence was that she had been told by her mother not to visit the accused, and she had admitted in her testimony that she had been worried that her mother would be angry with her for defying her. In light of this, the Court of Appeal felt that the girl's distress could have been due to this factor – fear of her mother's anger – rather than due to anything the accused might have done to her. The failure by the trial judge to explain this to the jury resulted in the quashing of the conviction.

Begg was followed by *Stobo v HM Advocate*,[69] in which the accused, a taxi driver, was charged with indecent assault by forcing a female passenger to have oral sex with him. The accused did not admit that there had been sexual contact. Indeed, he put forward a defence of alibi. Despite this, in his charge to the jury the judge stated that evidence of the complainer's distress, spoken to by third parties, could corroborate the alleged indecent assault. The judge, unlike his brethren in *Begg*, emphasised that the jury had to be satisfied that the complainer's distress was due to the indecent assault and not to some

---

64 1992 SCCR 505, p 511. See, also, *op cit*, Davidson, fn 50.
65 1983 SCCR 32.
66 *Moorov v HM Advocate* 1930 JC 68; 1930 SLT 596.
67 1983 SCCR 32, p 39.
68 1992 SLT 991; 1992 SCCR 171.
69 1994 JC 28; 1994 SLT 28; 1993 SCCR 1105.

other factor. Refusing the accused's appeal against conviction, the then Lord Justice General, Lord Hope, stated: 'I have no doubt that care must be taken not to use evidence of the complainer's distress beyond its proper limits'.[70] He later explained:

> I remain of the opinion that the question whether or not distress can afford corroboration of the complainer's evidence must depend on the nature of the activity she has described. Distress cannot of course corroborate her evidence as to the identity of her assailant, and it cannot provide corroboration in those cases of assault where the evidence that it resulted in physical injury requires to be corroborated. I continue to think that where corroboration of penetration is needed in rape cases distress will be incapable of providing this, because the other acts involved in the rape to overcome the complainer's resistance will be sufficiently distressing in themselves to explain the distress.[71]

The issue was again addressed in the case of *Smith v Lees*.[72] The accused was charged with using lewd and libidinous practices towards a 13 year old girl by causing her to handle his naked penis.[73] This was alleged to have occurred while the accused and complainer were in a tent. The Crown relied on the evidence of a witness, who spoke of the girl having left the tent shortly after the alleged incident 'with a tear in her eye' and 'clearly upset', as corroboration of the girl's own account. The question on appeal was whether the evidence of the witness as to the complainer's distress was in itself sufficient corroboration. Due to the importance of the issue, a bench of five judges was convened to hear the case.[74] It was held that while distress is capable of corroborating a complainer's evidence that she did not consent to the accused's behaviour, and that he had used force to overcome her will, the distress could not corroborate the complainer's account of the actual behaviour of the accused. *Stobo v HM Advocate* was overruled and the *dicta* in *Begg v Tudhope* and *McLellan v HM Advocate* were disapproved. The Lord Justice General, Lord Rodger of Earlsferry, emphasised:

> ... the jury must be satisfied that the distress was something which arose spontaneously due to the nature of the incident rather than to circumstances outside the incident. Where that is the nature of the distress, then I am satisfied that evidence of such distress can be used as corroboration of *certain aspects* of the complainer's account.[75]

His Lordship then clarified this with an example from the law of rape:

> Suppose a witness were to have seen the accused having intercourse with the complainer and, before either of them was aware of his presence, the witness

---

70 1994 JC 28, p 33.

71 *Ibid*, p 34.

72 1997 SCCR 139.

73 Contrary to the Sexual Offences (Scotland) Act 1976, s 5.

74 This is known as a 'full Bench decision'.

75 *Smith v Lees* 1997 SCCR 139, pp 143–44. Emphasis added.

noticed that the complainer was in tears or showing other signs of distress. In the subsequent trial it could hardly be suggested that the witness's evidence of seeing the complainer in distress during the intercourse would be irrelevant to the question of whether she had consented to the intercourse, as the accused was contending, or had submitted only due to force, as the complainer was contending. If the jury were satisfied that the signs of distress seen by the witness were genuine, then they would be entitled to find in the witness's evidence corroboration of the complainer's evidence that she had not consented to intercourse, but had simply submitted due to the force used by the accused.[76]

Smith v Lees was followed in the case of *Thomson v HM Advocate,*[77] in which the charge was a serious, but non-sexual, assault. The trial judge directed the jury that the complainer's distress after the assault could be used to corroborate his testimony that he had been assaulted. It was held on appeal that this was a misdirection, but that no miscarriage of justice had occurred since the evidence of the complainer's physical state could supply the requisite corroboration.

Can *Smith v Lees* really be distinguished from *Yates,* or *Cannon?* In a rape case in which the accused accepts that intercourse took place, both the complainer and the accused agree that 'something happened', and both agree that what happened was sexual intercourse. Where, of course, they disagree is over the consensual nature of that intercourse. In the case in which a child is sexually assaulted in the manner alleged in *Smith v Lees,* both agree that something happened, but they disagree about the very act which happened. This is why the courts are unwilling to allow the child's testimony to be corroborated by third party evidence as to the child's subsequent distress. What if the allegation was that the child was shown an obscene photograph by the accused, or that the accused exposed himself to her? The accused might accept that he had shown the child a photograph, or part of his body, but maintain that this was an innocent act – that he showed the child a picture of a puppy, not a pornographic picture, or that he showed her a tattoo on his arm, rather than his penis. The reasoning in *Smith v Lees* would suggest that the child's distress could not corroborate her account of what it was that she was shown. It is not regarded as sufficient for corroboration, since it is felt that the distress could be due to a number of factors. However, this same allegation is also frequently made in rape cases, in which it is claimed that it was the complainer's shame, or remorse, that caused the distress. Even if there are a number of reasons that could plausibly account for the distress, this is surely a

---

76 *Smith v Lees* 1997 SCCR 139, p 144. The defence counsel suggested that acceptance of this would lead to defence lawyers having complainers 'psychologically examined to check whether the symptoms of distress had been genuine or not'. The Crown would have to instruct its own experts, leading to a 'battle of experts'. The court thought that this was unlikely.

77 1998 SCCR 56.

matter of weight of evidence rather than sufficiency of evidence, hence is arguably best left to the jury.

Since *Smith v Lees*, there has been a further significant development in the principle of corroboration by distress, arising from the case of *Fox v HM Advocate*.[78] This was a case involving 'clandestine injury'. Reference has already been made to the fact that, in Scotland, sexual intercourse with a sleeping or self-intoxicated woman is not regarded as rape, but rather is termed 'clandestine injury to women'. In *Fox*, the essentials of a charge of clandestine injury were described as follows:

> ... (1) that the [accused] had intercourse with the complainer and (2) that at the time of the intercourse she was in such a state of intoxication as to be incapable of consenting or not consenting to sexual interference. The Crown therefore required to prove these elements by corroborated evidence.[79]

The case was important in respect of corroboration, since it had been argued by counsel for the accused that corroboration by distress could not be found where the distress could perhaps be attributed to factors other than the non-consensual nature of the incident.[80]

A court of five judges was convened to consider the issue. The complainer had testified that she had attended a party in the accused's home, after which she had been put to bed suffering from the ill effects of over consumption of alcohol. She awoke some hours later to find the accused having sexual intercourse with her. She was very much distressed by this, and several people, including the police officers whom she contacted shortly thereafter, witnessed her distress. The accused admitted that he had had sexual intercourse with the complainer but alleged that her distress was due to the fact that she had initially thought that she was having sexual intercourse with her boyfriend, but became upset once she discovered that she was mistaken about this. The complainer accepted that when she asked the accused to stop, he did so. Several alternative reasons for the complainer's distress were suggested to the jury by the trial judge. As well as the complainer's testimony that she was distressed to find the appellant having sexual intercourse with her, and the appellant's averment that her distress only resulted when she became aware that the person with whom she was having intercourse was not her boyfriend, the trial judge suggested that the complainer may have been distressed at finding herself in a strange house, or that her distress may have been due to the fact that her friends had left her in the house. The trial judge instructed the jury as follows:

---

78 1998 SCCR 115.

79 *Ibid*, p 121.

80 The cases of *Fox* and *Smith v Lees* are discussed in Brown, A, 'Two cases on corroboration' 1998 SLT (News) 71.

> The thing I need to emphasise is that the evidence of the complainer's distress can only be treated as corroborating her evidence of intercourse taking place against her will if you are satisfied that that event, that is, intercourse without her consent, rather than any other possible cause, is the explanation for the distress described by the witnesses.[81]

The Court of Appeal held that this was a correct direction; it was for the jury to determine the source of the complainer's distress, and the fact that alternative explanations for that distress were possibilities did not in itself prevent the jury from deciding that the distress was caused by the act of the accused in having intercourse with the complainer. An adminicle of evidence need not be unequivocally in support of the prosecution case to amount to corroboration.[82]

Is a complainer's distress really independent evidence? Although testimony is given by third parties to the effect that they witnessed the complainer's distress, this really is evidence which emanates from the same source as the evidence it is designed to corroborate: both derive from the complainer herself. Given that corroboration in rape cases is designed primarily to safeguard against a fabricated story, it might be argued that such a complainer would be equally capable of fabricating distress. *Stricto sensu*, her distress does not comprise evidence from an 'independent' source. In allowing distress to corroborate certain elements of a complainer's testimony in cases of rape and other sexual assault, the courts have arguably bent the rules of evidence close to their breaking point.

CONCLUSIONS

In light of this, there would seem to be two main options for reform: abolish the corroboration requirement for certain types of crimes only, such as for rape and other sexual assaults; or abolish the corroboration requirement in respect of all common law crimes. The suggestion that corroboration should be abandoned for certain crimes, but not others, is unlikely to meet with general approval. That rape is a serious crime is as much an argument for making its proof particularly difficult, as for making it easier for the prosecution to secure a conviction.

English law no longer requires corroboration in criminal cases, and the position in the majority of the US is similar. Rather than continue to provide exceptions for sexual offences, it may be time for Scots law to reconsider its approach to corroboration, in general. Given the extent to which corroboration

---

81   1998 SCCR 115, p 123.

82   The court overruled the case of *Mackie v HM Advocate* 1994 SCCR 227. For a discussion of the *Mackie* case, see Sheldon, D, 'Corroboration and relevance' 1998 SLT (News) 115.

has been watered down, it does not seem just that a rape case in which there is evidence of a scratch on the accused, or a bruise on the complainer, can be left to the jury, while one in which such real evidence is absent can be dismissed by the court.

Perhaps what is needed is for corroboration to be formally abolished in respect of *all* common law crimes; corroboration should no longer be a requirement, but instead a corroboration warning could be introduced in appropriate cases. It is already the practice for juries to be warned, in cases where the evidence is thin, about the danger of errors in identification evidence.[83] It may be argued that confession and identification evidence are highly susceptible to error and fabrication, and are thus the very types of evidence which ought to require clear corroboration.[84] In contrast to this, the evidence of a complainer in a rape or other sexual assault case as to the non-consensual nature of the intercourse is unlikely to be 'mistaken'; as we have already noted, the greater need for corroboration lies in the fear of a lying complainer. Such a warning would apply not just to female complainers, or to complainers in sexual assault cases, but to all cases where the only evidence adduced by the Crown was that of one witness. A jury should be warned that it is *always* dangerous to convict on the testimony of a sole witness, and that they should scrutinise the evidence particularly carefully. Where, however, they are convinced beyond a reasonable doubt that the witness is telling the truth and is not mistaken, they should convict the accused.

83 See *Brotherston v HM Advocate* 1995 SCCR 613; *Blair v HM Advocate* 1993 SCCR 483; *McAvoy v HM Advocate* 1991 SCCR 123.

84 According to Sheldon: '... research suggests ... that mistaken identification and unreliable confessions are the two most significant causes of wrongful convictions.' (Sheldon, D, *Evidence: Cases and Materials*, 1996, Edinburgh: Green, p 131.)

CHAPTER 9

THE USE OF SEXUAL HISTORY EVIDENCE IN RAPE TRIALS

Susan Easton

INTRODUCTION

The use of sexual history evidence in rape trials causes distress to complainants, can affect the outcome of the case and contributes to the low conviction rate for this offence. It also acts as a deterrent to reporting incidents of what is, in any case, already an under-reported crime.[1] Despite legislation introduced in the Sexual Offences (Amendment) Act 1976 designed to restrict the use of such evidence, the law has been used in ways which favour defendants rather than complainants.[2] Problems with the application of the law since 1976 are considered, as well as the new provisions on the use of sexual history evidence in the Youth Justice and Criminal Evidence Act 1999. Consideration is given to whether a woman's sexual past is ever relevant to consent or to her truthfulness. The experience of Canada is also examined.

It is argued that the use of this evidence conflicts with the basic principles of the law of evidence. This anomaly may be understood in the context of the law's perception of women as witnesses, which itself reflects the marginalisation of women. The legal rules which circumscribe the use of sexual history evidence reflect a particular construction of women's sexuality. The perception of past sexual conduct in the minds of judges, counsel and juries is constructed by myths and stereotypes about women's behaviour and sexuality, including the notion that women are mendacious on sexual matters. Rape is an area where myths and stereotypes have shaped the law but have also become more entrenched by the impact of discriminatory law. Rape myths are used to deny the harm of rape, to trivialise it and deny its impact, and to mitigate sentences.

---

1   I am grateful to participants at the Workshop on Feminist Perspectives on the Law of Evidence (sponsored by Cavendish Publishing), held at the University of Reading on 22 March 1999, for their comments on an earlier draft of this paper.

2   The term 'complainant' is used throughout this paper, as 'victim' implies passiveness and 'alleged victim' denies women the presumption of truthfulness; however, 'complainant' is criticised by Majury because it trivialises rape and reinforces the stereotype of the woman as a nag or whinger or as the vengeful mistress and still sees the woman as the problem. See Majury, D, '*Seaboyer* and *Gayme*: a study in inequality', in Roberts, JV and Mohr, RM (eds), *Confronting Sexual Assault*, 1994, Toronto: Toronto UP, pp 268–92.

THE HISTORY AND DEVELOPMENT OF THE LAW GOVERNING THE USE OF SEXUAL HISTORY EVIDENCE

When complainants have testified in court, they have often been subjected to cross-examination on the intimate details of the alleged rape and have been frequently questioned on their past sexual experience. In some cases, this questioning has been undertaken by the defendant himself, in effect himself forcing the complainant to re-live the rape.[3] This has led to demands for changes in the law, some of which have been included in the Youth Justice and Criminal Evidence Act 1999. The attack on the character of prosecution witnesses is, of course, not confined to rape cases, as Ellison[4] points out: all witnesses who give evidence may be subject to an attack on their character; cross-examination is an ordeal for many witnesses because of the latitude given to defence counsel to attack their credit. Recent research has shown that rape victims tend to be cross-examined for longer than victims of assault and find the cross-examination more traumatic.[5] The attack on character is particularly distressing for those complaining of sexual offences and especially damaging given the cultural climate in which sexual history evidence is received and in view of the fact that the conviction rate fell between 1985 and 1995 despite an increase in the reporting of rape.

The increase in reporting is often assumed to be a response to improved police procedures, but it could reflect a genuine increase. The offence of rape suffers from a high attrition rate as cases may not be reported, or even if reported do not proceed to prosecution and conviction. When cases are reported, the full extent of the crime may be masked by no-criming, downgrading of offences and plea-bargaining.[6] Harris and Grace[7] examined

---

3   Ralston Edwards cross-examined Julia Mason for six days on trial in 1996. The two complainants giving evidence at the trial of Milton Brown were also subjected to a humiliating cross-examination by the accused. This case prompted Lord Bingham to suggest that, if necessary, the judge himself should undertake the questioning to prevent an abusive cross-examination: *R v Milton Brown* [1998] 2 Cr App Rep 364.

4   Ellison, L, 'Cross-examination in rape trials' [1998] Crim LR 605. The treatment of witnesses was also criticised by the Royal Commission on Criminal Justice and more recently by the Home Office Report, *Speaking Up for Justice: Report of the Interdepartmental Working Group on the Treatment of Vulnerable or Intimidated Witnesses in the Criminal Justice System*, 1998, London: Home Office.

5   Brereton, D, 'How different are rape trials? A comparison of the cross-examination of complainants in rape and assault trials' (1997) 37 Br J Crim 242.

6   See Gregory, J and Lees, S, 'Attrition in rape and sexual assault cases' (1996) 36 Br J Crim 1. Grace, S, Lloyd, C and Smith, J, *Rape: From Recording to Conviction*, 1992, Research and Planning Unit, Paper No 71, London: Home Office. Even if the case proceeds and leads to a conviction, the sentence may be relatively low. Sentences for a first offence have increased since *Billam* [1986] 1 WLR 349, but not as much as the *Billam* guidelines recommended, and there are disparities between different areas.

7   Harris, J and Grace, S, *A Question of Evidence? Investigating and Prosecuting Rape in the 1990s*, 1999, Home Office Research Study No 196, London: Home Office.

483 cases initially recorded as rape in 1996 and followed their progress, interviewing lawyers, judges and complainants. They found that only 6% of cases initially recorded by the police as rape resulted in convictions and that cases broke down at each stage, no-criming, no further action, acquittals and downgrading to lesser offences. Cases involving acquaintances were most likely to be no-crimed and cases involving intimates were most likely to be no further actioned or to be discontinued by the CPS than cases involving strangers.

At common law, sexual activity with other men was seen as relevant to consent if the woman was a prostitute or notoriously immoral;[8] past sex with the defendant was also seen as relevant to consent and credibility. In these three cases witnesses could be called to testify on these matters.[9] Although the courts exercised some restraint when admitting this evidence in relation to consent, they freely admitted it to undermine the complainant's credibility, reinforcing the assumption that women who are sexually active are inherently untrustworthy. The complainant's sexual activity was seen as relevant to credibility although, when questioned, her answers were final and could not be contradicted, unless they fell within an exception to the finality rule. Although evidence was often introduced ostensibly because it went to credit, in practice it was likely to affect whether the jury believed she consented and defence lawyers were well aware of this. The jury's view of the credit of the complainant may be crucial in determining the outcome.

An Advisory Group on the Law of Rape[10] was set up in response to public concern.[11] The Heilbron Committee, which reported in 1975, argued that women's sexual experience with partners of their own choice was not indicative of truthfulness or relevant to the likelihood of her consenting. The report was very critical of the way a complainant's sexual past was subject to cross-examination and was used to prejudice the jury against her.

The committee proposed that questions concerning past sexual conduct with persons other than the defendant should be prohibited unless they fell into an exceptional case, namely, cases where there is a striking similarity between the sexual behaviour of the complainant on past occasions and the alleged behaviour in the present case, or if the defence wanted to adduce sexual history evidence to rebut evidence introduced by the prosecution. It also advocated the introduction of a statutory definition of rape, anonymity for complainants, and a minimum of four women jurors in rape cases.

The law was amended in 1976 to address some of these problems and to implement some, but not all, of the group's recommendations. The 1976 Act did not use the criterion of striking similarity, but focused on unfairness to the

---

8   *R v Clarke* [1817] 2 Stark 244.

9   *R v Riley* (1887) 16 Cox CC 191.

10 Heilbron Committee, *Report of the Advisory Group on the Law of Rape*, Cmnd 6352, 1975, London: HMSO.

11 Following concern over the judgment in the case of *DPP v Morgan* [1975] 2 All ER 347.

defendant rather than unfairness to the complainant or the effects on the fairness of the proceedings as a whole. This was a matter for the judge to decide when considering whether to allow questioning on sexual history. No guidelines were included in the statute, but subsequent case law focused on whether the jury would take a different view of the complainant's evidence than if questions were not allowed. But as this is precisely what will happen in most cases, the Act was frequently interpreted to favour defendants rather than complainants.

Section 2(2) of the Sexual Offences (Amendment) Act 1976 stated that:

(1) if at a trial any person is for the time being charged with a rape offence to which he pleads not guilty, then, except with the leave of the judge, no evidence and no question in cross-examination shall be adduced or asked at the trial, by or on behalf of any defendant at the trial, about any sexual experience of a complainant with a person other than the defendant;

(2) the judge shall not give leave in pursuance of the preceding subsection for any evidence or question except on an application made to him in the absence of the jury by or on behalf of a defendant; and on such an application the judge shall give leave if and only if he is satisfied that it would be unfair to that defendant to refuse to allow the evidence to be adduced or the question to be asked.[12]

Section 2 did not apply to sexual assaults other than rape and attempted rape, but in *Funderburk*[13] the court said the mischief at which s 2 is aimed should be borne in mind as a brake on cross-examination in other contexts. Although the legislative changes of 1976 were intended to reduce the use of sexual history evidence, this did not prove to be the case.

THE INTERPRETATION OF S 2

The impact of s 2 was limited, as counsel continued to ask questions on sexual history, and when leave was requested it was rarely refused, so the law did not have the desired effect. Moreover, where trial judges have refused such questioning, this has usually been successfully challenged on appeal.[14] Although trial judges are now more aware of the distress caused to complainants by such cross-examination, the Court of Appeal is further

---

12 The Criminal Justice and Public Order Act 1994, s 142, broadens the definition of rape to include male victims. The Act also removes 'unlawfully' from the statutory definition of rape. However, sexual offences, including rape, are primarily male crimes. In 1996, eg, over 11,000 men compared to 100 women were prosecuted for sexual offences.

13 [1990] 2 All ER 482.

14 See Temkin, J, 'Sexual history evidence – the ravishment of section 2' [1983] Crim LR 3.

removed from that process. The myths and stereotypes underpinning the old law survived.[15]

When trial judges tried to exclude evidence under s 2, the Court of Appeal was very willing to grant appeals because sexual history evidence had been excluded. The way in which this evidence was used was both constructed by and reinforced assumptions about women's sexuality. For in deciding whether evidence is relevant to either consent or credibility, judges' perceptions will be constructed through myths, stereotypes and prejudices about appropriate sexual behaviour.

Under s 2 the complainant could not be cross-examined on her previous sexual history with other men without leave of the judge. For leave to question, the judge had to be satisfied that it would be unfair to the defence to refuse to allow questions to be asked. In determining the question of unfairness, the judge would consider whether it would lead the jury to take a different view of the complainant's evidence. However, the problem was that, in practice, juries' assumptions about sexual behaviour are such that it is very likely that they will view the evidence differently if the woman has been sexually active.

The Court of Appeal said in *Viola*[16] that judges should allow questioning if the questions are relevant to consent rather than credibility, but as the Heilbron Committee[17] rightly argued, sex with other men is scarcely ever relevant to whether she consented to sex with the accused on the occasion in dispute. The court said that questions going simply to credit will 'seldom be allowed', but left open the possibility that there might be some circumstances in which questions going to credit might be permitted. The court also acknowledged that there is a grey area, lying between relevance to credit and relevance to consent. The court said that if the evidence of promiscuity is so strong or so close in time to the event in issue, it may reach that borderline. But if its relevance is slight, then the judge will be far from persuaded that it would be unfair to exclude it. The court argued that if there is strong evidence of promiscuity, then we are moving nearer to the borderline between credit and the issues in the case. But this seems to rest on the dubious assumption that a woman prepared to consent to several partners is more likely to have consented in this case. What constitutes promiscuity in the view of the court may be a relatively low level of sexual activity. In *Brown*,[18] the defence wanted

---

15 See Temkin, J, *Rape and the Legal Process*, 1987, London: Sweet & Maxwell; Lees, S, *Carnal Knowledge: Rape on Trial*, 1996, London: Penguin; Adler, Z, *Rape on Trial*, 1987, London: Routledge and Kegan Paul; see, also, Adler, Z, 'The relevance of sexual history evidence in rape: problems of subjective interpretation' [1995] Crim LR 769.

16 [1982] 3 All ER 73.

17 *Op cit*, Heilbron Committee, fn 10.

18 (1989) 89 Cr App R 97.

to adduce evidence that she had sex with her boyfriend and had a child by another man as evidence of promiscuity; the Appeal Court aid that this was a case 'near the borderline', between credit and the issues in the case, but the evidence of 'promiscuity' was not sufficiently strong or contemporaneous to the alleged rape to reach that borderline. The court said that whether the defendant's attitude to sex was material on which the jury could rely, in concluding she consented on the occasion in dispute, was in every case a matter of degree. There may be other features relevant to consent which would tip the balance between fairness and unfairness. A number of factors have been used to justify such questioning, including the fact that the complainant is under 17 and not a virgin.[19]

In its review of the law on sexual offences in 1984, the Criminal Law Revision Committee concluded that there was no evidence to support the claim that the law was not working effectively.[20] But Adler's study of rape cases heard at the Old Bailey in 1985 found that judges were still assuming that previous sexual experience was relevant to consent: '... the basic assumption that the victim's prior sexual experience is relevant in establishing consent has not been substantially altered by a procedural change in the law.'[21] She found that sexual history evidence was used most frequently by defendants involved in multiple rapes, where it was harder for the defence to establish consent. In her sample, there was a 75% success rate for applications under s 2. Moreover, in two cases, the judges themselves questioned the complainant on her history, even though the defence had made no application and without objection from the prosecution.

Lees[22] examined police records of all cases of sexual assaults reported to two London police stations over a two year period; she also monitored rape trials at the Old Bailey over four months, analysed 31 transcripts of rape trials in three courts and conducted a survey of survivors of rape and attempted rape. She found great dissatisfaction among complainants about their treatment by the criminal justice system and particularly in court. While treatment by the police improved in the 1990s in many areas, treatment in court did not progress at the same rate.[23] In Lees's study, over half the respondents were questioned about previous sex with men other than defendant, the effect of which was to make them feel as if they, rather than the

---

19 See, eg, *SMS* [1992] Crim LR 310. For a valuable discussion of the case law before 1999, see *op cit*, Temkin, fn 15.

20 Criminal Law Revision Committee, 15th Report, *Sexual Offences*, Cmnd 9213, 1984, paras 2.87–8.

21 *Op cit*, Adler (1987), fn 15, p 77.

22 *Op cit*, Lees, fn 15.

23 However, police practice has varied in quality. Temkin's research indicates that there is still some dissatisfaction on the part of complainants with their reception by the police and that guidelines are not always followed in practice. See Temkin, J, 'Reporting rape in London: a qualitative study' (1999) 38(1) Howard J Crim Justice 17.

accused, were on trial. There was a high acquittal rate in her sample, which made it even harder for women to come to terms with the rape. The one exception she cites is a case where the complainant was a lawyer and no questions were asked about her sexual history, which, Lees argues, provides a model for good practice. But in many other cases she surveyed, women were questioned at length on their past sexual behaviour. A survey by Victim Support of 590 rape cases in 1995 found that 41% of respondents felt angry, horrified and revictimised by the nature of cross-examination.[24] The rape trial may be experienced and conducted as a ritual humiliation. In Lees's study, one woman said the worst experience was having her underwear passed round the courtroom.[25]

Moreover, the use of sexual history evidence does influence the jury and has a significant effect on the outcome of the case. In Adler's study, only 44% of 80 defendants pleading not guilty were convicted, three of whom later had their convictions quashed. Complainants perceived as chaste and virginal achieved a 98% conviction rate, while those whose sexual reputation had been discredited had a 48% conviction rate.[26] In some cases acquittals were judicially directed.

The attack on sexual reputation can be an important ingredient of the verdict. Kalven and Zeisel's study of American juries showed that juries do focus on women's behaviour and are hostile to complainants whom they see as 'assuming a risk' of attack by drinking, dressing in certain ways or accepting lifts.[27] Sexual activity is one of a number of factors which adversely affect the complainant's prospect of success; others include the use of drink and drugs, living on welfare, mental disorder and depression. Such complainants are seen as more blameworthy and are less likely to win at trial compared to those complainants who meet the criteria of 'respectability'.[28] Sexual history provides a way of devaluing women, so their violation is seen as less significant than that of 'respectable' women.

Although a woman's reputation should be irrelevant to whether or not she has been raped, in practice her 'respectability', which in court is equated with sexual respectability, may be crucial in determining who is speaking the truth. The status of the woman's character, rather than the accused's, can become the centre of the trial; whether she survives the attack on her character may be crucial to the outcome of the case. In the context of a rape trial her character is primarily assessed in terms of her sexual history rather than her occupation or absence of a criminal record, whereas a man's sexual experience will be

---

24 Victim Support, *Women, Rape and the Criminal Justice System*, 1996, London: Victim Support.

25 *Op cit*, Lees, fn 15.

26 *Op cit*, Adler (1987), fn 15.

27 Kalven, H and Zeisel, H, *The American Jury*, 1966, Boston, Mass: Little, Brown.

28 See *op cit*, Lees; *op cit*, Adler (1987), fn 15. See, also, Clark, L and Lewis, D, *The Price of Coercive Sexuality*, 1977, Toronto: Toronto Women's Press.

construed differently by the jury. In the *Diggle* case (1995), where the accused was sexually inexperienced, this was reported on with amusement in the press and was seen as a failing rather than a virtue. When a man's good character is put in evidence, the attention is on his occupation, professional standing, social class and lack of convictions.

THE RELEVANCE OF SEXUAL HISTORY

The key problem is that if relevance is a matter of common sense as well as logic and experience, common sense views of women, which are often negative, will work against complainants. It is hard to see sexual history evidence as relevant unless we rely on myths and stereotypes of appropriate behaviour for women or we assume that sexual experience renders a witness unreliable or more likely to consent indiscriminately. The problem is that relevance is not a neutral concept, although the formulation of the concept in terms of statistical or mathematical probabilities may give this impression. There is plenty of scope for values, experience and common sense to influence the judge and the jury when considering the relevance of evidence. As L'Heureux-Dubé J said in her dissenting judgment in the Canadian case of *Seaboyer*:

> ... the concept of relevance has been imbued with stereotypical notions of female complainants and sexual assault. A decision on relevancy whether formed by experience, common sense or logic is a decision particularly vulnerable to the application of private beliefs and, thus, stereotype and myth. Once the mythical bases of relevancy determination in the area of sexual assault cases are revealed, the irrelevance of most evidence of prior sexual history is clear.[29]

The presumed relevance rests on myths that women lie about sex and sexually active women are more likely to do so, and more likely to consent indiscriminately, despite the lack of empirical evidence for these assumptions. The discourse of rape is shaped by the irrational fear of the man wrongly convicted by the lying, vengeful or neurotic woman. Yet there is no evidence to suggest that the number of false allegations is higher in relation to rape than other offences, notwithstanding the perception of lawyers, judges and police officers of such a problem.[30] Lees and Gregory in their study could find no evidence to indicate a serious problem of false allegations and neither could the Law Commission.[31] While some false allegations may be made, the extent

---

29 (1991) 83 Dom LR (46th) 193, p 197.

30 Patullo cites the New York Sex Crimes Analysis Survey of 1979, which found that only 2% of the allegations were false – the same as for other crimes: Patullo, P, *Judging Women*, 1983, London: National Council for Civil Liberties.

31 See *op cit*, Gregory and Lees, fn 6; Law Commission, *Corroboration of Evidence in Criminal Trials*, Working Paper No 115, 1990, London: HMSO.

of the problem has been greatly exaggerated and the few cases which do arise are given extensive publicity. Indeed, rape contrasts with other crimes in terms of the additional deterrents to malicious prosecution, including an intrusive medical examination, the humiliation of cross-examination on sexual conduct and the airing in public of intimate details of one's life. This view of women as prone to lie about rape nonetheless has a long history, and is found in the writing of Hale,[32] Wigmore,[33] Glanville Williams[34] and the Report of the CLRC on Sexual Offences.[35]

The use of sexual history evidence is hard to justify on the ordinary principle of relevance.[36] It is difficult to see its relevance except in very rare cases, and even then it may still be insufficiently relevant to outweigh the prejudicial effects of admission. Rather, it focuses the attention of the jury on collateral issues and diverts it from considering the guilt of the defendant. Defenders of the admission of sexual history evidence have usually focused on its contribution to the search for the truth as if this were an ungendered, neutral, objective process.

In discussions of relevance, critics of the exclusion of sexual history evidence have pointed to circumstances where it should be admitted. In *Seaboyer*,[37] examples cited by McLachlin J included establishing an honest belief in the complainant's consent, establishing bias or a motive to fabricate on the part of the complainant, showing that a person other than the accused caused the physical consequences of the alleged rape, as similar fact evidence and where it is relevant to evidence introduced by the prosecution.

But L'Heureux-Dubé J, dissenting, argued that the provision in question, s 276, excluded only irrelevant evidence and the defendant has no constitutional right to adduce irrelevant evidence. Sexual history evidence was properly excluded because it was so prejudicial and because assumptions of relevance are based on stereotypical assumptions about women.

To admit evidence excluded under s 276, she argued, would divert the jury from the search for the truth. Even if one accepts that the Charter of Rights and Freedoms is infringed, which is debatable, s 276 would be justified under s 1 as a reasonable limit given Parliament's goal to eliminate sexual discrimination in the prosecution of sexual offences and to encourage women to report offences. The law has to be seen in the context of the fact that most sexual assaults are committed against women by men, they cause extensive damage to women, they are mostly unreported because of women's fear of

---

32   Hale, M (Sir), *The History of the Pleas of the Crown*, 1971, London: Professional.

33   Wigmore, JH, *Evidence in Trials at Common Law*, 1970, Boston, Mass: Little, Brown, p 736.

34   Williams, G, *Proof of Guilt*, 1958, London: Stevens; *op cit*, Criminal Law Revision Committee, fn 20.

35   *Op cit*, Criminal Law Revision Committee, fn 20, para 186.

36   See McColgan, A, 'Common law and the relevance of sexual history evidence' (1996) 16 OJLS 275.

37   (1991) 83 Dom LR (4th) 193.

reprisals and if they are prosecuted, women are treated in a biased way by the courts.

Similar fact or pattern evidence, L'Heureux-Dubé J argued, is usually irrelevant but highly prejudicial. If it shows only propensity, it should be excluded. Consent is to a person, not to circumstances. Evidence of prior acts of prostitution is never relevant. Moreover, the evidence excluded by s 276 could not assist the jury in considering whether the defendant's belief in her consent was honestly held. It is also difficult to see how sexual history evidence *per se* can provide proof of bias or motive to fabricate unless we accept the stereotype of women as liars on sexual matters. Evidence that the complainant has made a prior allegation of sexual assault would already be admissible under existing legislation, as it would not involve admitting her past sexual history. Prior sex with the defendant was also admissible, as was evidence of mistaken identification. In any case, the exceptions to s 276 admitted a considerable amount of sexual history evidence.

The Heilbron Committee[38] did see the use of sexual history evidence as similar fact evidence, to show a pattern of behaviour on the part of the complainant, as relevant, where the pattern of sexual conduct is so distinctive and so closely resembles the accused's version of the event, it goes to prove that the complainant consented. The example given by the Committee is where the defendant is alleging that the complainant consented to sex, but then demanded money, and when payment was refused, she argued she had been raped; this could warrant admission of evidence of other men to show that she had sex with first acquaintances and demanded money from them. In this situation, the Committee thought, the evidence would be relevant to consent.

But past misconduct of the defendant is rarely admitted, and mere propensity or disposition has traditionally been seen as normally insufficient to warrant admission. On similar fact principles, mere relevance is not enough; the probative value of the evidence has to outweigh its prejudicial effect.[39] As sexual history evidence is very prejudicial, its probative value would need to be high and the number of cases reaching this level would be low. Adler found that most applications to question were granted even where relevance was minimal. The cases in which past sexual conduct has been adduced have fallen well short of the striking similarity exception envisaged by the Heilbron Committee and have included evidence on the age or ethnic group of previous sexual partners. The circumstances in which sexual history evidence would furnish independent evidence analogous to the similar fact rule would be very limited. McColgan[40] gives the example of a situation

---

38 See *op cit*, Heilbron Committee, fn 10; *R v Krausz* (1973) 57 Cr App R 466.

39 *DPP v P* [1991] 2 AC 477.

40 *Op cit*, McColgan, fn 36.

where the defendant is alleging sex at the instigation of the complainant, where the contact is of a very unusual nature. Here, evidence that she previously instigated this type of sex, but she is denying this, and at the time of the offence the accused was not aware of this, would make his account more believable. But, in most cases, this is unlikely to arise, and independent evidence is unlikely to be available. In the majority of cases where requests to question on sexual history are made, the justifications in terms of relevance are likely to be much weaker than this.

Evidence of past misconduct of the defendant is usually excluded precisely because of the fear that the accused will be convicted on the basis of past rather than present conduct and will divert the jury's attention from the particular case under consideration. Similarly, if past sexual conduct of the complainant is admitted, it diverts the jury from fully considering the guilt of the accused.

Relevance for legal purposes means more than mere probability; the principle of relevance excludes weakly relevant evidence. Relevant evidence may also be excluded because of other rules of evidence, such as hearsay, opinion evidence and privilege, in order to protect core values and principles, or where the evidence is unreliable or likely to distort the search for the truth, or arouse the prejudice of the jury or take an undue amount of time to hear. Even Bentham's[41] radical model of free proof acknowledged that relevant evidence should be excluded if it leads to unnecessary expense, vexation or delay.

Certainly, sexual history evidence would seem to be irrelevant in most cases and likely to divert the jury from the main issue in the trial – namely, determining the defendant's guilt or innocence – add to the length of the trial and cause unnecessary vexation to the complainant. Moreover, its effect is highly prejudicial when received in the context of prevailing views of women's sexuality.

The defence may also try to draw attention to similarities between her past sexual history with other men where she has no prior relationship with the accused, and the incident in dispute, focusing on her preference for a particular type of sexual partner or her sexual proclivities. In *Viola*, the instances of consensual sex on the same day with other men could only be deemed relevant if we accept that the fact of consensual sex with others should lead us to doubt later denials of consent. The assumption that a woman who has consented in the past to sex with other men is more likely to have consented on the occasion in dispute, nonetheless survives in the minds of juries and legal officials.[42]

---

41   Bentham, J, *Rationale of Judicial Evidence, The Works of Jeremy Bentham*, 1843, Edinburgh: William Tait.

42   See *op cit*, Harris and Grace, fn 7.

The relevance of sexual history to credibility is also peripheral. A woman's sexual preferences and behaviour would seem so unrelated to her reliability as to constitute a collateral fact. But, in practice, as empirical studies show, complainants are subjected to questioning on a range of personal matters of questionable relevance to consent or credit, including past abortions, their menstrual cycles, their medical and gynaecological histories and the colour of their underwear. Lees[43] found numerous examples of questioning used to undermine the complainant's 'respectability' by cross-examining her on her childcare arrangements, or stressing the fact that she was a single mother or that she drank alcohol. Even if it is hard to establish consent directly through past sexual activity, it will be effective in undermining credibility, which may well affect the jury's assessment of the disputed consent. The defence will also use indirect ways of suggesting promiscuity, for example, the fact that the complainant is on the pill is used to suggest this, even though there could be a medical reason for this, unrelated to sexual activity.

The relevance of previous consensual sex with the accused

If sex with other men is irrelevant, should previous consensual sex with the defendant be treated differently, when considering a claim of non-consensual sex with the accused? The view held by defenders of its relevance is that past sex with the defendant is relevant to the disputed consent as part of the context in which sex occurred, as part of an ongoing relationship.[44] But consent should be considered discretely in each particular case, and ongoing consent cannot and should not be inferred from a history of prior consent within a relationship, although of course the assumption of ongoing consent within a marriage contract survived in English law until 1991.[45] This is now accepted as outmoded and in conflict with principles of equality and autonomy in the context of marriage. As Lord Keith said in *R v R*, the proposition that a wife cannot retract consent suggests that 'by marriage a wife gives her irrevocable consent to sexual intercourse with her husband under all circumstances and irrespective of the state of her health or how she happens to be feeling at the time. In modern times any reasonable person must regard that conception as quite unacceptable'.[46] In entering any sexual relationship one does not give an ongoing permission for all future occasions, and no reasonable person would infer such a consent.

Defence lawyers are well aware that by focusing on prior sex with the accused, they can liken the alleged rape to normal sex. Moreover, where a

---

43   *Op cit*, Lees, fn 15.

44   See, eg, *op cit*, Heilbron Committee, fn 10.

45   *R v R* [1991] 4 All ER 481.

46   *Ibid*, p 484.

relationship has ended, the prior relationship can be used to suggest malice and spite as the reason for a false allegation and 'fitted' into the context of prevailing rape myths. In Adler's study, with one exception, all the cases where the complainant had prior sex with the defendant resulted in acquittal. The existence of a prior sexual relationship with the defendant has even been used in mitigation.[47]

The complainant is more likely to get a conviction if she is raped by a stranger than by an intimate. Acquaintance rape has a higher attrition rate than stranger rape. Harris and Grace[48] found, in the selection of cases they examined, that the relationship between the complainant and the suspect had a strong influence on the attrition process. No further action was more common with intimate rapes. Moreover, if there has been prior sexual contact between the parties, it becomes easier for the defence to present the alleged rape as normal sexual behaviour, to increase the chances of acquittal.

The assumption that a woman who has had consensual sex with the defendant in the past is more likely to have consented on this occasion, assumes an ongoing consent of the kind until recently attributed to wives and makes it very difficult to prosecute successfully cases where there is a prior relationship. Yet this assumption constitutes an inductive leap which would be totally unacceptable in other areas of criminal law. A reputation for charitable works would not indicate that a person is likely to have consented to the appropriation of his property by another, in cases of alleged theft. In medical law, consent for treatment has to be given on each separate occasion of invasive medical treatment and a physician could not presume an ongoing consent from the fact of consent to a past procedure. Neither should we infer future consent from past consent with the defendant or an indiscriminate consent from past consensual sex with other men. Yet the assumption seems to persist that being sexually active places a woman within a class of people who are more likely to consent to sex in the future than, say, those who are celibate as a matter of principle or policy. But this inference is problematic, as one can change one's mind on the issue of celibacy at any time: the sexually active person may opt for celibacy in the future while the celibate person may make an exception. Sexual choices are not predetermined or fixed for ever. Even if we accepted that, generally, people will act in the future as they have tended to act in the past, we are still a long way from presuming a specific consent to a specific individual.

The admission of sexual history evidence is one of a number of rules requiring special treatment of women as a class of witnesses, including the formerly mandatory corroboration warning. The assumption behind the rule

---

47   See *op cit*, Adler (1987), fn 15.

48   *Op cit*, Harris and Grace, fn 7.

was that women as a class are untrustworthy in contrast to other witnesses.[49] The suspect nature of rape complainants is also reflected in the exception to s 1 f(ii) of the Criminal Evidence Act 1898 (now s 1(3)(ii), as amended by the Youth Justice and Criminal Evidence Act 1999) for defendants in rape cases. Although *Selvey*[50] held that s 1(f)(ii) applied even when casting an imputation is necessary to the defence, the defendant can allege consent in rape cases without losing his shield, thus giving defendants to charges of rape a privileged status. This rule, which can be traced back to 1908,[51] needs to be rejected; this would place the accused in a rape trial in the same situation as other defendants, and would assist many complainants in prosecuting their cases.

THE USE OF SEXUAL HISTORY EVIDENCE IN CANADA

The use of sexual history evidence has been criticised in other jurisdictions and a range of ways of dealing with it can be found, including prohibition, discretionary approaches and time barred questioning, limited to recent or contemporaneous sexual history. Where States have removed judicial discretion in relation to sexual history and corroboration, such as Michigan in the 1980s, the conviction rate has increased.[52]

The issue of sexual history evidence was widely debated in Canada within and outside the courtroom in the 1980s and 1990s. The admission of sexual history evidence was barred in most cases in Canada in 1976. But in *Seaboyer*,[53] the rape shield law was declared unconstitutional. The majority of the Supreme Court in *Seaboyer* decided that s 276 of the Criminal Code, which prohibited evidence of prior sexual conduct except in limited circumstances, was unconstitutional. It infringed principles of fundamental justice and the right to a fair trial guaranteed by ss 7 and 11 of the Charter of Rights and Freedoms, because it precluded the court from considering relevant evidence.

---

49 The corroboration warning should not be left to discretion. In jurisdictions where the corroboration warning is discretionary, its impact has been limited. See *Longman v R* (1989) 168 CLR 79.

50 [1970] AC 304.

51 *R v Sheean* (1908) 21 Cox CC 561; see, also, *R v Turner* [1944] KB 463 and *R v Lasseur* [1991] Crim LR 53.

52 The Michigan Criminal Sexual Conduct Act 1974 arguably provides a good model to follow. It applies to prosecution and defence, because in practice it has sometimes been introduced by the prosecution. It comprises a general prohibition with exceptions for evidence of specific sexual activity to show the source of pregnancy, disease or semen, and past sexual conduct with the defendant, but the judge may admit evidence within the exceptional categories only where it is material to a factor in issue and its probative value exceeds its prejudicial effect.

53 (1991) 83 Dom LR (4th) 193.

Section 277, which excluded sexual history evidence for the purpose of challenging the credibility of the complainant, was deemed valid. The court accepted that evidence of sexual reputation or conduct could not, of itself, be logically probative of consent or credibility, if it is merely to show that a person with a sexual past is more likely to have consented to sex on the occasion at issue at trial or is less worthy of belief. However, if it is to be adduced for another purpose, because it goes to prove an issue at trial, and where its probative value is not substantially outweighed by the danger of unfair prejudice to the complainant, then it should not be automatically excluded.

After *Seaboyer*, the legislation was redrafted in 1992 to give judges more scope to admit sexual history evidence. The Department of Justice consulted women's groups, including the Women's Legal Education and Action Fund (LEAF). Most women's groups took the view that sexual history evidence is never relevant and that most judges cannot be relied on to determine relevance or weigh relevance against prejudicial effect, in a way which is free of stereotypes regarding women's sexuality and credibility.[54] In response to some of the recommendations, the availability of the consent defence was narrowed and precluded if based on self-induced intoxication, recklessness or wilful blindness. The new Bill referred to sexual history evidence as 'rarely relevant' rather than never relevant, while referring to the inherently prejudicial character of such evidence. The preamble to Bill C-49 recognised the incidence of sexual assault against women and children and the unique character of the offence and its impact. Evidence that the complainant has engaged in sexual activity with the accused or any other person is not admissible to support an inference that she is more likely to have consented or is less worthy of belief. No evidence shall be adduced by or on behalf of the accused that the complainant has engaged in any sexual activity other than the sexual activity which forms the subject matter of the charge, whether with the accused or any other person, unless the judge determines that the evidence is of specific instances of sexual activity, is relevant to an issue at trial and has significant probative value that is not substantially outweighed by the danger of prejudice to the administration of justice. In determining this, the judge shall take into account: the interests of justice, including the right of the accused to make a full defence; the interest of society in encouraging the reporting of sexual offences; whether there is a reasonable prospect that the evidence will assist in arriving at a just determination in the case; the need to remove from the fact-finding process any discriminatory belief or bias; the risk that the evidence may unduly arouse sentiments of prejudice, sympathy or hostility in the jury and the right of the complainant to personal security and the full protection of the law; and any other factor that the judge considers relevant.

---

54 See McIntyre, S, 'Redefining reformism – the consultations that shaped Bill C-49', in *op cit*, Roberts and Mohr, fn 2, pp 293–326.

If an application is made for it to go in, the applicant must specify the evidence he wishes to adduce and the jury and public must be excluded. When the judge has heard the evidence, she then reaches a decision and must give reasons for the decision, state what its relevance is to the issues at trial and record the reasons. Clearly, there is much more control over its admission than there has been in England. Nonetheless, since *Seaboyer*, the focus has shifted to obtaining disclosure of personal medical, psychiatric and counselling records and using them as a way of discrediting the complainant, achieving indirectly the results which cannot be achieved directly under s 276.[55]

REFORMING THE LAW

Section 2 clearly failed to provide an effective shield for the complainant. While a change in the law will not, on its own, solve the problem of sexual violence, it will go some way towards improving the situation for complainants and prevent the trial itself becoming a means of secondary victimisation. In Canada, the restrictions on the use of sexual history evidence in place before *Seaboyer* did reduce the secondary victimisation of complainants by the criminal justice process and made the experience of testifying less traumatic.[56]

In view of the widespread public criticism of the treatment of complainants and particularly the distress caused to complainants by being cross-examined by the defendant and the decline in conviction rates, the government has now introduced legislation to address this issue, as part of a package of measures to assist rape victims. These measures include a bar on the right of defendants to cross-examine complainants in court.

The report of the Home Office Working Group on the Treatment of Vulnerable or Intimidated Witnesses[57] in 1998 recognised that the law was not working well and proposed 'a more structured approach to decision taking' which sets out more clearly when the evidence of previous sexual history can be admitted. Evidence received by the working group indicated that the prospect of aggressive questioning on sexual behaviour in court was a significant factor influencing women's decisions not to proceed and contributed to the high attrition rate for rape cases. It recommended improving the treatment of rape complainants and amending the law on sexual history evidence.

---

55 See *R v Osolin* [1993] 4 SCR 595.
56 See Clark, S and Hepworth, D, 'Effects of reform legislation on the processing of sexual assault cases', in *op cit*, Roberts and Mohr, fn 2, pp 113–35.
57 *Op cit*, Home Office, fn 4.

The working group did not favour total exclusion of sexual history evidence because it accepted that there may be circumstances in which it is relevant and should be admitted to avoid a risk of wrongful conviction. It favoured the Scottish approach found in ss 274 and 275 of the Criminal Procedure (Scotland) Act 1995. In the Scottish legislation, in trials of sexual offences including assault, the court should not admit evidence to show that the complainant is not of good character in relation to sexual matters, is a prostitute, or has at any time been engaged with any person in sexual behaviour not forming part of the subject matter of the charge. But the court may allow questioning if it relates to sexual behaviour which took place on the same occasion as sexual behaviour forming the subject matter of the charge, or it would be 'contrary to the interests of justice' to disallow it. However, there have been problems in practice, because the rules are not followed or are unable to deal with subtle attacks on character or are used in ways which undermine the goals of the legislation.[58]

The working group also favoured the use of CCTV links to enable vulnerable witnesses to give evidence from outside the courtroom. There should be a rebuttable presumption that a victim who is a witness for the prosecution for rape and other serious sexual offences should have special measures available and witnesses generally should be treated with more respect by the courts. It supported a mandatory prohibition on cross-examination by the accused in rape cases.

These recommendations are now incorporated in the Youth Justice and Criminal Evidence Act 1999 (YJCEA), which provides, *inter alia*, that a witness (other than the accused) is eligible for special assistance if the court is satisfied that the quality of the witness's evidence is likely to be diminished by reason of fear or distress (s 17(1)). Under s 17(4), the court will treat complainants of a sexual offence as eligible for such assistance unless the witness has informed the court of the witness's wish not to be so eligible.[59] So there is a presumption that complainants of sexual offences will need the assistance of special measures. The court may discharge or vary a special measures direction if it appears to the court to be in the interests of justice to do so, and may do so either on application by either party or of its own motion (s 20(2)). The court must state in open court its reasons for giving or varying or refusing an application for a special measures direction (s 20(5)).

The special measures include screening the witness from the accused, allowing the witness to give evidence from outside the court by a live

---

58 Brown, B, Burman, M and Jamieson, L, *Sexual History and Sexual Character Evidence in Scottish Sexual Offence Trials*, 1992, Edinburgh: Scottish Office Central Research Unit.

59 The Act provides a package of special measures to assist witnesses who are vulnerable on grounds of age or incapacity or because of intimidation and to enhance the quality of their evidence.

television link and allowing the witness's evidence to be given in private. Other measures include allowing for a video-recording of an interview of the witness to be admitted as evidence-in-chief, and where such a recording has been admitted, to allow for any cross-examination or re-examination to be recorded by means of a video-recording. Statements made under a special measures direction which are not made in direct oral testimony will be treated as if made by the witness in direct oral testimony.

Further assistance to the complainant is made by s 34, which prohibits defendants charged with a sexual offences from cross-examining in person the complainant. If the accused is not represented, then the court must, if it considers it necessary in the interests of justice for the witness to be cross-examined by a legal representative, appoint a legal representative for him (s 38(3)). Where the accused is prevented from cross-examining the complainant under s 34, the judge must give the jury such warning (if any) as it considers necessary to ensure that the accused is not prejudiced by any inferences that might be drawn from the fact that the accused has been prevented from cross-examining the witness in person (s 39).

The YJCEA amends the statutory framework for asking questions or presenting evidence about the complainant's previous sexual history. The defence will have to apply to ask questions or introduce such evidence and the circumstances in which they will be allowed to do so will be strictly limited.

Section 41 provides that:

(1) If at a trial a person is charged with a sexual offence, then, except with the leave of the court –

(a) no evidence may be adduced, and

(b) no question may be asked in cross-examination,

by or on behalf of any accused at the trial, about any sexual behaviour of the complainant;

(2) the court may give leave in relation to any evidence or question only on an application made by or on behalf of an accused, and may not give such leave unless it is satisfied –

(a) that sub-s (3) or (5) applies, and

(b) that a refusal of leave might have the result of rendering unsafe a conclusion of the jury or (as the case may be) the court on any relevant issue in the case.

So there is a general prohibition on questioning with the exceptions set out in sub-ss 3 and 5:

(3) This sub-section applies if the evidence or question relates to a relevant issue in the case and either –

(a) that issue is not an issue of consent; or

(b) it is an issue of consent and the sexual behaviour of the complainant to which the evidence or question relates is alleged to have taken place at or about the same time as the event which is the subject matter of the charge against the accused; or

(c) it is an issue of consent and the sexual behaviour of the complainant to which the evidence or question relates is alleged to have been, in any respect, so similar –

   (i) to any sexual behaviour of the complainant which (according to evidence adduced or to be adduced by or on behalf of the accused) took place as part of the event which is the subject matter of the charge against the accused, or

   (ii) to any other sexual behaviour of the complainant which (according to such evidence) took place at or about the same time as that event,

   that the similarity cannot reasonably be explained as a coincidence.

(5) This sub-section applies if the evidence or question –

   (a) relates to any evidence adduced by the prosecution about any sexual behaviour of the complainant; and

   (b) in the opinion of the court, would go no further than is necessary to enable the evidence adduced by the prosecution to be rebutted or explained by or on behalf of the accused ...

The assumption behind sub-s 5 is that the defence must be able to challenge the prosecution's evidence, on the principle of equality of arms, but must go no further than contradicting or explaining the claims of the complainant.

The court, in reaching its decision, must be satisfied that one of the criteria in s 41 has been met, *and* that if the sexual behaviour evidence was not heard, the jury or magistrate might make an unsafe decision on an issue falling to be proved in the case. If questioning is allowed, then it must relate to specific instances of sexual behaviour. The procedure is that an application for leave will be heard in the absence of the press and public. When the application for leave has been determined, the court must state in open court (but in the absence of the jury) its reasons for giving or refusing leave and if it gives leave, the extent to which evidence may be adduced or questions asked.

The new provisions in the YJCEA are long overdue and do recognise the distress faced by witnesses giving evidence in rape cases. The special measures and the prohibition on cross-examination by the accused are particularly welcome, as is the requirement to give reasons for the decision to grant or refuse leave to question on sexual behaviour. These provisions also cover a broader range of sexual offences than rape alone (s 62). Sexual offences for the purposes of the Act include burglary with intent to rape, unlawful intercourse, indecent assault and forcible abduction, and indecent conduct towards a child under 14, incitement of a child under 16 to commit incest, and attempting, aiding, abetting, conspiring, procuring or inciting the commission of the substantive offences.

There is an explicit prohibition on allowing evidence or questioning on past sexual conduct with the defendant if it is adduced merely to suggest that the witness is not worthy of belief. If the court thinks the sole or main purpose is to undermine the complainant's credibility, it will not allow it (s 41(4)). In contrast to the 1976 Act, no distinction is drawn between the defendant and other men. The Act does focus on similar fact evidence as the Heilbron Committee originally recommended.

If the question or evidence relates to an issue of consent and the questioning or evidence relates to behaviour which occurred at or about the time of the alleged offence, then leave may be granted. It is expected that 'at or about the same time' will be interpreted as no more than 24 hours before and after the alleged offence.[60] It is not envisaged that showing that the complainant has a history of making unproven complaints of sexual offences would be treated as evidence of sexual behaviour, so it would still be possible for such evidence to be adduced.[61]

But the Act does not go far enough.[62] An issue of consent is defined in s 42(b) as any issue whether the complainant in fact consented to the conduct constituting the offence with which the accused is charged, and so does not include any issue as to the belief of the accused that the complainant consented. If the accused is claiming that, at the time of the offence, he honestly believed she was consenting, even though he now accepts she was not, sexual behaviour evidence can still be introduced. This lets in all the old problems and is likely to be exploited in many cases.

Furthermore, if the focus is on similar fact evidence, then it would be better if the appropriate test were used, namely, that the admission of sexual history evidence should be excluded unless its probative value exceeds its prejudicial effect.[63] Sexual history evidence should not be admitted unless it is relevant, but even if it is legally relevant, its probative value should outweigh its prejudicial effect for its admission to be justifiable and cases meeting this criterion would be extremely rare. As sexual history evidence is so prejudicial, the prejudicial effect is likely to outweigh the probative value of the evidence in most cases. By excluding sexual history evidence, the courts would be

---

60   See YJCEA 1999, explanatory note 148.

61   See *ibid*, explanatory note 150.

62   Although the provisions for other witnesses lie outside the scope of this chapter, it should be noted that the response of some commentators has been that the provisions will improve their position but do not go far enough. See Bates, P, 'The Youth Justice and Criminal Evidence Act – the evidence of vulnerable adults' (1999) 11(3) CFLQ 289.

63   As used in *DPP v P* [1991] 2 AC 477.

endorsing principles which lie at the heart of the law of evidence. Moreover, the relevance of this evidence itself rests on the acceptance of myths and stereotypes. Once they are relinquished, its relevance is no longer obvious. There should also be an explicit provision excluding evidence of past sexual conduct if it is adduced merely to suggest that the complainant is more likely to have consented by virtue of this fact.

If sexual history evidence is excluded, this would have a beneficial impact on the conduct and outcome of trial because the jury would then be in a position to focus on the important issues in the case, namely the *mens rea* and actions of the accused. Because this evidence does influence juries, its exclusion should improve the conviction rate for rape. Effective laws and procedures also give a message that complainants are taken seriously and that it is the defendant and not the complainant who is on trial. The loss of the right to cross-examine in person would not conflict with the accused's right to a fair trial under Art 6(1) of the ECHR, provided that there is mandatory legal representation.[64] But it is possible that cases on the exclusion of sexual history may be mounted if the new law is interpreted very narrowly, but the European Court of Human Rights has made clear that there is considerable scope for States to develop their own rules of evidence.

Awareness of the realities of rape also needs to be enhanced. Although it is argued here that the problem of sexual history evidence extends beyond judicial attitudes, the significance of judicial attitudes should not be underrated. Laws are only as effective as the judges interpreting and enforcing them. When some American States enacted rape shield laws prohibiting sexual history evidence, their effectiveness was undermined by conservative judicial attitudes. Similarly, in England, outmoded attitudes may survive. In retrospect, it was unwise for the decision on sexual history evidence to rest on judicial assessments of unfairness when judges' attitudes in the past were part of the problem.

Mack[65] argues that judicial resistance to implementing laws aimed at preventing sexual history questioning may undermine the legislation. It was necessary to narrow judicial discretion in South Australia for this reason. Some judges still see women as untruthful, and judicial scepticism conveys that women are not to be believed. Judicial education is therefore a key first step in improving understanding of the effects of rape.

---

64 See *Croissant v Germany*, 25 September 1992, Series A, Vol 237, where the European Court of Human Rights found that the requirement for mandatory legal representation satisfied Art 6. See, also, Ashworth, AJ, 'Art 6 and the fairness of trials' [1999] Crim LR 261.

65 Mack, K, 'Continuing barriers to women's credibility' (1993) 4 Criminal Law Forum 327.

CONCLUSION

Engaging with law has raised problems for feminists in entering a terrain constructed by masculinist values, but nonetheless procedural and evidential changes can improve the experience for women who testify in rape cases. The importance of reaching a verdict should also be stressed to the jury, and they should be allowed sufficient time to do so. The jury should also be warned that the absence of recent complaint does not indicate fabrication. Victim impact statements should be given and, in addition, expert witnesses should give evidence on the impact of rape and the range of responses to sexual assault.

The prosecution should be more active in cross-examining the accused on the circumstances of the alleged rape to shift the focus to the accused, to his state of mind and behaviour rather than the complainant's and in countering irrelevant evidence led by the defence. If the complainant is attacked, then the prosecution should be permitted to attack the character of the defendant. The exception to *Selvey*[66] for rape cases needs to be removed. Harris and Grace[67] recommend improvements in prosecution standards, contact between complainants and prosecution counsel prior to trial, better protection for witnesses and more support for complainants from reporting to the trial, and better collection of evidence, as they found some cases were dropped despite the fact that they involved violence.

Proposals to improve the treatment of rape complainants in court are often opposed by defence lawyers and others who argue that the court is undermining the defence's right to a fair trial. Durston,[68] for example, has defended the Court of Appeal's decisions on s 2 of the 1976 Act in terms of the priority necessarily given to the defendant's right to a fair trial. Recent responses in the press to the new legislation have also expressed the fear that this right is being undermined by the indulgence given to the complainant. Similarly, in Canada, the majority judgment in *Seaboyer* was strongly influenced by the accused's right to a fair trial. So the abstract rights of the defendant were given a privileged position in contrast to the real experience of women as targets of assault. But this rights-based critique of rape shield laws wrongly assumes that the complainant and male defendant are in a position of

---

66 [1970] AC 304.

67 *Op cit*, Harris and Grace, fn 7. Respondents in the Victim Support study also stressed that they would have liked contact with prosecution counsel before trial to prepare the case.

68 Durston, G, 'Cross-examination of rape complainants: ongoing tensions between conflicting priorities and the criminal justice system' (1998) 62 JCL 91.

equality as witnesses and that the law is neutral.[69] This purported neutrality of the law is difficult to reconcile with women's experience of prosecuting rape cases. As in many other areas of law, the law of evidence purports to be impartial and neutral, treating all parties equally and fairly, committed to the search for the truth. Yet in this case it is constructed on a particular concept of women's essential nature, namely, that women are inherently untrustworthy. The discriminatory nature of the law is reflected in the criteria used to reach decisions as well as procedures. In the case of sexual history evidence, the rules themselves have been injurious to complainants, regardless of how they have been applied in particular cases. Legal standards may perpetuate prejudice while presenting the law as a neutral and fair standard which is applied objectively.

If our starting point is one of gender inequality and the recognition that women have been systematically disadvantaged in the past by special rules which undermine women as witnesses, as well as being indirectly disadvantaged by their apparent powerlessness,[70] a more radical approach is required. The abstract problem of character evidence should be grounded in women's experience of violence as complainants also deserve the right to a fair hearing. Fairness to the complainant and the fairness of the proceedings as a whole should also be considered. In addition, the public interest in improving the conviction rate of rapists has to be taken into account as well as the defendant's rights.

---

69 For an excellent discussion of the limits of rights-based approaches for women, see McColgan, A, *Women Under the Law: The False Promise of Human Rights*, 2000, London: Longman. She highlights 'the tendency of entrenched rights to privilege traditional judicial perceptions of relevance over those which are the result of conscious attempts to eradicate discrimination from the law' (p 250).

70 *Op cit*, Mack, fn 65.

CHAPTER 10

EXPERT DISTRACTIONS: WOMEN WHO KILL, THEIR SYNDROMES AND DISORDERS

Anne Scully

In recent years, expert medical evidence has been utilised in order to present defences to murder, particularly the defence of provocation, for women who have killed violent partners. Whilst the use of such evidence is interesting in individual cases, what is at question is whether reliance on expert testimony will be constructive in the long term as a means of explaining the experiences and reactions of women subjected to systematic domestic violence. To resolve this issue, the role of expert medical evidence in the key cases in this field will be assessed to reveal the impact of such evidence on our understanding of battered women, and to discover why it is that expert evidence, as opposed to other forms of testimony, has been adopted by the legal profession in dealing with cases of this kind. Lastly, an alternative form of evidence for the defence, obviating the possible drawbacks of medical evidence, will be considered as a means of presenting to the courts the realities of battered women's choices and actions.

Generally, women who have killed violent partners have found that their motives and experiences are not reflected in the current law of homicide. As a result, those women are denied access to defences that are otherwise available to others, namely self-defence and insanity or the partial defences of provocation and diminished responsibility. The two justificatory defences of provocation and self-defence are particularly difficult for battered women who kill to claim. With regard to provocation, in 1949, in the landmark case of *R v Duffy*,[1] the court stated that a wife who had killed her violent husband could not expect the background of domestic violence to be taken into account in assessing her claim to the defence of provocation under s 3 of the Homicide Act 1957.[2] The prime reason for this was that Devlin J interpreted the requirement of 'loss of self-control' in s 3 as a requirement that the loss of self-control be 'sudden and temporary'.[3] Thus, a woman who had killed a violent spouse while he slept or while he was in a drunken stupor could not avail herself of the partial defence of provocation even though she herself found that it was at that particular point in time that she had felt so provoked that she could not take any more and had lost her self-control. Moreover, she could

---

1   [1949] 1 All ER 932.
2   *Ibid*, p 392F: 'It does not matter how cruel he was, how much or how little to blame ... What matters is that this girl had the time to say ... thou shalt not kill.'
3   *Ibid*, p 932H.

not claim that she had acted in self-defence because at the exact moment at which her husband was asleep or in a stupor her life had not been in immediate danger, despite the fact that she really did feel that she was constantly struggling to preserve her life.

Turning to the alternative defences of either diminished responsibility[4] or insanity, each of these necessitates an admission on the woman's part that she acted madly rather than out of necessity. Of particular importance to a battered woman whose self-esteem has already been considerably weakened by her abuser, is the fact that neither of these two defences allows for any consideration that she may have acted as any rational person would react given her situation. Thus, it becomes apparent that, at the time *Duffy* was decided, the only options open to battered women, compelled by the brutality of their male partners to kill them, were to claim before the court that they were either 'mad' via diminished responsibility or insanity, or 'bad',[5] neither of which reflects the experiences and motives of women who eventually killed men who had originally been loved ones.

Nonetheless, the principle enunciated in *Duffy* remained the legal standard until *R v Ahluwalia*[6] in 1992. Here the opportunity arose for the first time[7] to submit expert medical evidence to explain the impact of systematic domestic violence on the defendant and its relevance to her actions in killing her abusive partner. Thus, expert medical evidence could be adduced to enhance the likelihood of a successful claim to the partial defences of diminished responsibility or provocation where a mental abnormality could be proven[8] as a result of the background of domestic violence. Provocation, as noted above, is a preferable defence because it does not suggest that the defendant was mad when she acted but that she was reacting to the provocative actions or words of the deceased. In order to claim provocation successfully, the defendant must pass both a subjective and an objective test and expert testimony can be of importance in both tests. The subjective test requires the defendant to show that she herself was provoked by the words or deeds of the deceased. The

---

4 Homicide Act 1957, s 2: 'Where a person kills or is party to the killing of another, he shall not be convicted of murder if he was suffering from such an abnormality of mind ... as substantially impaired his mental responsibility for his acts and omissions in doing or being a party to the killing.'

5 For further discussion of this construction of women's identities as mad or bad, see Nicolson, D, 'Telling tales: gender discrimination, gender construction and battered women who kill' (1995) 3 FLS 185; Edwards, S, 'Mad, bad or pre-menstrual' (1988) 138 NLJ 456; Scully, A and Stanko, B, 'Retelling the tale', in Myers, A and Wright, S (eds), *No Angels: Women Who Commit Violence*, 1996, London: Pandora.

6 [1992] 4 All ER 889; [1993] Cr App R 133.

7 Nicolson, D and Sanghvi, R, 'Battered women and provocation: the implications of *R v Ahluwalia*' [1993] Crim LR 728.

8 Murphy, P (ed), *Blackstone's Criminal Practice*, 1999, London: Blackstone, p 2039, para F10.5: expert evidence is admissible in claims of provocation only where it concerns abnormality of mind.

objective test entails a decision as to whether a reasonable person with some of the same characteristics as the defendant would have been thus provoked. The notion of the reasonable person is one limited to a person having only the same defining characteristics of the defendant, for example, age or gender.[9]

The expert testimony submitted in *Ahluwalia* was based on Lenore Walker's work on 'Battered Woman's Syndrome'.[10] This testimony was accepted as proof that Kiranjit Ahluwalia was of diminished responsibility, but it was not deemed sufficient proof of an ongoing mental state to qualify as a defining characteristic of the 'reasonable man' for the purposes of a defence of provocation. Nonetheless, the admissibility of the expert evidence did mean that the defendant's experience of domestic violence at the hands of the deceased was brought before the court. Walker's research into Battered Woman's Syndrome need not be limited in its application to women, nor to heterosexual relationships; moreover, it can be applied in situations beyond homicide and may be used to raise defences of duress or self-defence in cases of non-fatal force, but it is perhaps in cases of women who kill violent male partners that, as a theory, it has had the greatest impact. Walker's work presents a cycle of behaviour in which a woman is defined as a battered woman if she is battered on more than one occasion and stays in the relationship. Once this has occurred, the pattern of abuse is developed in three cycles: first, minor abuse which builds tension; secondly, the infliction of brutal violence; and, thirdly, the 'loving respite' stage in which the batterer seeks the forgiveness of the battered woman and is particularly loving and attentive. During the repeated cycle of abuse, the woman develops what Walker calls 'learned helplessness', in which the battered woman's perception that there is no escape from the violent relationship becomes her reality, and in which mental state the only alternatives open to her are to attempt to mitigate the violence or to fight back. In fact, for many women this perception finds its roots in their batterer's assertions that he will not let them escape and will come after them if they do.[11] This syndrome explains a substantial mental impairment caused by the violence to which the women were subjected. Hence it was hoped that those women could present their actions to the court either as the result of diminished responsibility caused by the violent behaviour of their spouse or, preferably, as a response which differed from the

---

9   But see, also, *R v Morhall* [1996] 1 AC 90, where addiction is sometimes considered a defining characteristic. It seems that characteristics included do not have to be only unchangeable traits such as age or gender, but also, since *R v Smith* [1998] 4 All ER 387, features of one's personality which may not be permanent but which cannot be expected to be mastered by the defendant at that time. Eg, severe depression is included, but not explosiveness.

10 Walker, L, *The Battered Woman Syndrome*, 1984, New York: Springer.

11 For anecdotal evidence of the experience of learned helplessness, see Dobash, RE and Dobash, R, *Violence Against Wives*, 1980, London: Open Books; Gelles, R, *The Violent Home: A Study of Physical Aggression Between Men and Women*, 1972, London: Sage.

usual immediate response to provocation because of the violence they suffered at the hands of the deceased. In brief, in these types of cases, Battered Woman's Syndrome was adduced to explain a slow burn reaction as a legally acceptable response to provocative words or deeds.[12] Thus, the expert medical evidence serves to provide assistance to the jury in understanding the reactions of a victim of domestic violence and to dispel myths about responses to such brutality. This suggests that the expert evidence will open up the context of the defendant's actions and will result in a greater understanding within the legal system of the experiences of women and others in violent relationships. If defendants are to continue to rely upon such expert evidence, it is important to analyse to what extent the admission of expert medical or psychological evidence does advance women's claims to defences in murder cases or whether, as other commentators have suggested, expert evidence merely serves a function of distraction by diverting attention away from the problem of the imbalance of power in intimate relationships in a patriarchal society.

USING EXPERT MEDICAL EVIDENCE

The successful appeal made by Kiranjit Ahluwalia against her conviction for murder was celebrated[13] as a victory for battered women and medical or psychological evidence. At the initial trial, the judge had not allowed consideration of evidence of the defendant's depression, even though it was likely that the depression was the result of continued assaults over the duration of her marriage and that it was directly linked to her behaviour when she killed her husband. On appeal, evidence of depression was admitted under the umbrella of Battered Woman's Syndrome and was the basis for a verdict of diminished responsibility. However, what was more significant was that the door was left open for future submission of evidence of the syndrome in relation to other defences, including provocation. Indeed, the basis of Emma Humphreys' subsequent appeal[14] against the conviction for the murder of her abusive partner was the introduction of medical evidence as to her psychological disorder and the connection between her psychological state and her actions in killing Trevor Armitage. Humphreys had developed a habit of self-harming already and, after Armitage had threatened her, Humphreys had tried to slash her wrists. This can be viewed

---

12 It should be noted, however, that Battered Woman Syndrome is not limited to the partial defences to murder. It has been relied upon in Canada to support a self-defence claim by a woman who killed an abusive partner: *Lavallee* (1990) 55 CCC 3d 97.

13 Edwards, S, 'Battered Woman Syndrome' (1992) 142 NLJ 1350; McColgan, A, 'In defence of battered women who kill' (1993) 13 OJLS 508; *op cit*, Nicolson and Sanghvi, fn 7.

14 *R v Humphreys* [1995] 4 All ER 1008.

as a response to the expectation of imminent physical and sexual violence, either as a desperate attempt to evade that violence by distraction or, at a deeper level, the self-harm could be a manifestation of despair at her situation and self-loathing for being unable to do anything about the continuing violence. What is beyond question is that either interpretation of Emma Humphreys' actions in self-harming are a consequence of her position of powerlessness in an abusive relationship.

Nonetheless, in considering provocation, the court at first instance deemed the self-harm as attention-seeking behaviour and therefore not a defining characteristic to be included in the typification of the 'reasonable man' nor of relevance to the way in which she might react to what would to other people be relatively minor incidents. Thus, her behaviour did not fall within the definition of a medically prescribed psychological state which would raise the defence of provocation. On appeal, with the benefit of expert medical evidence, the 'attention-seeking behaviour' was regarded as a psychological illness akin to anorexia.[15] Once presented under the auspices of the 'psy' profession, the court found this evidence 'critical to the appeal'[16] and then made the logical progression of allowing the disorder to be admitted as a defining characteristic for the purposes of the objective test. As a result of this expert evidence, the past abuse, both physical and sexual, that Emma Humphreys had suffered at the hands of Trevor Armitage was considered as a context within which to understand why she would have been provoked by his taunts about her attempts to slash her wrists, and she won the appeal. Following *Humphreys*, then, it would have seemed that the way for women to introduce their experience of violence to the courts was through the submission of expert medical evidence.

As a consequence, Sara Thornton attempted to appeal a second time against her conviction for the murder of her violent husband. She had always maintained that she was not guilty of murder, but she said that she had taken the drastic action of threatening him with a knife because she had been provoked to such extremes as a result of his consistent violent behaviour towards her and fear that he would act on his threat to kill her. There had been a time lapse between the threat to kill her and her decision to find the knife, but she herself felt that she was acting under provocation. She thought that as she brought the knife towards him that he would deflect it. He did not.[17] At first instance, the claim to a defence of diminished responsibility was dismissed on the basis that the evidence did not demonstrate any abnormality of mind sufficient to impair her responsibility substantially. At the first appeal in 1992, the court upheld the decision of the court of first instance, but further stated that 'provocative acts in the course of domestic violence over a period

15   *R v Humphreys* [1995] 4 All ER 1008, p 1010.
16   *Ibid*.
17   *R v Thornton* [1992] 1 All ER 306, p 306.

of time which did not cause sudden and temporary loss of self-control did not amount to provocation in law, but might be considered by a jury as part of the context or background against which the accused's reaction to provocative conduct had to be judged'.[18] However, Sara Thornton was not judged to be sufficiently affected by the background of violence to warrant a decision on the basis of diminished responsibility, let alone access to the defence of provocation. Nonetheless, despite what was in the main a restatement by the court of the *Duffy* principle, it was the latter aspect of the court's reasoning on the admissibility of proof of domestic violence as a context which gave rise to the opportunity for Kiranjit Ahluwalia to introduce evidence of the violence she suffered during her marriage as a backdrop to her actions. Now, with her case coming full circle, as a result of the successful appeals by both Kiranjit Ahluwalia and Emma Humphreys, Sara Thornton lobbied for a second appeal. She was successful, and the Court of Appeal in *R v Thornton (No 2)* ordered a retrial on the basis that expert medical evidence on 'Battered Woman's Syndrome' would have had a significant impact on the original decision by raising provocation as an issue. It would do this in two ways. First, expert evidence would impact on the objective test for provocation: the characteristics of the defendant regarded as relevant to the construction of the reasonable man. Secondly, it would influence what would constitute provocative behaviour[19] for that particular defendant, that is, the subjective test. Although each of these points would remain an issue for the jury, they would be expected to listen to expert medical evidence to help them decide on the impact of systematic domestic violence because this was an issue which could not be expected to be within the realm of knowledge of an ordinary jury member.[20] Thus, the court recognised the value of medical evidence in opening up the context and complexities of an abusive relationship. In *Thornton (No 2)*, Lord Taylor CJ made it quite clear that what had influenced the court in ordering a retrial had been not only the recent clarification of the law on this point, but also the submission of new medical evidence on Thornton's behalf, which had been equally important. The new evidence testified to the severity of the personality disorder from which she suffered and the impact on her 'mental make-up'[21] of the violent abuse she had sustained at her husband's hands. At the retrial, Sara Thornton was found guilty of manslaughter and, because of the time she had already spent in prison, she was also found to have served her sentence.[22]

---

18 *R v Thornton* [1992] 1 All ER 306, p 307.

19 *R v Thornton (No 2)* [1996] 1 WLR 1174, p 1175.

20 *R v Turner* [1975] QB 834: the Court of Appeal decided that expert evidence was admissible on matters beyond the jury's ordinary human experience, but not otherwise.

21 *R v Thornton (No 2)* [1996] 1 WLR 1174, p 1182.

22 *Ibid*, p 1184: decision in the retrial given as a reporter's footnote to the report of the appellate court's judgment.

The judgments in each of the appeal hearings of *Ahluwalia, Humphreys* and *Thornton* clearly demonstrate that the motive for reconsideration was the newly submitted expert medical evidence. In each case, nothing that was factually new was presented to the courts, but the way in which facts about the defendants were presented was new. The defendants' stories were retold in terms of a disorder or a syndrome. Being able to label their experiences through the medium of expert psychological testimony thus elicited greater protection from the law than the evidence of abuse represented by a clearly documented list of broken bones and bruises, but protection nonetheless. This is particularly seen in the transformative process that Emma Humphreys' attention-seeking behaviour, which has never yet been classified as a psychological disorder by the medical profession,[23] underwent due to the support of an expert witness from the 'psy' professions by means of an analogy to anorexia.

So, in summary, where women defendants have framed their story, their actions and experiences within the boundaries of medical/psychological evidence, the injustice that would otherwise have been done to them by them rigid parameters of legal reasoning can be undone. The question then arises of whether reliance on the professionals comes without any cost.

DISSECTING THE DECISIONS: REAL ADVANCES OR TEMPORARY DIVERSIONS?

So, can it be that after consistently being convicted for murder when the death of a violent spouse seemed the only escape, all that women defendants needed to do was to turn to the medical and 'psy' professions to document their suffering in a way that would allow them to claim the defences to murder that men have always been able to utilise? The beneficial impact of expert medical evidence has been very real in the lives of women who have followed in the wake of Ahluwalia, Humphreys and Thornton. Such evidence may have prevented women being convicted for murder rather than manslaughter and may have also pre-empted unnecessary imprisonment and subsequent appeals. There are, however, two very serious problems inherent in relying upon expert medical evidence such as was admitted in these cases.

First, there is a problem with the requirement that medical evidence be adduced and, secondly, in the way in which that evidence is manipulated within our system of legal reasoning. Looking at the apparent requirement that a woman be supported by the medical profession in her claim to have been provoked, rather than simply being mad, gives rise to concern for future cases. Whilst in these individual cases it would appear that justice was

---

23 See *op cit*, Scully and Stanko, fn 5, p 64.

ultimately done and the context to these women's actions was, by various means, taken into account, the problem does arise that future women defendants may find that their experiences will only be validated by the criminal justice system if they can invoke either a *bona fide* disorder or they can rely, following *Humphreys*, on the goodwill and flexibility of the courts and the professionals to manufacture a disorder. This is acceptable at a very pragmatic level if the court wants to see justice done rather than have law 'done', but should women's access to criminal justice depend the goodwill and flexibility of the medical professional and the courts? By relying on expert medical testimony it is conceivable that women may not be following a path to liberation from the mad or bad stereotype but may be merely exchanging that for another set of classifications. Furthermore, it is interesting to note that, under the rules of evidence, expert medical testimony is admissible in support of claims of provocation only when mental abnormality is to be proven.[24] Thus, even though women who use medical expert evidence to show provocation may feel that they are avoiding the mad or bad stereotypes, presenting the rationality of their actions to the court, it seems that to adduce medical evidence in a defence of provocation is to admit to some level of 'madness'.

With regard to the way in which expert medical evidence is adopted within a system of legal reasoning, the decisions in these landmark cases claim to be within the boundaries of legal consistency and the system of precedent. However, if the definition of provocation as a sudden and temporary loss of self-control, given in *Duffy*, was previously exclusive of a battered woman's experience of provocation, how can the same law now fit with the new understanding of provocation from a woman's perspective? The answer lies in the introduction of expert medical evidence to the reasoning process. The question that arises next is whether admission of expert evidence on Battered Woman's Syndrome has resulted in a real and binding development of legal principle or whether the extension of admissibility of medical evidence has been a politically expedient response on the part of the legal system to a series of high profile cases.

In *Ahluwalia*, psychological depression brought on by systematic violence was regarded as the cause of substantial impairment of the defendant's responsibility for her actions and was presented consequently as proof of diminished responsibility. But, despite *obiter* comments on the effects of violence in creating defining characteristics relevant to provocation, the decision in this case was only a restatement, not a development, of legal principle because Kiranjit Ahluwalia's conviction for murder was commuted to a conviction for manslaughter on the basis that she was temporarily out of her mind, not that she was provoked. The discourse of law could not

24 *Op cit*, Murphy, fn 8, p 2039, para F10.5.

justifiably typify her as bad, owing to her utter conformity to stereotypical femininity at all times apart from when she killed her husband, so she fell into the only other conceivable category of feminine agency: she was mad. Arguably, *obiter dicta* in the judgment represents the possibility of developing legal principle so as to recognise the experiences of women in violent relationships by indicating the potential for evidence of psychological disorders to be adduced to support a claim of provocation. Notwithstanding this possibility, in reality, the judgment in *Ahluwalia* did not give women who kill violent partners full access to defences to murder. It is also interesting to note that those defences are already available to men charged with the murder of a spouse by virtue of the confluence of the way in which men react to provocation and the statutory definition of provocation. Moreover, it is as yet unclear that the promise of a defence of provocation reflective of women's experience, as held out in the *obiter* comments, has been fulfilled in any tangible sense.

Turning to the *Humphreys* case, it is equally disappointing in that it does not really deliver justice for battered and abused women generally. A defence of provocation, contextualised by men's victimisation of women via the medium of expert evidence, was explored more fully in this case than in previous cases. Emma Humphreys' reaction to her abuser's threats and ridicule was also understood as a consequence of the abuse to which she had systematically been subjected during their relationship. However, the court did not give a clear acknowledgment of the adoption of Battered Woman's Syndrome by legal discourse. Instead, it accepted the word of a medical expert that what Emma Humphreys had experienced was sufficient to alter her perception of the risk of violence. Once more, this is not a new development of legal principle. First, as a defence to murder, a serious abnormality of mind, such as a personality disorder, is already accepted within the defence of diminished responsibility. Secondly, the judgment in *Humphreys* is dependent, in part, on accepting that she acted to a degree with diminished responsibility and that this was at best combined with provocation. Thus, legal discourse persists in talking about women being 'mad' when they kill. Thirdly, the disorder which the court accepted as being of relevance to the issue of how the defendant might react to provocation was not a disorder described in court as being caused exclusively by the violence inflicted by her partner.

Therefore, in future cases, the judgment in *Humphreys* could be read narrowly to suggest that provocation can only be interpreted cumulatively where there is a pre-existing psychological disorder, not one caused directly by being battered; that is, the courts might in future rely on a narrow interpretation of *Humphreys* in order to return to the precedent set by *Ahluwalia* that Battered Woman's Syndrome is an insufficiently defining characteristic to be included as a notional characteristic of the 'reasonable man'. Thus, within the rules of precedent, and in less politically sensitive circumstances, it would be logically consistent for the courts to step back from the current interpretation of the effect of *Humphreys*. This would deny battered women the defence allowed to Emma Humphreys unless they, too, can bring evidence of a psychological disorder prior to the abusive relationship which could be counted as a defining characteristic of the reasonable man. The *Humphreys* decision is problematic because the court has not been sufficiently explicit in defining what constitutes a disorder which counts as a permanent characteristic and how disorders brought on by being subjected to systematic domestic violence fit within that definition. Without that explicit reasoning, the liberality that was shown in designating self-harm as a recognised disorder without prior medical terms of reference can be retracted as sympathy or political necessity ebbs away. Indeed, without a firm and rational foundation for defining certain behaviours as disorders, those behaviours can be redefined as just that, behaviour, and not a disorder of requisite permanence. Indeed, one interpretation of the judgment in *Humphreys* is that Emma Humphreys' behaviour and disorders contributed to an 'immaturity' which, of itself, is a sufficiently permanent characteristic to be taken into account[25] when considering the defence of provocation. On that reading, women have not explicitly been given access to the defence of provocation because they were cumulatively provoked by male violence. Thus, women are once again left without recourse to a defence easily available to male defendants in the same circumstances.

Thornton (No 2) further illustrates the predicament. On quashing Thornton's conviction for murder, although the judgment in the Court of Appeal raised the prospect of the evolution of a defence of provocation based upon either cumulative provocation, resting upon a sudden and temporary loss of self-control sparked by a minor but 'last straw' word or act[26] or the inclusion of Battered Woman's Syndrome in the characteristics of the reasonable person,[27] the retrial was actually decided on the basis of diminished responsibility.[28] So, to summarise, on a close reading of the reasoning in each of the three landmark cases not one of them was decided on the basis of murder as a reasonable response for a person provoked by extreme and systematic violence at the hands of the person they killed. *Ahluwalia* was decided on diminished responsibility; *Humphreys* was decided on attention-seeking and immaturity as characteristics of the reasonable man responding to provocation, not Battered Woman's Syndrome as a defining characteristic of the reasonable man; and lastly *Thornton (No 2)* was ultimately a case decided on diminished responsibility, not provocation. In each of these cases, the woman was found to some degree or other to be mad or not fully in

---

25 *R v Humphreys* [1995] 4 All ER 1008, p 1022.

26 *R v Thornton (No 2)* [1996] 1 WLR 1174, p 1181.

27 *Ibid*, p 1182.

28 Chan, W, 'Legal equality and domestic homicides' (1997) 25 Int J Soc Law 203.

control as an adult. Thus, while expert medical evidence offered the hope of a defence reflective of women's experience, what it delivered was a retreat into madness or a diversion into disorders inherent in the defendant prior to her exposure to systematic abuse.

The case of *Luc Thiet Thuan*,[29] heard at a similar time to that of *Thornton (No 2)*, initially indicated that the court has already moved to limit the potential of a broader interpretation of provocation as developed through the three landmark cases of *Ahluwalia, Humphreys* and *Thornton*. The defendant, Luc Thiet Thuan, did not succeed on appeal to have his mental infirmity taken into account as a characteristic of the reasonable man. Instead, mental infirmity was limited by the court to being of relevance to the subjective test for provocation only.[30] Therefore, the jury could not take the same syndrome into account in judging the ability of the reasonable man, sharing the same characteristics of the defendants, to control his response to the provocation. The reasonable man would not be formulated as sharing the psychological characteristics of the defendants.

However, Lord Steyn's dissenting opinion in *Luc Thiet Thuan*,[31] expressing his dissatisfaction with this development in the law of provocation and supporting the developments in *Thornton* and earlier cases, has more recently been mirrored in the Court of Appeal judgment in *R v Smith*.[32] It seems from *Smith* that the defendant's psychological condition can be considered as a defining characteristic of the reasonable man, even if it is not a permanent condition. In this case, the defendant's reaction to provocation was influenced by severe depression. What remains to be seen is whether Battered Woman's Syndrome will be considered as a psychological condition at the same level as severe depression, or whether it will continue to be indicative of diminished responsibility only. If that is the case, battered women will continue to be granted an excusatory defence only, rather than a justificatory defence, despite the admission of medical evidence.

What is of central concern, though, is that, even if battered women are recognised as being traumatised by systematic violence, by relying on medical evidence as to their states of mind when provoked, the focus for their actions continues to be their instability rather than the brutality of their abuser. If a man, such as the defendant in *Smith*, is provoked whilst depressed, that should be taken into account by the jury when considering the reactions of a person in his position. But when a man, who is not clinically depressed, is

---

29 [1996] 3 WLR 45.

30 However, after *R v Parker* [1997] Crim LR 760, it is questionable whether the decision of the Privy Council in *R v Luc Thiet Thuan* would be applied in preference to earlier Court of Appeal decisions.

31 [1996] 3 WLR 45, pp 60–66.

32 [1994] 4 All ER 387. See above, fn 9.

'provoked' by his wife's behaviour, he is not required to submit medical evidence as to his state of mind because the presumption of the law is that those conditions can be understood by the layman and hence an expert is superfluous. Why is it so difficult to understand the reactions of a woman who lives in fear of extreme violence without reference to an expert? The answer can only be that in a patriarchal society, the violence suffered by women at the hands of men can only be acknowledged if it is medicalised and reactions to it pathologised.

EXPERT MEDICAL EVIDENCE: THE CURE OR PART OF THE DISEASE?

Even if women's reactions to male violence must be pathologised via the medium of the medical professions in order to maintain the myth that male violence is unusual and incomprehensible, why does the admission of medical evidence as to state of mind continue to result in cases being decided on the basis of diminished responsibility rather than provocation? The answer to this question lies in the source of the evidence relied upon. Expert medical evidence derives from medical discourse; a discourse privileged in our society in much the same way that legal discourse is privileged[33] at the expense of other epistemologies. Medical and legal discourses are both privileged forms of knowledge because they both conform to the predominant social construction: patriarchy. The link between patriarchy, law and medicine can be comprehended in one of two ways: either patriarchy structures all knowledge, and so all forms of knowledge will be 'male',[34] or those forms of knowledge which are supported and privileged are discourses which share resonances with patriarchy, but are not completely subservient to patriarchy.[35] The former position is flawed in two ways. First, there are empirical problems in proving that any privileged discourse is simply a creation of patriarchy. Secondly, there are also reformative problems for feminists in taking this position: we must either accept that we are forever bound or limited by the current

---

33 Wells, C, 'Battered Woman Syndrome and defences to homicide: where now?' (1994) 14 LS 266, p 270.

34 On this point see, generally, MacKinnon, CA, *Toward a Feminist Theory of the State*, 1989, Cambridge, Mass: Harvard UP and *Feminism Unmodified*, 1987, Cambridge, Mass: Harvard UP. See, also, Smart, C, *Feminism and the Power of the Law*, 1989, London: Routledge, Chapter 4 for a discussion of MacKinnon's views on this point. On medical discourse in particular as a 'male' discourse, see Finley, LM, 'Breaking women's silence in law: the dilemma of the gendered nature of legal reasoning' (1989) 64 Notre Dame L Rev 886, reprinted in *Lloyd's Introduction to Jurisprudence*, 1994, London: Sweet & Maxwell, p 1141.

35 *Op cit*, Smart, fn 34, discusses this point with regard to the nature of law. A similar deconstruction of the nature of law, but taken from a Marxist stance, is made by Thompson, EP, *Whigs and Hunters: The Origin of the Black Act*, 1975, London: Allen Lane.

epistemology, or we must consciously engage in the creation of a new epistemology before we can resolve the material implications and subordinations of patriarchy. So, to envisage all forms of knowledge as 'male' is somewhat nihilistic. The latter standpoint, acknowledging a system of shared resonance and privilege, is less problematic. The connections between those whose gender is privileged and the discourses privileged by society are demonstrable. Patriarchy champions a masculine rationality, promoting universal truths and developing dualistic thinking,[36] thus making invisible other conceptions of truth and the world at large. This way of thinking is perpetuated by those who find this a 'natural' environment and who consequently are empowered by subscribing to the superiority of this form of knowledge. It is clear that legal discourse shares these characteristics: the win or lose adjudication, the truth of precedent and the preference for analogical argument. But does medical discourse share the same resonances? Clearly, with a scientific basis, medicine celebrates that which can be rationally proven, diseases are diagnosed on the premise of deduction by analogy and diagnosis represents the universal truth of the patient's condition: the power associated with medicine's truth is particularly apparent in the realm of mental health.

Once it is accepted that medicine is a discourse privileged by a patriarchal society in the same way that legal discourse is privileged, what consequence does this have for women caught up in the criminal justice system? Carol Smart has said that, as medical or 'psy' discourse has extended to new terrains and has been adopted as a modern form of regulation and surveillance, so law has developed a symbiotic relationship with medicine by which means law may also extend its realm of power.[37] Thus, on the basis of shared resonances, law and medicine interact to create an incontrovertible regulatory regime and the resonances they share promote and celebrate those identities and structures which possess similar qualities. The circle is completed: those in power recognise and support structures which reflect their own qualities and in turn those structures set the same qualities as accepted standards. Thus, the privileged discourses guarantee the full representation of those with power – men – and effectively suppress and silence those who do not reflect the universal truths disseminated by patriarchal discourse – women.[38]

Sylvia Walby supports this interpretation of the interaction between law, medicine and patriarchy when she conceptualises patriarchy as a set of

---

36 Young, IM, *Justice and the Politics of Difference*, 1990, Princeton, NJ: Princeton UP; Gilligan, C, *In a Different Voice*, 1982, Cambridge, Mass: Harvard UP.

37 *Op cit*, Smart, fn 34, p 96.

38 For discussions of examples of other instances in which women's voices have been silenced by medicine and law in combination, see Harrington, J, 'Privileging the medical norm: liberalism, self-determination and the refusal of treatment' (1996) 16 LS 348; Stern, K, 'Court-ordered caesarean sections: in whose interests?' (1993) 56 MLR 238; Bridgeman, J and Millns, S, *Feminist Perspectives on Law*, 1998, London: Sweet & Maxwell.

mutually supporting, yet independent, social structures and relations.[39] She depicts a society in which patriarchy is perpetuated by a variety of seemingly autonomous practices or institutions which nonetheless act together to strengthen patriarchy. Those institutions achieve the appearance of impartiality by presenting apparently diverse interests whilst actually functioning to reinforce the pervasiveness of patriarchal interests. For example, when it became untenable to suggest any longer that men and women charged with murdering their partners were afforded the same treatment by legal discourse, medicine presented what seemed to be an opportunity for equal justice: the inclusion of women's experience of provocation via Battered Woman's Syndrome. Ultimately, though, the spotlight on medical evidence served to distract from the real focus of inequality: that law is constructed to reflect and justify masculine experience, prescribes acceptable notions of femininity and demands excuses when women's behaviour deviates from those notions. Hence, Battered Woman's Syndrome has not developed as an effective route by which to adapt existing defences to murder so as to reflect women's truths and experiences because it has been formulated by medical discourse, and as such is patriarchally resonant. Whilst seeming to offer an opportunity for women to present their experiences to the court, Battered Woman's Syndrome is constructed in such a way as to be immediately familiar and yet is also constructed so as not to meet the very high threshold of proof for status as a defining characteristic of the reasonable person. This became very clear in the *Humphreys* judgment and despite some concessions in *Thornton (No 2)*, the threshold was still not considered to have been met by Sara Thornton.[40] At best, medical discourse illustrates an abstracted model of how a battered woman might act. At worst, the advent of Battered Woman's Syndrome has distracted legal personnel from the pursuit of other avenues by which to introduce the realities of the lives of abused women into the courts as evidence. Returning to the three key cases, it is apparent that recognition of Battered Woman's Syndrome by the courts, while opening up debate on the nature of battered women, has not directly resulted in an improvement of the way in which women charged with killing their partners are treated by the criminal justice system. Ultimately, those women are still excused from their behaviour by reason of madness through diminished responsibility, rather than justified in their actions as reasonable people responding to horrific brutality and granted a defence of provocation.[41]

---

39 Walby, S, *Theorising Patriarchy*, 1990, Oxford: Blackwell.

40 Indeed, Coughlin rejects completely the possibility that Battered Woman Syndrome can aid women's access to effective defences because it is the product of a masculine epistemology, just as law is. See Coughlin, AM, 'Excusing women' (1994) 82 California L Rev 1, p 79.

41 For a discussion of the significance of justificatory or excusing defences to murder, see Edwards, S, *Sex and Gender in the Legal Process*, 1996, London: Blackstone, p 231.

While there is an apparent consideration of the violence women suffer at the hands of their male intimates on the part of the courts and the 'psy' professions, the gains made by the invocation of medical expert evidence exist but are limited. Real gains include the qualified modification of 'sudden and temporary' loss of self-control as a component of provocation. In *Ahluwalia*, the court acknowledged that cooling off time would not negate the claim to provocation where there is a history of domestic violence, but the same cooling off time would be influential in rebutting the validity of defence of provocation.[42] Another gain is in the recognition of the psychological impact that systematic domestic violence has on women in addition to the more obvious physical impact. This was confirmed in *Thornton (No 2)* by the requirement that judges direct the jury to the admissibility of evidence of Battered Woman's Syndrome with regard to the subjective element of provocation. Thus, although there have not been any cases decided as yet explicitly on this basis, the Court of Appeal has given its blessing to the adoption of such a course of action. These are truly beneficial advances toward the acknowledgment of what really happens when a woman kills a violent partner. However, given the privileged position of medical discourse in patriarchal society, it is also conceivable that women may never be able to avail themselves of a full defence of provocation based on their status as battered women because medical discourse sets the syndrome at odds with the pervasiveness required for the objective element of the defence of provocation. Simply put, the existence of a possible medical basis for defence to murder does not mean that that defence will be any more realisable for women than their current chances of using the present defences to murder. Therefore, reliance on expert medical evidence may represent more a diversion than a real chance to achieve justice for women who find themselves in this situation. The outcome for patriarchy is that attention is focused on a means which may deliver a just outcome for battered women, but will do so only when it is the interests of patriarchy.

BEYOND DISTRACTION: EXPERT MEDICAL EVIDENCE MAY SERVE TO DAMAGE WOMEN WHO KILL

Despite the beneficial steps taken by the courts in condoning the introduction of expert medical evidence on the effects of domestic violence, a decision has not yet been given which has commuted a conviction for murder against a battered woman to one of manslaughter on the basis of provocation; either in the subjective test of cumulative provocation or in the objective element of defining mental characteristics. However, if expert medical evidence serves

42   *Op cit*, McColgan, fn 13.

only to distract women from effective engagement with the criminal justice system, that distraction can be overcome. What is problematic is the possibility that reliance on this type of evidence has done considerable damage to the way in which women are perceived in legal discourse. Chan suggests that utilising expert medical evidence on Battered Woman's Syndrome may create more problems than it solves. She summarises feminists' concerns as, first, the possibility of reinforcing existing stereotypes about women as passive and accepting in the face of violence or irrational when they react. By focusing on Battered Woman's Syndrome, the woman is represented as incapable of reasonable behaviour and in thrall to her syndrome. Secondly, Chan states that not only may expert medical evidence perpetuate old stereotypes, it may create new ones. By requiring expert testimony as to the symptoms of Battered Woman's Syndrome, a stereotype of the *'bona fide'* battered woman may emerge. Thus, women will be constricted not only as they are at present by the standard of how a reasonable man reacts to provocation, they will also be judged by an acceptable notion of a feminine reaction to provocation as approved by the 'psy' professions.[43] If women fail to fit the stereotype, it is unlikely they will be recognised at all as women who have been subjected to systematic violence. As McColgan says of experience in America:

> Where such (expert) evidence has been admitted it has frequently been used to construct a stereotypical battered woman, rather than to counter male perceptions of danger, immediacy and harm ... When women failed to fit the stereotype (where, for example, they had fought back before) the evidence then would often be put to one side and their conduct judged against the standard of the reasonable man ...[44]

The preservation of existing inaccurate stereotypes of women as mad or bad, and the formulation of new stereotypes, are risks inherent in invoking expert testimony. Although such testimony may have fortunate results in the short term, it may only serve to devalue women's voices more in the long term. Nevertheless, this is not the greatest harm done by turning to experts to validate women's experience of male violence. Significant harm is done in two ways: first, when women are seen to need an expert to give credibility to their response to physical and psychological abuse, they are doubted as being capable of explaining what they perceived of as provocative words or deeds, whereas a man's response to provocation caused by a woman is viewed as generally understandable. For example, men often claim that they were provoked to kill their female partner either by her infidelity or by her nagging.[45] It is accepted that nagging or adultery are provocative acts, and yet it is open to question as to whether being beaten by one's male partner is

---

43 *Op cit*, Chan, fn 28, pp 206–07.
44 *Op cit*, McColgan, fn 13.
45 See *op cit*, Edwards, fn 41, pp 397–400.

provocative or just part of a stormy relationship. An expert is needed to 'explain' how women might react to violence. The damage that this does is twofold: first, requiring expert evidence affirms the stereotype of women as sufficiently lacking in credibility so as to be believed without the corroboration of an expert; and, secondly, domestic violence is transformed by the mediation of expert testimony into something abnormal whilst at the same time suggesting that violence might be an acceptable component of intimate relationships. Ultimately, the invocation of expert medical evidence obscures and distracts from the reality of domestic violence.

The second means by which significant harm is done by the dependence upon expert evidence is by another form of distraction. As expert medical evidence focuses on the defendant's disorders or syndromes, it distracts attention from the violence committed by the deceased man. The violence he committed becomes of importance only to the extent to which it could be related to the onset of Battered Woman's Syndrome. Instead, the battered woman's decision to kill her violent partner would be better understood in direct relation to the extent of the violence she suffered at his hands. Then her actions could be considered as a reasonable use of force in response to the level of violence and abuse which was inflicted on her. Instead, the violence perpetrated by the man is used to humiliate the woman one more time by being used to assess whether she has a right to be termed sufficiently 'mad' or disordered to be given the protection of the partial defences to murder. It seems, following *Thornton (No 2)*, that even if a defence of provocation on the basis of Battered Woman's Syndrome is allowed, it will be on the basis of expert testimony as to the extent to which the woman's mental makeup has been transfigured by the violence she suffered. What would be preferable would be a defence premised on the concept that, for battered women, it is reasonable to respond to continued and considerable violence as they have done when they believe there is no alternative other than their own eventual death. A defence so defined would demand a close examination of the violence done by the deceased and would place it in a causal role with regard to his own death, rather than looking to how well or badly the woman coped mentally with the violence done to her. The proposed strategy of adoption of a defence based on the deceased's violence rather than on the woman's susceptibility to disorder and syndrome would still require expert medical evidence. This would be a detailed chronicling of the medical treatment received for violence done or the obvious absence of treatment in cases where women were prevented from seeking medical help. Whilst this would still entail a certain reliance on the medical profession, it should be remembered that expert medical evidence becomes problematic for women when it interprets the effects of abuse. If expert testimony is confined to factual confirmation of the existence of violence, then we may avoid inferences being drawn as to whether the defendant is 'deserving' of the label 'battered woman'.

Additionally, a defence to murder focused on the violence done by the deceased to lead the defendant to believe that she had no other option of escape would not be based solely on submission of medical evidence. A range of evidence would have to be submitted so as to present the full context in which the defendant acted to kill her alleged abuser. In this sense a less dualistic, more polycentric approach could be adopted into which any number of agents: social services, schools, GPs, neighbours, the police and the defendant herself could be incorporated. The evidence submitted by the defendant would be on the issue of honest belief as to her alternatives to escape the violence. Whilst this may seem a wholly subjective test, the concept of honest belief is already employed in the criminal justice process. With regard to rape, the subjective test of belief as to consent is in place and works to give the male defendant the benefit of the doubt. This is supported by factual medical evidence as to lack of struggle or absence of force used.[46] In the same way, a defendant's honest belief as to the danger in which she found herself would be corroborated by physical and psychological examination as to the existence of past abuse and the network of context surrounding her. A defence in this form would place the abusive partner at centre stage and would place firmly in focus a social commitment not to accept the violent physical, verbal or psychological abuse of one person by another whilst demanding that any action as grave as taking another's life must be an absolute last resort.

CONCLUSION

The use of expert medical evidence has been advantageous for battered women who kill their violent partners in that it has created a space in which the problem of domestic violence can be discussed. It has also been useful in that it has rectified some myths and mistakes about how women might react to provocation and what effects domestic violence has on those reactions. In a pragmatic sense, it has resulted in the release of women who were convicted of murder when they had been fighting for their own preservation. However, any defence predicated upon a notion that the disorders and syndromes caused by systematic violence are of greater relevance to a battered woman's actions than the violence done to her by the 'loved one' she ends up killing is in desperate need of refocusing. The central factor in deciding the fate of battered women who kill should be the extent of the violence done to them by the deceased, not how mad or disordered that violence has made them. Expert medical testimony must not be allowed to distract us from that focus.

---

46   *Op cit*, Finley, fn 34.

Nevertheless, it seems, on a close consideration of the nature of medical expert testimony and the manner in which it has been employed by the courts, that, until the shared resonances of patriarchy, medicine and law can be surmounted, it is unlikely that women will be granted the same access to the range of defences to murder as are currently available to men, and in fact may continue to be hindered in their search for such equality by the very means they are employing to achieve that equality of access to criminal justice.

CHAPTER 11

THE CHARACTER OF THE ACCUSED

Mary Childs

INTRODUCTION

One of the most complex and contradictory areas of the English law of criminal evidence is that dealing with evidence of the accused's character. Technicalities abound, and the inconsistency and contradiction within the case law has given rise to considerable criticism and debate. The search for a clearly stated and easily applied scheme for governing the admission of character evidence has occupied scholars and judges in most common law jurisdictions, and the one apparently universal conclusion is that the matter is not susceptible to such ready solutions.[1] In 1996, the Law Commission for England and Wales produced a Consultation Paper of epic length, acknowledging the unsatisfactory state of the law and finally concluding, with a tone of resignation as much as satisfaction, that the way forward was to make some minor amendments to the existing unsatisfactory system.[2]

It would be foolhardy to attempt, in this brief chapter, to develop a newer, better, simpler or more rational approach to the admissibility and use of character evidence. Instead, I propose to offer a few partial and exploratory feminist thoughts about certain aspects of the law relating to character evidence, and to raise a few questions about what it tells us about the law's construction of identity, agency, and gender. I will do so by looking at arguments for and against the greater use of character evidence, by considering debates about the treatment of 'similar fact evidence' in sexual offence cases, and by asking how the law should regard evidence contradicting previous acquittals. In all these contexts, the approach adopted will be feminist in the broadest sense of being concerned with the way legal rules affect the position of men and women within the legal system, and seeking to expose and articulate gendered differences in both assumptions and effects.

In undertaking this limited and tentative exercise, I start from the position that the proper concern of evidence scholars is not simply the study of rules of

---

1   The Criminal Law Revision Committee described this as 'by far the most difficult of all the topics which we have discussed': 11th Report: *Evidence (General)*, Cmnd 4991, 1972, para 70.

2   Law Commission, *Previous Misconduct of a Defendant*, Consultation Paper No 141, 1996, London: HMSO.

admissibility. As the evaluation of evidence is equally central to the allocation of risk in the trial process, its assessment (by either lay or professional fact-finders) is as crucial to the legal system, and as important a matter of consideration by evidence scholars.[3] Equally, thinking about evidence means thinking about social context and fact construction as well as rules of law,[4] and these rules cannot be properly understood without consideration of the insights offered by psychology and the social sciences.[5] Nothing is a 'piece of evidence' *in abstracto*; it becomes evidence by virtue of a chain of reasoning linking it to an issue in the case. The case law and academic discussion of character evidence presents us with insights into the assumptions about men and women which permeate those reasoning processes.

In the context of character evidence issues, as with many other aspects of evidence law, issues in relation to sexual offences have prompted the most feminist analysis and criticism. There are several reasons for this focus: first, the obviously sex-specific nature of most sex offences in English law.[6] Secondly, the undeniable fact that even when sexual offences are framed in gender neutral terms, the majority of complainants are female and the overwhelming majority of defendants are male. Thirdly, the broader social impact upon all women of the fear of rape and other sexual assaults. The response of the criminal justice system to rape and sexual assault cases is an important focus of feminist study not only because its perceived ineffectiveness contributes to women's fears of crime, but also because it exposes social and legal constructions of men, women, and sexual behaviour.

As one commentator has observed, the history of English evidence law in relation to character evidence has been largely a history of cases dealing with sexual offences, particularly offences against children.[7] The use of such evidence was especially significant in these cases because until recently the jury had to be warned of the dangers of convicting on the testimony of the complainant alone, and would be advised by the judge to look for

---

3   See Stein, A, 'The refoundation of evidence law' (1996) 9 Canadian J Law & Jurisprudence 279.

4   Twining, W, *Rethinking Evidence: Exploratory Essays*, 1990, Oxford: Blackwell.

5   The later years of the 20th century saw a flourishing of interdisciplinary writing on evidence and proof, sometimes referred to as 'the new evidence scholarship': Lempert, R, 'The new evidence scholarship: analyzing the process of proof' (1986) 66 Boston UL Rev 439; Jackson, J, 'Analysing the new evidence scholarship: towards a new conception of the law of evidence' (1996) 16 OJLS 309; Twining, W, 'Recent trends in evidence scholarship', in Nijboer, JF and Reijntjes, JM (eds), *Proceedings of the First World Conference on New Trends in Criminal Investigation and Evidence*, 1997, Lelystad, The Netherlands: OU Press.

6   Until 1994, English law limited the physical act of rape to penile-vaginal penetration; although this definition has been broadened to encompass anal rape and rape of men, it remains the case that only a man can commit rape as the principal offender.

7   Mirfield, P, 'Similar fact evidence of child sexual abuse in English, United States and Florida law: a comparative study' (1996) 6 J Transnational L & P 7.

corroborative evidence.[8] Given the likelihood that the offences took place in private, and the rule that corroborative evidence had to emanate from a source independent of the complainant, the only other corroborative evidence might be evidence relating to the character of the accused, such as evidence of other similar offences.

CHARACTER EVIDENCE IN ENGLISH LAW

In English criminal trials the accused may adduce evidence of good character for two purposes. First, to suggest that he or she is not 'that sort of person' – that is, the sort who would commit the offence charged.[9] Secondly, to bolster the credibility of the accused who chooses to testify.[10] If the accused chooses to offer evidence of good character, then those claims may be rebutted by cross-examination of the accused or by the testimony of other witnesses. But the accused has the option of not putting character in issue, and in that case, the general rule is that evidence will be excluded if it shows the bad reputation or previous misdeeds of the defendant. A few statutory exceptions either permit character evidence to be admitted to prove some element of the offence,[11] or make previous convictions an element of the offence itself,[12] but these are rare. The protection of the accused against attacks on character takes two forms: a protection (which may be forfeited in certain circumstances) against cross-examination about extraneous misconduct, and a prohibition on introduction by the prosecution of evidence concerning the accused's bad character or previous convictions (misleadingly referred to as 'similar fact evidence').

A number of reasons have been advanced for the exclusion of character evidence from the trial:[13] that it lacks probative force, that its admission would unduly complicate and extend the trial, and that admissibility of bad character evidence would encourage police and prosecutors to 'round up the

---

8   The requirement of a corroboration warning in sexual cases was abolished by the Criminal Justice and Public Order Act 1994, s 32.

9   *R v Stannard* (1837) 7 C & P 673.

10 *R v Bellis* [1966] 1 All ER 552.

11 Eg, Official Secrets Act 1911, s 1(2); Theft Act 1968, s 27(3).

12 Eg, Firearms Act 1968, s 21. One statutory provision which has the effect of introducing such evidence (albeit not explicitly) is the requirement in the Street Offences Act 1959 that only a 'common prostitute' can be convicted of soliciting for the purpose of prostitution. Magistrates are thereby given notice that the accused has on two or more previous occasions been cautioned by police who identified her as a prostitute. The Home Office has recommended abolition of this system, which disadvantages defendants without adequate justification and suggests a view of sexually transgressive women as in a criminal class of their own and suitable for treatment as second class citizens: *The Rehabilitation of Offenders Act 1974 and Cautions, Reprimands and Final Warnings: A Consultation Paper*, 1999, London: Home Office, Annex B.

13 *Op cit*, Law Commission, fn 2, paras 7.1–7.28.

usual suspects' instead of properly investigating offences. Central to the debates about admissibility of 'similar fact evidence' is the fear that its admission will create undue prejudice to the accused and thereby undermine the rectitude of verdicts.

The probative value of most character evidence lies in the common sense assumption that people tend to behave in predictable ways, and that therefore, information about the conduct of the defendant on a previous occasion can give the trier of fact useful insights into how the defendant may have behaved in relation to the offence charged.[14]

The theory underpinning this assumption is that people have personality characteristics which manifest themselves more or less consistently in a range of situations. Thus, someone who lied in one situation would be likely to do so in other circumstances. An extreme version of this approach is reflected in the rule that a defendant who chooses to make character an issue in the case cannot do so selectively; character is said to be indivisible, so if a claim of good character is made with respect to sexual matters, then the defendant may be exposed to cross-examination about prior acts of dishonesty.[15]

But psychologists do not agree about the extent to which people can be viewed as possessing consistent and persistent traits or personality characteristics. Some psychological research suggests that, in fact, behaviour varies dramatically across different situations. The idea that one can speak of relatively fixed characteristics such as 'dishonesty' appears to conflict with research based upon observation of subjects given the opportunity to be dishonest in a range of situations. The fact that one was dishonest in one situation is not very helpful as a way of predicting honesty or dishonesty in dissimilar situations.[16]

Experienced mental health professionals who thoroughly investigated the behaviour and history of violent mentally ill patients were wrong in predictions of future violence two out of three times – as Mendez argues, it may be prudent to think carefully before inviting jurors to make similar assessments on the basis of much less evidence.[17]

What does feminism have to say about character evidence? One initial response might be to say that such evidence should be viewed with caution due to the problematic nature of its assumptions about human nature. Feminist concerns about the dangers of essentialism[18] suggest we should be

14 Zuckerman, A, 'Similar fact evidence: the unobservable rule' (1987) 103 LQR 187.

15 *R v Winfield* (1939) 27 Cr App Rep 139.

16 Davies, SM, 'Evidence of character to prove conduct: a reassessment of relevancy' (1991) 27 Criminal Law Bulletin 504.

17 Mendez, M, 'Character evidence reconsidered: "people do not seem to be predictable characters"' (1998) 49 Hastings LJ 871; Mendez, M, 'The law of evidence and the search for a stable personality' (1996) 45 Emory LJ 221.

18 Spelman, E, *Inessential Woman: Problems of Exclusion in Feminist Thought*, 1988, London: The Women's Press; Harris, A, 'Race and essentialism in feminist legal theory' (1990) 42 Stanford LR 581.

wary of making assumptions that groups or individuals can be described and understood in terms of fixed 'natures'. If we accept descriptions of people as 'dishonest' or 'avaricious', can we resist other descriptive terms such as 'feminine' or 'emotional' or 'promiscuous'? Some postmodern feminist theorists draw upon psychoanalytic theory, with its emphasis on the role of the unconscious, to question whether individual subjects can ever be 'known' even to themselves.[19] Conceptions of subjectivity as 'heterogeneous and decentred' suggest that it may be impossible ever fully to understand others as unitary and consistent characters.

But, as anti-essentialist critiques acknowledge, the political force of feminism largely depends upon the claim that shared identities and affiliations are linked to certain commonalities of experience and perception.[20] The tension between individualising witnesses and making general claims can also be seen in feminist debates about evidence of Battered Woman's Syndrome and rape trauma syndrome. The value of such evidence depends upon claims that victims of rape or domestic violence tend to respond in consistent and predictable ways.[21] Some feminists have argued, however, that the use of such syndrome evidence is dangerous for women whose reactions do not fit the standard pattern of the syndrome.[22] They may find that, if they do not fall within the standard model, their circumstances may be entirely disregarded.

Concerns about the generalisations inherent in character evidence may be met, however, with the observation that excluding character evidence from the trial will not keep stereotypes and generalisations out of the minds of jurors and judges. They will still form opinions and impressions of the characters of the witnesses, but will do so on the basis of the limited information available to them.[23] Where there is little information available other than appearance and demeanour while testifying, jurors are likely to form impressions of character based upon stereotypes, including gendered stereotypes. An alternative might be to permit introduction of more expert evidence in relation to the character of the individual witness or defendant, as a way of advancing the feminist goal of moving to more individualised and

---

19 Young, IM, 'The ideal of community and the politics of difference', in Nicholson, L (ed), *Feminism/Postmodernism*, 1990, London: Routledge, Chapter 12.

20 *Op cit*, Spelman, fn 18; Ramazanoglu, C, *Feminism and the Contradictions of Oppression*, 1989, London: Routledge.

21 One scholar has described it as 'group character evidence': Mosteller, R, 'Syndromes and politics in criminal trials and evidence law' (1996) 46 Duke LJ 461.

22 Raeder, M, 'The double-edged sword: admissibility of Battered Woman's Syndrome evidence by and against batterers in cases involving domestic violence' (1996) 67 Colorado L Rev 789; Mahoney, M, 'Legal images of battered women: redefining the issue of separation' (1991) 90 Michigan L Rev 1. See, also, Scully, Chapter 10, in this volume.

23 Park, R, 'Character at the crossroads' (1998) 49 Hastings LJ 717, pp 740–41.

contextual justice as well as increasing the likely accuracy of the character assessment.[24] If juries are already making character assessments part of their decision making (even if unconsciously), should they not be helped to make those assessments more accurately? As jurors may be unaware of the rules excluding character evidence, they may simply assume that if they don't hear about prior misdeeds, then none occurred.[25]

But will introducing more character evidence advance feminist goals? In some cases, it appears that the real function of good character evidence is to increase the chance of jury nullification – an acquittal derived not from a lack of proof with respect to the offence charged, but rather because it is thought inappropriate to punish this defendant. If a defendant is allowed to appeal to the jury to acquit on the basis of character, those most likely to benefit may well be those who fit conventional models of proper behaviour, including hegemonic models of acceptable masculine and feminine lifestyles. The principle that defendants should be tried for what they have *done*, not for who they *are*, seems consistent with feminist concerns about equal treatment and the need to minimise prejudice to marginalised or unconventional persons,[26] but it might also be argued that the incorporation of a feminist 'ethic of care' in evidence law would weigh in favour of admitting more character evidence as part of a move to more individualised and contextualised justice.[27]

David Leonard has suggested that permitting the defendant to offer character evidence serves what he calls the 'cathartic function' of a trial by giving the central party an opportunity to be fully heard and acknowledged as a person, to seek the fullest possible understanding by the jury of their situation.[28] This view recognised that trials have myriad social functions, not simply that of factual investigation.

In this way, expanding the use of character evidence might be viewed as consistent with feminist endeavours to have women's stories heard in court. Aviva Orenstein has written of the potential use of character evidence to enrich and enhance the narratives told in rape trials, thereby contextualising

---

24 Taslitz, A, 'Myself alone: individualizing justice through psychological character evidence' (1993) 52 Maryland L Rev 1. Taslitz suggests that this would help jurors overcome pre-existing biases and would also further important moral and political goals. In England and Wales, this would be problematic, owing to the rule in *R v Turner* [1975] 1 All ER 70: expert psychological evidence is only admissible in respect of abnormal mental states.

25 Orenstein, A, 'No bad men! A feminist analysis of character evidence in rape trials' (1998) 49 Hastings LJ 663.

26 Baker has pointed out that letting in more evidence of previous convictions will have a disparate impact upon members of highly policed and disadvantaged ethnic minorities. Baker, K, 'Once a rapist? motivational evidence and relevancy in rape law' (1996) 110 Harv L Rev 563.

27 See Nicolson, Chapter 2, in this volume.

28 Leonard, D, 'The use of character to prove conduct: rationality and catharsis in the law of evidence' (1986–87) 58 Colorado UL Rev 1.

justice and educating jurors to understand things in a way which takes them beyond stereotypes and rape myths.[29]

Still, one has only to think of recent high profile prosecutions of 'bad' women to see the dangers of admitting character evidence in relation to those who are seen as immoral or transgressive of social norms – in the cases of both Sara Thornton[30] and Rosemary West,[31] for instance, evidence was given of unconventional social and sexual behaviour, and it was widely thought that this may have contributed in part to their convictions. Equally, it has been argued by Peter Tillers[32] that an overlooked reason for excluding character evidence generally is the moral and political one of respect for the autonomy and integrity of the individual defendant, and the desirability of sparing them the humiliation and intrusion of exposing their entire personal history to the scrutiny and judgment of strangers. Feminists who have criticised the way the adversarial system treats victims should think carefully about the implications of increased reliance on character evidence in trials, as it seems likely to exacerbate the distress of witnesses, whether defendants or others.

A concern raised by Katherine Baker is that use of character evidence by the prosecution is likely to add to the disadvantage of groups already overrepresented as defendants in the criminal justice system.[33] In most cases, legally aided defendants will lack the resources to investigate the character of prosecution witnesses, while the prosecution will be able to obtain criminal records and other damaging information about the defendant and any defence witnesses. The temptation to 'round up the usual suspects', knowing that their criminal records could be used against them, would be most likely to affect members of marginalised groups. It cannot be consistent with feminist principles to overlook the undesirable consequences of reform proposals which risk exacerbate existing inequalities.

WHY EXCLUDE EVIDENCE OF PREVIOUS MISCONDUCT?

Central to the protection of the accused against evidence of previous misdeeds is the fear that its admission would create an unacceptable risk of prejudice. Broadly, there are two types of prejudice to the accused which may arise if the trier of fact is aware of the accused's criminal record or other misdeeds. The first kind is sometimes called 'reasoning prejudice', while the second is

---

29 *Op cit*, Orenstein, fn 25.

30 See the discussion in Nadel, J, *Sara Thornton: The Story of a Woman Who Killed*, 1993, London: Victor Gollancz, especially Chapter 7.

31 Masters, B, *'She Must Have Known': The Trial of Rosemary West*, 1996, London: Doubleday.

32 Tillers, P 'What is wrong with character evidence?' (1998) 49 Hastings LJ 781.

33 *Op cit*, Baker, fn 26.

referred to as 'moral prejudice'. Both types tend to reduce the likelihood that criminal trials will result in accurate and acceptable verdicts.

Briefly, 'reasoning prejudice' refers to the fear that the court will overestimate the probative value of the evidence. Although, in the common law system, issues of admissibility and weight are often regarded as conceptually distinct, certain exclusionary rules are justified, at least in part, on the principle of reducing the risk of inferential error. The rule against character evidence is one such rule. As discussed later in this chapter, fact-finders (whether jurors or magistrates) who lack accurate information about the prevalence of offending may be thought prone to overestimate its significance.

'Moral prejudice' refers to a different sort of risk; the risk that the trier of fact will disregard the evidence relating the offence charged, and instead convict the accused on the basis of a feeling that this individual is deserving of punishment (less strongly, they may simply feel inclined to convict on the basis of a lower degree of certainty than otherwise, feeling that the accused has probably committed other offences or is less worthy of protection against wrongful conviction). This has sometimes been described as the risk of 'nullification prejudice'.[34]

'SIMILAR FACT' EVIDENCE

As indicated in the discussion above, there are certain circumstances in which the prosecution may introduce evidence of the accused's previous misdeeds or bad character as part of the prosecution case. The circumstances in which such evidence will be admitted are not easily described, however.

The leading case setting out the general parameters of the doctrine is *Makin v AG for New South Wales*,[35] in which it was stated that evidence of bad character or acts extraneous to the facts of the present case was generally inadmissible to show guilt via propensity reasoning, although it might be admitted to show design, or to rebut a defence open to the accused. This approach gave rise to a number of decisions in which the courts approached the question of admissibility by searching for a recognised line of argument falling within the permitted category of arguments justifying admission of the evidence. The exercise was purely one of categorisation of the argument, with admissibility flowing almost automatically from a finding that the reasoning

---

34 Park, R, 'Character issues in the OJ Simpson case – or, rationales of the character evidence ban, with illustrations from the OJ Simpson case' (1996) 67 Colorado UL Rev 747.

35 [1894] AC 57.

employed was other than simply that of the accused's propensity to commit such offences.[36]

The *Makin* test was significantly changed (although not expressly overruled) in *DPP v Boardman*,[37] in which the House of Lords declared that the true reason for admission of such evidence was that, in some cases, its probative force might be such that it would be an affront to common sense to exclude it. The question in each case should be whether the prejudicial effect of the evidence was outweighed by its probative force. This probative force might arise in a number of ways, but the one which came to dominate the post-*Boardman* cases was the notion of 'striking similarity'; judges were reluctant in some cases[38] to admit evidence of bad character unless satisfied that there was some unusual similarity between it and the offence charged.

The requirement of 'striking similarity' as a precondition of admissibility was rejected in *DPP v P*.[39] The House of Lords restored the convictions, and said the fundamental test for admission was whether the probative force of the evidence made it just to admit it despite its prejudicial effect. The only category of cases in which 'striking similarity' might be required would be those in which the identity of the perpetrator was in issue.

Why might these rules affect men and women differently? The simple answer is that a greater willingness to admit such evidence in sex cases is likely to result in more convictions of male rapists and child abusers. The overwhelming majority of those charged with sexual offences are male, and the majority of their victims (both adult and juvenile) are female; a measure which shifts the balance in favour of conviction may provide greater protection for victims. As these offences typically take place in private, and the trial often consists principally of a contest between the credibility of the accuser and that of the accused, anything which can be used to bolster the prosecution case may have a significant impact on enforcement of sexual offences. Women have historically been viewed as less credible witnesses than men, and have been regarded as particularly suspect when appearing as complainants in sexual offence cases.[40] Where one woman alleges rape or sexual assault, her word alone may not persuade the jury beyond a reasonable

---

36 Although the judge did have a general discretion to limit the introduction and use of such evidence in order to preserve the fairness of the trial.

37 [1975] AC 421; [1974] 3 WLR 673.

38 But not all; in some cases, the courts regarded the test as one of 'positive probative value'.

39 [1991] 2 AC 447.

40 Mack, K, 'Continuing barriers to women's credibility: a feminist perspective on the proof process' (1993) 4 Criminal Law Forum 327; Hunter, R, 'Gender in evidence: masculine norms vs feminist reforms' (1996) 19 Harv Women's LJ 127; Scheppele, K, 'Just the facts ma'am: sexualised violence, evidentiary habits, and the reversion of truth' (1992) 37 NYLS L Rev 123.

doubt, but it may be a very different story if other women testify to similar incidents, as Susan Estrich explained when discussing the exclusion of character evidence from the sexual assault trial of William Kennedy Smith:

> ... one woman might lie, but four? One might have a motive to fabricate, but all of them? And if four women are all saying the same thing about one man, maybe it's the man who's lying.[41]

Despite the move away from the rigidity of the *Makin* categories and the post-*Boardman* preoccupation with 'striking similarity', it has been argued that courts are still too reluctant to admit similar fact evidence in rape cases, with the result that serial rapists are walking free. Susan Lees describes cases in which men were accused of rape by a number of different women but acquitted each time; the rapes were said to be 'acquaintance rapes' because the complainants were known socially (although not well known) by the defendants, and at each trial the defendant successfully argued consent.[42] One man had been reported to the police by 11 different women, but only three cases went to trial and he was acquitted each time. Lees argues that, in such cases, the rules relating to similar fact evidence should be relaxed to permit multiple counts to be tried together, or to permit evidence of other rapes to be adduced.[43] Given this concern that the exclusion of character evidence in rape cases is contributing to an unacceptably high acquittal rate, what reforms might be adopted to address the problem?

A special rule for sexual offences?

The use of similar fact evidence in sexual offence cases has been given special status in the US, where Rule 413 of the Federal Rules of Evidence[44] provides that, in rape cases, the prosecution may adduce evidence of the defendant's prior rapes. The Law Commission briefly considered the desirability of introducing a similar rule in England and Wales, but rejected it.[45] I contend that they were right to do so. Although the adoption of Federal Rule of Evidence 413 might be viewed as a desirable advance, it has been condemned

---

41 Estrich, S, 'Palm Beach stories' (1992) 11 Law & Phil 5, p 13.

42 Lees, S, *Carnal Knowledge: Rape on Trial*, 1997, London: Penguin, pp 159–80.

43 *Ibid*, p 252.

44 www.law.cornell.edu/rules/fre. Although the Federal Rules of Evidence are technically applicable only to limited areas within federal criminal jurisdiction, they are highly influential upon development of criminal procedure at State level.

45 *Op cit*, Law Commission, fn 2, paras 9.24–9.36.

by feminists[46] and other evidence scholars[47] alike. There are several reasons for this criticism, and they relate to both reasoning prejudice and moral prejudice.

Sexual offences and reasoning prejudice

Recidivism and probative force

One criticism of the Federal Rules of Evidence approach is that it rests upon, and may reinforce, existing undesirable myths about rape and sexual assault which lead to an overestimate of the probative force of previous sex crimes convictions. The rationale behind Federal Rule of Evidence 413 appears to be that rapists are somehow more prone to recidivism, or more aberrant in some way than other types of offenders. There appears to be no clear statistical evidence to suggest a higher rate of recidivism;[48] in fact, a 1989 recidivism study in the US found that only 7.7% of released rapists were re-arrested for rape, as opposed to 33.5% of released larcenists re-arrested for larceny, 31.9% of released burglars re-arrested for burglary, and 28.4% of drug offenders re-arrested for drug offences.[49] Of course, it is generally accepted that many rapes go unreported, but it is equally true that many burglaries go unsolved, and there is no reason to think that these figures grossly misrepresent recidivism rates.[50] It is sometimes asserted that sexual offences differ from other crimes by virtue of being caused by some psychological abnormality rather than by a 'rational' economic or other motive, and that this peculiarity increases the risk of recidivism.[51] One proponent of the sexual offence Federal Rule of Evidence stated:

---

46 *Op cit*, Baker, fn 26; *op cit*, Orenstein, fn 25.

47 Duane, J, 'The new Federal Rule of Evidence on prior acts of accused sex offenders: a poorly drafted version of a very bad idea' (1994) FRD 95; Natali, LM and Stigall, S, '"Are you going to arraign his whole life?" How sexual propensity evidence violates the due process clause' (1996) 28 Loyola U Chi LJ 1; McCandless, J, 'Prior bad acts and two bad rules: the fundamental unfairness of Federal Rules of Evidence 413 and 414' (1997) 5 W & M Bill of Rights J 689; Ellis, M, 'The politics behind Federal Rules of Evidence 413, 414 and 415' (1998) 38 Santa Clara L Rev 961; Pickett, JG, 'The presumption of innocence imperiled: the new Federal Rules of Evidence 413–414 on the use of other sexual offence evidence' (1995) 70 Wash L Rev 853.

48 Imwinkelreid, E, 'Undertaking the task of reforming the American character evidence prohibition: the importance of getting the experiment off on the right foot' (1997) 22 Fordham Urb LJ 285; Park, R, 'Character at the crossroads' (1998) 49 Hastings LJ 717; *op cit*, Baker, fn 26.

49 Cited in *op cit*, Baker, fn 26, pp 578–79.

50 All such crime figures are unreliable to some extent for a variety of well known reasons, but, with respect to re-arrest rates, it might be thought that police might find it easier to arrest a recidivist rapist rather than burglar, as most rapists are known to their victims and can be identified by them; the same cannot be said with respect to burglars.

51 Richard Posner has described rapists as having a 'taste' for rape as an end in itself, a taste not shared by most men. In contrast, he thinks a thief has a taste for money – a 'normal' desire, but simply pursued by unconventional means. Posner, R, 'An economic approach to the law of evidence' (1999) 51 Stanford L Rev 1477.

Ordinary people do not commit outrages against others because they have relatively little inclination to do so, and because any inclination in that direction is suppressed by moral inhibitions and fear of the practical risks associated with the commission of crimes. A person with a history of rape or child molestation stands on a different footing. His past conduct provides evidence that he has the combination of aggressive and sexual impulses that motivates the commission of such crimes, that he lacks effective inhibitions against acting on these impulses, and that the risks involved do not deter him.[52]

What this analysis omits, of course, is the acknowledgment that the same could be said of any of a range of offences, from robbery to non-sexual assaults; there is no explanation of why these arguments are particularly weighty with respect to sexual offences. The reason may, however, be found in the same author's statement that 'evidence showing the defendant has committed sexual assaults on other occasions places him in a small class of depraved criminals'.[53] Jenny McEwan has also argued that sexual offenders are different from 'career criminals' because they are mentally or emotionally sick, and the progression of their illness is often reflected in a progression from relatively minor to more serious and dangerous behaviour.[54]

But psychological research has repeatedly indicated that most rapists are not psychologically distinguishable from the ordinary male population, and when Sue Lees asked rape victims to describe their rapists they overwhelmingly said these men appeared to be completely 'normal' individuals.[55] It is true, of course, that some sex offenders display highly deviant behaviour and mental abnormality,[56] but not all sex offenders will fall into this category. Moreover, to the extent that this image of the 'monster' rapist persists, juries may be less likely to believe that a defendant who does not seem monstrous could be a rapist. It is commonly believed that 'nice men' – educated, affluent, middle class and white – do not commit rape;[57] this view of rapists as an aberrant minority permits others to dismiss the magnitude of the problem while absolving 'non-monsters' of responsibility.[58]

The establishment of a registration system for those convicted of sexual offences suggests a belief that defendants are prone to recidivism,[59] but Home

---

52 Karp, D, 'Evidence of propensity and probability in sex offense cases and other cases' (1994) 70 Chicago-Kent L Rev 20.

53 *Ibid*, p 24.

54 McEwan, J, *Evidence and the Adversarial Process*, 2nd edn, 1998, Oxford: Hart, p 67.

55 *Op cit*, Lees, fn 42, pp 223–24.

56 An example is *R v Straffen* [1952] 2 QB 911. Another is *R v Beggs* [1989] Crim LR 898, discussed in *ibid*, McEwan, p 67 as an example of the court failing to appreciate the aspects of the sex offences which gave them probative force.

57 Taslitz, A, 'Patriarchal stories I: cultural rape narratives in the courtroom' (1996) 5 S California Rev Law & Women's Studies 387.

58 *Op cit*, Orenstein, fn 25, p 683.

59 Sex Offenders Act 1997.

Office research studies indicate a lower reconviction rate for sexual offenders than for other types of offenders. One study showed a reconviction rate of 7% in four years for a sample of released prisoners.[60] It is true that this is likely to be a serious underrepresentation of true offending levels, but whether recidivism is particularly underrepresented in sexual cases is not proven. Annual statistics show the numbers of sexual offences reported each year, and numbers of convictions, but do not indicate whether these represent repeat offences. Research looking at cohort samples suggests that about one in 90 men born in 1953 had a conviction for a serious sexual offence[61] by age 40.[62]

Prevalence and probative value

Of course, the probative value of a previous crime with respect to a later incident of the same offence will be greater if the base rate of commission in the population is low, even if the recidivism rate is also low. Roger Park offers a helpful explanation: if burglary by parachute were a crime distinct from other forms of burglary, and one rarely committed, then a 30% recidivism rate for parachute burglars and for common burglars would render similar fact evidence of parachute burglary far more probative than similar fact evidence of common burglary.[63] It is this reasoning which leads Park to disagree with those who argue that the recidivism study makes it illogical to relax the character evidence prohibition for sex crimes rather than for offences with higher recidivism rates. He takes the view that, since rape is an offence less commonly charged than burglary or larceny, even with a lower absolute recidivism rate a previous conviction may carry greater probative force than is the case for more common offences. He claims that this is the statistical insight which lies behind the old 'common sense' view that certain offences thought to be very rare were more easily admitted as similar fact evidence.

One well known example of this sort of reasoning in English law is the case of *Thompson v R*,[64] in which the accused was charged with offences of gross indecency committed with two boys. When Thompson was arrested he was found in possession of powder puffs, and at his home the police found indecent photographs of young boys. This evidence was admitted to rebut his defence of 'innocent association' (mistaken identity), despite its only relevance

---

60 Marshall, P, *Reconviction of Imprisoned Sexual Offenders*, Research Bulletin No 36, 1994, London: Home Office.

61 Defined as: rape; buggery; indecent assault; unlawful sexual intercourse; incest; abduction; and gross indecency with a child. Marshall, P, *The Prevalence of Convictions for Sexual Offending*, Research Findings No 55, 1997, London: Home Office Research and Statistics Directorate.

62 *Ibid*, Marshall, fn 61.

63 *Op cit*, Park, fn 48, p 760.

64 [1918] AC 221.

being via the reasoning that Thompson was disposed to commit homosexual offences. The House of Lords upheld this decision, Lord Sumner saying that:

> Experience tends to show that these offences against nature connote an inversion of normal characteristics which, while demanding punishment as offending against social morality, also partake of the nature of an abnormal physical property ... Persons who commit the offences now under consideration seek the habitual gratification of a particular perverted lust, which not only takes them out of the class of ordinary men gone wrong, but stamps them with the hallmark of a specialised and extraordinary class as much as if they carried on their bodies some physical peculiarity.[65]

For some time, *Thompson* was interpreted as creating a special category of admissibility for evidence of homosexuality, although this was rejected in *Boardman*.[66] Although *Thompson* illustrates the 'common sense' application of the reasoning explained by Park, it also shows its dangers. We no longer view homosexuality as extremely rare, although there is still no clear consensus about its prevalence. The statements in the case were based upon base rate assumptions now thought to represent a severe underestimation of the incidence of homosexual activity or orientation. It was once thought that paedophilia was also extremely rare, but unfortunately it appears to be far more common than once imagined. Where the prevalence of an offence is underestimated by a court, the effect is likely to be a corresponding overestimate of the probative force of previous convictions for that offence.

How prevalent is rape? Baker argues that one problem with Federal Rule of Evidence 413 is that it rests upon an assumption that rape is also a very rare crime, something feminists have argued is not the case. It is commonly agreed that rape is an underreported offence, but the extent of that underreporting cannot be estimated with any confidence. Research in the US has also found remarkably high numbers of men prepared to say that they would engage in coercive sex or had done so in the past. In one survey of male college students, 43% reported having had sex with a woman despite her protests; other surveys have reported lower percentages, but still far greater numbers of men self-reporting sexual assault than ever come to the attention of the police.[67] Victim surveys suggest most rape victims choose not to report the incident to the police, and reports from Rape Crisis centres also indicate that many of the women who seek their assistance do not report the rape. In the US, Diana Russell's survey of 930 women found that 41% said they had been raped, but very few of these rapes had been reported to the police.[68] In the UK, a survey

---

65 [1918] AC 221, p 235.

66 [1894] AC 57. In *Boardman*, the passage quoted above was described as 'like a voice from another world'.

67 Cited in *op cit*, Baker, fn 26, p 576.

68 Russell, D, *Sexual Exploitation: Rape, Child Sexual Abuse, and Workplace Harassment*, 1984, London: Sage.

of 1,500 female Cambridge students found that approximately one in five had experienced an attempted or actual rape, but only one in 50 had reported the incident. A similar survey of 2,000 young women in Oxford indicated that only 6% of those who said they had been raped had reported it to the police.[69] These patterns may be changing, although we have insufficient information. What is clear is that the number of rapes reported to the police in England and Wales rose significantly in the 1990s,[70] but nobody can say with certainty whether this reflects increased incidence or increased reporting rates.

It appears, therefore, that there is currently no consensus as to the prevalence of rape in England and Wales. What is true is that the number of reported rapes continues to rise steadily, suggesting that either rape is not as rare as once thought, or that it has been rare, but for some reason is increasing in prevalence. In either case, it suggests that the probative value of similar fact evidence in rape cases may be less than might have been thought on the basis of crime figures from only a few years ago. As Baker says, the class of rapists is not a 'small group of depraved criminals', as they were described by the proponents of Federal Rule of Evidence 413, but rather a 'large class of normal human beings'.[71]

All rapes are not the same

A rule of blanket admissibility for similar fact evidence in sexual offence cases would lump together a wide range of disparate offences, as Baker has observed.[72]

This obscures the very real differences between different rapes, although feminist work on rape has sought to show that sexual assaults and rapes take place in many different contexts and for many different reasons. Rapes occur as part of a pattern of domestic violence, as a manifestation of rivalry with other men, as an expression of hostility in wartime, and to establish control over other men in prisons. The drunken teenager who uses force to obtain sex with his girlfriend is not the same as a violent serial rapist who seeks to vent his rage against women.[73]

---

69 *Op cit*, Lees, fn 42, p 215.

70 The number of reported rapes trebled between 1985 and 1996, from about 2,000 to about 6,000 per year. Some of the change may be attributable to changes in police recording practice. The number of 'stranger' rapes did not increase significantly; the rise was almost entirely accounted for by a huge increase in the number of 'acquaintance rapes' reported. Harris, J and Grace, S, *A Question of Evidence? Investigating and Prosecuting Rape in the 1990s*, Home Office Research Study 196, 1999, London: Home Office.

71 *Op cit*, Baker, fn 26, p 576.

72 *Op cit*, Baker, fn 26.

73 For a discussion of rape as an expression of anger, see Groth, A, Burgess, AW and Holmstrom, LL, 'Rape: power, anger and sexuality' (1977) 134 Am J Psychiatry 1239.

Both have committed rapes, but the two rapes are different in motivation and meaning. Some rapists use power to get sex, others use sex as a way of establishing power, and still others rape as an expression of hostility.[74] To treat all previous rape convictions as sufficiently probative to warrant admission in any subsequent rape trial runs counter to feminist work intended to move perceptions of sexual imposition away from the narrow stereotypes, such as the view that the only 'real rapes'[75] are those in which the perpetrator is a violent stranger and the victim a virginal girl. One aim of feminist work on rape has been to show the similarities between very different rapes, but that does not mean the multidimensionality of rapes should be overlooked. As Baker observes, 'it is not at all clear that the commission of one kind of sexual assault is probative of a likelihood to commit another kind of sexual assault'.[76]

Sexual offences and 'moral prejudice'

One troubling difference between sexual offence convictions and other types of similar fact evidence lies in the extent to which it may lead the jury to render a decision on the basis of 'moral prejudice', deciding that the defendant is less worthy of protection than otherwise, regardless of the strength of evidence with respect to the offence charged. A sense that this may be especially problematic in respect of sexual offences is reflected in the approach taken by the courts to severance of counts. Different counts are more likely to be severed and tried separately where they are charges of sexual crimes, as the risk of prejudice is thought to be higher than when multiple counts of non-sexual offences are tried together.[77]

The Law Commission Consultation Paper reported the findings of a study carried out in 1995 by the Oxford Centre for Socio-Legal Studies.[78] The research, commissioned by the Home Office, studied the effects upon mock jurors of information about the criminal record of an accused. It was aimed at investigating, *inter alia*, whether different types of previous convictions created different types or degrees of prejudice against the defendant.

Certain types of offences were more likely than others to create general prejudice against a defendant – to lead the mock jurors to regard the defendant as more likely to have committed the offence currently charged, more deserving of punishment, more likely to have got away with criminal

---

74 *Op cit*, Baker, fn 26.

75 Estrich, S, 'Real rape', 1987, Cambridge, Mass: Harvard UP. For a study of the effects of this idea on the processing of rape cases, see Stewart, M, Dobbin, S and Gatowski, S, '"Real rapes" and "real victims": the shared reliance on common cultural definitions of rape' (1996) 4 FLS 159.

76 *Op cit*, Baker, fn 26, p 576.

77 *Op cit*, Law Commission, fn 2, para 2.99.

78 *Op cit*, Law Commission, fn 2, Appendix D.

offences in the past, and more likely to lie in court. The offences most likely to create this general negative impression were offences of indecency against children, and, to a lesser extent, offences of indecent assault on a woman. The degree of prejudice was strongest with respect to recent offences similar to the one charged.

This research suggests that there may be good reason to exercise special care with respect to admission of similar fact evidence relating to sexual offences, and especially sexual offences involving children. Although the use of mock juries has certain limitations as a way of assessing the likely behaviour of real jurors, it cannot be dismissed as an indicator of the very real problem of this type of prejudice. And while it may be possible to correct for the effects of 'reasoning prejudice' by giving jurors more information about the prevalence and recidivism rates for specific offences, it is difficult to se how 'moral prejudice' can be dealt with other than by excluding evidence of such previous convictions from the trial.

The risks of both reasoning prejudice and moral prejudice are especially high in rape cases, and are associated with a view of rape as rare and monocausal deviant behaviour, a view challenged by feminist work on sexual assault. If such evidence were admitted automatically in sexual offence cases, this 'category' approach would represent a retrograde move, akin to a return to the 'ticket to admissibility' approach which followed *Makin* and was rejected in *Boardman*. It would be likely to result in more rape convictions, but there is no guarantee that they would necessarily be accurate convictions. If judges can be made to understand the probative force of genuinely relevant previous convictions, then there may be an increase in the use of similar fact evidence where it is genuinely appropriate, without the damaging consequences of a blanket rule.

It might also be seen as problematic to seek blanket admissibility of character evidence in relation to defendants in sexual case, while simultaneously supporting restrictions on admission of the complainant's sexual history. The reasons for exclusion are not identical, of course,[79] but it is likely to prove difficult to maintain a position that character should be irrelevant with respect to the complainant but not the defendant. Advocates of blanket admissibility should be wary of providing support for the practice of rape cases being conducted as competitive character attacks.

---

79 Restrictions on admission of complainants' sexual history evidence are intended in part to prevent the prospect of such cross-examination from deterring victims from coming forward.

ALTERNATIVES TO THE CATEGORY APPROACH

If it is acknowledged that the Federal Rules of Evidence approach is undesirable, but the current approach is unsatisfactory, the next logical question to ask is whether any alternative proposals offer better prospects for reform. Lees suggests that the way to improve the use of similar fact evidence in rape cases might be to educate judges by showing them patterns in the rapist's behaviour which connect different incidents and give them sufficient probative force to warrant admission: types of women assaulted, types of sexual acts, strategies, language and syntax used.[80]

Another option is to think of less dangerous ways of pursuing the same goal – that of rebutting the average juror's presumption that a 'normal' defendant is highly unlikely to be a rapist. Orenstein suggests an alternative which would be less intrusive and more educative, that of introducing expert testimony to debunk rape myths.[81] An example is the California case of *McAlpin*,[82] in which a police officer was permitted to testify that there was no such thing as a 'typical child molester', that such persons might come from any social background, and that they might have impeccable reputations in the community. Orenstein calls this 'group character' evidence, but Baker has described it as 'anti-character' evidence because its purpose is 'to help purge jurors of their tendency to think in character types'.[83]

CHARACTER EVIDENCE AND THE CONTRADICTION OF ACQUITTALS

One peculiarity of character evidence is that, in one context, the rules of admissibility have until recently been superseded by a rigid exclusionary rule which may have particular impact in cases of sexual offences. This prohibited the introduction of evidence tending to contradict the defendant's previous acquittal. The rule still applies to cross-examination of the accused.[84] The rule was overturned by the House of Lords in the case of *R v Z*,[85] the facts of which illustrate the unfortunate effects of the rule and why its operation might be particularly problematic in rape cases.

---

80 *Op cit*, Lees, fn 42, p 186.

81 *Op cit*, Orenstein, fn 25.

82 *People v McAlpin* 812 P 2d 563 (Cal 1991). The prosecution adduced the evidence in anticipation of the defence calling evidence of the accused's blameless reputation.

83 Baker, K, 'A Wigmorean defense of feminist method' (1998) 49 Hastings LJ 861, p 867.

84 In respect of cross-examination, it derives from the wording of the Criminal Evidence Act 1898: *R v Pommell* [1999] Crim LR 576.

85 (2000) *The Times*, 23 June.

The offence charged was rape, and the defence sought to argue both consent and a genuinely held belief in consent. The prosecution sought leave to introduce evidence of four previous incidents involving the defendant and four other women as complainants. In each of the four cases, the defence was either consent or mistaken belief in consent. In three of the four cases, the defendant had been acquitted. The prosecution argued that rape had occurred in all four cases, despite the three acquittals, and the judge was of the view that the four incidents possessed sufficient probative force to warrant admission. The probative force was derived from similarities between the previous incidents and those of the offence charged. The defence relied upon the rule in *Sambasivam v Public Prosecutor, Federation of Malaya*.[86] That rule prevented the prosecution in a later trial from asserting, or adducing evidence to show, that the accused was actually guilty in respect of a charge in respect of which he or she was acquitted. The rule was sometimes regarded as a species of estoppel, and had also been seen as an aspect of the rule against double jeopardy, although the accused was not exposed to a risk of conviction for the previous offence.[87] The trial judge held that the *Sambasivam* rule meant that evidence of all the previous allegations must be excluded, as the evidence of the sole conviction did not carry sufficient weight by itself to justify admission despite its prejudicial effect. The Court of Appeal agreed that the evidence could not be admitted, but the House of Lords decided that the rule should no longer be applied.

It is not surprising that this issue arose in the context of a rape prosecution; rape is a crime with a very low conviction rate,[88] and recidivist rapists may be more successful in escaping conviction than recidivist perpetrators of other offences. Thus, a rule which precluded contradiction of previous acquittals might well have had a disparate impact upon rape prosecutions. My argument here is not that rapists are more likely to be recidivists than are other types of offenders, but rather that recidivist rapists may be acquitted at trial more often than other types of recidivist offenders.[89] Thus, they were more likely than other offenders to benefit from the consequences of this exclusionary rule.

The rule was also inconsistent with the admission of similar fact evidence in respect of offences which had never given rise to any prosecution. Had the previous rape cases never proceeded to trial, the rule in *Sambasivam* would have been of no application. Similarly, had the charges been heard together, the evidence of each complainant could have been cross-admitted to support the evidence of the others. To exclude such evidence after an acquittal would provide a disincentive for the prosecution to proceed with charges in a timely

---

86 [1950] AC 458.

87 See the discussion of the rule in Law Commission, *Double Jeopardy*, Consultation Paper No 156, 1999, London: HMSO.

88 In 1996, only one in 10 recorded rape cases in England and Wales resulted in conviction: *op cit*, Harris and Grace, fn 70.

89 For obvious reasons, this cannot be proven or disproven.

fashion. The prosecution would have been in a stronger position had they failed to prosecute the accused on the previous occasions, and had instead waited for more complainants to come forth with allegations. The unacceptability of such an approach is obvious, and a rule which might suggest it (even if it is unlikely that the prosecution would be delayed in any but the most exceptional cases) is therefore undesirable.[90]

The rule also ran counter to the reasoning which underpins the rationale for admission of similar fact evidence; as Mance LJ commented:

> ... the coincidence of similar facts may have an evidential force not possessed by the facts of any one case alone. There can, therefore, be no incongruity in allowing a jury in a later case to look back at earlier incidents, even if they have, when viewed individually, led to acquittals. The jury's verdict will be confined to the later case. If the jury can observe a previously unidentified pattern, which assists it to a result different from that to which it might otherwise have come, the interests of justice will have been served in respect of the later case.

The point was well made in a an article by Jenny McEwan:[91]

> ... if in *Smith* [(1916) 11 CAR 229] the defendant had been accused of the murder of his second wife, who was found dead in her bath, he might well have been acquitted for want of convincing evidence. But when his third wife was found dead in her bath, bringing the total of Brides in the Bath to three, it would be absurd if the prosecution could not adduce evidence of both former incidents, in order to prove the murder of the third wife, notwithstanding a previous acquittal in relation to one of them.

The facts of *R v Z* illustrate the point perfectly – the number of rape allegations was crucial to the ruling on admissibility, as the sole conviction lacked sufficient probative force to be admitted even if the evidence of the other allegations was inadmissible.

The argument that previous acquittals are final statements of innocence was rejected as a justification for the *Sambasivam* rule, and again this point is one which has significance in relation to the prosecution of sexual offences. A previous conviction can properly be regarded as proof of guilt, but the acquittal of a defendant shows no more than that the court had a reasonable doubt. Unfortunately, it also appears that, in some rape cases, juries have been prepared to acquit not due to lack of proof that the events in question took place, but instead because they either viewed the complainant as

---

90 And, even if that option were open for serious consideration, it might well fall foul of the fair trial provisions in the European Convention on Human Rights. A defendant might argue that the older charges should have been dealt with promptly, and it would have been difficult to contend that avoidance of *Sambasivam* issues would be a justifiable reason for delay.

91 McEwan, J, 'Law Commission dodges the nettles in Consultation Paper No 141' [1997] Crim LR 93.

'contributorily negligent' or thought the accused was not a 'real rapist'.[92] It is to be hoped that such attitudes are diminishing (although the prohibition on jury research[93] in England makes it difficult to tell how prevalent such views are here or have been in the past), but, even if they are no longer widespread, they may have been responsible for some past acquittals. If that is so, it undermines any claim that past acquittals are tantamount to a finding of innocence. If jurors in a previous prosecution have refused to apply the law despite finding facts which amounted to rape, that does not necessarily mean that a subsequent jury should be bound by that previous decision.

Recent advances in forensic technology make it increasingly likely that previous verdicts may be found unsafe, whether convictions or acquittals. If an individual was acquitted of a rape 15 years ago due to lack of identification evidence, but now DNA testing indicates that he was the perpetrator, it would be unduly rigid to deny the prosecution the opportunity to challenge the previous acquittal.[94] For this reason, as well as those given above, the decision of the House of Lords to abandon the *Sambasivam* rule should be welcomed.

CROSS-EXAMINATION AS TO CHARACTER

The general rule in English law is that the ordinary witness may be subjected in cross-examination to attacks on character intended to shake the witness's credibility[95] in the eyes of the trier of fact. Some limited protection against sexual history character attacks has been introduced for complainants in sexual offence cases,[96] but the only witness who enjoys a broad protection against attacks on character is the defendant.

---

92 *Op cit*, Baker, fn 26; *op cit*, Orenstein, fn 25; Pollard, P, 'Judgments about victims and attackers in depicted rapes: a review' (1992) 31 Br J Soc Psy 302; Johnson, I and Sigler, R (eds), *Forced Sexual Intercourse in Intimate Relationships*, 1997, Aldershot: Dartmouth.

93 Contempt of Court Act 1981, s 8.

94 Of course, the proportion of rape prosecutions in England and Wales in which identity is in issue is diminishing, as more and more cases turn upon issues of content: see *op cit*, Harris and Grace, fn 70.

95 The witness may be discredited on grounds of lack of knowledge or capacity, by evidence of previous inconsistent statements or by evidence of bias, corruption, previous convictions, discreditable conduct or general untruthfulness. But these matters of credibility are collateral to the main issues in the trial, and so the witness's denial cannot be rebutted by other evidence. The sole statutory exception is for previous convictions: Criminal Procedure Act 1865, s 6. Of course, in rape cases, the line between credibility and consent is particularly problematic, with the result that the Court of Appeal has said that evidence may be called to rebut a complainant's denials of previous sexual experience: *R v Funderburk* (1990) 90 Cr App R 467.

96 With limited effectiveness: see Easton, Chapter 9, in this volume.

This protection does not apply to matters evidence of which could be adduced in chief by the prosecution, nor to matters which have already been made known to the court before the cross-examination takes place. Apart from these limitations, the accused may forfeit the protection in several ways: by putting his or her character in issue through the introduction of good character evidence, by giving evidence against a co-accused, or by casting imputations on the character of prosecution witnesses or the victim of the offence. This last limitation is the one I wish to examine.

The rule that casting imputations on the prosecution leads to loss of the shield is stated in s 1(3)(ii) of the Act; its rationale is 'tit for tat'; if the jury are to be told that bad character makes the prosecution witnesses less credible, then the same latitude must be given to the defence.[97] As commentators have observed, however, this approach overlooks the very different positions of such witnesses: the prosecution witness whose character is attacked may be disbelieved, but does not run a risk of conviction. Equally, the rule permits the prosecution to attack defence witnesses with impunity, even more so when the defendant has a criminal record and thus is inhibited from retaliation.[98]

Numerous cases have turned upon the interpretation of the word 'imputations'; in theory, any suggestion that the prosecution witnesses are lying might be thought to constitute an imputation, although the courts have acknowledged the need to allow the defendant some latitude in respect of such claims.[99] Things which have been held to constitute imputations include allegations that the witness or victim fabricated evidence,[100] committed the crime himself,[101] was prone to violence,[102] or extorted the accused's confession.[103]

But imputations have not been confined to matters of criminality or dishonesty, things which might be thought directly relevant to the credibility of the witness, and therefore to warrant retaliatory attacks on the credibility of the accused. In some cases, imputations have concerned sexual immorality, and in these cases the courts have exhibited a troubling degree of inconsistency. In cases where legal and consensual homosexual conduct was alleged in respect of a male witness, that was held to be an imputation which caused the accused to lose his shield against cross-examination as to character, but the same strict approach has not been applied in rape cases. Thus, in *Selvey v DPP*,[104] the accused lost his shield after making an allegation that the

---

97 This reasoning was offered in the case of *R v Preston* [1909] 1 KB 568.
98 See, eg, Tapper, C, *Cross and Tapper on Evidence*, 9th edn, 1999, London: Butterworths, pp 409–10.
99 *R v Rouse* [1904] 1 KB 184; *R v Britzman and Hall* [1983] 1 All ER 369.
100 *R v Clark* [1955] 2 QB 469.
101 *R v Hudson* [1912] 2 KB 464.
102 *R v Wainwright* [1998] Crim LR 665.
103 *R v Cook* [1959] 2 QB 340.
104 [1970] AC 304.

male complainant in a buggery case was a homosexual prostitute; in contrast, in *Turner*,[105] it was held not an imputation to allege that the female complainant in a rape case had not only consented, but had also willingly participated in an act of gross indecency prior to intercourse.[106] It might be argued that the difference is that prostitution is regarded as less morally acceptable than promiscuity generally, and that therefore the allegations in *Selvey* were more serious than those in *Turner*, but this argument is inconsistent with the case of *Bishop*.[107] In *Bishop*, the accused was charged with burglary; it was alleged that he had stolen things from the witness's bedroom, a room in which Bishop's fingerprints had been found. In his defence, Bishop sought to explain the presence of his fingerprints in the room by alleging that he had engaged in homosexual acts there with the victim. The allegation of consensual homosexual activity was held to constitute an imputation despite its legality; the Court of Appeal was of the view that legality was not synonymous with morality, and that most people in 1974 regarded an allegation of homosexuality as in imputation on the character of the witness.

There is, therefore, an obvious disparity in treatment; the sexual behaviour of a female rape complainant can be questioned without any loss of the shield against cross-examination, while allegations regarding the lawful homosexual conduct of a male witness will not have the same result, whether made in the context of a sexual offence (as in *Selvey*) or of a property crime (as in *Bishop*). There is no principled explanation of this discrepancy; it has been stated in a leading evidence text that the rape cases may be regarded as *sui generis* or explained on the ground that they are no more than an allegation of consent and a claim that the prosecution has failed to establish one element of the offence.[108] A more frank acknowledgment of the position can be found in another text which states that this is an arbitrary limitation on the scope of the proviso in s 1(3)(ii), and an example of the way the law of evidence has systematically discriminated against complainants in rape cases.[109] It offers a possible alternative explanation of the anomaly: that an allegation of consent *simpliciter* does not by itself suggest immorality on the part of the complainant, and is for that reason not an imputation. That cannot be convincing as an explanation of its origins, however, and regardless of whether the allegation of consent is regarded as an allegation of sexual immorality it remains true that it is an assertion that the complainant is either deceitful or seriously deluded. An equivalent allegation that a witness in a

105 [1944] KB 463.
106 The rule can be found even earlier, in the case of *R v Sheean* (1908) 21 Cox CC 561.
107 [1975] QB 274.
108 *Op cit*, Tapper, fn 98, p 408.
109 Dennis, I, *The Law of Evidence*, 1999, London: Sweet & Maxwell, pp 639–40.

non-sexual case was lying might well lead to the loss of the defendant's protection.[110]

Given the presence of this inconsistency, what should be done to rectify it? To treat rape and other cases equally must be the goal, as there is no principled justification for the current anomaly. One option would be to regard any attack on the sexual behaviour of the witness as an imputation leading to loss of the defendant's shield, but the desirability of that option is solely its consistency of treatment of prosecution witnesses. It overlooks the larger problem of the proviso – the shaky foundation of the 'tit for tat' rule as a basis for permitting the defendant's character to be attacked. The rule has been broadly criticised as illogical, as it permits the introduction of evidence which could not have been adduced otherwise because its probative force is not sufficient to justify admission.

It might also be argued that the proviso serves a useful function in deterring defence counsel from character assassination of prosecution witnesses. This justification is much the same as that for the restriction on sexual history evidence, and it might be thought that feminist critics would therefore seek preservation or even extension of its scope.[111] However, the proviso can have no function in deterring unfair character attacks where the accused chooses not to testify or has no criminal record which might be disclosed in retaliation. The protection of prosecution witnesses against unacceptably hostile or irrelevant cross-examination should not be contingent upon such factors; if the witness should be protected that protection should apply in all cases regardless of the accused's criminal record.[112]

Of course, there may be some situations in which imputations regarding prosecution witnesses are essential to the defence case.[113] In such cases, it must be wrong to inhibit the defence of an accused with previous convictions. Although the courts may exercise discretion to protect the accused in such

---

110 But only if it went beyond a mere denial of the prosecution case: *R v Britzman and Hall* [1983] 1 All ER 369.

111 The Heilbron Committee on the Law of Rape recommended the solution proposed by the Criminal Law Revision Committee – the accused would be exposed to cross-examination if the attack on a rape complainant's character was not central to the defence: Heilbron Committee, *Report of the Advisory Committee on the Law of Rape*, Cmnd 6352, 1975.

112 For this reason, the Australian solution considered by the Law Commission – limiting the scope of the proviso so that the shield is lost only with respect to imputations not relating to the witness's conduct in the events or investigation in question – is only a slight improvement. It would help the accused with prior convictions who alleges, eg, police misconduct, but would still draw an unacceptable distinction generally between defendants with criminal records and those without. See *op cit*, Law Commission, fn 2, para 12.71.

113 In cases where it is alleged that a confession was falsified or obtained improperly, or that the witnesses have deliberately lied.

cases,[114] it is not desirable to leave this protection up to the exercise of a discretion rather than a rule.

The proper approach must be to address the problem of witness harassment directly, through judicial intervention in questioning,[115] or through protective measures such as those introduced for vulnerable witnesses through the Youth Justice and Criminal Evidence Act 1999. Previous convictions of an accused do not become more relevant to culpability or credibility simply because other witnesses have been attacked, and it cannot be right to allow in such prejudicial information as a limited, inconsistent and indirect method of deterring improper conduct on the part of some defendants.

CONCLUDING THOUGHTS

The problem of how to deal with evidence of character in criminal trials is one which has troubled lawyers for many years and which will undoubtedly continue to generate debate. This brief examination of some aspects of the relevant law has attempted to draw out questions of whether contextualising justice through character evidence is desirable, why we should think carefully about the tendency to view sexual offences as 'different', and how some aspects of the current law may have differential impacts upon the protection of female victims of crime.

What can feminist theory tell us about the way forward in dealing with character evidence? One cautionary note is that we must remember that problems with evidential matters are not necessarily the causes of problems with respect to rape trials or any other criminal trials. Rather, they manifest a set of social and cultural beliefs about sexuality, about risk, and about the nature of men and women. The rules of evidence alone cannot eradicate these underlying problems. Equally, the relaxation of exclusionary rules to admit more character evidence may help women to be better heard and understood, but may also prejudice those who violate gendered norms of acceptable behaviour. Feminist critiques cannot provide definitive answers to how the law should deal with character evidence, but their contributions are essential to the ongoing debate.

---

114 And apparently do so with regularity; the Law Commission observed in *op cit*, fn 2, para 12.27, that: 'It is unusual and unsatisfactory to have a statutory rule so comprehensively undermined by a discretion.'

115 See Ellison, Chapter 3, in this volume.

BIBLIOGRAPHY

Anon, 'Developments in the law – privileged communications' (1985) 98 Harv L Rev 1450

Anon, 'Functional overlap between the lawyer and other professionals: its implications for the privileged communications doctrine' (1962) 71 Yale LJ 1226

Anon, 'How do lawyers stack up against other professionals?' (1994) *American Lawyer*, September, p 56

Adams, W, 'The judiciary and anti-discrimination law' (1986) 11 Legal Service Bulletin 247

Adler, Z, 'The relevance of sexual history evidence in rape: problems of subjective interpretation' [1985] Crim LR 769

Adler, Z, *Rape on Trial*, 1987, London: Routledge and Kegan Paul

AG's Advisory Committee, *Charge Screening, Disclosure, and Resolution Discussions*, 1993, Ontario: AG's Advisory Committee

AG's Department, *Reducing Delays in Criminal Cases: Pegasus Taskforce Report*, 1992, Melbourne: AG's Department

Alison, A (Sir), *Practice of the Criminal Law of Scotland*, 1833, Edinburgh: W Blackwood

Althouse, A, 'Beyond King Solomon's harlots: women in evidence' (1992) 65 S California L Rev 1265

Althouse, A, 'The lying woman, the devious prostitute, and other stories from the evidence casebook' (1994) 88 Northwestern UL Rev 914

Anderson, T and Twining, W, *Analysis of Evidence*, 1991, London: Weidenfeld & Nicolson

Ashworth, A, *The Criminal Process*, 1994, Oxford: Clarendon

Ashworth, AJ, 'Article 6 and the fairness of trials' [1999] Crim LR 261

Atiyah, PS, 'Judges and policy' (1980) 15 Israel L Rev 346

Australian Bureau of Statistics, *1995: Australian Criminal Courts*, 1997, Canberra: Australian Bureau of Statistics

Babcock, B, 'Feminist lawyers' (1998) 50 Stanford L Rev 116

Baer, J, *Women in American Law: The Struggle Toward Equality from the New Deal to the Present*, 1993, New York: Holmes and Meier, Vol 2

Bailey, P and Devereux, A, 'The operation of anti-discrimination laws in Australia', in Kinley, D (ed), *Human Rights in Australian Law*, 1998, Sydney: Federation

Baker, 'Once a rapist? Motivational evidence and relevancy in rape law' (1996) 110 Harv L Rev 563

Baker, K, 'A Wigmorean defense of feminist method' (1998) 49 Hastings LJ 861

Baldwin, J and McConville, M, *Negotiated Justice: Pressures to Plead Guilty*, 1977, London: Martin Robertson

Bargen, J and Fishwick, E, *Sexual Assault Law Reform: A National Perspective*, 1995, Canberra: Office of the Status of Women

Barnett, H, *Introduction to Feminist Jurisprudence*, 1998, London: Cavendish Publishing

Barry, D, 'Hey, guys, I'm talking to you' (1992) *Chicago Tribune Magazine*, 21 June, p 27

Bartlett, KT, 'Feminist legal methods' (1990) 103 Harv L Rev 829

Bates, P, 'The Youth Justice and Criminal Evidence Act – the evidence of vulnerable adults' (1999) 11(3) CFLQ 289

Becker, M, 'Maternal feelings: myth, taboo, and child custody' (1992) 1 S California Rev Law & Women's Studies 133

Bell, C and Fox, M, 'Telling stories of women who kill' (1995) 5 SLS 471

Bell, R, *Worlds of Friendship*, 1991, London: Sage

Bennett, WL and Feldman, MS, *Reconstructing Reality in the Courtroom*, 1981, London: Tavistock Feldman

Bentham, J, 'An introductory view of the rationale of evidence for the use of lawyers as well as non-lawyers', in Mill, J (ed), *The Works of Jeremy Bentham*, 1810, London: Simkin, Marshall

Bentham, J, *Rationale of Judicial Evidence*, 1827, London: Hunt and Clarke, Vol 5

Bentham, J, *Rationale of Judicial Evidence: The Works of Jeremy Bentham*, 1843, Edinburgh: William Tait

Berger, M and Robinson, K, 'Gender bias in the American Bar Association Journal: impact on the legal profession' (1998) 13 Wisconsin Women's LJ 75

Berger, V, 'Man's trial, woman's tribulation: rape cases in the courtroom' (1977) 1 Columbia L Rev 86

Bishop, J, *Prosecution Without Trial*, 1989, Sydney: Butterworths

Blackstone, W, *Commentaries on the Laws of England*, 1809, London: Strahan, Bk 1

Blake, M and Ashworth, A, 'Some ethical issues in prosecuting and defending criminal cases' [1998] Crim LR 1

Blumstein, P and Schwartz, P, *American Couples*, 1983, New York: William Morrow

Bottomley, A (ed), *Feminist Perspectives on the Foundational Subjects of Law*, 1996, London: Cavendish Publishing (2nd edn, forthcoming 2001)

Brereton, D, '"Real rape", law reform and the role of research: the evolution of the Victorian Crimes (Rape) Act 1991' (1994) 27 A & NZ J Crim 74

Brereton, D, 'How different are rape trials? A comparison of the cross-examination of complainants in rape and assault trials' (1997) 37 Br J Crim 242

Bridgeman, J, and Millns, S, *Feminist Perspectives on Law*, 1998, London: Sweet & Maxwell

Bronitt, S, 'The rules of recent complaint: rape myths and the legal construction of the "reasonable" rape victim', in Easteal, P (ed), *Balancing the Scales: Rape Law Reform and Australian Culture*, 1998, Sydney: Federation

Brown, A, 'Two cases on corroboration' 1998 SLT (News) 71

Brown, B, Burman, M and Jamieson, L, *Sex Crimes on Trial: The Use of Sexual Evidence in Scottish Courts*, 1993, Edinburgh: Edinburgh UP

Brown, B, Burman, M and Jamieson, L, *Sexual History and Sexual Character Evidence in Scottish Sexual Offence Trials*, 1992, Edinburgh: Scottish Office Central Research Unit

Buhrke, R and Fuqua, D, 'Sex differences in same- and cross-sex supportive relationships' (1987) 17 Sex Roles 339

Burgess, A and Holmstrom, L, 'Rape trauma syndrome' (1974) 131 Am J Psychiatry 981

Burnett, *A Treatise on Various Branches of the Criminal Law in Scotland*, 1811, Edinburgh: G Ramage

Burnett, AL, 'Permeation of race, national origin, and gender issues from initial law enforcement contact through sentencing: the need for sensitivity, equalitarianism and vigilance in the criminal justice system' (1994) 31 Am Crim LR 1153

Byrne, P, 'Plea bargaining' (1988) 62 ALJ 799

Cahn, E (ed), *Courts on Trial*, revised edn, 1970, Princeton, NJ: Princeton UP

Cahn, NR, 'A preliminary feminist critique of legal ethics' (1990) 4 Georgetown Journal of Legal Ethics 2475

Cahn, NR, 'Styles of lawyering' (1992) 34 Hastings LJ 1039

Campbell, S, 'Catholic sisters, irregularly ordained women and the clergy-penitent privilege' (1976) 9 University of California Davis L Rev 523

Capra, D, 'Communications with psychotherapists and social workers' (1996) New York LJ, 12 July, p 3

Carlen, P and Worral, A (eds), *Gender, Crime and Justice*, 1987, Milton Keynes: OU Press

Chambers, G and Millar, A, 'Proving sexual assault: prosecuting the offender or persecuting the victim?', in Carlen, P and Worral, A (eds), *Gender, Crime and Justice*, 1987, Milton Keynes: OU Press

Chambers, G and Millar, A, *Investigating Sexual Assault*, 1983, Edinburgh: Scottish Office Central Research Unit

Chambers, G and Millar, A, *Prosecuting Sexual Assault*, 1986, Edinburgh: Scottish Office Central Research Unit

Chan, W, 'Legal equality and domestic homicides' (1997) 25 Int J Soc Law 203

Chiss, M, 'Troubling degrees of authority: the continuing pursuit of unequal marital roles' (1993) 12 Law and Inequality J 225

Chodorow, N, *The Reproduction of Mothering: Psychoanalysis and the Sociology of Gender*, 1978, Berkeley, CA: California UP

Christie, M, *Breach of the Peace*, 1990, Edinburgh: Butterworths

Clark, P, 'The public prosecutor and plea bargaining' (1986) 60 ALJ 199

Clark, L and Lewis, D, *The Price of Coercive Sexuality*, 1977, Toronto: Toronto Women's Press

Coates, J, 'Language, gender and career', in Mills, S (ed), *Language and Gender: Interdisciplinary Perspectives*, 1995, London: Longman

Coates, J, 'Women's friendships, women's talk', in Wodak, R, *Gender and Discourse*, 1997, London: Sage

Coates, R, 'What are the problems from the defendant's perspective?', in Australian Institute for Judicial Administration, *Reform of Court Rules and Procedures in Criminal Cases* (collection of papers presented at AIJA Conference, Brisbane, 3–4 July 1998), 1998, Carlton, : AIJA

Comment, 'Underprivileged communications: extension of the psychotherapist-patient privilege to patients of psychiatric social workers' (1973) 61 California L Rev 1050

Commonwealth Director of Public Prosecutions, *Prosecution Policy of the Commonwealth*: www.nla.gov.au/dpp/prospol.html

Conley, J, O'Barr, W and Lind, E, 'The power of language: presentational style in the courtroom' (1978) Duke LJ 1375

Cotterrell, R, *The Sociology of Law: An Introduction*, 1984, London: Butterworths

Coughlin, AM, 'Excusing women' (1994) 82 California L Rev 1

Covey, J, 'Making form follow function: considerations in creating and applying a statutory parent-child privilege' (1990) Illinois UL Rev 879

Crawford, M, *Talking Difference: On Gender and Language*, 1995, London: Sage

Criminal Justice Commission, Research and Co-ordination Division, *Evaluation of Brisbane Central Committals Project* 1996, Brisbane: Criminal Justice Commission

Criminal Law Revision Committee, 11th Report, *Evidence (General)*, Cmnd 4991, 1972, London: HMSO

Criminal Law Revision Committee, 15th Report, *Sexual Offences*, Cmnd 9213, 1984, London: HMSO

Damaska, M, *Evidence Law Adrift*, 1997, New Haven: Yale UP

Davidson, FP, 'Corroboration in distress' (1997) 2 Scottish Law and Practice Quarterly 30

Davies, M, *Asking the Law Question*, 1994, Sydney: LBC

Davies, SM, 'Evidence of character to prove conduct: a reassessment of relevancy' (1991) 27 Criminal Law Bulletin 504

Dennis, I, *The Law of Evidence*, 1999, London: Sweet & Maxwell

Derlega, V and Winstead, B (eds), *Friendship and Social Interaction*, 1986, New York: Springer

Derlega, V, Metts, S, Petronio, S, and Margulis, S, *Self-Disclosure*, 1993, Newbury Park, CA: Sage

Devereux, A, 'Human rights by agreement? A case study of the Human Rights and Equal Opportunity Commission's use of conciliation' (1996) 7 Aust Dispute Res J 280

Devlin, P, *The Judge*, 1979, Oxford: OUP

Diamond, I and Quinby, L (eds), *Feminism and Foucault: Reflections on Resistance*, 1988, Boston, Mass: Northeastern UP

Dindia, K and Allen, M, 'Sex differences in self-disclosure: a meta-analysis' (1992) 112 Psych Bulletin 106

Dinnerstein, D, *The Rocking of the Cradle and the Ruling of the World*, 1987, London: Warren

Director of Public Prosecutions (SA), *Statement of Prosecution Policy and Guidelines*, July 1999, Adelaide: DPP

Dobash, RE and Dobash, R, *Violence Against Wives*, 1980, London: Open Books

Dolgin, K and Minowa, N, 'Gender differences in self-presentation: a comparison of the roles of flatteringness and intimacy in self-disclosure to friends' (1997) 36 Sex Roles 371

Dolgin, K, Meyer, L and Schwartz, J, 'Effects of gender, target's gender, topic, and self-esteem on disclosure to best and middling friends' (1991) 25 Sex Roles 311

Dorgan, C (ed), *Statistical Handbook of Working America*, 1995, Detroit, Mich: Gale Research

Douzinas, C and Warrington, R, *Justice Miscarried: Ethics, Aesthetics and the Law*, 1994, London: Harvester Wheatsheaf

Downs, DA, *More Than Victims: Battered Women, The Syndrome Society and the Law*, 1996, Chicago, IL: Chicago UP

Du Cann, R, *The Art of the Advocate*, 1993, London: Penguin

Duane, J, 'The new Federal Rule of Evidence on prior acts of accused sex offenders: a poorly drafted version of a very bad idea' (1994) FRD 95

Dublin Rape Crisis Centre, *The Legal Process and Victims of Rape*, 1998, Dublin: Dublin Rape Crisis Centre

Duck, S, *Friends, for Life*, 1983, Hemel Hempstead: Harvester Wheatsheaf

Duck, S, *Understanding Relationships*, 1991, New York: Guilford

Durston, G, 'Cross-examination of rape complainants: ongoing tensions between conflicting priorities and the criminal justice system' (1998) 62 JCL 91

Easteal, P (ed), *Balancing the Scales: Rape, Law Reform and Australian Culture*, 1998, Sydney: Federation

Edwards, A and Heenan, M, 'Rape trials in Victoria: gender, socio-cultural factors and justice' (1994) 27 A & NZ J Crim 213

Edwards, S, 'Battered Woman Syndrome' (1992) 142 NLJ 1350

Edwards, S, 'Mad, bad or pre-menstrual?' (1988) 138 NLJ 456

Edwards, SSM, *Sex and Gender in the Legal Process*, 1996, London: Blackstone

Ehrenreich, N, 'OJ Simpson and the myth of gender/race conflict' (1996) 67 Colorado UL Rev 931

Ehrlich, S and King, R, 'Consensual sex or sexual harassment: negotiating meaning', in Bergvall, V, Bing, J and Freed, A (eds), *Re-Thinking Language and Gender Research: Theory and Practice*, 1996, London: Addison Wesley Longman

Ellis, M, 'The politics behind Federal Rules of Evidence 413, 414 and 415' (1998) 38 Santa Clara L Rev 961

Ellison, L, 'Cross-examination in rape trials' [1998] Crim LR 605

Ellison, L, 'The protection of vulnerable witnesses in court: an Anglo-Dutch comparison' (1999) 3 Int J of Evidence and Proof 29

Emmelmann, D, 'Gauging the strength of evidence prior to plea bargaining: the interpretive procedures of court-appointed defense attorneys' (1998) Law & Soc Inq 927

Emmelmann, D, 'Trial by plea bargain: case settlement as a product of recursive decision making' (1996) 30 Law & Soc Rev 335

EOC (Vic), *Annual Report 1996–97*, 1997, Melbourne: Victorian Government

Eser, A, 'Collection and evaluation of evidence in comparative perspective' (1997) 31 Israel L Rev 429

Estrich, S, 'Palm Beach stories' (1992) 11 Law & Phil 5

Estrich, S, 'Real rape', 1987, Cambridge, Mass: Harvard UP

Evans, K, *Golden Rules of Advocacy*, 1993, London: Blackstone

Farr, K, 'Administration and justice: maintaining balance through an institutionalised plea negotiation process' (1984) 22 Criminology 291

Ferguson, PR, 'Controversial aspects of the law of rape: an Anglo-Scottish comparison', in Hunter, R (ed), *Justice and Crime: Essays in Honour of The Right Honourable The Lord Emslie*, 1993, Edinburgh: T & T Clark

Field, D, and Raitt, F, *Evidence*, 1996, Edinburgh: Green

Findlay, M, Odgers, S and Yeo, S, *Australian Criminal Justice*, 2nd edn, 1999, Melbourne: OUP

Finley, LM, 'Breaking women's silence in law: the dilemma of the gendered nature of legal reasoning' (1989) 64 Notre Dame L Rev 886, reprinted in *Lloyd's Introduction to Jurisprudence*, 1994, London: Sweet & Maxwell

Fishman, K, 'Therapy for children' (1991) *The Atlantic*, June, p 47

Flanagan, O, *Varieties of Moral Personality: Ethics and Psychological Realism*, 1991, Cambridge, Mass: Harvard UP

Flood-Page, C and Mackie, A, *Sentencing Practice: An Examination of Decisions in Magistrates' Courts and the Crown Courts in the Mid-1990s*, Home Office Research Study No 180, 1998, London: HMSO

Foucault, M, 'Afterword', in Dreyfus, M and Rabinow, P, *Michel Foucault: Beyond Structuralism and Hermeneutics*, 2nd edn, 1983, Chicago, IL: Chicago UP

Fox, M, 'Legal responses to "battered women who kill"', in Bridgeman, J and Millns, S (eds), *Law and Body Politics*, 1995, Aldershot: Dartmouth

Frank, J, *Courts on Trial*, Cahn, E (ed), revised edn, 1970, Princeton, NJ: Princeton UP

Frank, J, *Law and the Modern Mind*, 1949, New York: Stevens

Fredman, S, *Women and the Law*, 1997, Oxford: Clarendon

Freyer, J, 'Women litigators in search of a care-orientated judicial system' (1995) 4 Am UJ Gender and Law 199

Friedman, R, 'Thoughts from across the water on hearsay and confrontation' [1998] Crim LR 697

Friedman, RD, 'Answering the Bayesioskeptical challenge' (1997) 1 E & P 276

Frohmann, L, 'Convictability and discordant locales: reproducing race, class and gender ideologies in prosecutorial decision making' (1997) 31 Law & Soc Rev 531

Frohmann, L, 'Discrediting victims' allegations of sexual assault: prosecutorial accounts of case rejections' (1991) 38 Social Problems 213

Frug, MJ, *Postmodern Legal Feminism*, 1992, London: Routledge

Galanter, M, 'Why the "haves" come out ahead: speculations on the limits of legal change' (1974) 9 Law & Soc Rev 95

Gelles, R, *The Violent Home: A Study of Physical Aggression Between Men and Women*, 1972, London: Sage

General Council of the Bar of England and Wales, *Code of Conduct of the Bar of England and Wales*, 1991, London: Bar Council

Gilbert, G, *The Law of Evidence* (1754), 1754, Dublin: A Strahan

Gilligan, C, *In a Different Voice: Psychological Theory and Women's Development*, revised edn, 1993, Cambridge, Mass: Harvard UP

Gilligan, C, *In a Different Voice: Psychological Theory and Women's Development*, 1982, Cambridge, Mass: Harvard UP

Grace, S, Lloyd, C and Smith, J, *Rape: From Recording to Conviction*, Research and Planning Unit, Paper No 71, 1992, London: Home Office

Graham, KW, 'There will always be an England: the instrumental ideology of evidence' (1987) 85 Michigan L Rev 1204

Grant, Y, 'The penetration of the rape shield: *R v Seaboyer* and *R v Gayme* in the Ontario Court of Appeal' (1989–90) 3 CJWL 592

Graycar, R, 'The gender of judgments', in Thornton, M (ed), *Public and Private: Feminist Legal Debates*, 1995, Adelaide: OUP

Green, K, 'Thinking land law differently' (1995) 3 FLS 131

Gregory, J and Lees, S, 'Attrition in rape and sexual assault cases' (1996) 36 Br J Crim 1

Groth, A, Burgess, AW and Holmstrom, LL, 'Rape: power, anger and sexuality' (1977) 134 Am J Psychiatry 1239

Hale, M (Sir), *The History of the Pleas of the Crown* (1736), 1971, London: Professional

Hall, L and Lloyd, S, *Surviving Child Sexual Abuse*, 1989, Lewes: Falmer

Harrington, J, 'Privileging the medical norm: liberalism, self-determination and the refusal of treatment' (1996) 16 LS 348

Harris, A, 'Race and essentialism in feminist legal theory' (1990) 42 Stanford L Rev 581

Harris, J and Grace, S, *A Question of Evidence? Investigating and Prosecuting Rape in the 1990s*, Home Office Research Study No 196, 1999, London: Home Office

Hartsock, N, 'Foucault on power: a theory for women?', in Nicholson, L (ed), *Feminism/Postmodernism*, 1990, London: Routledge

Hartsock, N, 'Rethinking modernism: minority versus majority theories' (1987) 7 Cultural Critique 187

Hastie, R (ed), *Inside the Juror*, 1993, Cambridge: CUP

Haxton, D, 'Rape shield statutes: constitutional despite unconstitutional exclusions of evidence' [1985] Wisconsin L Rev 1219

Heath, M and Naffine, N, 'Men's needs and women's desires: feminist dilemmas about rape law reform' (1994) 3 Aus Fem LJ 30

Heenan, M and McKelvie, H, *Evaluation of the Crimes (Rape) Act 1991*, 1997, AG's Legislation and Policy Branch, Melbourne: Department of Justice

Heenan, M and McKelvie, H, *Evaluation of the Crimes (Rape) Act 1991*, 1997, AG's Legislation and Policy Branch, Melbourne: Department of Justice

Heenan, M and McKelvie, H, *The Crimes (Rape) Act 1991: An Evaluation Report*, 1997, Melbourne: Victorian Department of Justice

Heenan, M, 'Sex crimes and the criminal justice system' (1997) 9 Aus Fem LJ 90

Heidensohn, F, *Women and Crime*, 1985, London: Macmillan

Heilbron Committee, *Report of the Advisory Committee on the Law of Rape*, Cmnd 6352, 1975, London: HMSO

Heinzelman, S and Wiseman, S (eds), *Representing Women: Law, Literature and Feminism*, 1994, Durham, NC: Duke UP

Helgeson, V, Shaver, P and Dyer, M, 'Prototypes of intimacy and distance in same-sex and opposite sex relationships' (1987) 4 Journal of Social and Personal Relationships 195

Henderson, LN, 'Legality and empathy' (1987) 85 Michigan L Rev 1574

Hendrix, K, 'When women turn to matters of the mind' (1992) *Los Angeles Times*, 19 April, p E1

Henham, R, 'Bargain justice or justice denied? Sentence discounts and the criminal process' (1999) 62 MLR 515

Henning, T, 'The impact of evidence and procedure upon victims', paper given at the Second Annual Evidence Teachers' Conference, February 1999, Sydney

Henning, T, *Sexual Reputation and Sexual Experience Evidence in Tasmanian Proceedings Relating to Sexual Offences*, 1996, Hobart: Tasmania UP

Herman, R, 'The growing presence of women in psychiatry' (1991) *Washington Post*, 1 October, p Z9

Heyn, D, *Marriage Shock: The Transformation of Women into Wives*, 1997, New York: Dell

Hill, B and Fletcher-Rogers, K, *Sexually Related Offences*, 1997, London: Sweet & Maxwell

Hite, S, *Women as Revolutionary Agents of Change (The Hite Reports: Sexuality, Love and Emotion)*, 1993, London: Sceptre

Home Office, *Speaking Up For Justice: Report of the Interdepartmental Working Group on the Treatment of Vulnerable or Intimidated Witnesses in the Criminal Justice System*, 1998, London: Home Office

Howard, M, Crane, P and Hochberg, D, *Phipson on Evidence*, 1990, London: Sweet & Maxwell

Human Rights and Equal Opportunities Commission, *Annual Report 1997–98*, 1998, Sydney: HREOC

Hume, D, *Commentaries on the Law of Scotland Respecting Crimes*, Bell, BR (ed), 4th edn, 1844 (reprinted 1986), Edinburgh: Butterworths

Hunt, A, *Explorations in Law and Society: Toward a Constitutive Theory of Law*, 1993, New York: Routledge

Hunter, R and Leonard, A, *The Outcomes of Conciliation in Sex Discrimination Cases*, Working Paper No 8, 1995, Centre for Employment and Labour Relations Law, University of Melbourne

Hunter, R and Mack, K, 'Exclusion and silence: procedure and evidence', in Naffine, N and Owens, RJ (eds), *Sexing the Subject of Law*, 1997, Sydney: LBC

Hunter, R and McKelvie, H, *Equality of Opportunity for Women at the Victorian Bar*, 1998, Melbourne: Victorian Bar Council

Hunter, R and Stubbs, J, 'Model laws or missed opportunity?' (1999) 24 Alt LJ 12

Hunter, R, 'Gender in evidence: masculine norms vs feminist reforms' (1996) 19 Harv Women's LJ 127

Hunter, R, 'Having her day in court? Violence, legal remedies and consent', in Breckenridge, J and Laing, L (eds), *Challenging Silence: Innovative Responses to Sexual and Domestic Violence*, 1999, Sydney: Allen & Unwin

Hunter, R, 'Litigants in person in contested cases in the Family Court' (1998) 12 AJFL 171

Hunter, R, 'Sex discrimination legislation and Australian legal culture', in Thacker, A (ed), *Women and the Law: Judicial Attitudes as they Impact on Women*, 1998, Geelong: Deakin UP

Hunter, R, *Family Law Case Profiles*, 1999, Sydney: Justice Research Centre

Hutchins, R and Slesinger, D, 'Some observations on the law of evidence: family relations' (1929) 13 Minnesota L Rev 675

Illich, I, *Gender*, 1993, London: Marion Boyars

Imwinkelreid, E, 'Undertaking the task of reforming the American character evidence prohibition: the importance of getting the experiment off on the right foot' (1997) 22 Fordham Urb LJ 285

Interdepartmental Working Group on the Treatment of Vulnerable or Intimidated Witnesses in the Criminal Justice System, *Speaking Up For Justice: Report of the Interdepartmental Working Group on the Treatment of Vulnerable or Intimidated Witnesses in the Criminal Justice System*, 1998, London: Home Office

Jack, R and Jack, DC, *Moral Vision and Professional Decisions: The Changing Values of Women and Men Lawyers*, 1989, New York: CUP

Jackson, B, *Law, Fact and Narrative Coherence*, Liverpool: Deborah Charles

Jackson, B, 'Narrative models in legal proof' (1998) 1 International Journal for the Semiotics of Law 225

Jackson, J, 'Analysing the new evidence scholarship: towards a new conception of the law of evidence' (1996) 16 OJLS 309

Jamieson, L, 'The social construction of consent revisited', in Adkins, L and Merchant, V, *Sexualising the Social: Power and the Organisation of Sexuality*, 1996, London: Macmillan

Johnson, F and Aries, E, 'Conversational patterns among same-sex pairs of late-adolescent close friends' (1983) 142 J Genetic Psychology 225

Johnson, F and Aries, E, 'The talk of women's friends' (1983) 6 Women's Studies International Forum 353

Johnson, I and Sigler, R (eds), *Forced Sexual Intercourse in Intimate Relationships*, 1997, Aldershot: Dartmouth

Jonakait, RJ, '"My God!" Is this how a feminist analyzes excited utterances?' (1997) 4 W & MJ Women & Law 263

Jones, A, *Women Who Kill*, 1991, London: Victor Gallancz

Jones, P, *Lawyer's Skills*, 1997, London: Blackstone

JUSTICE, *Negotiated Justice: A Closer Look at the Implications of Plea Bargains*, 1993, London: JUSTICE

Kalven, H and Zeisel, H, *The American Jury*, 1966, Boston, Mass: Little, Brown

Karp, D, 'Evidence of propensity and probability in sex offense cases and other cases' (1994) 70 Chicago-Kent L Rev 37

Katsoris, C, 'Confidential communications – the accountants' dilemma' (1966) 35 Fordham L Rev 51

Kelly, L, *Surviving Sexual Violence*, 1988, Cambridge: Polity

Kenny, A, 'The expert in court' (1983) 99 LQR 197

Kinports, K, 'Evidence engendered' (1991) Illinois UL Rev 413

Komarovsky, M, *Blue Collar Marriage*, 1967, New York: Vintage

Konradi, A, 'Preparing to testify: rape survivors negotiating the criminal justice process' (1996) 10 Gender and Society 404

Koss, M, Gidyez, C and Wisniewski, N, 'The scope of rape: incidence and prevalence of sexual aggression and victimization in a national sample of higher education students' (1987) 55 J Consulting and Clinical Psychology 162

Krattenmaker, T, 'Interpersonal testimonial privileges under the Federal Rules of Evidence: a suggested approach' (1976) 64 Georgetown LJ 613

Krattenmaker, T, 'Testimonial privileges in federal courts: an alternative to the proposed federal rules of evidence' (1973) 62 Georgetown LJ 61

Kronman, AT, *Max Weber*, 1983, London: Edward Arnold

Lacey, N, 'On the subject of sexing the subject', in Owens, R and Naffine, N (eds), *Sexing the Subject of Law*, 1997, Sydney: LBC

Lacey, N, 'Unspeakable subjects: sexuality, integrity and criminal law' (1997) 8(2) Women: A Cultural Review 143

LaFree, G, *Rape and Criminal Justice: The Social Construction of Sexual Assault*, 1989, Belmont, CA: Wadsworth

Lakoff, R, *Language and Woman's Place*, 1975, New York: Harper

Law Commission, *Corroboration of Evidence in Criminal Trials*, Working Paper No 115, 1990, London: HMSO

Law Commission, *Criminal Law – Evidence in Criminal Proceedings: Hearsay and Related Topics*, Consultation Paper No 138, 1995, London: HMSO

Law Commission, *Double Jeopardy*, Consultation Paper No 156, 1999, London: HMSO

Law Commission, *Evidence in Criminal Proceedings: Hearsay and Related Topics*, Consultation Paper No 138, 1995, London: HMSO

Law Commission, *Evidence in Criminal Proceedings: Hearsay and Related Topics*, Consultation Paper No 245, Cm 3670, 1997, London: HMSO

Law Commission, *Previous Misconduct of a Defendant*, Consultation Paper No 141, 1996, London: HMSO

Lees, S, 'Judicial rape' (1993) 16 Women's Studies International Forum 26

Lees, S, *Carnal Knowledge: Rape on Trial*, 1996, London: Hamish Hamilton

Lees, S, *Ruling Passions: Sexual Violence, Reputation and the Law*, 1997, Buckingham: OU Press

Lempert, R, 'A right to every woman's evidence' (1981) 66 Iowa L Rev 725

Lempert, R, 'The new evidence scholarship: analyzing the process of proof' (1986) 66 Boston UL Rev 439

Lennon, K and Whitford, M, *Knowing the Difference: Feminist Perspectives in Epistemology*, 1994, London: Routledge

Leonard, D, 'The use of character to prove conduct: rationality and catharsis in the law of evidence' (1986–87) 58 Colorado UL Rev 1

Levinson, S, 'Testimonial privileges and the preferences of friendship' (1984) Duke LJ 631

Levy, E, *Examination of Witnesses in Criminal Cases*, 2nd edn, 1991, Toronto: Carswell

Linton, N, 'The witness and cross-examination' (1965) X Berkeley J Soc 7

Lloyd, G, *The Man of Reason: 'Male' and 'Female' in Western Philosophy*, 1984, London: Methuen

Louisell, D, 'Confidentiality, conformity and confusion: privileges in federal court today' (1956) 31 Tulane L Rev 100

Lynch, D, 'The impropriety of plea agreements: a tale of two counties' (1994) 19 Law & Soc Inq 115

MacCrimmon, M, 'The social construction of reality and the rules of evidence' (1991) 25 British Columbia UL Rev 36

Mack, K and Anleu, S, *Pleading Guilty: Issues and Practices*, 1995, Melbourne: Australian Institute of Judicial Administration

Mack, K and Roach Anleu, S, 'Sentence discount for a guilty plea: time for a new look' (1997) 1 Flinders J Law Reform 123

Mack, K, 'An Australian perspective on feminism, race and evidence' (1999) 28 Southwestern UL Rev 367

Mack, K, 'Continuing barriers to women's credibility: a feminist perspective on the proof process' (1993) 4 Criminal Law Forum 327

Mack, K, 'Gender awareness in Australian courts: violence against women' (1995) 5 Criminal Law Forum 788

MacKinnon, C, *Feminism Unmodified: Discourses on Life and Law*, 1987, Cambridge, Mass: Harvard UP

MacKinnon, C, *Toward a Feminist Theory of the State*, 1989, Cambridge, Mass: Harvard UP

MacPhail, I, *Evidence*, 1987, Edinburgh: Law Society of Scotland

Mahoney, K, 'International strategies to implement equality rights for women: overcoming gender bias in the courts' (1993) 1 Aus Fem LJ 115

Mahoney, M, 'Legal images of battered women: redefining the issue of separation' (1991) 90 Michigan L Rev 1

Majury, D, '*Seaboyer* and *Gayme*: a study in inequality', in Roberts, JV and Mohr, RM (eds), *Confronting Sexual Assault*, 1994, Toronto: Toronto UP

Marshall, P, *Reconviction of Imprisoned Sexual Offenders*, Research Bulletin No 36, 1994, London: Home Office

Marshall, P, *The Prevalence of Convictions for Sexual Offending*, Research Findings No 55, 1997, London: Home Office Research and Statistics Directorate

Martin, B, 'Feminism, criticism, and Foucault', in Diamond, I and Quinby, L (eds), *Feminism and Foucault: Reflections on Resistance*, 1988, Boston, Mass: Northeastern UP

Mason, G, 'Reforming the Law of rape: incursions into the masculinist sanctum', in Kirkby, D (ed), *Sex, Power and Justice*, 1995, Melbourne: OUP

Massaro, T, 'The dignity value of face to face confrontations' (1988) 40 Florida UL Rev 863

Masters, B, *'She Must Have Known': The Trial of Rosemary West*, 1996, London: Doubleday

Matoesian, G, 'Language, law and society: policy implications of the Kennedy Smith rape trial' (1995) 29 Law & Soc Rev 669

Matoesian, G, *Reproducing Rape – Domination through Talk in the Courtroom*, 1993, Cambridge: Polity

McAllister, B, 'Pressure's up to $100 million a month' (1998) *Washington Post*, 12 March, p A13

McBarnet, D, 'Victim in the witness box – confronting victimology's stereotype' (1983) 7 Contemporary Crises 293

McBarnet, D, *Conviction: Law, the State and the Construction of Justice*, 1981, London: Macmillan

McCandless, J, 'Prior bad acts and two bad rules: the fundamental unfairness of Federal Rules of Evidence 413 and 414' (1997) 5 W & M Bill of Rights J 689

McColgan A, 'A feminist's perspective on general defences', in Nicolson, D and Bibbings, L (eds), *Feminist Perspectives on Criminal Law*, 2000, London: Cavendish Publishing

McColgan, A, 'Common law and the relevance of sexual history evidence' (1996) 16 OJLS 275

McColgan, A, 'In defence of battered women who kill' (1993) 13 OJLS 508

McColgan, A, *Women Under the Law: The False Promise of Human Rights*, 2000, London: Longman

McConville, M and Baldwin, J, *Courts, Prosecution and Conviction*, 1981, Oxford: Clarendon

McConville, M, 'Plea bargaining: ethics and politics' (1998) 25 JLS 562

McEwan, J, 'Documentary hearsay evidence – refuge for the vulnerable witness?' [1989] Crim LR 642

McEwan, J, 'Law Commission dodges the nettles in Consultation Paper No 141' [1997] Crim LR 93

McEwan, J, *Evidence and the Adversarial Process*, 2nd edn, 1998, Oxford: Hart

McGlynn, C, *The Woman Lawyer*, 1998, London: Butterworths

McMillan, C, *Women, Reason and Nature: Some Philosophical Problems with Feminism*, 1982, Princeton, NJ: Princeton UP

McNaughton, J (ed), *Wigmore on Evidence*, 1961, Boston, Mass: Little, Brown

Mechtenberg, D, 'Women need to plan for financial future' (1998) *Denver Post*, 17 May, p L6

Mendez, M, 'Character evidence reconsidered: "people do not seem to be predictable characters"' (1998) 49 Hastings LJ 871

Mendez, M, 'The law of evidence and the search for a stable personality'(1996) 45 Emory LJ 221

Menkel-Meadow, C, 'Portia in a different voice: speculations on a women's lawyering process' (1985) 1 Berkeley Women's LJ 39

Menkel-Meadow, C, 'Portia *redux*: another look at gender, feminism and legal ethics', in Parker, S and Sampford, C (eds), *Legal Ethics and Legal Practice*, 1995, Oxford: Clarendon

Menkel-Meadow, C, 'The trouble with the adversary system in a post-modern, multi-cultural world' (1996) 1 J Inst Stud Leg Ethics 801

Mill, J (ed), *The Works of Jeremy Bentham*, 1810, London: Simkin, Marshall

Miller, T, 'Women surge into accounting' (1996) *Accounting Today*, 16 December, p 20

Minow, M, 'Stripped down like a runner or enriched by experience: bias and impartiality of judges and jurors' (1992) 33 W & ML Rev 1201

Mirfield, P, 'Similar fact evidence of child sexual abuse in English, United States and Florida law: a comparative study' (1996) 6 J Transnational L & P 7

Mitchell, M, 'Must clergy tell? child abuse reporting requirements versus the clergy privilege and free exercise of religion' (1987) 71 Minnesota L Rev 723

Moseley-Braun, C, 'Women's retirement security' (1996) 4 Elder LJ 493

Mosteller, R, 'Syndromes and politics in criminal trials and evidence law' (1996) 46 Duke LJ 461

Mueller, C and Kirkpatrick, L, *Modern Evidence: Doctrine and Practice*, 1995, Boston, Mass: Little, Brown

Murphy, P (ed), *Blackstone's Criminal Practice*, 1999, London: Blackstone

Murphy, P, *A Practical Approach to Evidence*, 3rd edn, 1985, London: Blackstone

Murphy, P, *Murphy on Evidence*, 6th edn, 1997, London: Blackstone

Murphy, S, 'Assisting the jury in understanding victimisation: expert psychological testimony on Battered Women Syndrome and rape trauma syndrome' (1992) 25 Columbia Journal of Law and Social Problems 277

Nadel, J, *Sara Thornton: The Story of a Woman Who Killed*, 1993, London: Victor Gollancz

Naffine, N and Owens, R (eds), *Sexing the Subject of Law*, 1997, Sydney: LBC

Naffine, N, *Law and the Sexes: Explorations in Feminist Jurisprudence*, 1990, Sydney: Allen Unwin

Nagel, T, *The View from Nowhere*, 1986, Oxford: OUP

Napley, D, *The Technique of Persuasion*, 1991, London: Sweet & Maxwell

Natali, LM and Stigall, S, '"Are you going to arraign his whole life?" How sexual propensity evidence violates the due process clause' (1996) 28 Loyola U Chi LJ 1

New South Wales Bureau of Crime Statistics and Research, *New South Wales Criminal Court Statistics 1993*, 1994, Sydney: New South Wales Bureau of Crime Statistics and Research

Nice, J and Trubek, L, *Cases and Materials on Poverty Law: Theory and Practice*, 1997, St Paul, Minn: West

Nicholson, L (ed), *Feminism/Postmodernism*, 1990, London: Routledge

Nicolson, D and Sanghvi, R, 'Battered women and provocation: the implications of *R v Ahluwalia*' [1993] Crim LR 728

Nicolson, D and Webb, J, *Professional Legal Ethics: Critical Interrogations*, 1999, Oxford: OUP

Nicolson, D, 'Facing facts: the teaching of fact construction in university law schools' (1997) 1 E & P 132

Nicolson, D, 'Telling tales: gender discrimination, gender construction and battered women who kill' (1995) 3 FLS 185

Nicolson, D, 'Truth, reason and justice: epistemology and politics in evidence discourse' (1994) 57 MLR 726

Nicolson, D, 'What the law giveth, it also taketh away: gender-specific defences to criminal liability', in Nicolson, D and Bibbings, L, *Feminist Perspectives on Criminal Law*, 2000, London: Cavendish Publishing

Nietzsche, F, *The Will to Power*, Kaufmann, W and Hollingdale, RJ (trans), 1968, New York: Random House

Nolan (Lord) and Sedley, S (Sir) (eds), *The Making and Remaking of the British Constitution*, 1995, London: Blackstone

NSW Department for Women, *Heroines of Fortitude: The Experiences of Women in Court as Victims of Sexual Assault – Summary Report*, 1996, Sydney: Department for Women

O'Barr, W and Atkins, B, '"Women's language" or "powerless language"', in McConnell-Ginet, S, Borker, R and Furman, N (eds), *Women and Language in Literature and Society*, 1980, New York: Praeger

O'Barr, W, 'Asking the right questions about language and power', in Kramarae, C, Schulz, M and O'Barr, W (eds), *Language and Power*, 1984, London: Sage

O'Connor, P, *Friendships Between Women: A Critical Review*, 1992, Hemel Hempstead: Harvester Wheatsheaf

O'Donovan, K, 'Defences for battered women who kill' (1991) 18 JLS 219

O'Donovan, K, 'Law's knowledge: the judge, the expert, the battered woman, and her syndrome' (1993) 24 JLS 427

O'Donovan, K, *Family Law Matters*, 1993, London: Pluto

O'Donovan, K, *Sexual Divisions in Law*, 1985, London: Weidenfeld & Nicolson

Office of Crime Statistics, *Crime and Justice in South Australia 1997 – Police, Adult Courts and Corrections*, 1998, Adelaide: AG's Department

Oh, C, 'Questioning the cultural and gender-based assumptions of the adversary system' (1992) 7 Berkeley Women's LJ 125

Orenstein, A, '"My God!" A feminist critique of the excited utterance exception to the hearsay rule' (1997) 85 California L Rev 159

Orenstein, A, 'Apology excepted: incorporating a feminist analysis into evidence policy where you would least expect it' (1999) 28 Southwestern UL Rev 221

Orenstein, A, 'Evidence in a different voice: some thoughts on Professor Jonakait's critique of a feminist approach' (1997) 4 W & MJ of Women & Law 295

Orenstein, A, 'Feminism and evidence', in Taylor, B, Rush, S and Munro, RJ (eds), *Feminist Jurisprudence, Women and the Law – Critical Essays, Research Agenda and Bibliography*, 1999, Littleton, CO: Fred B Rothman

Orenstein, A, 'No bad men! A feminist analysis of character evidence in rape trials' (1998) 49 Hastings LJ 663

Palmer, A, *Principles of Evidence*, 1998, Sydney: Cavendish Publishing

Park, R, 'Character at the crossroads' (1998) 49 Hastings LJ 717

Park, R, 'Character issues in the OJ Simpson case – or, rationales of the character evidence ban, with illustrations from the OJ Simpson case' (1996) 67 Colorado UL Rev 747

Patullo, P, *Judging Women*, 1983, London: National Council for Civil Liberties

Pennington, N and Hastie, R, 'The story model for juror decision making', in Hastie, R (ed), *Inside the Juror*, 1993, Cambridge: CUP

Pickett, JG, 'The presumption of innocence imperiled: the new Federal Rules of Evidence 413–414 on the use of other sexual offence evidence' (1995) 70 Wash L Rev 853

Pleck, J, 'Man to man: is brotherhood possible?', in Glazer-Malbin, N, *Old Family, New Family*, 1975, New York: Van Nostrand

Pollard, P, 'Judgments about victims and attackers in depicted rapes: a review' (1992) 31 Brit J Soc Psy 302

Porter, E, *Feminist Perspectives on Ethics*, 1999, London: Longman

Posch, P, 'The negative effects of expert testimony on the Battered Woman's Syndrome' (1998) 6 Am UJ Gender & Law 485

Posner, R, 'An economic approach to the law of evidence' (1999) 51 Stanford L Rev 1477

Raeder, M, 'The double-edged sword: admissibility of Battered Woman Syndrome evidence by and against batterers in cases involving domestic violence' (1996) 67 Colorado UL Rev 789

Raine, J and Smith, R, *The Victim/Witness in Court Project: Report of Research Programme*, 1991, London: National Association of Victim Support Schemes

Raitt, FE and Zeedyk, MS, *The Implicit Relation of Psychology and Law: Women and Syndrome Evidence*, 2000, London: Routledge

Ramazanoglu, C, *Feminism and the Contradictions of Oppression*, 1989, London: Routledge

Reisman, J, 'Intimacy in same-sex friendships' (1990) 23 Sex Roles 65

Rembar, C, *The Law of the Land*, 1989, New York: Simon & Schuster

Rhodes, DL, 'Gender and professional roles' (1994) 63 Fordham L Rev 39

Roberts, P, 'Expert evidence in Canadian criminal proceedings', in Reece, H (ed), *Law and Science*, 1998, Oxford: OUP

Robinson-Jacobs, K, 'When it comes to pay, it's still a man's world' (1998) *Los Angeles Times*, 23 April, p D1

Rock, P, *The Social World of the English Crown Court*, 1993, Oxford: Clarendon

Rogers, S, 'The ethics of advocacy' (1899) 59 LQR 259

Royal Commission on Criminal Justice, *Report of the Royal Commission on Criminal Justice*, 1993, London: HMSO

Rubin, L, *Just Friends: The Role of Friendship in our Lives*, 1985, New York: Harper and Row

Rumney, P and Morgan-Taylor, M, 'Recognizing the male rape victim: gender neutrality and the law of rape' (1997) 26 Anglo-Am L Rev 198

Rush, P and Young, A, 'A crime of consequence and a failure of legal imagination: the sexual offences of the model criminal code' (1997) 9 Aus Fem LJ 100

Russell, D, *Sexual Exploitation: Rape, Child Sexual Abuse, and Workplace Harassment*, 1984, London: Sage

Sallmann, P, *Report on Criminal Trials* 1985, Melbourne: AIJA

Schafran, L, 'Writing and reading about rape: a primer' (1993) 66 St John's L Rev 979

Scheppele, KL, 'Just the facts ma'am: sexualised violence, evidentiary habits and the revision of truth' (1992) 37 NYLS L Rev 123

Scheppele, KL, 'Manners of imagining the real' (1994) 19 Law & Soc Inq 995

Scottish Law Commission, *Hearsay Evidence in Criminal Proceedings*, No 149, 1995, Edinburgh: Scottish Law Commission

Scottish Office, *Towards a Just Conclusion – Vulnerable and Intimidated Witnesses in Scottish Criminal and Civil Cases*, 1998, Edinburgh: Scottish Office

Scully, A and Stanko, B, 'Retelling the tale', in Myers, A and Wright, S (eds), *No Angels: Women Who Commit Violence*, 1996, London: Pandora

Seabrook, S, *The Efficient Disposal of Business in the Crown Court*, 1992, London: General Council of the Bar

Sedley, S (Sir), 'Law and public life', in Nolan (Lord) and Sedley, S (Sir) (eds), *The Making and Remaking of the British Constitution*, 1995, London: Blackstone

Sheehy, E, Stubbs, J and Tolmie, J, 'Defending battered women on trial: the Battered Women Syndrome and its limitations' (1992) 16 Crim LJ 369

Sheldon, D, 'Corroboration and relevance' 1998 SLT (News) 115

Sheldon, D, *Evidence: Cases and Materials*, 1996, Edinburgh: Green

Sheldon, S and Thomson, M, *Feminist Perspectives on Health Care Law*, 1998, London: Cavendish Publishing

Sherrod, D, 'The influence of gender on same-sex friendships', in Hendrick, C (ed), *Close Relationships*, 1989, Newbury Park, CA: Sage

Shuman, D and Weiner, M, 'The privilege study: an empirical examination of the psychotherapist-patient privilege' (1982) 60 North Carolina L Rev 893

Siann, G, *Gender, Sex and Sexuality*, 1994, London: Taylor and Francis

Simon, HA, *Reason in Human Affairs*, 1983, Oxford: Blackwell

Sippel, J, 'Priest-penitent privilege statutes: dual protection in the confessional' (1994) 43 Catholic UL Rev 1127

Smart, C, 'Law's power, the sexed body, and feminist discourse' (1990) 17 JLS 194

Smart, C, *Feminism and the Power of Law*, 1989, London: Routledge

Sopinka, J, Lederman, S and Bryant, A, *The Law of Evidence in Canada*, 1992, Toronto: Butterworths

Spelman, E, *Inessential Woman: Problems of Exclusion in Feminist Thought*, 1988, London: The Women's Press

Spencer, G, 'Cuomo proposes Bill to replace "Son of Sam" law' (1992) New York LJ, 24 March, p 1

Spencer, J, 'Hearsay reform: a bridge not far enough?' [1996] Crim LR 29

Stanchi, K, 'The paradox of the fresh complaint rule' (1996) 37 Boston College L Rev 441

Stein, A, 'Judicial fact finding and the Bayesian method: the case for deeper scepticism about their combination' (1996) 1 E & P 25

Stein, A, 'The refoundation of evidence law' (1996) 9 Canadian J Law & Jurisprudence 279

Stern, K, 'Court-ordered caesarean sections: in whose interests?' (1993) 56 MLR 238

Stewart, M, Dobbin, S and Gatowski, S, '"Real rapes" and "real victims": the shared reliance on common cultural definitions of rape' (1996) 4 FLS 159

Stone, J, *Social Dimensions of Law and Society*, 1966, London: Stevens

Stone, M, *Proof of Fact in Criminal Trials*, 1984, Edinburgh: Green

Stone, S and Taylor, T, *Testimonial Privileges*, 1993, Colorado Springs, CO: Shepard's/McGraw-Hill

Strick, A, *Injustice for All*, 1996, New York: Barricade

Strong, J (ed), *McCormick on Evidence*, 1992, St Paul, Minn: West

Sweeney, L, 'The competitive negotiator' (1992) J Law Soc Scotland 49

Tannen, D, *You Just Don't Understand*, 1990, New York: Ballantine

Tapper, C, *Cross and Tapper on Evidence*, 9th edn, 1999, London: Butterworths

Taslitz, A, 'A feminist approach to social scientific evidence: foundations' (1998) 5 Michigan J Gender & Law 1

Taslitz, A, 'Gender and race in evidence policy: what feminism has to offer evidence law' (1999) 28 Southwestern UL Rev 171

Taslitz, A, 'Myself alone: individualizing justice through psychological character evidence' (1993) 52 Maryland L Rev 1

Taslitz, A, 'Patriarchal stories: cultural rape narratives in the courtroom' (1996) 5 S California Rev Law & Women's Studies 387

Taslitz, AE, *Rape and the Culture of the Courtroom*, 1999, New York: New York UP

Taylor, B, Rush, S and Munro, RJ (eds), *Feminist Jurisprudence, Women and the Law – Critical Essays, Research Agenda and Bibliography*, 1999, Littleton, CO: Fred B Rothman

Temkin, J, 'Prosecuting and defending rape: perspectives from the Bar' (2000) 27 JLS 219

Temkin, J, 'Rape in court' (1998) *The Guardian*, 27 October, p 17

Temkin, J, 'Reporting rape in London: a qualitative study' (1999) 38(1) Howard J Crim Justice 17

Temkin, J, 'Sexual history evidence – the ravishment of section 2' [1983] Crim LR 3

Temkin, J, *Rape and the Legal Process*, 1987, London: Sweet & Maxwell

Thompson, EP, *Whigs and Hunters: The Origin of the Black Act*, 1975, London: Allen Lane

Thornburg, E, 'Metaphors matter: how images of battle, sports and sex shape the adversary system' (1995) 10 Wisconsin Women's LJ 13

Thornton, M, 'Board's first decision' (1979) 4 Legal Service Bulletin 180

Thornton, M, 'Equivocations of conciliation: the resolution of discrimination complaints in Australia' (1989) 52 MLR 733

Thornton, M, *The Liberal Promise: Anti-Discrimination Legislation in Australia*, 1990, Melbourne: OUP

Tillers, P, 'What is wrong with character evidence?' (1998) 49 Hastings LJ 781

Torrey, M, 'When will we be believed? Rape myths and the idea of a fair trial in rape prosecutions' (1991) 24 University of California Davis L Rev 1013

Tronto, JC, *Moral Boundaries: A Political Argument for an Ethic of Care*, 1993, London: Routledge

Twining, W, 'Freedom of proof and the reform of criminal evidence' (1997) 31 Israel L Rev 439

Twining, W, 'Hot air in the redwoods: a sequel to *The Wind in the Willows*' (1988) 86 Michigan L Rev 1523

Twining, W, 'Recent trends in evidence scholarship', in Nijboer, JF and Reijntjes, JM (eds), *Proceedings of the First World Conference on New Trends in Criminal Investigation and Evidence*, 1997, Lelystad, Netherlands: OU Press

Twining, W, *Rethinking Evidence: Exploratory Essays*, 1990, Oxford: Blackwell

Twining, W, *Theories of Evidence: Bentham and Wigmore*, 1985, London: Weidenfeld & Nicolson

Tyler, D and Easteal, P, 'The credibility gap' (1998) 23 Alt LJ 211

van Kessel, G, 'A summary of Mirjan R Damaska's *Evidence Law Adrift*' (1997–98) 49 Hastings LJ 359

Veniegas, R and Peplau, L, 'Power and the quality of same-sex friendships' (1997) 21 Psychology of Women Quarterly 279

Verhovek, S, 'Record for women in Washington legislature' (1999) *New York Times*, 4 February, p 18

Victim Support, *Women, Rape and the Criminal Justice System*, 1996, London: Victim Support

Wagenaar, WA, van Koppen PJ and Crombag, HFM, *Anchored Narratives*, 1993, Hemel Hempstead: Harvester Wheatsheaf

Walby, S, *Theorising Patriarchy*, 1990, Oxford: Blackwell

Walker, L, *The Battered Woman Syndrome*, 1984, New York: Springer

Warren, E, 'She's gotta have it now: a qualified rape crisis counselor-victim privilege' (1995) 17 Cardozo L Rev 141

Watts, W, 'The parent-child privileges: hardly a new or revolutionary concept' (1987) 28 W & ML Rev 583

Weiss, S, 'How we constructed "the jury": a look at narrative storytelling' (1997) 12 Berkeley Women's LJ 73

Welch, S, 'The truth of liberation theology: particulars of a relative sublime', in Diamond, I and Quinby, L (eds), *Feminism and Foucault: Reflections on Resistance*, 1988, Boston, Mass: Northeastern UP

Wellborn, OG, 'Demeanour' (1991) 76 Cornell L Rev 1104

Wellman, FL, *The Art of Cross-Examination*, 4th edn, 1997, New York: Simon & Schuster

Wells, C, 'Battered Woman Syndrome and defences to homicide: where now?' (1994) 14 LS 266

Wigmore, JH, 'The problem of proof' (1913) 8 Illinois L Rev 77

Wigmore, JH, *Evidence in Trials at Common Law*, 1970, Boston, Mass: Little, Brown

Wigmore, JH, *Wigmore on Evidence*, 1937, Boston, Mass: Little, Brown

Williams, G, *Proof of Guilt*, 1958, London: Stevens

Willis, 'New wine in old bottles: the sentencing discount for pleading guilty' (1995) 13 Law in Context 39

Winstead, B, 'Sex differences in same-sex friendships', in Derlega, V and Winstead, B (eds), *Friendship and Social Interaction*, 1986, New York: Springer

Wise, S and Stanley, L, *Georgie Porgie: Sexual Harassment in Everyday Life*, 1987, London: Pandora

Wood, L and Rennie, H, 'Formulating rape: the discursive construction of victims and villains' (1994) 5(1) Discourse and Society 125

Woolf (Lord), *Access to Justice: Final Report*, 1996, London: HMSO

Wright, EW, 'Victoria's approach to reducing criminal case delays: specific initiative', AIJA Eighth Annual Conference, 1989, Carlton, Vic: AIJA

Wright, C and Graham, K, *Federal Practice and Procedure*, 1980, St Paul, Minn: West

Wundersitz, J, Naffine, N and Gale, F, 'The production of guilt in the juvenile justice system: the pressures to "plead"' (1991) 30 Howard J of Crim Justice 192

Yaroshefsky, E, 'Balancing victim's rights and vigorous advocacy for the defendant' (1989) Annual Survey of American Law 152

Young, IM, 'The ideal of community and the politics of difference', in Nicholson, L (ed), *Feminism/Postmodernism*, 1990, London: Routledge

Young, IM, *Justice and the Politics of Difference*, 1990, Princeton, NJ: Princeton UP

Zacharias, F, 'Rethinking confidentiality' (1989) 74 Iowa L Rev 351

Zuckerman, A, 'Law Commission's Consultation Paper No 138 on Hearsay: (1) the futility of hearsay' (1996) Crim LR 4

Zuckerman, A, 'Similar fact evidence: the unobservable rule' (1987) 103 LQR 187

INDEX

Acquittals 228

Adler, M 172, 176, 179

Adversarial proceedings

  advocacy 45–46

  alternative

    dispute resolution 35, 37

  fact-finding 34–35

  legal representation 35–36

  rape 39–57

  sexual offences 11–12

Advocacy

  adversarial 45–46

  rape 45–46

Alternative

  dispute resolution 35, 37

Anleu, SR 10–11, 12

Anti-discrimination,
See Discrimination

Appeals

  informal tribunals 107–08

  sexual history 170–71

Aries, E 64

Attorney-client

  privilege 84–87

Australia

  complaints 106

  discrimination 10, 105–09

  harassment 105–26

  hearings 105–09

  informal tribunals 105–26

  rape 54–56

  rules of evidence 105–26

  sexual history 187

  sexual offences,

    without trial 10–11

Bailey, A 109

Baker, K 217, 225–26

Bar Council

  Code of Conduct 47–48

Bargen, J 128

Battered Woman's

  Syndrome 8, 191–209

  bias 204

  character

    evidence 215

  cooling off 20–21, 205

  cycle of 193

  definition 193

  depression 194, 198–99, 201

  diminished

    responsibility 16–17, 192–95, 198–200, 202

  epistemology 203

  experts 12, 191–209

  facts 33

  hearsay 67–68

  medical evidence 191–92, 194, 196–98, 202–208

  murder 7–8, 12, 16–21, 191–209

  patriarchy 202–04, 209

  privileged

    gender 203

  provocation 16–17, 19–21, 191–202, 204–08

  psychological

    evidence 194–95, 197

  psychological

    disorders 194–95, 199–202

research 193
self-defence 191–92
self-harm 194–95, 200
stereotyping 199, 206
United States 206
victimisation 199
Bayes Theorem 5
Bentham, J 2, 3, 14
Best evidence rule 61–62, 73
Bias
  battered women 204
  gender 59–76
  hearsay 59–76
  privilege 83, 89
Brereton, D 46
Bronitt, S 146
Bullying 43–44

Canada
Charter of Rights
  and Freedoms 4, 180
  sexual history 174, 180–82
CCTV 50–51, 53–56, 183–84
Chan, W 206
Character evidence 12
  acquittals 228–31
  admissibility 211–35
  Battered Woman's
    Syndrome 215
  children 212, 227
  consistent traits 214
  credibility 213, 219
  cross-examination 231–35
  English law 213–17
  essentialism 214–15
  experts 215, 216, 228
  generalisations 215

imputations 232–34
juries 216
Law Commission 211, 220–21, 226
marginalised
  groups 217
  prejudice 216, 217–19, 221
    moral 226–27
    reasoning 221–27
  prevalence 223–26
previous misconduct,
  excluding
    evidence of 217–18
probative
  value of 214, 218–19, 221–25
  rape 216–217, 220–35
  trauma
    syndrome 215
  types of 225–28
  recidivism 221–23, 227, 229
  sexual history 168, 231
  sexual offences 211–12, 220–28, 230–31, 234–35
  similar fact
    evidence 211, 214, 218–27, 229–30
  stereotyping 215
  striking similarity 219–20
  subjectivity 215
  United States 220, 224
Children 212, 227
Childs, M 12

Civil proceedings
  and relaxation of
    evidential rules   2–3
Clergy   87–90
Clinton, B   79
Coates, J   69
Communication
  female   63–64
  gender   63–68
  male   63–68
  witnesses   69–70
Confessions   154
Confidentiality   79–103
Convictions
  rape   137
  rates   130–32
  reasonable
    prospect of   129–34
  registration of   222–23
  research   130–32
  sexual offences   129–37, 149
Corroboration
  abolition   164–65
  children   161–62
  confessions   154
  distress, by   75, 158–164
  English law   151–52, 164
  hearsay   65, 74–75
  miscarriages
    of justice   154
  mistake   155, 165
  rape   65, 151–64
  reform   164–65
  Scotland   11, 65, 149–65
  sexual history   179–80
  sexual offences   11, 133–34,
                                      149–65

United States   164–65
warnings   133–34,
                                    151, 155,
                                  165, 179–80
Courtroom language   68–72
Crawford, M   64
Criminal proceedings
  exclusionary rules   3
  guilty pleas   129
  hearsay   61–62
  legal professional
    privilege   86–87
Cross, R   14
Cross-examination,
  See, also, Sexual
    history
  character evidence   231–32
  harassment   117–19
  language   70–71
  objections   117–19
  rape   40–49, 70–71

Damages
  experts   121–22
  psychological
    harm   121–22
Defence   136–38
Depression   194,
                                  198–99, 201
Development of
  evidence law
    and scholarship   4–12
Devereux, A   109
Difference feminism   28–29
Diminished
  responsibility   16–17, 192–95,
                                198–200, 202

Discrimination,
    See, also, Sex
        discrimination
    Australia   10, 105–09
    indirect   59
Dispute resolution   35, 37
    Australia   127–48
    sexual offences   127–48
Distress   158–64
Doctor/patient
    privilege   90–93
Domestic violence,
    See Battered women
Durston, G   188

Easton, S   11
Edwards, A   145
Ellison, L   11–12, 168
Enlightenment
    epistemology   14, 22–25
    ontology   14
Epistemology
    battered women   202
    Enlightenment   14, 22–25
    ethics   13–37
    facts   33
    foundationalism   20, 32
    gender   13–37
    knowledge   25
    rationalism   28
    stereotyping   32
    truth   32–33
Essentialism   214–15
Estrich, S   220
Ethics
    epistemology   13–37
    gender   13–37
    legal representation   35–37

European Convention
    on Human Rights   187
Experts,
    Battered Woman's
        Syndrome   12, 191–209
    damages   121–22
    harassment   121–22
    hearsay   66
    informal tribunals   121–22
    rules of evidence   121–22

Fact-finding   13, 15–16,
                                        20–22
    adversarial
        proceedings   34–35
    battered women   33
    epistemology   33
    reconstructions   31–37
Fair trials   187, 188
False allegations   42, 155
Feminism and
    evidence   5–12
Ferguson, P   11
Fishwick, E   128
Foucault, M   32, 36
Foundationalism
    epistemology   20, 32
    post-modernism   29–30
Fragmented testimony   79

Gender   8–9
    bias   59–76
    communication   63–68
    courtroom language   68–72
    epistemology   13–37
    ethics   13–37
    hearsay   59–76

indirect
  discrimination   59
  language   10, 63–68
    courtroom, of   68–72
  neutrality   24–25
  positivism   17–18
Generalisations   215
Gilligan, C   27, 56
Grace, S   188
Graycar, R   145
Gregory, J   174–75
Guilty pleas   129, 134–43

Hale, M   175
Harassment
  Australia   105–26
  complaints   106
  cross-examination   117–19
  experts   121–23
  hearings   105–09
  hearsay   119–20
  informal tribunals   105–26
  interruptions   117–19
  length of hearings   114–16
  medical evidence   121–23
  number of cases on   110–13
  objections   117–19
  protection, lack of   123–24
  psychological harm   121–22
  research   109–11
  rules of evidence   105–26
  sexual history   123–24
  similar fact evidence   120–21
Harris, J   188
Health care
  professionals   90–93

Hearings
  Australia   105–09
  harassment   105–09
  informal tribunals   105–09
  length of   114–16
  rules of evidence   105–09
Hearsay
  admissibility   61–63
  battered women   67–68
  best evidence   61–62, 73
  bias   59–76
  corroboration   65, 74–75
  criminal
    proceedings   61–62
  exceptions   72–76
  exclusion,
    reasons for   61–62
  experts   66
  gender   59–76
  hearsay   59–76
  incest   66
  indirect
    discrimination   59
  informal tribunals   119–20
  judiciary   62
  Law Commission   62–63,
                             73, 75–76
  oaths   62
  oral traditions and   10
  prior statements   75–76
    consistent   74
    content of   61
    occurrence of   61
  professional
    opinions   66
  proof
    process and   61–63
  res gestae   74

Scotland 62–63, 73–75
sexual offences 65, 67, 74–75
witnesses 73
Heenan, M 41–44, 50,
54, 145, 147
Hite, S 64
Human Rights
Act 1998 4
Hunter, R 10, 12

Impartiality,
See Bias
Imputations 232–34
Incest 66
Informal tribunals
appeals 107–08
Australia 105–26
experts 121–23
harassment 105–26
hearings 105–09
length of 114–16
hearsay 119–20
legal
representation 108
medical evidence 121–23
objections 117–19
rules of evidence 105–26
similar fact
evidence 120–21
Interruptions 117–19
Intimidation 43–44,
117–19
Intoxication
rape 150–51, 163
Scotland 150–51

Johnson, F 64
Judiciary
hearsay 62
rape 48–49
sexual history 170–71, 187
Jury trials
character evidence 216
reduction in 36
sexual offences 129–30
Justice
rationalism 18
reconstructions 25–31

Kalven, H 173
Kinports, J 8, 10
Knowledge
epistemology 25
positivism 22

Language
courtroom 68–72
cross-examination 70–71
fragmented
testimony 70
gender 10, 63–72
legal
representation 68–72
rape 70–72
witnesses 69–70
Lees, S 41, 172–74,
178, 222, 228
Legal professional
privilege 84–87
Legal representation
adversarial
proceedings 35–36, 45–46
Bar Code
of Conduct 47–48

ethics 35–37
informal tribunals 108
language 68–72
Leonard, D 216
Logic 18

Mack, K 10–11, 12, 60, 187
MacKinnon, C 60, 124–25
Marginalisation 217
Marital privilege 97–102
Matoesian, G 72
McColgan, A 176–77, 206
McEwan, J 44, 222
McKelvie, H 41–44, 50, 54, 147
Meaning of 'evidence' 1–3
Medical evidence
  battered women 191–92, 194, 196–98, 202–08
  harassment 121–22
  informal tribunals 121–22
  rules of evidence 121–22
Mendez, M 214
Menkel-Meadow, C 56–57
Mental health
  professionals'
    privilege 93–96
Miscarriages of justice 154
Murder
  battered women 7–8, 12, 16–22, 191–209
  diminished
    responsibility 16–17, 192–95, 198–200, 202

provocation 16–17, 19–21, 191–202, 204–08

Nicolson, D 9–10, 12
Nietzsche, F 20
Noddings, N 27

Oaths 62
O'Barr, W 72
Objections 117–19
Opinions
  hearsay 66
  professional 66
Oppression 29, 31
Orenstein, A 216–17

Parent/child
  privilege 101–02
Park, R 223
Pleas
  criminal
    proceedings 129
  guilty 129, 134–43
  negotiation 128,138–41
  rape 138,140
  sentencing 138–41
  sexual offences 128, 134–43
Positivism
  fact 14–21
  gender 17–18
  knowledge 22
  patriarchal law 15–21
  rationalism 16
  reason 18–19
  truth 16, 18–19

Post-modernism
  difference
    feminism 28–29
    foundationalism 29–30
Prejudice 176, 177, 181, 216–19, 221–27
Prior statements 61, 74–77
Privilege 10, 79–103
  bias 83, 89
  clergy 87–89
  confidential
    communications 79–103
  criminal
    proceedings 86–87
  gender 96
  health care
    professionals 90–93
  legal professional 84–87
  mental health
    professionals 93–96
  parent-child 101–102
  psychotherapists 93–96
  recognising 80–81
  relationships that
    should be
      privileged 82–102
  spouses 96–102
  United States 79–103
Professional
  opinions 66
Prosecutors 134–36, 147
Provocation
  battered women 16–17, 19–21
  cooling off 20–21, 205
  cumulative 199–200, 205–06
  murder 16–17, 19–21
  reasonableness 193, 195, 199–201, 206

self-control,
  sudden loss of 191–92, 196, 198, 205
  test for 192–93
Psychiatrists'
  privilege 93–95
Psychological
  disorders 194–95, 199–202
Psychological
  evidence 194–95, 197
Psychological harm 121–22
Psychotherapists 93–95

Raitt, F 10
Rape,
  See, also, Sexual
    history 7
  adversarial
    advocacy 45–46
  adversarial
    proceedings 39–57
  attrition 39
  Australia 54–56
  Bar Code of
    Conduct 47–48
  bullying tactics 43–44
  categories of 225–26
  CCTV 50–51, 53–56, 183–84
  character
    evidence 215–17, 220–35
  children 161–62
  clandestine
    injuries 163
  consent 65, 150–51, 156–57, 162

constraints,
   inadequacy of   46–49
convictions   137
corroboration   65, 151–64
court, giving
   evidence in   49–56
credit, cross-
   examination as to   41–42
cross-examination   40–49,
                         70–71
   credit, as to   41–42
definition   149–50
delay in reporting
   offence   42
false allegations   42, 155
giving evidence
   in court   49–56
guilty pleas   138
injuries caused by   156–58
intimidation   43–44, 51
intoxication   150–51, 163
judiciary, role of   48–49
language   70–72
medical
   examinations   157
mistake   155, 165
pleas   140
reporting   224–25
rules of evidence   128
Scotland   150–51
screens, use of   50–51, 52–55
sentencing   140–41
similar fact
   evidence   220, 228
stereotyping   42, 44, 146
stranger   179
survey   40–41, 43
trauma syndrome   215
use of force   156–59

victims   142–43
video links   50–51, 52
video recorded
   interviews   53
victims'
   treatment
     in court   40–41, 51–53
vulnerable
   witnesses,
     report on   51–53
weapons, use of   158–59
withdrawal of
   complaints   39
Rationalism   14, 15, 23
   epistemology   28
   justice   18
   positivism   16
   reason   18
Reason   23
   positivism   18–19
   rationalism   18
   reconstructions   25–31
Recidivism   221–23,
                      227, 229
Rennie, H   71
Res gestae   74
Roberta, P   66
Rock, P   46, 47
Rules of evidence
   Australia   105–26
   experts   121–23
   harassment   105–26
   hearings   105–09
   hearsay   119–20
   informal tribunals   105–26
   intimidation   117–19
   medical evidence   121–23
   objections   117–19
   protection, lack of   123–24

rape 128
similar fact evidence 120–21
strategic uses
of the rules of 117–24
Russell, D 224–25

Scholarship,
development of 4–12
Scotland
corroboration 11, 65, 149–65
hearsay 62–63, 73–75
intoxication 150–51
rape 150–51
sexual history 183
sexual offences 11, 149–65
Screens 50–51, 52–55
Scully, A 12
Self-defence 191–92
Self-harm 194–95, 200
Sentencing
discounts 138–41
guilty pleas 138–41
rape 140–41
sexual offences 138–41
Sex discrimination
Australia 105–26
gender 59
harassment 105–26
hearsay 59
indirect 59
Sexual harassment,
See Harassment
Sexual history
appeals 170–71
Australia 187
Canada 174, 180–82
CCTV links 183–84
character,
attacks on 168

consent,
relevance to 169, 171–72,
177–81, 186
corroboration 179–80
credibility 178, 181, 186
Criminal Law
Revision
Committee 172
defendants,
examination by 184–85
deterrent to
reporting 167
development of
law governing 168–70
fair trials 187, 188
false allegations 174–75
harassment 123–24
Heilbron
Committee 169–70, 176
history of law
governing 168–70
Home Office
Working Group 182–83
judiciary 170–71, 187
past misconduct,
evidence of 176–77
prejudice 176, 177, 181
previous
consensual sex,
evidence of 178–80, 186
promiscuity 171–72
rape 41–42,
70–71,
167–89
reform 182–87
relevance of 174–78,
181, 186
reporting 168–69
deterrent to 167
research 172–73

respectability 173–74, 178
Scotland 183–84
sexual offences 11, 132–33
similar fact
  evidence 176, 186
special measures 183–84
stereotyping 167, 174,
  176, 181
stranger rape 179
United States 173, 180, 187
victimisation 182
Sexual offences,
  See, also, Rape;
    Sexual history 7
acquittals 228–31
adversarial
  offences 11–12
Australia 10–11, 127–48
character
  evidence 211–12,
    220–28,
  230–31, 234–35
construction of 127–48
convictions 129–37, 149
corroboration 11, 133–34,
  149–65
defence 137–38
dispute
  resolution 127–48
guilty pleas 134–43
hearsay 65, 67, 74–75
jury trials 129–30
pleas
  guilty 134–43
  negotiation 128, 138–41
prosecutors 134–36, 147
registration 222–23
Scotland 11, 149–65

sentence
  discount 138–41
similar fact
  evidence 12
stereotyping 134–35, 138
trial, without 10–11
victims 142–43
witness
  credibility 134–35
Similar fact evidence
  admissibility 120–21
  character evidence 211, 214,
    218–27,
    229–30
  children 227
  harassment 120–21
  informal tribunals 120–21
  rape 220, 228–35
  rules of evidence 120–21
  sexual history 176, 186
  sexual offences 12
  striking similarity 219–20
Smart, C 145–46
Spencer, J 75
Spouses' privilege 96–102
Starr, K 79
Stereotyping 8–9
  battered women 199, 206
  character evidence 215
  epistemology 31
  rape 42, 44, 146
  sexual history 167, 174,
    176, 181
  sexual offences 134–35, 138
  witnesses 134–35
Stone, M 68–69

Taslitz, AE	41, 126	rape	142–43
Temkin, J	48, 71, 220	sexual offences	142–43
Thornburg, E	45	Video links	50–51, 52
Thornton, S	16–18, 20–21, 37, 195–204, 217	Video recording interviews	53
Tillers, P	217	Walby, S	203–04
Tribunals,		Walker, L	193
See Informal tribunals		West, R	217
		Wigmore, JH	14, 82, 97, 175
Truth		Williams, G	175
epistemology	32–33	Witnesses	
oppression	29	character	
positivism	16, 18–19	evidence	219
reconstructions	25–31	communication	69–70
Twining, W	4, 13–14	credibility	134–35, 219
		cross-examination	40–49
United States		hearsay	73
battered women	205	impressions	
character		given by	69–70
evidence	220, 224	language	69–70
privilege	79–103	rape	40–49, 51–53
sexual history	173, 180, 187	sexual offences	134–35
Use of force	156–59	stereotyping	134–35
		vulnerable	51–53
Victimisation	182, 199	Wood, L	71
Victims			
construction of	142–43	Zeisel, H	173
'ideal'	142–43